Chaiyo!

KING VAJIRAVUDH AND
THE DEVELOPMENT OF
THAI NATIONALISM

King Vajiravudh in Ceremonial Dress for the Declaration of War (Statue at Vajiravudh College).

Chaiyo!

KING VAJIRAVUDH AND THE DEVELOPMENT OF THAI NATIONALISM

Walter F. Vella

ASSISTED BY

Dorothy B. Vella

*Published with the
support of The Maurice
J. Sullivan & Family
Fund in The University
of Hawaii Foundation*

THE UNIVERSITY PRESS OF HAWAII · HONOLULU

Copyright © 1978 by The University Press of Hawaii. All rights reserved.

No part of this work may be reproduced or transmitted in any form or by any means, electronic or mechanical, including photocopying and recording, or by any information storage or retrieval system, without permission in writing from the publisher.
Composition by Asco Trade Typesetting Limited, Hong Kong.
Manufactured in the United States of America.

Designed by Dave Comstock

Library of Congress Cataloging in Publication Data

Vella, Walter Francis, 1924–
  Chaiyo! King Vajiravudh and the development of Thai nationalism.

  Bibliography: p.
  Includes index.
  1. Nationalism—Thailand—History. 2. Thailand—History. 3. Vajiravudh, King of Thailand, 1881–1925. I. Vella, Dorothy B., joint author. II. Title.
DS583.V44   959.3′04′0924 [B]   78–1060
ISBN 0-8248-0493-7

*The song that nerves a nation's heart
Is in itself a deed.*

Tennyson

Contents

    Illustrations   viii
    Preface   ix
    Note   xii
    Introduction   xiii
1. Prince to King   1
2. The King Consecrated   13
3. The Wild Tigers   27
4. The Monarchy   53
5. National Survival and Militarism   79
6. The West as Model   126
7. The Concept of Nationality   176
8. The Past as Model   202
9. The Media   243
10. An Assessment   257
    Notes   273
    Bibliography   325
    Index   337

Illustrations

King Vajiravudh in Ceremonial Dress for the Declaration of War	frontispiece
Prince Vajiravudh at His Tonsure Ceremony	11
Public Audience on Coronation Day	18
Cartoon: Royal Leadership in Siam	65
Cartoon: Appeal for Contributions to Cruiser Fund	96
Cartoon: Royal Support for Education	162
Cartoon of Prince Purachatra by King Vajiravudh	245
King Vajiravudh Memorial	271

Frontispiece and photographs on pages 18 and 271 are by Eric and Paul Vella.

Preface

Chaiyo means victory, it means hurrah. It is a cheer, a rallying cry, coined by a king whose overall program of nationalism is the subject of the following pages. This book is devoted to one basic aim: to examine Siamese nationalism during the reign of King Vajiravudh as thoroughly and completely as my talents and the sources—the Thai archives, printed works in Thai and Western languages, and the memories of Thai friends—permit. I have resisted temptations to digress into an overall history of the reign or an examination of theories of nationalism. Yet I hope, of course, that the work will contribute to the general understanding of this period of Thai history and also provide information for political theorists on the nationalistic process.

The biases of an author who is not a polemicist are apt to be what he is least aware of and least likely to admit. I have tried to examine my biases in two areas of vulnerability: my views on nationalism and my feelings toward Thailand. I regard nationalism as far from

Preface

an unalloyed blessing. Like any system of loyalty, it has its virtues and its faults. Its good lies in its power to unite; its bad lies in its power to divide. Perhaps the history of mankind is the story of the search for larger and larger loyalties. Just as King Vajiravudh saw the development of a family spirit, a team spirit, a school spirit as the stepping stones to a national spirit, perhaps the development of a national spirit is the necessary prelude to an international spirit. On Thailand my views are less ambiguous and, for that very reason, more likely to be subjective. In one of the most stimulating talks given at the Association for Asian Studies in recent years, Professor Herbert Phillips surveyed American research on Thailand and concluded, with respect to the researchers, that, despite their vast differences in field, background, and methodology, all shared one attitude. That attitude was love for Thailand and the Thai. Even writers "critical" of Thai institutions wrote their criticisms in a spirit of affection. I write, then, as objectively as I can, write truths as I see them, but the affection is there. As a historian, further, I have often experienced personally, seen the living reality of, the Thai view—indeed the Southeast Asian view—of what history is, or should be. History to the Thai is not the cold compilation of facts and analysis of events, the piling up of stories, good and evil, with no aim except objective truth. History's aim is not to be, in Thucydides' phrase, "an exact knowledge of the past as an aid to the interpretation of the future," but rather a setting forth of the moral good of the past, of the virtues of the past, to serve as a moral guide to the future. This view of the uses of history commands my respect as those who expressed it to me in intimate conversation command my respect. In the end, however, I remain a Western historian of Siam, not a Siamese historian. My intellectual progenitor is Thucydides.

The "assisted by" on the title page needs a word of explanation. Dorothy B. Vella, my wife, played an extraordinary role in the development of this book—as a researcher, a consultant, and an editor. She did all the research in the English-language newspapers. Every thought and idea, every draft and redraft, was tested out on her. And the final editing was hers. Credit for the book we share, but the blame for error I must assume alone. For I wrote the words, and, in cases of conflict, I played the autocrat.

To give proper acknowledgment of aid given me in this study over the years is awesome. First of all, heartiest and fullest thanks are due to those Thai who lived during the reign and were willing to reminisce for my benefit: Netra Poonwiwat, Rian Srichandr, and

Preface

Charoon Sattamet, three members of the coup party of 1912 who were willing to bare to a stranger painful periods of their lives; Prince Dhani Nivat; Princess Poon Pismai Diskul; Princess Charubhatra Abhakorn; Prince Sitthiporn Kridakara; Phraya Harnklangsamuth; Sathitya Semanil; Phraya Prichanusat; M. L. Pin Malakul; Phra Mahamontri; Phra Maha Dhep Kasatarasanuha; Phraya Borihara Rajamanob; Phraya Noradhebprida; Udom Kalyanamitra; Khunying Chalow Anirutdeva; Nai Kuad Humphrae; M. R. Kukrit Pramoj; and Princess Elisabeth Chakrabongse. Belonging to this list, but meriting most particular thanks for answering my questions repeatedly in person and by letter, is Chamun Amorn Darunarak. He and his wife Uthumporn have become more than correspondents; they have become my very good friends.

Another category of acknowledgment is due the Thai friends, librarians, teachers, and students who helped me in such diverse ways as finding a needed book or helping me puzzle out a poetic line: Vilaileka Buranasiri, Vina Sritanratana, Dr. Kajorn Sukabanij, Sulak Sivaraksa, Captain and Mrs. Bisdarn Chulasevok, Robert and Kanok Vil, Maenmas Chavalit, Choosri Sawasdisongkram, Neon Snidvongs, Niramol Kangsadara Pachinburavan, Phraya Bharataraja, Lt. Bhakorn Subhajalasaya, Dr. Malai and Khunying Ubol Huvanandana, Kamol T. Chaisuwan, and Vilai Grandstaff. Also in this category of friend and helper is Ramphai Charumas, who did more than any other individual to arrange introductions to people I wanted to meet and to track down books and collections of books I needed to read and who aided me in other ways too numerous to recall.

Invaluable in providing much of the wherewithal for my sabbatical year of research in Thailand in 1969–1970 was the American Council of Learned Societies, which awarded me a research grant. Thai institutional cooperation was also exceedingly generous; particularly noteworthy in this regard were the National Research Council, the National Archives, the National Library, the Damrong Library, and the Siam Society.

Among the inspirers and facilitators of any work that arises out of academe are countless people in one's university—colleagues, students, librarians, administrators, and members of the secretarial staff. Colleagues venture ideas, students react to notions. Complete attributions are impossible here. But worthy of particular mention for indispensable aid in searching and securing titles are two members of the University of Hawaii's Asia Collection staff: Joyce Wright, head, and Mrs. Lan Hiang Char, librarian. A researcher's obligation to his institution—in my case, the University of Hawaii—is im-

Preface

measurable. I am grateful to the university for granting me the research time and sabbatical leave that made this study possible and for aiding me in countless other ways such as awarding special funds for microfilming materials related to my research. A final word of heartfelt thanks goes to the loyal and indefatigable band of secretary-typists at the university, particularly Gayle Ing, Machiko Tsuruya, and Jo Ann Yamashita, who succeeded in translating the almost illegible scrawl of my first draft into readable type and who thereafter faced mounds of retyping with undiminished good cheer.

Note

All Thai words except personal names are rendered in the so-called general system outlined in the *Journal of the Thailand Research Society* of March 1941. For personal names, the transliterations adopted by the Thai individuals themselves are used; when a person's preference is not known, however, the general system is again followed.

In accordance with the official designations for the periods, the term Siam is used for the name of the country during the Vajiravudh years, Thailand for the country today. The adjective Siamese is used when the reference is to the political entity of the time, the adjective Thai when the reference is to things linguistic, ethnic, or cultural, regardless of time.

Introduction

The parade of the world's leading propagandists for nationalism is one of almost infinite variety. Led off by a little Corsican drumbeater for liberty, equality, and brotherhood, the march continues with romantic poets paired with red-shirted revolutionaries, men in shabby dhotis striding side by side with reincarnated Caesars. In this mixed company in which the daring, the loud, the common outnumber the sedate, the reflective, the traditionalist, walks a figure more unusual than most: a king of Siam, continuer of a 600-year-old monarchy, inheritor of the status of god-king, diffident, dignified, and soft spoken.

Vajiravudh of Siam, absolute monarch of his country from 1910 to 1925 and sixth ruler of his dynasty, was a paradoxical combination of traditional autocrat and modern nationalist. He was indeed the founder of modern nationalism in his country. His espousal of nationalism as an instrument of national strength was as deliberate, as unrevolutionary as were the actions his predecessors had taken to ease Siam into the modern world.

Introduction

The policy of making adjustments to the Western presence and power by accepting Western "improvements" was deliberately begun by King Mongkut, Vajiravudh's grandfather, in the 1850s. This policy was continued by King Chulalongkorn. Both these monarchs considered the policy of Westernization necessary for Siam's survival; they believed that it was necessary to adopt Western techniques in order to preserve Siam's political independence, its society, its essential culture. But neither king fully appreciated the underlying danger to Thai values in their policy; neither realized that the adoption of Western techniques would change the character of what they were trying to save. By 1910 many traditional Thai arts and crafts, for example, had disappeared. Little had been done by Mongkut or Chulalongkorn to stop this trend and, in the view of a long-time foreign resident in Siam, "it is doubtful indeed if they desired it"; one of the "dominating passions" of Chulalongkorn's life was to "Europeanize his country . . . and the fact that some of his reforms were quite unsuited to the climate and habits of the people, never deterred him from introducing them."[1]

Vajiravudh was much better able to understand the force of Western culture—partly because he came later in time, partly because he had had a thorough schooling in things Western, including nine years of study in England. Vajiravudh therefore perceived that unthinking acceptance of Western ways of doing things must endanger Thai ways of looking at things. Continuance of Thai values, heretofore taken for granted, must be actively pursued if Thailand were to remain Thai. Yet how was Thailand to become more Westernized and more Thai at the same time? For "Westernization" and "Thaiification" worked at cross-purposes: the more egalitarianism, the less hierarchy of respect; the more science and technology, the less abstraction from the material world.

Vajiravudh's answer to the challenge of Westernization was to embark on a program of nationalism for his country, a method of fighting fire with fire that has won global acceptance. The inspiration for Vajiravudh's nationalist program was, first and foremost, Great Britain, the Western nation that Vajiravudh knew best, at this time a nation caught up in imperialist enthusiasm. Other influences on the King were emergent Japan, whose defeat of Russia had made a strong impression on him, and the rising nationalist groups in China, which had had an influence on the Chinese in Thailand. Sources for nationalist inspiration were not hard to find in the years immediately before, during, and after World War I.

Nationalism, to be worthy of the name, requires more than an

Introduction

eloquent spokesman. Unless the leader has a mass following, unless numbers of people are caught up in the "ism," the nationalist proponent is merely a voice, and the ideology he espouses remains inert, lifeless. Machiavelli in the sixteenth century could call for the "valor of an Italian spirit," could speak of Italy's being "ready and willing to follow any banner" that would lead the battle for redemption from foreign occupation and bring unification. But he spoke as a visionary whose message, while undoubtedly attractive to Lorenzo Medici, his patron, had little effect on the Italian population at large. Machiavelli may have been a nationalist, but Italian nationalism was another 400 years in coming.

Was Vajiravudh a similar prenationalist voice, a propagandist but not a leader of a new loyalty? This is hard to judge. For he was the king, and his people perforce followed. The crucial question is whether those who followed did so out of obligation or out of conviction. Did Vajiravudh persuade the Thai people to love their nation above all else, or did he merely impose on them outward behavior that seemed to betoken nationalism?

However the question be answered—and some answer will be attempted—the position of Vajiravudh remains central. Whether he was the leader of an emergent nationalist land or an ideologue whose policies, later espoused by others, would produce a people aware of their uniqueness as a nation, Vajiravudh remains a key figure in the analysis of Thai nationalism. The history of Thai nationalism must start with Vajiravudh.

An overview of the nationalism of King Vajiravudh of Siam reveals many similarities with nationalistic expressions in other times and other places. The enlistment of tradition, of history, in the nationalistic cause is not new; nor is the empirical search for sources of national strength; nor is the effort to contrast the nation and national characteristics favorably with those of foreigners.

What is remarkable about Vajiravudh's nationalism no doubt owes much to the peculiar historical circumstances of Siam in the early twentieth century. Siam had managed to maintain its political independence, as a formality at least, in a century of expanding colonialism. The upsurge of anticolonial nationalism in the rest of Southeast Asia therefore bypassed Siam. The Thai people had been lulled into a feeling of relative complacency. Yet the Western-trained Vajiravudh saw that nationalism had a utility beyond its role in the achievement of independence; it had a utility in state-building. And so this traditional monarch worked assiduously to promote nationalism among a somewhat reluctant people.

Introduction

The difficulty of rousing nationalistic fervor in a country whose people by and large were "too content with themselves" was enormous. The difficulty was in no way diminished by the fact that the task was undertaken by a national leader acting very much on his own. "Be loyal to your king" may have been a good nationalistic aim, but it undoubtedly raised some eyebrows because it was pronounced by the King himself.

The injunction of the King to avoid imitating foreign ways also rang a bit false. For there was no greater imitator of Western ways in the Thailand of his day than the King himself. In addition to a governmental program that was essentially one of Westernization, Vajiravudh's nationalism and even many of its slogans (including the necessity for loyalty to nation, religion, and king—analogues to the British "God, King, and Country") were Western imports. Vajiravudh's strong stand against imitation meant, in the last analysis, only that the delicate choice of what should be introduced from the West was a choice that the King felt he alone was capable of making. Vajiravudh here was again the traditional monarch making the crucial decisions for his people.

The nationalistic program of Vajiravudh was, all in all, moderate, almost exclusively hortatory. Vajiravudh was no demagogue. His most xenophobic comments were directed against the Chinese, but even in these he did not descend into verbal mire. He launched no pogroms; in fact, no anti-Chinese legislation at all was issued during his reign.

The paradox of competing values in Thailand is nowhere clearer than in the picture of King Vajiravudh introducing the Western concept of nationalism to his people in the manner of a tolerant moral exemplar in the finest tradition of the benevolent autocracy of old Siam.

1

Prince to King

When Chulalongkorn died on October 23, 1910, he had been king for forty-two years. Most of his subjects could remember no other. The special royal word for the death of a king (*sawannakhot*) felt strange on the lips to older courtiers; it was meaningless to the young.

Despite the length of his rule—the longest in Thai history—the King was not old; his death was totally unexpected. Chulalongkorn had celebrated his fifty-seventh birthday a month before his death. Although he had had periodic bouts of illness over the years, he had not been ill for some time before his fatal attack. The progress from the first complaint of "stomach trouble" to coma and death was but a week. Not even the highest princes in the court knew the seriousness of the King's condition. Less than forty-eight hours before he died the First Queen had reported that "His Majesty has improved in all respects."[1]

Crown Prince Vajiravudh, whose residence at Saranrom Palace put him some distance away from Dusit Palace, where the King had

Prince to King

been staying, was probably less well informed about his father's illness than most. In fact, on the morning of the King's final day, Vajiravudh had had to be awakened to be summoned to Dusit Palace.[2]

Certainly in the short view the practical and emotional period of preparation of Vajiravudh for assuming the royal authority was brief. In the long view, however, his preparation, while not ideal, was better than that of most of his predecessors.

The first advantage he had was early assurance of becoming king. In 1886 Chulalongkorn, in order to ensure a peaceful succession, had appointed his son Vajirunhis Crown Prince, the first Crown Prince in Thai history. When Vajirunhis died in 1895, Chulalongkorn named Vajiravudh, then his oldest son of the highest princely rank, the new heir.[3] In the following fifteen years Vajiravudh, the royal family, and all the Thai people had become thoroughly used to the prospect of Vajiravudh's succession. The intention of Chulalongkorn in naming an heir was entirely fullfilled on his death, and the indecision, deliberating, politicking, and even open warfare that had characterized periods of change of rule in traditional times were completely avoided. Vajiravudh stepped into his new role unchallenged.

Other advantages of the new monarch included his intelligence, his age, his training, and his knowledge and experience. Vajiravudh's intelligence hardly requires proof. His mind was agile, inquisitive, logical, and retentive. Vajiravudh acceded at the age of twenty-nine, in the words of one Thai prince "a splendid age to succeed to a throne."[4] While age alone is no qualification, accession at too few years could be a distinct disadvantage, as Chulalongkorn himself had discovered when he had become king at fifteen, full of royal dignity but powerless.

The training of Vajiravudh was certainly exceptional. He was the first Siamese king to have been educated abroad, to have traveled extensively, to have visited many foreign courts and capitals. He left Siam for his education in England in 1893, when he was twelve, and stayed for nine years. He acquired a general education under a number of tutors and received special military training at Sandhurst and through service with several British infantry and artillery units. In 1900 he went up to Oxford, where he studied history and law. His social education was not neglected: he conversed with European royalty (starting by taking tea with Queen Victoria in 1894), learned horsemanship and lawn tennis, visited the London theater (he was always fond of plays), and represented his father at various functions. Throughout the European years he visited France, Belgium, Italy, Hungary, and Spain; on the way home, the United States and Japan.

Prince to King

The training of Vajiravudh in Thai traditions did not entirely lapse while he was abroad. Preceptors were periodically sent to Europe to instruct him—and the other sons of Chulalongkorn sent abroad for study—in the Thai language, in Buddhism, and in Thai culture. Further, the King on occasion sent letters of moral instruction to the young princes to help them keep their Thai values intact.[5] He advised his sons to write him regularly—in Thai as well as in a European language. For knowledge of Thai was indispensable. Chulalongkorn put this clearly in one letter:

> I would at this point impress upon you the fact that in sending you abroad for a European education, it is not my object to have you useful solely through your knowledge of foreign languages and European methods of work. Your own language and literature must ever be in constant use.... Knowledge of a foreign language is merely the means of acquiring further learning.[6]

On his return to Siam in January 1903, Vajiravudh gained additional experience. He became inspector general of the army, commander of the royal guards, an army general, an assistant private secretary to King Chulalongkorn, president of the National Library, president of the Commission on Exhibitions, chairman of a drafting committee for the military penal code, and temporary head of the Ministry of Justice. The Prince also on occasion accompanied the King to meetings of the Council of Ministers and was shown drafts of key documents—both as part of his preparation for eventual rule. The highest position the Prince was entrusted with in the years before his accession was that of head of the caretaker government, together with the Regency Council and Council of Ministers, during Chulalongkorn's second trip to Europe (for his health) from March to November 1907.

All these experiences, including the last as "acting king," carried less responsibility than might appear. In no case was Vajiravudh able to operate on his own. He was at the most a contributor to the work of a council, at the least an observer, expected to learn by seeing rather than by doing. During his father's absence in 1907, Vajiravudh fully filled the King's functions in only one role—that of performer of royal ceremonies in the countless Brahmanic and Buddhist rites that made up a large part of the royal duties. In deliberations of the Regency Council or the Council of Ministers, the Prince served as chairman, but key problems were cabled to the King for decision; and matters that required more immediate action were decided on by the councils, who were instructed to rely on their knowledge

Prince to King

of Chulalongkorn's earlier policies or, where such knowledge was lacking, on their best estimates of the King's probable course of action. All that was done from March to November 1907 had a *pro tem* character to it and had to pass Chulalongkorn's scrutiny on his return.[7]

Saranrom Palace

There was one area in which the Prince had considerable freedom of action, and that was the governance of his own household. It was the custom for young princes to leave the king's palace—where the considerable female royal entourage also resided—at an early age. Vajiravudh followed this custom late in 1904, taking up residence in Saranrom Palace. Here he was to develop a style of life and some of the special interests that he carried forward into his reign as king.

Saranrom Palace in the days when it served as residence of the Crown Prince was quite a world to itself. Located in spacious walled grounds east of the Grand Palace, the site even today preserves remnants of its former splendor—a Chinese-style pagoda tower, a Cambodian-style monument, various Victorian-style buildings elaborate with wooden Hansel-and-Gretel fretwork, walks and lanes that at one time bordered carefully laid out gardens and forested parks. This was Vajiravudh's domain for six years; this, his little empire, the setting of his princely court, the stage for his enterprises.

Among the preferred activities at Saranrom were amateur theatricals, classical dancing practice, war games, literary production, and newspaper publishing. These activities were organized and managed by the Prince personally. For the classical dance form called *khon* ("masked drama"), an amateur troupe (Khon Samak Len) was established.[8] Trained teachers and musicians were hired, but the troupe itself was made up of young courtiers. The Crown Prince wrote the texts and directed the troupe's frequent performances. In the program notes for a performance at the opening of the school of military cadets on December 25, 1909, the Prince wrote that the wish of the volunteer performers was only to give pleasure and to remind the Thai that the art of the dance was not exclusively Western, that the Thai had traditional arts that ought not be allowed to fall into ruin.[9] This basic purpose was to underlie many aspects of Vajiravudh's nationalism after he became king. The Prince also took keen interest in plays—production, writing, acting. At least four of his full-length plays date from Saranrom times.[10]

Literary activities of all kinds had long interested the Prince. Even during his days in England he had been productive, turning out

Prince to King

student publications and a historical thesis for Oxford.[11] Two earmarks of the writer—voracious reading habits and the keeping of a diary—were among the earliest habits of Vajiravudh.[12] At Saranrom much of the literary work was directed into the publication of a monthly journal entitled *Thawipanya* (Enhancement of Knowledge). The Prince was editor and chief contributor to the journal, which printed poems and articles with political and nationalistic overtones as well as purely literary pieces. Aside from contributions to *Thawipanya*, Vajiravudh also produced three travel accounts: one of a trip to the North with his father in 1905;[13] one of a trip to the South in 1909;[14] and, the most interesting, a long narrative account of his trip in 1907 to the region of Thailand's first capital, Sukhothai.[15] The Sukhothai account, published in 1908, is a remarkable journey into Thailand's past, both in terms of the physical journey by elephant and on foot through rough, often uncleared jungle trails that had once been royal highways and in terms of the intellectual encounter at sites of palaces and temples of onetime grandeur. The Prince, in his preface to this work, made his purpose clear. He hoped the work would be of use to archaeologists and historians, but he also had other hopes for it:

> Perhaps it will make the Thai more aware that our Thai race is not a new race and is not a race of jungle folk or, as the English say, uncivilized .... We should feel ashamed today to compare ourselves not only to other peoples but also to our own ancestors .... The ancient Thai had the concepts and the diligence to make structures that were large and beautiful and long-lasting. Thai today do nothing but destroy the old things or let them decay because of their infatuation with new things in Western style. They do not know how to choose what is appropriate for our country.[16]

Many of the preoccupations at Saranrom Palace have been generally regarded as "games." Some indeed were; the Prince certainly took his moments of relaxation. He liked to tell stories to the young pages. One courtier particularly remembers the ghost stories—the deliberately dimmed lights, the close huddle round the Prince, the real fright of many, some of whom later had trouble getting to sleep.[17] Other popular amusements were charades, riddles, and treasure hunts.[18]

Games in at least one category had, or were to develop, a serious side; these were the war games and police games. The war games apparently started in 1905 and were played in the environs of Saranrom. They were elaborately staged. There were two teams, each

Prince to King

headed by a command staff which planned the strategy to be carried out by the commissioned and noncommissioned officers and the men. Each side wore a distinguishing color, red or green, and the various grades of soldiers wore appropriate insignia. Firecrackers were used to help produce realism. The games were taken seriously, and the operations were judged by referees. The Crown Prince usually served as the principal referee, although on occasion he commanded one of the combatant teams instead. A general strike of Chinese merchants in Bangkok in June 1910 inspired a variation of the war games: police action against "Chinese" strikers.

All the games, including the war games, took place at night after dinner, beginning around 10 P.M. Ordinary games usually lasted until 3 A.M., but the war games went on until 4 or 5 A.M. The relaxed Prince and exhausted pages would be off to bed with the sounds of the waking city—the sound of the reveille bugle at the nearby military cadet school and the clatter of streetcars bringing early workers to their jobs. It is obvious that, when the war games were held, they absorbed the major energies of the Prince and his courtiers. The fact that they were held late at night and in the early morning hours was in keeping with the traditional regimen in Thai court circles.

The war games were also conducted during the Prince's vacation months away from Bangkok at his bungalow in Nakhǫn Pathom. There the games took place during the day; the uniforms were more elaborate; "artillery" units with teak-log cannon were added; and the whole operation was even more strenuous and serious, partly because local people—officials and farmers—came to watch.[19]

A game of somewhat similar nature occupied the Prince and young pages for a time at Parusakawan Palace. Here a model municipality was built, consisting physically of a long, narrow building, divided into rooms, with two pages to a room, and ideationally of a self-governing community with its own government leaders, its own fire department, police, bank, newspaper, and town meetings. The fire department drilled by sprinkling the lawn and shrubbery; the bank received deposits the pages were able to make from their small monthly stipends.[20]

An indispensable element in all the Prince's activities in the closed world within his own control was his attempt to build a body of loyal and like-minded retainers and to develop a spirit of camaraderie within it. One of his first acts at Saranrom was to create a club called Thawipanya Samosǫn, or the Enhancement of Knowledge Club.[21] Membership was drawn from both courtiers and individuals outside the Saranrom court. By Thai standards of the time, the Thawipanya Club was remarkably egalitarian: commoners far outnumbered those of princely rank, and all members were treated equally. The club had its own officers; its principal officer was elected annually (the Crown Prince always won), and he chose all the other officers.[22] The club published the journal *Thawipanya*.

The club was much like a British club. Members used the clubhouse, in the Saranrom Gardens, to lounge about and read the foreign and domestic newspapers or to play billiards, ping pong, chess, or card games. Outdoor sports included tennis, cricket, croquet, and hockey. These games were all very new in Thailand, and their popularity rapidly grew—no doubt in large part because of the princely favor shown them. The membership also held general meetings two or three times a week. These meetings were usually devoted to formally organized debates on topics such as "This group believes in ghosts" (the affirmative won) or "Electric lights are better than lanterns" (the negative won).[23]

The Thawipanya Club also sponsored amateur theatricals. A small playhouse was built in the gardens, and frequent performances were given. At times outside guests were invited. Even Westerners, on occasion, were part of the audience, and one foreign journalist recalled in later years "the happiest memories of evenings in that theatre in the garden."[24]

The Prince's predilection for dramatics was not universally appreciated. His mother was one outstanding critic. Queen Saowapha came to one performance in which Vajiravudh had a part, and after the performance Her Majesty remonstrated with him. She said that she had enjoyed the play but could not get over the feeling that it was not right for the Prince himself to be on stage, interacting with other people in a way not suitable for one of his rank and station. The Prince yielded nothing in his reply: acting was an art; acting required one to play the role of the character portrayed, not oneself; there was nothing unseemly in actions that were part of developing a characterization. In short, the Prince made it clear that he intended to keep on acting.[25] And he did so, even as king.

One other action by Vajiravudh as Crown Prince that was indicative of his interests was the establishment of a special school in 1907. Most of the pages went to school off the palace grounds. For pages who had completed primary education but had not yet entered government service or one of the military academies, and for pages enrolled elsewhere but with some free time, special classes were held

Prince to King

at Saranrom in law, government, economics, military science, geography and history, and English. The Prince designed the curriculum and was the principal instructor.

In a sense, at Saranrom the Crown Prince himself was the principal student. He was organizing; he was leading; he was expressing ideas and carrying out notions. There are foreshadowings of many of his later state policies in his games, clubs, and literary proclivities. But the view of Saranrom as a training period for serious state ideas must not be carried too far. Saranrom was also Vajiravudh's place of relaxation, of play for play's sake. This was in no way unusual. Highborn princes were expected to enjoy themselves. Chulalongkorn, for example, had been established in his own separate residence at a much earlier age; he had held many parties there, had become something of a collector, and had become a father by two of his concubines—all before he reached the age of fifteen, when his father died.

There were some aspects of Vajiravudh's life at Saranrom that stimulated criticism. His playacting was one, as has already been mentioned. Even more important was the Prince's failure to marry. The entourage at Saranrom was entirely male. For a prince to reach his late twenties without acquiring a concubine was unusual and a disappointment to those anxious for the future of the dynastic line. Here again his chief critic, the only one to speak directly to him on the subject, was his mother. The Queen's personal physician reported that Vajiravudh's refusal to marry "was a source of continual distress and irritation to his mother." She argued; she pleaded; she reasoned; she tempted him by putting some "charmingly dressed" cousins in his way. All to no avail. The son remained an enigma to his mother. He remained adamant, and she accepted defeat—although none too graciously.[26]

Another source of some criticism was the Prince's extreme loyalty to the retainers, courtiers, and pages immediately around him. Some of the Prince's closest attachments were made within the circle of Saranrom, attachments that continued throughout the period of his reign as king. It was to be expected that some individuals outside this circle should resent their exclusion. There is no evidence, however, that their criticisms had any real effect upon the Prince or deflected him from pursuing his own goals in his own way.

A Victorian Siamese Prince

By October 23, 1910, Vajiravudh had been schooled, had been cast in public roles, had developed a private style of life. He had also

Prince to King

fitted out the furnishings of his mind. His overall perceptions as to what his small country, Siam, would need in order to survive had been formed; he was already convinced that Siam's first requirement was the development of a national esprit. Indeed, many of the specifics toward this goal had been partly conceptualized.

The cast of thought of the Prince was a reflection of his upbringing and of his time. He was a Victorian Siamese prince.

The impact of England on the Prince had been profound. His written and spoken English was excellent. He knew and admired the manners of British gentlemen. In Europe he had been *au courant* with the best restaurants (e.g., Claridge's), the best theaters. He could comment after viewing the ballet *Sylvia* at the Theatre Marie in St. Petersburg that its prima ballerina "danced very nicely. She has improved since last winter."[27] He read and enjoyed English periodicals, including *Punch*, *The Tattler*, and *Strand*.

Aside from admiring and acquiring the elite manners of Europe's premier state, Vajiravudh had been impressed with the ethos of Victorian society. England in the 1890s and early 1900s, the period of Vajiravudh's stay there, was not merely a powerful nation, it was the arbiter of Europe, the center of world empire. And assumptions about the reasons for this premiership surrounded Vajiravudh.

The Englishman of the late Victorian years was convinced that he lived in man's best times in man's best land. The criteria for evaluation were the technological proofs of progress: everything was bigger and better, and England had the biggest and best. In 1897, three years after Vajiravudh's arrival, England celebrated Victoria's Diamond Jubilee. Victoria's record-breaking reign "was symbolic, for England was also engaged in record breaking—she held the records for Empire, for wealth, for commerce, for sea-power, for the size of her metropolis, for social prosperity."[28]

Other proofs and symbols of England's preeminence abounded. In art the age of Wilde and Beardsley was seen as the beginning of a new Renaissance; a renaissance had certainly taken place in the theater with the plays of Jones, Pinero, and Shaw. In sports England was supreme; "the idea that foreigners could compete with Englishmen in any sort of athletic pursuit would have been scouted as too absurd for words."[29] And in the realm of imagination Kipling's "ten-year British sodger" brought the common man a hero who, by combining the discipline of the barracks with love of the Queen, became world conqueror. This loyalty of the Englishman, his belief in his great and well-deserved destiny, his willingness to work for it, to make any sacrifice to help the "team" win a soccer cup or to

Prince to King

help the Queen win the championship of the world, made a deep and long-lasting impression on the young Siamese prince in England.

Yet Vajiravudh did not become a converted Englishman. He did not become an uncritical Anglophile. His earliest schooling as a Siamese prince, reinforced by the princely life he resumed after the English interlude, inevitably determined his outlook. The outlook of the Siamese elite was not easily abandoned. The privilege, even adulation, accorded Siamese royalty was a deference that permeated the whole of the Thai social order and depended philosophically on the Buddhist belief that one was born to the existence he had earned in previous incarnations. The hierarchy of deference reached its peak in members of royalty and was expressed in forms beyond anything that could be imagined in Victorian England. Vajiravudh's place in this system had been confirmed by numerous royal ceremonies held for him from an early age—his establishment with his royal name and title and own retinue at the age of eight, his tonsure at the age of eleven, and his installation as Crown Prince at the age of fourteen. The tonsure ceremony, for example, was a week-long affair involving the construction of a forty-foot artificial "holy" mountain at the top of which King Chulalongkorn, as the god Siva, apotheosized his son as the god Ganesa. A onetime member of the Department of Royal Pages commented:

> However ignorant of the meaning of the complicated rites the young prince may be, he must at least subconsciously realize that this festival signifies a break with childhood days, that he must begin to take life seriously, and that he is a person of great importance on whom will eventually rest the responsibility for the welfare of the people .... no finer training for a possible heir to the throne in regal bearing and the duties that might later be required of him could possibly be conceived.[30]

There are abundant indications that Prince Vajiravudh fully appreciated the dignity of his social position. The one adverse report on record from his English tutor apparently arose from the tutor's lack of understanding of the social standing of the Prince among his own people: Vajiravudh had apparently acted imperiously toward two of his military aides, and the tutor reported that he was afraid the disposition of the Prince had turned sour. The Thai adults who investigated the matter saw only the normal behavior of a Siamese prince toward his commoner servants.[31]

The shuttling between East and West—both physically and ideologically—produced tensions and scars in Vajiravudh (and in other princes of his generation). The attempt to create an English club

Prince Vajiravudh at His Tonsure Ceremony.

atmosphere at Saranrom Palace by authoritarian means is a typical expression of his dilemma. On the personal level, Vajiravudh's shyness, his reluctance to establish close relationships with members of his own family, his didacticism, his love of children's games, and his sensitivity to criticism all bespeak a complicated man attempting to resolve his internal confusions on his own, by his own lights. Vajiravudh's reaction to criticism is particularly revealing: instead of modifying his behavior, Vajiravudh almost invariably retaliated with a devastating criticism of the critic.

The insecurity that can be perceived in the Prince's character undoubtedly had its psychological sources. The first Crown Prince, Vajirunhis, who died at the age of sixteen, was obviously much beloved by his parents; Vajiravudh must have felt, at times at least, that he was only a "second choice." Moreover, there are strong indications that both of Vajiravudh's parents were fonder of his full brother Chakrabongs than of Vajiravudh.[32] These facts may well have had their impact. And the insecurity of Siam itself may have affected his psyche. Just thirty-eight days before the young Prince left for his studies in England, French gunboats entered the Chaophraya River and anchored at Bangkok to underline demands for Siamese territorial concessions in favor of French Indochina. The Siamese survived this most serious challenge to their sovereignty only by making broad concessions. Vajiravudh, although young, could not help but be moved by the near panic this French move of 1893 caused in court circles.[33] King Chulalongkorn could not mask his fears. He secretly deposited a large sum of money in England to take care of his son in case the worst should happen and Vajiravudh should one day find that he had no country to return to. And he informed the twelve-year-old Prince of what he had done.[34]

Despite the thread of insecurity that was woven into his character, the visible fabric of Vajiravudh's personality showed no weakness. However strong his father had been, however great his contributions to his country, Vajiravudh on balance was convinced that mistakes had been made and that he, thanks to his broader knowledge of the outside world, would be able to bring Siam the kind of rule and the vital policies it needed for survival.

2

The King Consecrated

I wish no honor greater than that of being my father's son who, having inherited the throne, walks in his footsteps in order to help to complete the tasks necessary for the progress of the country.[1]

The earliest speeches of Vajiravudh as king abound in declarations of his intention of following in his father's footsteps. And his earliest actions were in no way disruptive of the past. In fact, traditional Thai administrative practices worked against rapid change of men or policies at the highest levels of government. For a monarch inherited the entire apparatus of his predecessor's government; the principal ministers were never removed from their posts or power. Vajiravudh had no immediate desire to disturb old officials who were inclined to regard the edifice of state created by Chulalongkorn as embodying "all that was absolute and right" and were "inclined instinctively to regard any possible reversal or even modification of . . . policy as

The King Consecrated

a sort of sacrilege."[2] He recognized the hold of "antiquated traditions" and appraised his situation realistically: "Just at first things are bound to move rather slowly, because of the many difficulties I have to surmount."[3]

Further, there was not much time in the early months of the reign for important change. There were countless ceremonies to be got through: the rites preliminary to the cremation of Chulalongkorn; the coronation of Vajiravudh on November 11; and, finally, the cremation of Chulalongkorn on March 16, 1911.

Yet Vajiravudh felt the need for something to signify that new directions would be pursued, to impress on his own people and the world outside that a new era had begun in Siam. The something decided on was a second grand coronation to be held at the end of 1911, well after the last obsequies for Chulalongkorn would be over.[4]

The coronation of kings in Thailand is an elaborate Brahmanic rite in which the royal name is inscribed on a golden tablet and the king takes a purificatory bath, receives the waters of consecration—eight waters brought from the eight directions of the kingdom—while sitting on an octagonal throne and facing in the appropriate direction, accepts the royal regalia (the crown is merely one of these), performs various kinds of almsgiving, holds ceremonial audiences with princes and ministers, and makes progresses around the capital by land and water. The ceremonies signify, in ancient Brahmanic thought, the king's assumption of divinity. In Siam the king could not claim the full powers and name of king until the key rite of consecration had taken place. And so the coronation ceremony was usually held within a week—in no case longer than a month—after accession to power.

Such a ceremony was conducted in November. Meanwhile, preparations were already going on for the second grand coronation to take place a little over a year later.[5]

The decision to hold a second coronation must have been made very early, possibly even before Vajiravudh acceded. For the first coronation omitted the traditional, though not essential, processions around the capital.[6] The idea of holding a European-style coronation celebration was undoubtedly stimulated by Vajiravudh's participation in the accession ceremonies of Alfonso XIII of Spain in 1902 and in the coronation festivities of Edward VII of England in the same year. For Siam to hold a similar celebration, with Vajiravudh hosting representatives of royal houses and ruling parties of the leading states of the world, would give Siam unprecedented prominence and dignity.

The King Consecrated

Some Thai were apprehensive, before the second coronation took place, that the ceremony itself would be conducted on Western lines.[7] Such fears were unfounded. Vajiravudh had no intention of having anything but a typical Thai coronation to which would be added festivities for foreign guests and the Thai population.

Vajiravudh's reasons for respect for Brahmanic ritual, particularly in relation to Thai coronations, were made manifest in one of his essays.[8] He argued against those "modernists" who would abandon old rituals in favor of Western models by pointing out that Siam was not a Western country, that modern Western notions should be adopted only when their utility was unmistakable, and that abandonment of Siam's past was to bring Siam back to the jungle, to make the Thai a primitive folk without a history or heritage. Insofar as the Brahmanic rites were concerned, he argued that, although it was true that the Thai were not Hindus but Buddhists, some aspects of life were not the concern of Buddhism. Buddhist monks might chant at coronations, for example, but the heart of the ceremony in Siam had always been not Buddhist but Brahmanic. And so, if for no other reason than to insure legitimacy in the installation of new kings, Brahman priests should be retained and supported.

Other traditions were highlighted even before the grand coronation. Among the most important were those associated with auguries. Supernatural signs of favor were eagerly sought at beginnings of reigns. Such signs were common throughout Indianized Southeast Asia, and ranged from earthquakes to showers of gemstones.[9] Vajiravudh's reign started with a succession of highly regarded portents: discoveries of some ancient bronze pieces—first, a flag standard bearing designs of a monkey and a *garuda* (a mythical bird); then, a bow and some arrows. These ancient articles, it was speculated, were once used in Brahmanic ceremonies. All these bronze pieces were presented to the King, who had replicas made for use in subsequent ceremonies. Also within the first months of the reign an albino elephant was found and presented to the King. In Siam and Burma the so-called white elephant was very highly regarded, and the discovery and capture of one at the beginning of a reign was considered very auspicious indeed.

Much was made of all these signs by high officials and the King. Vajiravudh, for example, ordered Prince Damrong, head of the Ministry of the Interior, to publicize the portentous acquisitions by printing a letter by the King about them in the journal of local government (*Nangsŭ thesaphiban*); the King noted that all government servants would thereby be inspired to work more industriously for

The King Consecrated

the benefit of the country.[10] One official publicly stated that, by these omens of highest import, "we are...convinced that Your Majesty was destined to be the great leader of our race."[11] Vajiravudh drew special joy from these "boons of supernatural power" and "objects of transcendent virtue."[12] He recalled from history the story of an ancient king who had found jewels and pearls on the shores of the sea and was still famous for his meritorious rule. He took particular pleasure in the bow and arrows, which he named "The Bow and Arrows of Rama's Strength," deriving meaning from the symbolism of these objects as weapons: "sure manifestations that warriors have not yet ceased to exist in the Land of the Thai."[13] He made much of their presumed association with Rama, the Hindu god whose name Vajiravudh was later to appropriate, and of the fact that at the end of one of the arrows was a trident (*wachira*, or *vajira*), a symbol Vajiravudh favored because it was part of his name: "almost as if made for me, and so all the more pleasing."[14]

The Grand Coronation

The coronation proper, with its key ceremony of consecration on December 2, was essentially a repeat of the time-honored ritual conducted a year earlier. This is not to say that the new coronation was devoid of emotional impact. In a remarkably intimate letter to his younger brother Chakrabongs, written on the evening of "this the greatest day of my life," Vajiravudh confided, "When the water of consecration fell first upon my head this morning, my tears fell with it. They were tears of mingled joy and sorrow."[15]

The most significant changes in the coronation proper were made in the concluding rites. For the first time, they were held in the handsome hall called Dusit Maha Prasat. Ordinarily this building was used for the long lying-in-state rituals and therefore was unavailable for coronations. In 1911, however, the hall was available, and Vajiravudh had the building renovated, removing some interior pillars that obstructed the view.[16] So the final ceremonies of accepting the royal regalia and conducting audiences were held in this grand hall, in the presence of many princes, officials, and foreign guests.

In the eyes of the foreigners present, the "supreme moment" was the crowning of the King by himself. The crown was a dazzling golden spire glittering with diamonds. When the crown came to rest, a "loud peal of joy burst out. All the ancient musical instruments were played with energy; the troops presented arms; the bands played the royal anthem; the four kinds of cannons used in ceremonies were fired; and the sound was taken up by the guns of the Army

The King Consecrated

and the Navy firing a salute of 101 guns. The bell at every temple throughout the Kingdom was beaten seven times, and in every monastery the monks assembled and prayed for a blessing on the King."[17]

After the ceremonies inside Dusit Maha Prasat were completed, an unprecedented new spectacle was staged. Between the entrances at the top of the parallel flights of stairs at the north face of the hall is a high and magnificently carved and heavily gilded balcony that faces a courtyard. On the balcony is a spired, gilded throne. A grander setting for a ceremony could hardly be imagined, and it was here that Vajiravudh held the final audience of his coronation day—the audience for the people. The princes and high officials had witnessed the ceremonies within the hall; now Vajiravudh wanted to show himself to the lower ranks and the general population, groups that had never before been so intimately associated with a coronation. These groups were represented by lesser civil and military officials, who were assembled in the courtyard facing the balcony. The crowd was large, larger than any that could have been accommodated inside a royal hall. And Vajiravudh's appearance before them was strikingly dramatic. All three sides of the balcony were draped, concealing the throne from the view of the crowd in the courtyard. The King entered by a rear door. At a signal the drums were beaten, the music flared, the soldiers presented arms, and the drapes were drawn—suddenly revealing the King seated on the throne, glittering in the sun above the crowd.[18]

Starting with the evening of the coronation day, there followed a round of parading and partying such as the old capital, used as it was to royal merrymaking, had never before seen crowded into such a short space of time. Vajiravudh's purposes in this grand display are clear. He wanted to draw into the mood of joy as many of his people as he could, to bring them together, have them share together, feel together the exhilaration of the time. And he wanted to impress his Western guests with Siam's progress, strength, and unity. The drums and bells, the fetes and pageants signaled not only the start of a new reign but also the bold entrance of nationalism as a state policy.

The most novel part of the coronation activities was the involvement of foreigners. Not that the presence of foreigners was entirely unprecedented. Chulalongkorn in 1873 and, before him, Mongkut in 1851 had invited foreigners to their inaugural rites.[19] The foreign guests on those earlier occasions, however, had been merely individuals who happened to be resident in Bangkok at the time. Vaji-

Public Audience on Coronation Day (Mural in Anantasamakhom Throne Hall).

The King Consecrated

ravudh's innovation was to adopt the European fashion and send invitations directly to the capitals of countries with whom Siam had treaty relations. The foreign guests he aimed for, and by and large got, were thus in the category of royal equals, of courtly "kin," rather than the less dignified status of local representatives of the diplomatic corps.

Who came? Although no reigning sovereign did—time and distance in the age before jet, or even prop, travel prevented that— the list of guests was impressive. Altogether there were some twenty-five royal representatives and special representatives (plus their entourages) representing fourteen governments. Ten of the guests were members of royal families. The great powers—England, France, Russia, Germany, the United States, and Japan—were all represented. The editorial writer of a local English-language newspaper reflected the general view: "Siam is feeling very proud and a little anxious. Never before have there been gathered in this capital so many Princes of foreign Reigning Families. Such a gathering of Royalties, the guests of the Sovereign, is comparatively a rare thing in a European capital, and is without precedent outside Europe."[20]

The preparations for impressing this distinguished foreign assembly were unstinting in labor and expense. As early as July the press caught the "general expectation that previous records in magnificence will be surpassed."[21] The whole capital was involved in a face-lift. People living along procession routes were ordered to paint their houses. Some 2,000 men were set to work refurbishing the Grand Palace. One royal building was turned into a museum to display "the priceless gold and silver vessels of ancient Siamese design and the collection of old time instruments of war." Another hall was extensively remodeled and fitted with lavish appointments to serve as "Theatre Royal" for the dramatic productions to be staged for the coronation festivities. And many palaces about town, including Saranrom, Amphọn, and the group in Dusit Park, were spruced up to serve as residences for the foreign guests. In those which lacked Western-style bathrooms, these facilities were installed. Some 750 tons of furniture were ordered from abroad as part of the program to provide the guests with nothing but the best.[22]

Foreign guests began arriving at the end of November. They were immediately caught up in a swirl of entertainments. Prince Chakrabongs, who was the heir presumptive and had represented Siam at the coronation of George V in England just five months before, was appointed the King's official greeter. He met the guests on arrival and saw them to their accommodations. On at least four occasions

The King Consecrated

before the coronation, the King himself met with groups of foreign guests. Foreigners were admitted to all the important coronation ceremonies. And luncheon and dinner parties, theatrical performances, illuminations, troop displays and parades, trips to temple fairs, and excursions to the old capital at Ayutthaya and the palace at Bang Pa-in were arranged. All high Thai royalty—including Queen Mother Saowapha, Prince Chakrabongs, Prince Yugala, Prince Paribatra, Prince Damrong, Prince Devawongse, and Prince Chira—were involved as hosts, wining and dining the visitors.

But the principal host was the King himself, who started the postcoronation round of partying with a gala performance of the Thai masked drama at the Theatre Royal on the evening of December 2. The King was also host of the Coronation Ball on December 6—not Siam's first such fancy dress affair, but one that "surpassed any that had gone before."[23] Throughout the days to December 10, when the final banquet and last fireworks display took place, Vajiravudh gave extraordinary personal attention to the guests, overcoming, in the words of Swedish Prince William, his "first shyness" to become a lively conversationalist.[24]

A Grand Success

The products of this trouble were all that had been desired. The foreign press and foreign guests were lavish and, presumably, sincere in their praise. The local English-language press editorialized: "Siam does well to be proud of the position she has attained, and of the sympathy and friendship shown her by all the other nations with which she has relations."[25] The coronation received wide and complimentary attention from the overseas press, with photographs and feature articles appearing in such publications as *The National Geographic*[26] and the *Daily Mirror*.[27] The American minister, in his birthday greetings to the King on January 1 on behalf of the entire diplomatic corps, referred to the coronation as "graced by the approval of such a representation of the World's Powers as never before was seen in Siam," as "successful beyond the expectations of her most ardent friends," and as having "given this People a new place among the World's family of Nations."[28] Prince William, who stayed on a while after the other foreigners had gone, was much impressed with the coronation, noting "I have never seen a crowned head sustain his dignity better than did Maha Vajiravudh on December 2, 1911";[29] he also wrote of "the truly magnificent Oriental hospitality that was shown us by our royal host."[30]

The Siamese themselves thought they had done well. The

The King Consecrated

Minister of Local Government termed the coronation "an event unparalleled in success and splendour in the history of our nation."[31] Finally the King, who acknowledged that the presence of so many high foreign dignitaries had at first filled all with "grave anxiety" lest anything go wrong and bring Siam worldwide criticism, noted with joy that the affair had achieved success "beyond our most sanguine expectations." He complimented everyone for helping "to bring about this satisfactory issue," which, he stated, "shows that we Siamese are yet far from the path of decline as a nation, and have no reason to be ashamed of ourselves before the nations who are ever watching us." Vajiravudh took special pride that of all Asian peoples "we Siamese . . . are the first nation to have attempted, and accomplished with unqualified success, such a great undertaking" involving "the great nations of the world." The King was confident that the coronation had won Siam the "good opinion" of the nations and had "demonstrated to the world" the strength of Thai national unity.[32]

The unity "demonstrated" by the participation of the populace in the coronation festivities was in fact a deliberate goal the King hoped the festivities would help realize. Never had so many people from so many strata of society been as actively participant in a coronation before. The route of the royal progress by land on December 3 followed a long path through the city. The procession stopped first at a large temporary pavilion especially constructed on the grounds of the city's great square, the Royal Plaza (*sanam luang*), where the King received an address of welcome from the people. The procession also stopped at another pavilion in the northern sector of town to exchange courtesies with representatives of the European resident community. And it stopped at two temples en route. On December 4 the progress by water took place. On December 5 the King returned to the pavilion at the Royal Plaza to address the students. On the sixth, various regiments of the army were presented with colors at the same site. And on the next day, His Majesty reviewed the troops. On the eighth, Vajiravudh drove to the heart of the business district to receive the compliments of the Chinese and Indian communities. The ninth and tenth were devoted to the King's special volunteer corps called the Wild Tigers.

Every effort seems to have been made to attract as many people as possible to most of these affairs. The line of march was always dense with people. The students' homage brought an assembly of 10,000 children. The military displays involved 30,000 troops, including many brought in from distant provinces.

The King Consecrated

The speeches given on the several occasions were full of formal compliments and well-wishing on one side, grateful thanks on the other. But there was more. The King was conveying an important message: in his remarks to his own people—the general populace, the students, the military—he set forth for the first time before large public assemblies the need for the unity of his people and, in brief form, some of his principal notions of Thai nationalism. The address to the people is typical. In it he pointed to the heritage of the Thai as a free people, thanks to the "patriotic self-denial" and "great sacrifice, even to the giving up of life" of the "noble ancestors of our Race." He said that Siam's essential strength was derived from the devotion of the people to their nation, to their religion, and to their king. He pledged never to spare himself or his personal comfort in pursuit of his sacred duty to preserve Siam's absolute independence. But, he stated, he could not discharge his high mission unaided; he needed the "mutual help and accord" of all. The people should perform their duties, obey the laws, show "mutual consideration," set aside "self-indulgence." If the Thai people were imbued with "patriotic intentions" and if they strove in unison to further the best interests of the country, Siam's future existence "as a free and independent nation will be absolutely assured." He concluded:

> Let no person of the Thai Race forget these high principles. Remember that we are born free and that our nation is known to the world as the Nation of the Free. Help, therefore, each other with your whole heart to maintain and uphold our precious independence unto eternity.[33]

Signs of popular excitement during the festive coronation days were not lacking. Most were undoubtedly expressions of simple natural exuberance, a holiday mood. For, on top of everything else, the time of the coronation coincided with that of the usual winter carnival celebrations that the Thai, basically an agricultural people, had traditionally enjoyed in the times between harvest and new planting. In one surprising moment, the King himself literally got carried away by the crowd. He and his sister, Princess Walai, were returning from a late reception given by the navy. They entered their carriage, and before anyone knew what was happening a group of sailors took up the carriage and pulled it out into the road "amid the cheers of the guests and of the naval men." The sailors moved at a run. They approached the palace. "Here the enthusiasm became infectious and the large crowds who had been watching the theatricals joined the procession. With an impetuosity that would not be denied, they rushed past the shocked palace guards . . . and only

The King Consecrated

halted when they had brought the Sovereign to his Home. The King smiled his thanks and retired within the Palace."[34] This incident is remarkably similar to one that occurred at Queen Victoria's Jubilee in 1887, when a mob of working men ran alongside the Queen's carriage "shouting with the full strength of their lungs, 'Go it, Old Girl! You done it well! You done it well!'" and the Queen responded "to the 'Old Girl' greeting with jolly nods and laughter that had in them nothing of ceremony or stateliness."[35]

A similar kind of infectious good feeling was evident on the day the children presented their homage. The children had listened to the King's call that they study hard and be a credit to their nation; they had marched; they had sung songs, including a special patriotic song composed by the King. When the King was preparing to depart, they began to cheer him, and the cheering "from the wide open mouths of healthy youngsters . . . surprised everyone by its strength. The school flags, and handkerchiefs were waved, hats thrown in the air, and the motions of the bandsmen were the only signs that the National Anthem was being played. The cheering continued long after His Majesty had passed out of sight. . . ." After the festivities the "highly excited" children were reluctant to go home; their parents had a hard time rounding them up: "The moon was high before the last batch got away and enthusiasm still ran high—so much so that the lads went marching and singing through the streets to their homes."[36]

The efforts to bring about a wave of popular enthusiasm for the King and his policies through the coronation celebration seem to have been as successful as were the efforts to impress the Western visitors. The local press was convinced that the children, for example, had proved their ability to respond to the King's appeal to their sense of loyalty. "Most significant of all," the press editorialized, the coronation showed that "the enthusiasm of the people has been growing. They are become more than ever proud of their King, and more than ever eager to co-operate in the realisation of his ideals."[37] The King reached essentially the same conclusion. In his annual birthday address on January 1, 1912, he commended all his people for making "the great national event" a success. The success that it was, the lack of "a single disturbance of any kind," constituted "undoubted proof that the people recognised that the event was not merely a ceremony for the King alone but the supreme demonstration and expression of the national independent existence. . . ."[38]

The equation of public fervor with national devotion was an easy one to make for someone familiar with European thought of the times.

The King Consecrated

Certainly the causal pairing of joy and loyalty was common in late nineteenth-century England. Tennyson summed it all up in these lines in "On the Jubilee of Queen Victoria":

> You then joyfully, all of you,
> Set the mountain aflame to-night,
> Shoot your stars to the firmament,
> Deck your houses, illuminate
> All your towns for a festival,
> And in each let a multitude
> Loyal, each, to the heart of it,
> One full voice of allegiance,
> Hail the fair Ceremonial
> Of this year of her Jubilee.[39]

None of this kind of loyal jubilation was part of Thai heritage. Most ceremonies, including coronations, had been private affairs, terrible in their magic, performed by and for a god-king to ensure the potency of his divine powers. In the end the ceremonies were for the benefit of the people, but that certainly did not mean they should be staged for the people's benefit. Quite the contrary. The need to ensure ritual purification was paramount. The defilement of ceremonies was not merely *lèse majesté*, it struck back at the defiler by reducing royal potency and thus adversely affected the whole kingdom. Even the royal progresses by land and water at the coronation's end were not originally for the benefit of public observers but signified ritual "possession" of the state. People were expected to stay indoors, out of sight, so they would not be harmed by the awesome power of His Majesty's gaze.

Change in this attitude toward ceremonies had been started by King Mongkut in the 1850s. Mongkut, who had spent twenty-seven years before his accession as a Buddhist monk, deemphasized some Hinduist elements and added Buddhist elements in court ritual, thus bringing the crown closer to the people. Chulalongkorn continued this policy. In fact, Chulalongkorn apparently wished for more Western-style public displays than his people would dare to give him; he "hankered for a more spontaneous welcome from the people, for something nearer to that which was accorded to European royalty when they went on tour." His officials tried to teach the people to "cheer and wave their hats," but these efforts failed: "to the country people the King was still a deity, someone to be feared"; they dared not "take familiarities with the gods that they were not accustomed to."[40] Vajiravudh, so much closer to the West than either of his

24

The King Consecrated

predecessors, and farther away than they from the ideal and ethos of the god-king, wanted the public displays even more and was willing to go to far greater lengths to get them.

Similarly with the desire to impress the West. The desire was not new. Mongkut delighted in exhibiting his knowledge of Western science, language, and culture. Chulalongkorn gave lavish dinner parties, constructed extravagant marble palaces in the Italian style. Vajiravudh built upon this public relations approach to international affairs that, ephemeral and "unproductive" as it may have seemed, had proved to be effective in convincing Westerners that Siam was truly becoming modern and progressive.

The price for all the festivities and foreigners' approbation was high. The second coronation was an enormously expensive affair. The costs totaled almost two million dollars, or nearly 8 percent of the national budget for 1911. The amount spent was about ten times the amount initially allocated. In the view of many commentators writing long after the event, such a huge outlay of money for a showy spectacle was a waste, the kind of waste of public money characteristic of Siam's most extravagant, most prodigal king. Although at the time the King did not hear such criticisms—"for no one speaks out loudly enough to reach my ears"—he was aware of their possible existence. In his diary he wrote, "I admit we certainly did spend a lot of money." But he reasoned that, far from being a waste, coronation expenses were a worthwhile investment. The state could be compared to a business concern: capital had to be risked for a business to thrive. "We Thai," he wrote, "are too shortsighted to be good businessmen . . . we are similarly shortsighted in state affairs." "My purpose," said the King, "is to lead Thai thought into broader and larger paths. And this ceremony was part of that policy."[41]

The money spent was certainly not all wasted. It is true that Vajiravudh loved show. And perhaps he bought more show than was really required. It is difficult, of course, to put a fair price on "nationalism"; it is easier to estimate the cost of a dam, a bridge, or a power plant. Perhaps Vajiravudh did unconsciously spend some of the money for ego fulfillment, yet his conscious aim was to use the coronation to further a program of nation building by swelling his people's awareness of nation. He realized the limits of the coronation as a means of doing this. And he said so. In summing up the hectic coronation time, he reminded his people that they must not be carried away by exultation at the coronation's success and "forget that there are other duties that have to be performed." He warned the Thai that they must not let foreigners "look upon us as only fit to make

The King Consecrated

useless grand outward displays." He concluded, however, that the display would not prove useless if we "set our minds to make the unanimity existing in our nation more intensified" and "always bear in mind that the interests of the State and nation stand first and foremost."[42] The coronation was but the means to implant an idea, and that idea was nationalism, from which all good things would flow.

3

The Wild Tigers

While the second coronation was being planned, but before it actually took place, Vajiravudh inaugurated what he undoubtedly regarded as his most important means for building nationalism, the Wild Tiger Corps. The corps was basically a paramilitary organization, a kind of home guard, made up of volunteers who were recruited at first from among the members of the civilian bureaucracy.

No creation of the King's was a better vehicle for his nationalistic ideas, and no concept for carrying out his nationalistic program was more fully realized. Further, no organization was dearer to his heart. The corps was his child, his delight. Its members were his comrades, his fellow "club" members, his companions at arms, his students. The Wild Tiger clubhouse was a place where the King could relax. The whole corps idea hearkened back to Saranrom Palace and the Thawipanya Club atmosphere, the "war maneuvers" of the pages and courtiers, with the King as absolute director and manager, although in a "democratic," that is, comradely, way.

The Wild Tigers

The creation of the corps was officially announced on May 1, 1911—six months and eight days after Vajiravudh became king.[1] On May 6 the formal ceremony inaugurating the corps and its first members was held in the Chapel Royal of Wat Phra Kaeo. The ceremony consisted of the customary lighting of candles, professions of faith, and reading of scriptures by monks. The King accepted the position of captain general, deposited some strands of his hair in a receptacle at the top of the staff of the corps banner, and then, bearing the banner, led the men to a formation in front of the chapel. There Prince Vajiranana, the Buddhist patriarch, delivered a sermon praising the corps, then blessed the members and banner with holy water and with Pali stanzas from the *Temiya Jataka*, to which he added a final stanza:

> By the power of these words
> I ask that the fortune of victory be yours,
> I ask that this volunteer Corps
> Be united and free from danger,
> And that it endure.[2]

The ceremony was private, it was quiet, it was relatively brief. But it was by no means casual. The presence of Prince Vajiranana, the careful preparation of the banner, and the selection of the members of the first company (*kǫng*) from among those courtiers closest to the King and from the ranks of ministers of state, high princes in government, and representatives of departments of the civil service, all showed that an event of great importance had taken place.[3]

The ceremony itself and the initial comments of the King also showed that the idea of the corps had been long forming in the King's mind. In the same month the corps was established the King stated that he had been planning for many years to create such an organization and that indeed, without such preparation, he would never have been able to move so fast and so well with the idea. The King traced the corps' genesis back to the war games he had introduced among his court pages at Saranrom Palace in 1905. These war games, he stated, were the initial experiments with the Wild Tiger idea. He wrote: "I acted quietly because one does not wish to make too much of a thing before one is sure that it will succeed."[4] The specific, practical planning sessions for the establishment of the corps, however, started as late as April 26, 1911, when the King and a small party of his closest courtiers, during a trip on the royal yacht in the Gulf of Siam, set up the basic framework and compiled the first list of volunteer members.

The Wild Tigers

The inspiration for the corps, of course, did not come from experiments or meetings. The corps had a meaning for the King that undoubtedly went far back in his history. The times, he saw, were ripe for the corps. Indeed, international times seemed ripe, for the heightened nationalism and superpatriotism, the urgently felt need for preparations of total populations for some great national endeavor, were obvious throughout Europe in the years prior to World War I. Sir Robert S. Baden-Powell's Boy Scout movement, which began in England in 1908 and spread like a grass fire through the receptive dry lands of Germany, France, Russia, and the United States, was but one symbol of the readiness of an idea. The Boy Scout movement was not the inspiration for the Wild Tiger movement, although the King knew of Baden-Powell and may have been stimulated by some of his ideas. The Wild Tiger Corps, true enough, had its germ in European ideas, in the King's appreciation of the strength of European nationalism; the same perceptions prompted both Baden-Powell and Vajiravudh. But Baden-Powell's organization came too late to have been responsible for the Wild Tiger idea, and the Wild Tiger concept was certainly not a literal or even close approximation of the entirely youth-directed, essentially nonmilitary concept of the Boy Scouts. The outward similarities of the Tiger Corps to the Boy Scouts were definitely not the sign of an imitation with "comic" overtones, as one Westerner of the time implied.[5]

Original Purposes of the Corps

The King's original aims for the corps in furthering national policies are made clear in a number of his writings and speeches,[6] particularly in a series of addresses he gave to corps members in May, June, and July of 1911.[7] The King evidently saw the organization as a new instrument for bringing the Thai nation together; breaking the narrow interests, personal and departmental, of civil servants; stimulating martial values; and, above all, creating among the Thai people a new national spirit, the spirit of the Wild Tigers.

The King cast his arguments for the corps in historic terms. The very name Wild Tigers, he said, was an old one, used in former times for men who kept watch on the frontiers of the country, observing enemy movements, sending back reports to aid the Siamese army. These Wild Tigers of former days had qualities of ruggedness, loyalty, and fearlessness combined with expert knowledge of nature and warfare. And it was their presence and the presence of many others with the Wild Tiger spirit, including "nearly all the kings," that made it possible for the Thai nation to prosper and survive.[8]

The Wild Tigers

The old society which possessed this Wild Tiger spirit, said the King, also had the advantage of not being divided into civilian and military groups. All young men served their country in war; only after such service and after they had established families were men considered civilians. Small as Siam then was, and surrounded by enemies, it expected all men to become strong, to know how to defend the country, to gain expertise in arms, to begin to learn the arts of war "as soon as they were able to walk." Principal ministers of government functioned as leaders in both peace and war. It was only after prolonged peace that the country became soft, that government officials began using the labor of soldiers for their own personal ends in the departments under their control, that enterprising men sought ways to avoid service, that military service became unpopular and even regarded as shameful. This theoretical sketch, which had some basis in history, set the scene for the King's essential arguments in favor of the Wild Tigers.[9]

In support of the purely military advantages of the Wild Tigers the King stressed the military danger Siam faced:

> How many countries close to us have already fallen to European power? Do you know? Burma, which was once our competitor, is a possession of the British. Cambodia, which was once a brilliant nation and was once the master of us Thai, is now a possession of the French. Vietnam is a possession of the French. More than half of Malaya is a possession of the British. Java, once very magnificent, is a possession of the Dutch.[10]

And on he went with India and Korea. Only four countries were still independent, but two of these, Persia and China, were in chaos. Only Japan and Siam were still free and orderly. "Of those two countries, which is the more respected in the world? I'm sorry to have to answer that it is Japan. Why? Because Japan has clearly demonstrated to the world that it still has able soldiers."[11] Siam in contrast, said the King, was weak. Its people were asleep. And it would be too late to awaken when the enemy was at the door. Siam had to learn to be prepared, even in peacetime, for "when other countries see we are prepared to fight, they are likely to give up the attack, for an attack on a country that is prepared to resist to the fullest becomes too costly to pursue."[12]

The military services, of course, had to bear the chief burden of defense, but civilians with proper military training, that is, the Wild Tigers, could support the military in time of need. The Wild Tiger Corps would enhance the country's military strength by giving civilians the opportunity to harden their bodies and commit their minds

The Wild Tigers

and spirits to the nation, as soldiers do. Once again, as in the proud past, all men of Siam would share in the task of defending the country.

The value of the military strength of the Wild Tiger Corps was, however, far outweighed in the King's mind by its spiritual strength, by the contribution it would make toward national unity by uniting civilian and military, by uniting the various civil sections of government, and, finally, by uniting the entire people in Wild Tigerism, that is, nationalism.

The corps, by blurring the lines between civilian and military, would ally these two social elements in a common cause:

> We should understand that although we have two separate names for soldier and civilian, the truth is that we have one name that applies to both, and that is the word *Thai*. Soldiers are one part of the Thai people, civilians are one part of the Thai people; how can they then be separate groups? Every soldier is also a civilian. Every civilian likewise ought to be a soldier.[13]

The overriding fact was that civilian and soldier must both see themselves as part of the Thai nation, equally willing to do their jobs, equally willing to make sacrifices of personal comfort, personal advantage, even life itself, for the good of the nation. It was not for soldiers to sacrifice and civilians to be comfortable. All must sacrifice; civilians must learn to be something in the way of soldiers themselves.

A real problem that had bedeviled Vajiravudh's father, King Chulalongkorn, in his program of reforming government administration was that of interministerial, interdepartmental, and interpersonal rivalry.[14] The problem stemmed from traditional administrative practices that made it difficult to remove high officials from office and that produced an extraordinary bond of loyalty and continued service between a high official and his staff. Vajiravudh saw the problem clearly. He stated: "Officials often seem to believe that their first and only debt of loyalty is due to the particular Ministry or Department in which they serve; they must do all they can to advance the interests and prestige of that Ministry or Department even at the cost of another branch of the service." Chulalongkorn, Vajiravudh said, "was well aware" of the problem and sought remedies in education, "which requires much time," and in conscription, "which was not popular with certain classes" (that is, the official classes). What was to be done, he asked, to break down parochial interests, to bring all civil servants into one discipline?

The Wild Tigers

Suppose something of a military nature were tried? But although military, it must be something with an element of freedom in it. It must be a military organization with liberty to join or not as the individual pleased. Hence the origin of the Wild Tiger Corps.

The King made explicit his expectation that the Wild Tiger Corps, although cast in a military form, would educate his officials in the idea that the interests of the individual and the department or ministry were subservient to those of the state, that the good of the country was paramount.[15]

The very structure of the Wild Tigers was designed to shake up the loyalties and ranks of the civil bureaucracy, for Wild Tiger positions did not correspond to regular department positions. A person high in a ministry might well be a common soldier in the Wild Tigers —a revolutionary approach to station in Siam, where customarily a person's rank in the bureaucracy determined not only his salary and the number of subordinates he supervised but also the prestige accorded him, the language with which he was addressed, and virtually every other aspect of his social status. The King justified his approach by citing the general who, aboard ship, must obey the captain; the high prince who, in school, must obey his teacher. So in the Wild Tigers every man, no matter what position he might hold outside, must obey his Wild Tiger officer. The King generalized that the discipline and the stability of any group depended on everyone's obeying the orders of those whose responsibility it was to give them.[16]

By bringing citizen and soldier together, by inculcating in civil sectors of life the values of sacrifice and unity he saw in the military, Vajiravudh hoped to bring a new spirit of unity to the nation. This unity of purpose would prompt everyone to do his duty toward the nation, which would be "the best way for one to demonstrate that he loves his nation more than he loves himself." For only by acting in harmony with the interests of the group could any individual survive. The nation was the highest group; if its constituent parts did not work together, the nation could not survive. Individuals who worked for their personal advantage in ways that harmed the group, helped destroy the group and, in the end, themselves as well. He compared the individuals in a group to the parts of a human body:

> ... if the hand feels that it has done enough work and will not bring food to the mouth, what will happen? No food goes to the stomach, which is ready to digest the food that does not come. So, lacking food, there is nothing to sustain the blood. The blood thins and is unable to

The Wild Tigers

care for the flesh and sinews of various body parts. So they weaken. The body emaciates. And the hand that refused to take up the food dies along with the rest.

So with nations. A nation, he said, is nothing other than many groups of people joined together in a great body; these groups must be in agreement if the organism is to escape destruction.[17]

Combining and surpassing all the King's particular aims for the Wild Tigers was his vision of the Tigers as bringing about a "true national feeling," a "Wild Tiger spirit," an ideal of nationalism among all his people. This was the only aim of the Tigers he mentioned in an important speech he gave on December 3, 1911, at coronation time:

> The aim of this national institution is to instil in the minds of the people of our own race love and loyalty towards the High Authority that controls and maintains with justice and equity the political independence of the nation, devotion to Fatherland, Nation, and our Holy Religion, and, not least of all, the preservation of national unity and cultivation of mutual friendship. These qualities form the strongest foundation on which our national existence will rest and not belie its name as the Nation of the Free. Thus shall we deserve well of our ancestors who gave their life's blood in firmly planting the home of our ancient race in this land of Siam.[18]

This message of three-in-one loyalty to king, nation, and religion —undoubtedly inspired by the British "God, King, and Country"— was a foundation of the King's nationalistic ideas and was continually developed before Wild Tiger audiences. These general nationalistic concepts, which will be developed in later chapters, were imparted to Wild Tiger groups more fully than to any others. The King obviously saw the corps as playing a large role in the dissemination of his basic nationalistic ideas. This large role included such specifics as supplying the nation with slogans and goals. The motto of the Wild Tiger Corps, emblazoned on its flags, badges, and signs, read "Give up life rather than honor." This motto, although coined for the Tigers, was clearly meant to set a standard of patriotism for the whole of the Thai nation.

The King assigned a new specific duty to the Wild Tigers in an order issued on June 20, 1911.[19] This order made it a duty of the Tigers to help preserve public order and called for them to aid local authorities in suppressing crimes, fighting fires, protecting the person of the king, and performing humanitarian deeds. Proper reports were to be made of such activities; those who had done outstandingly

The Wild Tigers

meritorious acts were to be cited in the *Čhotmaihet sǔapa* (Wild Tiger Documents) on pages figuratively called "plates of gold," and those who had failed their trust were to be listed on pages of "dog hide."[20]

There were other royal purposes, or possible purposes, with regard to the Wild Tigers that are not made explicit in the King's writings or speeches. Some of these purposes may even have been unconscious. When the King spoke to the Wild Tigers of very broad nationalistic aims and ideals, for instance, it seems hardly possible that he expected the corps to convert these ideals into reality. The corps at the outset was too small in numbers, too limited to the Bangkok bureaucratic elite, to convey these ideals to provincial and village Siam. It would appear that the King gave his speeches to the Tigers—on a regular weekly schedule for a long period of time—in large part because he needed an audience for his ideas, and the corps, his own creation, gave him an audience that was congenial and receptive.

The Tiger Corps was indeed congenial to the King; it functioned as a kind of club for His Majesty and was an extension of the club atmosphere he had earlier tried to establish as a prince at Saranrom Palace. Although all ministries and departments of government in a sense "belonged" to the King, in another sense none did. The Wild Tiger Corps, however, transcended bureaucratic offices, was superministerial, and was the King's own. Vajiravudh composed the Tigers' mottoes, he wrote the Tigers' songs, he designed the Tigers' uniforms, he led the Tigers' parades, he organized the Tigers' maneuvers, he established the Tigers' oath, he wrote the Tigers' rules of discipline—he engaged himself in every minute detail of Tiger activities. And he loved doing all these things. Faced with a government led by older ministers who were set in their ways and had the prestige of having worked closely with King Chulalongkorn in formulating state policies, Vajiravudh hoped consciously that the Tigers would help him bring this old order into his grasp. One cannot help but feel that unconsciously, however, he leaned on the Tigers to provide him with the sense of total control that the regular government was not providing him. It is too simple to say that the Tiger Corps was a toy for a frustrated monarch, but it undoubtedly had something of that meaning.

Vajiravudh in one early speech denied vehemently—perhaps too vehemently—that the Wild Tiger Corps was his "party":

> But, all of you, don't misunderstand. Don't think that, for my personal advantage, I am ordering or pressuring anyone into joining the Wild Tiger Corps. Don't make the further mistake of thinking that if someone

The Wild Tigers

doesn't join the Wild Tigers he won't be able to advance in government service. For this is not my group. I give you my word I have no such desires and wishes. I regard the whole of the Thai people as my group.[21]

In fact, of course, the corps did function as the King's group, and it was clearly so regarded by some individuals in the government whose later opposition to the corps constituted a serious problem for King Vajiravudh.

The special relationship of the Wild Tigers to the King was made explicit in June 1911 when the corps was given the assignment of protecting the King, of forming a kind of elite royal guard.[22] The traditional royal guard, drawn from the regular army, was maintained. But in addition to this guard, the King expected the Wild Tiger Royal Guards, a company composed of his closest courtiers, to keep a cordon surrounding him when he went to crowded places. If for any reason the Tiger Royal Guards were not sufficient in number, other Tigers were to help perform this service. It has been suggested that this royal use of the Tigers betrayed a lack of confidence in the army.[23] Although this would be hard to prove, at least for 1910–11 it is a possibility. It seems more likely, however, that this use of the Tigers as an elite royal guard merely reflects the fairly common desire, by no means peculiarly Siamese, of a new monarch to keep closest to him as protectors those whom he particularly trusts—probably the same desire that led the young King Chulalongkorn in 1868 to create an elite company of guards from among his court pages to ensure his personal safety.[24]

Initial Organization and Activities of the Corps

As the King's special creation, the Wild Tiger Corps from the outset was provided with extremely detailed definitions of its administration, its drills and exercises, its dress, its insignia, its rules. The corps regulations and orders were all written either by the King personally or by his chief lieutenants following his instructions. These regulations were, during the history of the corps, constantly being changed, amended, expanded, clarified.

First of all, it was declared that membership in the corps would be voluntary. Legally it was. But the King knew that "the Siamese as a people are ready to follow an example or a leader"; by his becoming the corps' leader and gaining the "hearty approval" of his ministers of state, "the success of the movement was assured."[25] Although the King repudiated the idea that success in the Wild Tigers assured success in the bureaucracy, undoubtedly many men joined in the hope that somehow their display of patriotism and self-sacrifice would come to the notice of the King and help their careers. Mere proximity to the king in Siam, in fact, was (and still is) regarded as portentous; the "magic" of the king had beneficial powers that were stronger the closer one got to him.[26] On men who were not so positively influenced, negative pressures undoubtedly had their effect. A foreign commentator stated that, in fact, membership in the corps became obligatory, so that anyone who was not enrolled "was regarded as a suspicious and untrustworthy person."[27] This statement may well be too strong, but there is certainly evidence that some overzealous officials put pressure on their subordinates to join in order to make a good impression on the King.[28] To what extent the King was aware of this practice is not known. On one occasion he denied the need for one group of officials to be released from Wild Tiger drill, on the grounds that the corps was voluntary and no special release was required; members could be excused on the legitimate grounds of pressing government work, or they could resign.[29] On another occasion, however, the King ordered the Ministry of the Palace to have a list prepared of all officials in the Secretariat Department who had not yet become Wild Tigers. Although no explanation for the order was given, the implications are obvious.[30]

To be accepted into the corps, the applicant had to be a Thai citizen, at least eighteen years of age, of good character, a civilian, and a Buddhist. (There was some later relaxation of the rules, e.g., acceptance of non-Buddhists.)[31] A member also had to have the requisite entrance fee of fifty baht (about twenty dollars at the time) and the funds to buy a uniform and to pay the annual dues of thirty baht (about twelve dollars). A member's status remained probationary until he had drunk the waters of allegiance in a special ceremony before the King. At this ceremony the Wild Tiger received a "commission" from the King, a mark of dignity equal to that accorded regular members of the civilian and military bureaucracy. The ranks in the corps, which resembled those in the military, were awarded by the King on the basis of the person's presumed knowledge of Wild Tiger qualifications, that is, military drill, and it was not unusual to see, in the words of a foreign commentator, "striplings of twenty . . . commanding gray-haired men of fifty."[32] The special criteria for rank in the Wild Tigers are shown in the composition of the first 122 appointments to the corps on May 6, 1911. Nineteen officers were appointed. Seven of these were court pages; none were nobles of the highest title; and only one was a prince of conferred (*krom*)

The Wild Tigers

title. Among the enlisted men, however, were one noble of the highest title and nine princes of conferred title.[33]

In addition to regular members, there were a number of other categories of members: reserve, subsidiary, special, probational, outside, and suspended.

Members of the corps were immediately recognizable as different from any other group in Siam. The colors of the original dress of the members were an appropriately tigerish black and yellow. The hat was black felt, wide brimmed, turned up on the right side and secured by a black and yellow cockade, in the center of which was a badge shaped like a tiger's face; it also had a black leather chin strap and a yellow hat band with black tiger markings. The tie was black satin; the trousers were black with yellow braidings; the boots were black; and the cloak was black with yellow lining. This was the "ordinary service uniform"; there were numerous variants for mounted guards and other special and provincial units, and there were different uniforms for field exercises. There was a bewildering procession of changes in the details of Tiger dress over the years. And, it should be remembered, Tigers were required to purchase their own uniforms.

Other special identifying symbols included special flags for corps units; three units were awarded flags at a formal ceremony on February 17, 1912, for example.[34] Even individual officers had flags designed for them with suitable symbols: a Lieutenant Bua (lotus) was given a flag with a lotus cluster; Prince Damrong was given a flag with a genuflecting angel, his special identifying symbol.[35]

The basic unit of the Wild Tiger administration was the company. By the end of 1911 there were four companies in Bangkok, and each provincial government circle (*monthon*) had at least the beginnings of a local company. Companies in the capital were to consist of 266 men; those in the provinces were to be half that size. Figures are hard to come by, but there were probably about 4,000 corps members by early 1912.[36] The overall administration, headed by the King as captain general, was in Bangkok.

Administrative divisions of the corps constantly changed, but one distinction was made from the outset between the ordinary Wild Tiger units (in Bangkok or elsewhere) and those units designated "Royal Guards," sometimes translated "His Own." The Royal Guards units were much closer to the King and were drawn largely from his palace retinue.

All corps units were expected to have drill fields and clubhouses. The clubhouse functioned as the meeting hall for lessons and lectures,

The Wild Tigers

and as unit headquarters for enlistment and record keeping. The clubhouse was also to serve as a social hall, as a gathering place for members in off hours, and as a site for indoor games. In the clubhouse would then develop the kind of social atmosphere that the King had learned of in England, the atmosphere of camaraderie, of group loyalty and esprit that Siam, he felt, so sorely needed. The first clubhouse, located near Dusit Palace, was opened on July 22, 1911, with a benediction by the Prince Patriarch and other monks, followed by the contribution by His Majesty of a dinner party for officers and a motion picture show for all.[37]

The principal activities of the Wild Tigers were to learn and put into practice proper discipline, to learn how to march and drill, to participate in various ceremonies and fetes, and to practice field exercises on maneuver.

The rules of discipline laid down by the King in several orders were precise and rigorous. They covered modes of attire, modes of requesting leave, and modes of saluting.[38] They also prescribed the penalties for infractions, which varied from payment of fines to expulsion from the corps. Ten "tardy" notices a month, for example, resulted in a fine not to exceed ten baht (about four dollars at the time); a second similar offense resulted in demotion to the suspended-member category.[39]

Great stress was placed on military drilling and marching. The Wild Tigers were expected to meet daily at 4:00 P.M. and, on most days, drill for two hours or so.[40] Other drills apparently also took place; officials of the Ministry of the Interior, "anxious to join the Corps," had preparatory drilling in July 1911 from seven to nine every morning.[41] Drill masters with experience were borrowed from military units. Before special events, drilling was particularly intensive. An inspection of the Chiangmai unit was preceded by drilling "every morning and evening," and as a result, it was reported, "many of the members feel their bones aching."[42]

One provincial official of the time, who praised the Wild Tigers, recalled in his autobiography an incident that shows the seriousness of the King's interest in drill and the burden it put on civil officials. The official entered the corps early and soon became an officer. In 1913 he led his troop to a large Wild Tiger gathering in the capital. He marched his unit proudly before the King at the royal parade grounds. Vajiravudh, visibly upset, stopped the troop. He ordered the official to repeat his march and correct the error. The march was repeated. It was repeated over and over, but never to the King's satisfaction. The official was about to faint. The King, still angry,

38

The Wild Tigers

told the official that the fault was not that of the troop, but of its leader. He ordered the troop dismissed and then commanded the official to drill by himself. Commented the official: "If anybody had been there to see, they would have thought me out of my mind." Finally, in sheer exhaustion, the official said, "I'm just not able to do it and beg your leave." The King relented and told the official of his error: he had been taking three steps too many. That evening, to show that his anger was not personal, the King came to the official's quarters, drove him to a shop, and asked him to choose some clothing at the King's expense.[43]

Marches and parades of properly drilled Wild Tigers were held frequently. The first public march, on June 17, 1911, was led by the Royal Bodyguard Band, followed by the standard bearer. Heading the Royal Tiger Company was His Majesty. This parade attracted thousands of onlookers.[44] A similar parade on June 29, in which some 800 men marched "smartly," again attracted thousands.[45] Important ceremonies, such as the coronation and celebrations of the King's birthday, regularly included parades of Wild Tigers as well as of the regular military.

A special effort was made during the coronation days to give prominence to Wild Tiger participation. An all-out effort was made to bring as many Tigers to the capital as possible. Reportedly some 4,230 officers and men came.[46] The Wild Tiger day was December 9, and the field display before foreign and local guests began at 3:00 P.M. with marches and flag presentations. At 4:40 the King made his entrance on horseback, accompanied by the mounted company of Wild Tiger Guards. Salutes, flag raising, music, and speeches followed. Enthusiastic cheers, a "rush-up" to attend the King, and a royal presentation of a pin of remembrance of the day concluded the affair.[47]

Shortly after the coronation, there were two important Wild Tiger fetes: the final coronation party on December 10 and a historical pageant of Wild Tiger traditions early in January.

The Wild Tiger party was held in the clubhouse grounds, which were converted into "a veritable enchanted land" with numerous booths, stalls, and entertainments.[48] One booth, the product of the Fourth Royal Bangkok Company, was fashioned in the form of a large tiger's head; its open mouth was the entrance, its stomach a cafe, and its sides the exits.[49] At the stalls, besides food and drink, Wild Tiger souvenirs of handkerchiefs, badges, and booklets were given away. The evening closed with a fireworks display in which the outstanding set pieces were the King's monogram and a tiger's head with the motto of the corps.[50]

The Wild Tigers

The Pageant of Wild Tiger Traditions was an elaborate affair, lasting for three days (January 3, 4, and 5, 1912). The pageant was officially presented to the King in honor of his birthday. In fact, however, the King himself was the chief planner, stager, and organizer of the pageant; he was indeed, as he was formally designated, the "Master of the Pageant."[51] Other top officers of government were called upon to lend their special talents: Prince Damrong, the Minister of the Interior, was historical assistant; Prince Paribatra, the Minister of Marine, was musical director.[52]

The pageant, held outdoors on the Wild Tiger drill field, lived up to its advance billing as "a magnificent spectacle." Said a foreign observer of the players:

> With their excellent scenic arrangements they gave a good idea of the history of Siam from the earliest times to the present day. The costumes were historically correct, and no pains had been spared to make the performances as realistic as possible. Nor were battle elephants wanting, richly hung with costly trappings and jewelled ornaments.[53]

The pageant announcement made it clear that the King's concept of Wild Tiger traditions was as broad as the country itself, "since the 'Wild Tigers' of old were the makers of Siamese history."[54] Altogether nine historic episodes were enacted, and the last episode on the last night was followed by the trooping of the colors and the singing of a patriotic song, "Love of Our Race and Our Fathers' Land."

There were other not-so-formal social activities of corps members during the initial year. A cryptic newspaper item told of at least one: "His Majesty the King took part in two plays at Phrapatom last week, when a number of members of the Wild Tigers comprised the audience."[55]

In addition to discipline, drill, and social diversion, which were year-long corps activities, members were expected to make a concerted effort to attend and fully participate in annual military maneuvers. In the first year of corps history, these maneuvers were held in stages from January 20 to March 2, 1912. The center of the maneuvers was Nakhǫn Pathom (about thirty-six miles west of Bangkok), where the King had built a "winter palace," theater, parade grounds, and Wild Tiger clubhouse.

The purposes of these maneuvers, in addition to the obvious aim of preparing the Tigers to play their role of supporting the army in time of war,[56] were succinctly spelled out by the King.[57] First, participation in war games would heighten civilian appreciation of the

The Wild Tigers

Thai soldiery, would convince civilians that soldiers' duties were onerous and required endurance. Such appreciation would lead to greater harmony between civilian and soldier. Second, the shared efforts and hardships experienced in the war games would bring civil servants closer together. Instead of just meeting in their official capacities, in which true characters are masked, real bonds of sympathy, understanding, and trust would emerge from the fellowship that field exercises would elicit. Third, war games would bring out the true man in each person, the man who had faced adversity and trial, who had endured them rather than be shamed before others, and who in the end would take pride in his achievement and so become a better person and worker for it.

The essential format of the war games was simple. One contingent of Tigers was designated the defender; the other, the aggressor. A neutral party judged each action and issued a final report on who won and why. The first engagement took place on January 20 and 21 at Nakhǫn Pathom between two of the Bangkok companies, one designated the red team and the other the green. The green team, acting as aggressor, was defeated by the red, whose second-in-command was the King.[58]

A much larger exercise was conducted between February 2 and 6, when various provincial units were added to the Bangkok companies. All in all, almost two thousand people were involved. The importance the King gave to these maneuvers can be judged from the fact that a special royal request was sent to every government ministry for the release of all men who could be spared.[59] The response was good; for example, Prince Devawongse of the Ministry of Foreign Affairs released twenty-nine of his staff and kept only ten in Bangkok.[60] In those maneuvers the yellow team, defending Nakhǫn Pathom, was headed by the Minister of Local Government, Chaophraya Yommarat; the red team, attacking from Ban Pong, was headed by the King. After four days, the red team was declared the winner and the exercises came to an end.[61]

In subsequent weekends through February, maneuvers of smaller scale took place. On February 10 a unit of Royal Tigers led by the King attacked the bungalow of Prince Damrong, defended by the Prince and a local Tiger unit. A newspaper reported that the issue was somewhat indeterminate, but the Prince "would have appeared to have escaped any serious injury since he was seen out motoring the following afternoon."[62] On subsequent weekends, maneuvers were held at Nakhǫn Pathom and at Hua Hin.[63] The King appears to

The Wild Tigers

have spent all of February at Nakhọn Pathom, being joined there by various units from the capital and elsewhere for the weekend maneuvers.

In addition to enduring the rigors of the war games themselves, the Tigers were subjected to the various deprivations of camp life. They were allowed to bring only two sets of clothes; no luggage was allowed, nor was there any place for storing personal articles of value. The Tigers rose at 5:00 A.M. If there were no games during the day, they drilled and played field sports. In the evenings they prayed, sang patriotic songs, and went to bed at eight o'clock. Leaving camp was forbidden; all gates were monitored, and guards were posted in town to catch truants. Men who were used to the comforts of home and servants found that they even had to wash their own clothes. Of course food, medical services, and lodging—such as they were—were supplied free, and money not spent on liquor and entertainments was money saved.[64] But full acceptance of the war games depended on belief in their high purpose. Some men undoubtedly did share the King's enthusiasm. It seems likely, though, that most accepted the experience passively.

The Boy Scouts

One branch of the Wild Tigers which was certainly not lacking in enthusiasm was the Boy Scouts. The Boy Scout organization was established by royal decree on July 1, 1911; in the decree it was clear that the scouts, literally the "Tiger Cubs" in Thai, were to be a junior edition of the adult corps, with the same aims as the parent body. The decree stated:

> Boys in their adolescent years should also receive both physical and mental training of the sort given Wild Tigers so that when they become older they will know their proper duties as Thai men. Everyone should do what is useful to the nation and country, to the land of one's birth. And the instilling of the proper spirit must begin when one is still young. A tree that is to be shaped into a pleasing form can be most easily trained when it is young and supple.[65]

The King, who was scout chief, spelled out these aims further in an address on December 5, 1911, when he enumerated the scout principles as loyalty to the sovereign, love of nation, and loyalty to the community.[66] And in an address on December 3 he pointed out that his wish was to inculcate in the minds of the younger generation the high patriotic qualities of the Wild Tigers.[67]

The training of the Boy Scouts in Siam closely mirrored that of

The Wild Tigers

the Wild Tigers; they drilled, paraded, took part in the war games. In the maneuvers at Nakhǫn Pathom in early February 1912, only three units were cited for outstanding performance of duties; one was a Boy Scout unit, and another was a Boy Scout and Tiger unit combined. The scouts threw themselves so enthusiastically into the maneuvers that it appears one group of them actually succeeded in capturing the King.[68] According to one source, the King saved himself from "capture" at the last moment by having the royal trumpeter blow the royal anthem, which forced the "invaders" to stand at attention while His Majesty proceeded to slip away.[69]

The devotion of the Boy Scouts is well illustrated by a letter of one Thai scout which was published in the London *Daily Mirror*. The scout, describing the rigors of camping, told of the scouts' cooking for themselves, "even though some of us did not know how to," and tramping knee-deep through muddy paddy fields, and ended with:

> I once had to run in the mud, and when I got out of the difficulty I felt so tired that I could hardly breathe and could not run any further. But, being ashamed before the other scouts, I leapt down into a trench without being seen, and there I rested until I recovered.
>
> Fortunately for me I was not conspicuous by my absence. If I was found out while being in the trench, what should I do? I had to make a hole in the ground and put my head in for shame.[70]

The enlistment of boys in the scout movement was phenomenally rapid. By December there were more than 2,000 in 63 units in the capital alone;[71] by 1922 the number had increased to 21,500 in 177 units.[72]

The boys' enthusiasm was matched by government efforts of support. Scoutmasters had to go through special training and be examined on, among other things, the proper methods of instilling the spirit of the Wild Tigers, i.e., nationalism.[73] Instruction in scouting principles had entered the regular school curriculum by 1913.[74] Scouts who had rendered outstanding service, such as helping put out fires, aiding the police to arrest criminals, and rescuing people from drowning, had their names inscribed on scrolls of honor. And men who had completed their scouting days were entered into the reserves, exhorted to retain their principles, and given a special medal as a gift from the King to serve as a constant reminder, a talisman, an amulet to help the wearer adhere to the good and to ward off evil temptations.[75]

The stress on nationalism persisted in the Boy Scout movement throughout the reign. Indeed the question once arose in the press as to whether the "good deed for the day" aspect of international scoutism was "being urged" upon Thai boys at all.[76] While there was always some attention paid to doing valorous deeds for the good of the nation, it appears that not until fairly late was there any explicit advice given scouts to perform small useful acts. Not until 1920 were scouts urged to help children cross streets or to pick up bits of broken crockery on the footpaths and to ask themselves at bedtime "What good deed have I done today?"[77] Attention to crafts such as carpentry, tailoring, mat making, and mechanics seems also to have come late[78] and may have been part of an effort to stimulate Thai interest in the manual arts, hitherto largely left to the Chinese.[79] The marches, drills, exercises, sports, and war games, however, remained central. Years after their scouting days, men remembered particularly these aspects of scouting.[80] One Thai writer recalled in particular the song scouts sang in their marches:

> All of us Scouts are completely at the service of Your Majesty
> Who established both the Tigers and the Scouts for the good of the Thai.
> We are most loyal and determined to help our nation and faith,
> To defend our Thainess and the honor of our king
> So the Thai will be Thai forever and never be brought to dust.[81]

Reactions against the Corps

There are indications of some rumblings and grumblings about the Wild Tiger Corps almost from the moment of its inception. The defensive tone taken in some of the early orders, and some modifications made in the corps, indicate that some of these criticisms reached the ears of the King. The earliest complaint, that uniforms were too expensive, was cited in a document refuting this charge, which stated that, although there were three Wild Tiger uniforms, only one, the field uniform, was really necessary and that it cost only forty-six baht (about eighteen dollars at the time).[82] The early establishment of a "suspended-member" category was apparently motivated by the need to accommodate individuals who were unable to live up to the drill and discipline regimen of regular members.[83]

The strongest expression of antipathy to the corps appeared in the remarks of a group of young army officers who were arrested in February 1912 for complicity in a planned coup d'état.[84] The coup group of 1912 and its motives deserve to be discussed fully (and shall be in the next chapter); it is obvious, however, that the hostility to

The Wild Tigers

the Wild Tigers expressed in extreme form by this group was present to some degree in various circles of the bureaucracy.

The members of the coup group of 1912 were extremely jealous of the Wild Tigers. The Tigers, first of all, were obviously very close to the King's heart; he spent much time, attention, and money on them. The young army officers felt that the army, and they themselves, were not being properly appreciated. In their view the Tigers represented a waste of money and energy, since the army represented the real defense of the nation. On the other hand, it was also a sore point that military men were not allowed to join the regular Tiger Corps (a few high officers were designated members of a "special" category); the theory was that the military did not need the kind of training the corps members were receiving. Also, many of the courtiers closest to the King, who dominated the Royal Guards Company of the corps, were individually resented for their "superiority."[85]

How much of this resentment, this antipathy, this criticism was general, of course, cannot be known for certain, for the press treated the subject very gingerly indeed. But that it went beyond the 1912 coup group is clear. One coup leader reflected that he, then a drill master but not a member of the corps, felt tired for the old men he had to march and said that he knew they were "forced" to be part of the corps.[86] Another indication of the generality of criticism is the report of a foreign observer who undoubtedly was relaying some of the adverse comments he heard in Bangkok in early 1912.[87]

The adverse criticisms that had circulated underground beforehand and were brought to the surface by the discovery of the coup plans clearly influenced several discussions within the Wild Tiger Royal Guards in 1912. The first meeting was held on March 12, presumably to provide at the King's request an evaluation of the Wild Tiger organization as it neared the end of its first year of activities. It is undoubtedly significant that the King did not attend this meeting. At the meeting, the guards did cite some of the Wild Tiger achievements but also suggested that means be found to open the membership to the less affluent and to men in the military.[88]

A second series of meetings was held in late March. Again the King was absent. A special committee of five members was chosen by general election to take the sense of the meetings and draft proposals for change to be submitted for a final decision by the King. Although the five-man committee had no executive power, its composition, the result of a vote of 6,669 members, is revealing. The five "winners" were, in order of popularity, Prince Chakrabongs,

The Wild Tigers

Prince Damrong, Prince Paribatra, Čhaophraya Yommarat, and Prince Charoon. The leading vote-getter had the reputation, deserved or not, of being opposed to the Wild Tigers. None of the five, with the exception of Čhaophraya Yommarat, could be considered Wild Tiger enthusiasts.[89]

The Wild Tiger meetings of late March were spirited and open. The members voted against property restrictions for members; they voted for allowing entry to army officers; they voted for medical examinations for prospective members; they voted for institution of an examination for the promotion of officers; they voted for the automatic transference of a Tiger to reserve status after six months' service; they voted to cut the entrance fee from fifty baht per year to ten baht. Some matters were discussed but not voted on because the King's views on these matters were already known. For example, the sentiment was in favor of cutting drill time, but it was already known that the King favored making drill compulsory only once a week; the view was also expressed that the King's favorite Palace Guard Company should be eliminated, but the King's declared intention of retaining this elite guard made discussion of this issue pointless.[90]

On April 12, King Vajiravudh called a general Wild Tiger meeting on his own to discuss the various proposals. His Majesty was obviously incensed at what had taken place in late March; he chided the members for calling a meeting "which greatly exceeded its powers" by discussing matters beyond its purview. He accused those who had participated in the March meetings of "sinning behind my back." But, he said, he would let "bygones be bygones." As to the specific recommendations, some he could accept, some he could not. Annual dues could not be cut until a survey was made. As for withdrawal from the Wild Tigers, he would allow special withdrawals for those pressed by work or pressured by superiors. But he added, in a note of sarcasm, that if he did not have the duty to head the Wild Tiger movement, he might consider going into the reserves himself, "for I have much government business to do." The tone of the rest of the meeting remained icy. The King presented his new rules for entry into the Tiger reserves and invited expressions of opinion on these rules, but he prefaced his invitation by saying, "I don't have to ask your views." Čhaophraya Yommarat was the only commentator, and he ventured to say that the rules were good. As for the committee of five, the King summarily dismissed them with the remark that too many were princes who had too much

The Wild Tigers

else to do, and, in the interest of speed and efficiency, he would undertake the task of revision himself.[91]

On April 16, 1912, one small but significant suggestion for reform was made by Prince Chakrabongs, the King's most outspoken brother and Army Chief of Staff. He pointed out that commissions to military officers bore only the royal seal whereas commissions to Wild Tigers were accorded a royal signature. This minor distinction, said Prince Chakrabongs, was leading to the erroneous conclusion that the King held the Tigers in higher regard than he did his soldiers. Prince Chakrabongs did not suggest how the King ought to handle commissions; he urged only that His Majesty treat them all alike.[92]

Despite his pique, the King did bring about some reforms. Drill hours were reduced, and only one drill day a week was required of long-term members.[93] Some effort seems to have been made to reduce the charge of favoritism by opening up the ranks of aide-de-camp Wild Tigers to men other than those in the palace retinue.[94] And Wild Tiger commands outside that of the Royal Guards were allowed to set their own dues schedule. By the end of 1913, one command had reduced its entrance fee from fifty to five baht and its annual dues from thirty to twelve baht.[95]

Later History of the Corps

Although the aborted coup of 1912 and the open criticism of the Wild Tigers somewhat chastened the King, he by no means abandoned the movement. There seems to have been some diminution of Wild Tiger activity for several months after March, but by fall the pace had picked up again. A second Pageant of Wild Tiger Traditions was held in early January,[96] and the annual maneuvers were given as much attention as ever in 1913. One of the clearest evidences of the King's continued interest in the Wild Tigers was his authorship in 1913 of a play, *Huačhai nakrop* (Soul of a Warrior), that was essentially a propaganda piece extolling the virtues of the Tiger Corps and of the Boy Scouts.

The later history of the corps reveals two essential facts: first, that the corps continued to expand; second, that some new emphases were developed.

With regard to the elaboration of the corps along original lines, there is no need here to go into extensive detail. There were constant revisions of administrative organization—the names and numbers of units, the grouping of units. And there were frequent changes in insignia and dress; a comprehensive revision in 1917 embodying all such changes since 1914 took up 130 pages of the Royal Government Gazette.[97] New functional units of the Tigers—including an artillery unit, an ambulance section, and a marine division—were periodically added. New clubhouses in the capital and the provinces were continually being opened. Although the annual Pageant of Wild Tiger Traditions was not continued after 1913, the staging of plays and fairs by Wild Tiger groups was expanded. The King's use of Wild Tiger units as sounding boards for his ideas on nationalism also continued.[98] The practice of having an end-of-the-year evaluation of Wild Tiger activity seems also to have continued, although the reporting committees in all the years after the first one were largely made up of the King's own men and nothing critical seems to have emerged.[99] And, lastly, annual maneuvers were held without fail. The King's undiminished interest in the maneuvers is evidenced by a letter to the Minister of the Palace in 1916 informing him not to schedule any ceremonies for February because the King planned to be away the whole month on Wild Tiger maneuvers.[100] Plans for the maneuvers of 1926 were under way when the King died.

Expansion in numbers of Wild Tigers seems also to have continued in later years. Although total figures are lacking, there are spotty records that show the addition of almost 2,000 new full members in 1915.[101] The total membership by 1924 was reported to be over 10,000.[102] Much of the growth seems to have occurred in the provinces, and news of provincial activity, such as locally organized maneuvers and drills, became particularly prominent in the later years. On trips that the King made to the provinces, much attention was paid to Wild Tiger displays. The trip to the southern provinces in 1915 was made complete with marches, displays, and maneuvers of Wild Tiger units, and the King was convinced that the Wild Tiger purpose of bringing government officials closer together was being fully served.[103] In another trip to the South in 1917 in which Wild Tiger units again outdid themselves, the King was so pleased that he conferred the designation "His Majesty's Own Guard" on the company at Phuket.[104]

The most marked change in emphasis in the Wild Tiger Corps after the abortive coup of 1912 was an obvious effort to bridge the gap between the military and the paramilitary organizations.

The Wild Tiger maneuvers of 1913 were remarkable for having military units involved in the war games for the first time. The leader of the White Team (opposed to the King's Red Team) was, in fact, a regular army general, the Commander of the Fourth Infantry Regiment.[105] Although the stated purpose in adding regular army

The Wild Tigers

units was to give Wild Tigers the experience of contending with trained troops, the unstated purpose was surely to lessen the jealousy of the regular military forces. Another formula for conciliation was adopted in 1915 and followed through the rest of the reign: after the regular Wild Tiger maneuvers were held, the King attended the army maneuvers, becoming, according to the press accounts, the first Siamese sovereign "to share the hardships of his troops in peace time."[106]

The King's attention to the regular military, already evident in 1913, was greatly intensified in the years of World War I.[107] And the war years also gave the King the opportunity to see the Wild Tigers in a new light, although he denied the newness of his insights. The range of his aims remained much the same, but the relative importance of the various aims changed. Emerging as the most important task for the Wild Tiger Corps by 1914 was its role of backing up the military, becoming Siam's second line of defense. Siam's army had to bear the chief burden of defense, said the King, but if an enemy really did come to take over the country, the army was too small to hold off long. And Siam lacked the resources and the time to build up a fully effective army. Meanwhile the Tigers would be the people's militia, relieving the army from the burden of securing internal order so that it might concentrate on the external enemy.[108]

In a long essay written in October 1914 the King gave a reasoned argument for the importance of the Boy Scouts and Wild Tigers in wartime. Both, he said, were of particular importance in a small country which had no large population from which to draw conscripts and so had to depend on all men to help defend the country and to do so willingly. The only thing that could substitute in war for large numbers was bravery and personal ingenuity. Volunteer trainees could be of inestimable value in protecting the countryside, in securing roads and communications networks, in supplying the army with information, in preserving internal order.[109]

In speech after speech during the war years Vajiravudh repeated the theme that Wild Tigers must look on the soldiers as their elder brothers, as the prime defenders of the nation whom the Tigers must support. The theme could not help but be gratifying to the regular military.[110] On July 21, 1917, the day before Siam declared war, a Royal Decree on the Duties of the Volunteer Wild Tiger Corps To Preserve the General Peace was issued that spelled out the supportive military role the King had already generally defined.[111]

An indication that the King's new desire for a united effort, stimulated by the war in Europe, did effect something of a recon-

The Wild Tigers

ciliation with army ranks may be present in a remarkable address given by Prince Chakrabongs on the occasion of his receiving a special rank in His Majesty's Own Wild Tiger Mounted Guards on April 9, 1917. In the speech Chakrabongs referred for the first time publicly to the "long-time rumor" that he disliked the Wild Tigers. He remarked that the rumor astonished him and must have arisen from a misunderstanding. The Prince declared, "I am a servant of His Majesty who founded the Wild Tigers. How then could I hate the Wild Tigers?" The Prince admitted that he was outspoken, that when he saw something that deserved criticism, he criticized. He went further and allowed that he had noticed deficiencies in some aspects of the corps and in some individuals in the corps. But, he said, this did not constitute an overall judgment; his overall judgment remained favorable to the corps. Finally, Prince Chakrabongs expressed hope that his reception into the mounted guards would prove his good wishes and still all unfavorable rumors.[112]

At the conclusion of World War I the King evidently believed that the reconciliation of the Wild Tigers and the regular army was complete. The soldiers were proud of their wartime effort and were now, said the King in an address to the Wild Tigers, "holding out open arms to us like brothers, which is not what once was."[113]

Evaluation

Evaluations of the Wild Tiger Corps in Thailand today tend to assume polar opposites of high praise or utter condemnation.

Critics who condemn the corps do so usually on the grounds that it was a useless, wasteful, gaudy show. There is no doubt that the corps cost money. But the money came largely from either the privy purse or the pocketbooks of members. Two early attempts to charge Wild Tiger travel expenses to ministries were unsuccessful; the requests were regarded as not "in the spirit" of the Wild Tiger movement.[114] Apparently some corvée labor was used in the preparing of camp sites at maneuver grounds.[115] And from time to time in the last five years of the corps various money-raising schemes were tried, including benefit play performances,[116] sports displays,[117] car races,[118] issuance of special Wild Tiger postage stamps,[119] and special lotteries and fairs.[120] Out-and-out appeals for donations[121] and the creation of a Society for the Furtherance of the Wild Tiger Scout Movement[122] with dues of five baht per year also helped raise money. Most of these fund-raising activities were organized in 1919 and 1920 to provide funds for 10,000 rifles for use in Wild Tiger training.[123]

In the end, the financial argument against the Wild Tigers must

The Wild Tigers

rest on the conclusion that the corps brought little of real value to Siam. An argument can indeed be made that the corps produced rivalry and division in Thai society. Elements in the civil and military bureaucracy remained antagonistic to the corps. The elitist Royal Guards were particularly resented. Vajiravudh was aware of the jealousy his guards stimulated, but he justified the special attention they were accorded on the grounds that they were not a territorial unit but a group whose main function was to protect His Majesty. Further, he said, the guards were the "experimental" unit of the Tigers; they were the Tigers who would try out new drill methods, new weaponry.[124] Lastly, the King rationalized his attention on the basis of the very hard work and special devotion to duty the guards exhibited: the King suggested that, rather than envy the guards their special insignia and uniforms, other Wild Tigers ought to emulate them in energy and hard work.[125]

As to the Tiger movement as a whole, at first the King was rhapsodic. In his diary for September 1911 he spoke of the popularity of the corps and its success in producing national unity. Membership in the corps had transformed weak men into strong men, drunkards into sober men, selfish men into self-sacrificing men. The King in those first months looked on the corps as his monument "more solid than any statue or stone that might have been built at much greater cost."[126] In later times the King continued to praise the movement as a success, excoriating those who opposed it. But he undoubtedly felt the corps had not realized his early high expectations. At the end of World War I he praised the defense role played by the corps and sarcastically referred to his desk-bound bureaucrats as men who were "sitting in an office playing at making black ink marks on paper" and, when and if war came, could only "splash ink on the faces of the enemy or beat their heads with paper."[127] Yet the King undoubtedly knew of reports in the 1920s that admitted failures. One such report claimed that, given the voluntary nature of the corps, little improvement could be expected. Several reports referred to the serious falling off of interest in drilling; by 1922, said the report of one official, "virtually no members at all" were coming in for training and the officers themselves were not coming in to supervise the exercises.[128]

On the positive side of an evaluation of the Wild Tigers, several arguments can be made.

The military aspects of the movement certainly had some effects. By and large, European observers were impressed with what they saw in the way of discipline and national unity demonstrated by the Wild

The Wild Tigers

Tiger movement. In the neighboring colony of French Indochina, the French were aware that "The King and the Siamese aristocracy have created and are maintaining a Nationalist movement that it would be a mistake to ignore."[129] Several articles appearing in the *Courrier d'Haiphong* and the Saigon *Opinion* even raised questions about Siam's intentions and pointed to the need for France to develop the defensive military position of its colonies.[130]

But no evaluations of the Wild Tigers that rest primarily on its specifics—its finances, its military role—can come to grips with the substance of a true judgment. For the Wild Tiger movement was first and last a means to bring about a feeling of nationalism among the Thai people. The movement succeeded to the extent that it stirred in the Thai people a devotion to nation, a commitment to national unity. Here it cannot be denied that the movement achieved success; how much success remains the question. From the accounts and memoirs of some former members of the corps, there can be no doubt that many were stirred.[131] Some men and many boys who had never before thought of dying to protect their king, nation, and religion had the concept, as expressed in the very language of the King, permanently etched on their minds. And the example of the King living, eating, and sleeping in the field with his Wild Tiger comrades proved to many the King's sincerity.[132] Yet the total group affected was, after all, small. When the corps was abolished by Rama VII, no one rose to defend it; the corps as an institution was nothing without its "golden bo tree shelter."[133] The essential idea behind the institution, however, had a life beyond the institution itself and its founder.

4

The Monarchy

On February 29, 1912, a fairly obscure army captain rushed from a meeting in a modest second-floor law office in Bangkok to deliver some urgent news to a fellow officer who taught at the army cadet school.[1] On receiving the news, the cadet school instructor, who had connections higher up, led the captain to Prince Phanthuprawat, chief of a unit of army engineers. Prince Phanthuprawat took the news to the top, to Prince Chakrabongs, the Army Chief of Staff and Acting Minister of Defense.

The Abortive Coup of 1912

The news was startling, and it was bad. For the captain's story was that he had just attended a meeting of junior military officers who were plotting a revolt against the leadership of King Vajiravudh. The government moved fast. Prince Chakrabongs rushed to Nakhọn Pathom to inform the King. By the following day arrests were under

The Monarchy

way. On the morning of March 2 a government press release indicated that matters were under control.²

The abortive coup of 1912 was more than a dramatic episode in the history of modern Thailand. The motives of its leaders showed the spread of Western political ideas, including the idea of nationalism, among the Thai people. Some of these ideas, in the forms in which the coup leaders expressed them, bear unmistakable traces of His Majesty's own rhetoric. The abortive coup of 1912, then, in some respects constituted an indirect tribute to the effectiveness of Vajiravudh's nationalistic message.

The essential aims of the 1912 coup group were not entirely in the category of political idealism. Dissatisfaction with the King on a much more personal level was, in fact, the first stimulus to revolutionary thought. The coup idea seems to have originated in an incident that occurred shortly before Vajiravudh became king. A small group of soldiers got into a quarrel with a group of pages of the then Crown Prince Vajiravudh over the favors of a girl who sold betel nut. The quarrel ended with the soldiers, armed with sticks, chasing the pages back into the safety of Parusakawan Palace. The following day the Crown Prince demanded redress for the insult to his position by the application of an old provision of the palatine law that called for lashing on the back with a rattan rod. King Chulalongkorn at first resisted. So did the Minister of Justice, Prince Rabi, who pleaded that the new Westernized penal code made lashing with the rattan outmoded. (Undoubtedly both the King and the Prince were concerned over the possible bad effects that the resumption of such "barbaric" practices would have on Western states at the very time Siam was seeking to achieve removal of treaty restrictions on its juridical sovereignty.) The Crown Prince insisted. The beatings were administered, and the seeds of embitterment with Vajiravudh were planted among the military and among some members of the legal profession.³

Personal antipathy to the Prince intensified after he became king in 1910. Testimonies of those involved in the 1912 abortive coup show a wide range of criticisms: coup members spoke not only of Vajiravudh's insistence on the "shameful" beatings but also of his "absorption in putting on plays" and indulgence in other extravagant diversions; his overfondness for the Wild Tiger Corps, whose maneuvers were no better than "playacting"; his waste of money in "building various palaces"; and his excessive devotion to "officials in the royal household" who were "eating up the kingdom" and who insulted those beneath them. Some criticisms circulated in the form of

The Monarchy

rumors.⁴ These criticisms were generalized into comments such as "The King does not pay attention to the government" and "Our country will be in danger of foreign exploitation because of the wickedness of one person."

The personal antipathy to the King on the part of some of the coup members, however, became part of a larger picture. It merged with, and can hardly be separated from, the conviction that absolute monarchy in Siam was outmoded and must go. None of the coup leaders held that the removal of "one person" was the whole solution to Siam's problems. The coup leaders spoke against "obligation to one solitary person"; they spoke for "faithfulness to the Thai nation."

In the area of political ideology, the ideas of the coup party of 1912 were far from mature. A few of the coup members knew something of outside events and attempted to instruct the others in the idea that absolute monarchy was an unprogressive and dying institution, that virtually all other states in the world were either constitutional monarchies or republics. They told less-well-read members about the forms of governments in Europe and America, the success of Japan after its adoption of a constitution, the movement of the Young Turks, the democratic revolution in Portugal, and finally and above all, the victory of the Kuomintang in China. Siam, they said, was behind the times; Siam also needed a parliament, in which the people could have a voice in government, in order to progress economically, socially, politically. The coup group, however, had not yet crystallized its thoughts on the form of government best suited to Siam. Some opted for a republic. The majority appear to have favored having a king under law, that is, a constitutional monarchy. But no constitution had been drawn up, no clear political path for the future had been agreed upon.

The lack of a precise political goal, however, was not seen as an obstacle to taking political action in the interests of the nation. The nationalistic purposes of the coup group are hard to question. Patriotic slogans abounded and were convincingly phrased. The nation's lack of progress, the poverty of the people, the susceptibility of the country to foreign domination were all cited as real ills. All Thai had to love their country and put its interests before all else. Death was preferable to national slavery. It is paradoxical that many of the remarks and slogans of the coup party closely reflected the ideas of the King himself. Said one coup member, "We are Thai and must love our nation and religion and land of our birth"—a paraphrase of the King's own "nation, religion, and king," with "land of our

The Monarchy

birth" substituted for "king." The motto of the coup party was "Give up life rather than nation"—almost identical to the Wild Tiger motto "Give up life rather than honor."[5]

Although the coup members focused mainly on internal affairs, they took an occasional glance at the presumed reaction of the outside world. The prevailing thought seemed to be that foreigners who looked down on the Thai as unprogressive, who even criticized the Thai king for his judicial practices, would be favorably impressed by a move toward constitutionalism. The view was also put forth that the existing government was exercising too harsh a policy with respect to local Chinese, that this policy had to be changed or it might lead to revolts of the Chinese in Siam and to severe action on the part of the Chinese republican government.[6]

The King's very stress on the crucial need for national defense was used by the coup party, and used against him. The argument here repeated the King's own comments that long peace in Siam had led to national weakness and consequent disadvantage in terms of outside power. The coup members, almost all of whom were soldiers, however, faulted the King for not giving adequate support to the regular armed forces. The army, they said, lacked weapons; its leaders were ignored.[7] The real defense of the kingdom was not being prepared to do its job. The cry "Can all of us soldiers and Thai just silently watch our Thai nation be destroyed?" yielded the answer "No, of course not." Indeed, the coup leaders argued, soldiers were the only element in society brave enough and in a strong enough position to do something to remedy the situation.

Some of the coup leaders undoubtedly had selfish motives as well as political and nationalistic ones, but the self-serving motivation appears not to have been dominant. Only a few of the secret, and often extremely frank, testimonies refer at all to the relatively poor wages and the slow promotions in the army. Perhaps if the coup party had grown larger in numbers, and with such growth had appeared more likely to succeed, the numbers of those who joined in the hopes of gaining personal advantage would have become more significant.

The organization and tactical plans of the 1912 coup party had serious weaknesses. What started out as barracks-room talk, in which some junior officers of like mind discovered each other, was formalized in an organizational meeting of a core group of seven officers on January 13, 1912. This meeting was followed by some ten or eleven subsequent meetings through the rest of January and all of February. The main purposes of the meetings were recruitment and indoctrination. Recruitment was on a person-to-person basis. By the end of February somewhat over one hundred people had attended meetings, and recruitment among provincial military units had just begun. Although most recruits came from army units in Bangkok, a few civilians—mostly lawyers and translators—and some three or four young naval officers had joined the coup party by the end of February. Members were asked for financial support[8] and help in spreading the word. The coup group members were very young; almost all were in their early twenties.[9]

The recruitment arguments followed the antimonarchic and pronationalistic lines already presented above. Appeals were also made to new members to be with the times, to be modern and not old-fashioned. Hints that the group was large, numbering into the hundreds, and had friends in high places among senior officers were also used by original coup members. Although the direct and unsupportable claim that Prince Chakrabongs was sympathetic to the group seems not to have been made, new members were well aware that the coup party leader, Dr. Leng Sichan (an army captain, with the title of Khun Thawaihanphithak), was the personal physician to the Prince and his family. Recruits were encouraged to think that if Dr. Leng were the head of the party then there must be important men in the nation backing it.[10]

It would appear from some of the testimonies of those arrested that they became involved by deception: they were invited to a meeting to "shoot birds" or to have a social evening only to discover that they were listening to conspiratorial talk; then they were pledged to secrecy, usually by the administration of an oath, solemnized by a ritual in which a bullet was dropped into a glass of liquor, which was passed around for all to drink. The claim to innocent or reluctant involvement is hard to credit, however; it seems to have been the natural defense of men accused of a serious crime. More than one coup member specifically denied the innocence of anyone who went to meetings and asserted that men were carefully screened before they were invited to an indoctrination session.[11]

The original plans of the nucleus coup group were for ten years of preparation, but it became clear by the second meeting that it would be impossible to maintain secrecy for such a long period. The new plans, far from complete by the end of February, called for action in early April at the annual ceremony in which the King would accept the oath of allegiance of his officials. Coup members who formed part of the royal guard would then surround His Majesty and compel him to yield to their demands. Those demands, although not yet decided on, would at a minimum be for King Vajiravudh to promise to grant his people a constitution and place himself under law; if the King were unwilling to make this concession, he would be replaced by Prince Chakrabongs. Some coup members suggested that Prince Chakrabongs be named constitutional monarch from the outset. Still others suggested that the monarchy be completely abolished and a republic instituted, with Prince Rabi installed as first president. Of these three plans, the second, calling for installation of Chakrabongs as king, seems to have been most popular by the end of February. The coup members, of course, expected to have all of March to perfect their plans and make their final decisions.

Two other "plans" emerge from the sources, but neither is well substantiated. One called for the coup group to take no action other than to petition the King for a constitution; this "plan," articulated by a small number of those arrested, sounds like an after-the-fact attempt to reduce culpability. As violent as the petitioning-plan was mild was the second "plan": a plot by coup members to "do violence" to the King. According to some rumors, the plotters had planned to kill the King.[12] The charge of violence was, in fact, made by the court martial judges and by the King.[13] It was, however, heartily denied by all those implicated both at the time of the coup and later, and seems to have been based primarily on an ill-advised attempt by one of the coup members, after the arrests had taken place, to threaten government leaders with a cannonading unless those arrested were freed. This threat apparently transformed the early lenient disposition of the King into a mood of bitterness and harshness.[14]

Discussions among coup members about the best alternative to King Vajiravudh as leader of Siam reveal something of coup mentality. Prince Chakrabongs, although completely oblivious of the fact, was undoubtedly the leading contender. He was, first of all, an army man and would therefore presumably be most sympathetic to the specific army grievances held by the majority of coup members. Further, he was seen as an honest man whose heart was with the people; on maneuvers, for example, he sloshed with his troops in the rain. A second choice among the princes was Prince Paribatra, the Minister of Marine, whose candidacy was supported by the naval officers. The only other name to be put forward was that of Prince Rabi (the Prince of Ratburi), who had a reputation for fairness, based, no doubt, on his opposition, as Minister of Justice, to the flogging of the army officers.[15] Prince Rabi was the favored candidate for the Thai presidency among those who wanted a republic. At no time, apparent-

The Monarchy

ly, was it even vaguely suggested that Dr. Leng or other leaders of the coup party should themselves take over top positions in the government.

The sentences given the coup members were made public on May 5, 1912. Ninety-one persons were found guilty of conspiracy. Three were sentenced to death; twenty, to life imprisonment; the remainder, to prison terms of twenty, fifteen, or twelve years. The King, in an act of clemency to show that he did not "entertain any feelings of revenge,"[16] immediately reduced all sentences: the death penalty was reduced to life imprisonment; life imprisonment was reduced to twenty years; the remaining sixty-eight prison sentences were reduced to suspended sentences.[17] In a final act of clemency twelve years later, in November 1924, all prisoners were freed.

It is difficult to measure the real effect of the abortive coup of 1912 on the thinking of the King or other Thai of the times. The foreign-language press in Bangkok speculated that the "present disaffection" and the "mutinous doctrines" were but the manifestations of the spirit of "liberty and progress" and the "wave of unrest" then sweeping through Asia; that the coup movement, although it did not "touch the masses," did indicate the existence of a "growing force of public opinion" that "requires guidance."[18] Editorials saw the coup as showing that "patriotism is an enormously greater force than it was a score or so of years ago."[19] But, the press pointed out, "the new reign has furnished evidence enough that the progress of the nation continues unhasting and unresting, and that the new spirit is understood and appreciated by the monarch."[20] The King's reduction of the sentences of the coup members was seen by one paper as giving "full proof" that

> he holds liberal views, that he has not desired nor does desire to withhold that discussion of public questions which is the right of a free people, so long as the expression of these views does not harm his country. His Majesty desires to see the people capable of taking their part in the affairs of state and has no intention of restricting their free speech during the interval that must elapse before the public are fit for the high duties involved .... The wise decision of the King to treat the conspiracy more as a youthful exaggeration than a serious endeavor will draw the teeth of demagogues and at the same time satisfy the legitimate aspirations of the people.[21]

The opinions in the foreign press on the effects of the coup seem largely wishful thinking. There is little evidence that the discovery of the coup plans resulted in any important change in public policy;

The Monarchy

there is no evidence that it fundamentally shook the King's confidence in the monarchic institution.

Among the relatively minor changes that may be attributed to coup influence were two that came in April. One was the transfer of the highest court of appeal in the country from the office of the King to the Ministry of Justice. This move was seen as "a modification of the constitution in the direction of extending the reign of law."[22] A second change that seems likely to have been a response to coup leaders' criticisms of the King's prodigality was the King's removal of the Privy Purse Department from a tax-exempt category. By this action all the King's personal lands and properties were to be subject to the same taxes as those levied on properties of ordinary citizens, for, as the King explained, "Apart from the official side, I consider myself as being on the same footing as any ordinary person."[23] Other changes of some significance included various efforts to enhance the prestige of the army and to modify the training of Wild Tigers.[24]

The army, for its part, made one innovation that seemed calculated to improve the overall image of the army in the King's eyes. This was the formation in May 1912 of a voluntary Association to Promote the Army of Siam. To show their love of land and king, association members agreed to forgo a portion of their pay (1 percent was the minimum) to raise funds to buy the army some heavy artillery.[25]

Defense of the Monarchy

King Vajiravudh, like his father before him, saw kingship as natural to Siam, essential to Siam's progress. He saw Siam's successes in history as the results of wise royal leadership. And he saw loyalty to the monarch as one of the three necessary loyalties for the further development of Siam as a united, progressive, modern state. Together with loyalty to nation and religion, loyalty to the king was part of his definition of nationalism.

The essentiality of loyalty to the king is stressed again and again and again in Vajiravudh's writings and addresses; it is a perennial theme throughout his reign. In an essay of 1915, for example, Vajiravudh made loyalty to the king part of the very definition of a "true Thai."[26] In some speeches and essays the theme is developed at length. It is the entire subject of a speech to the Wild Tigers in June 1911. Indeed, the first part of the Wild Tiger oath was an oath of loyalty to the king. In the 1911 speech Vajiravudh told why.[27]

First of all, Vajiravudh made clear that he supported the pledge of loyalty to the king not because *he* was king; it was the institution

The Monarchy

he supported. And his support was based on belief in a Hobbesian history of man in a primitive state, with the device of a leader finally being adopted by tribal groups in order to achieve external protection and internal order. The leader, or king, received the delegated power of the group and used that power for the benefit of the group. So the show of honor and respect to the king was in effect a show of honor and respect to the entire group, each of whose members had yielded power so that it could be combined in the person of the king. And, by the same token, deprecation of the king amounted to self-deprecation. The withholding of respect or obligation to the king simply amounted to a loss of power for the leader, making him less able to do the tasks that he was delegated to do for the group. The King proceeded to give examples showing the necessity to delegate power. Ships needed captains, and captains must command. Similarly with the ship of state, whose captain was the king. Further, the king had symbolic significance. For power is an abstract term and, like such terms as good and evil, was hard for earlier peoples to understand unless anthropomorphized. Just as good was personified as a god or an angel, and bad as a devil or demon, so power was seen in the form of a king; the king became the visible expression of the glory of the land. That glory belonged to everyone in the nation, and it was the duty of all to protect it and defend it. Anyone who would harm the king could only be considered as someone who was exceedingly evil and would do harm to the nation, would destroy the peace and welfare of the group.

From these abstractions and rationales for royal power, the King in his June 1911 speech dropped to a more personal level. He chided those who thought being king was a desirable job, a job with an enormous income, all kinds of personal perquisites, and freedom from any restraint. If a king could merely indulge himself, do nothing but devote himself to pleasure, then his position would be enviable. But the duties of a conscientious monarch were onerous indeed. And Vajiravudh could be nothing but conscientious, a king who would do his duty "to the best of my ability and strength," a king who was "prepared to sacrifice my pleasures, my body, even my life for the good of the nation." All he asked of the Wild Tigers and of his people was that they work with him, for "if we sink, we all sink; if we are saved, we are all saved." In any case, however the ship might fare in the stormy seas, "I will not abandon you, I will not flee."[28]

In an extension of his remarks on royal conscientiousness, Vajiravudh depicted himself as the moral exemplar of the state. In an

The Monarchy

address to students at the Royal Pages School in 1915 he likened the task of students and of government officials to that of a mountain climber. He said, in part:

> I try to climb the mountain every day. The mountain I climb is much higher than yours. Yours is but a small hill whose top is soon reached. But the mountain I climb—its top cannot be seen. Therefore I ask you to bear in mind that whatever the dimensions of your difficulties, I also experience difficulties and fatigue. I do not believe I am in any way better off than you.[29]

More than moral exemplar, the king, in Vajiravudh's view, was the ultimate source of all power in the state. Since all power and justification for authority ultimately went back to the throne, officials should not assume that they had any authority in their own right. Officials should not expect commoners to respect them for their ranks or titles. They should not be respected because of their high birth, their position as "gentlemen" (*phudi*). For a "gentleman"—the Thai word literally means "good person"—who behaves poorly is no gentleman, and an ordinary man of good deportment is.[30] An official must earn his title of respect and his label of gentleman by rigorously adhering to the royal will and by serving, as the monarch himself does, as a moral example to all the people.[31] In the end the official is but the pale reflected light of His Majesty's brilliance. And the people know this:

> Why do people respect the nobles? Only because they know the nobles convey a part of royal power. They do not respect the *persons* of the nobles as such. If you don't believe me, imagine what would happen if someone went into the countryside claiming he was a *čhaophraya* by virtue of his commission from the King of Cambodia or the King of Burma. Would he get the people's respect? Not at all![32]

While Vajiravudh was not loath to have his people believe in the traditional special powers, the karmic royal virtues, that Thai kings were thought to possess,[33] in his public remarks he stressed the human rather than superhuman qualities of the king and the pragmatic benefits of kingship. In his Wild Tiger addresses he was fond of speaking of himself as just another Thai citizen or as a friend; in his addresses to young people he asked that his words be regarded as those "of a teacher and not those of the king."[34] The Thai king, he pointed out, was not like the ancient king of China whose face could not be looked upon; the Thai people wanted to see their king, and Vajiravudh did not separate himself from his people. Indeed, he moved among them.

The Monarchy

In other lands kings were regarded as angels or gods, but in Siam the king was regarded as a human being. Vajiravudh described himself as but a Thai, with thoughts like those of Thai in general.[35]

The humanity and accessibility of the Thai monarch are contrasted strongly with the seclusion of the Japanese emperor in a newspaper article the King wrote in 1912 under the pseudonym "Asvabahu, a travelled Siamese." Vajiravudh remarked that he had long pondered the deeper meanings behind the degree of exposure of the monarch and his relationship with his people. There were advantages and disadvantages to seclusion and to exposure. The secluded monarch tended to preserve his dignity better, was regarded with more reverence. "It is one of the peculiarities of human nature," said the King, "to prefer showing reverence only to mysteries." And, "the very mysteriousness of the Emperor of Japan ensures reverence in him." On the other hand, what the sovereign who exposed himself to his people lost in reverence, he gained in better understanding of his people's wants and needs and in ability to create a bond of human sympathy between himself and his subjects. The accessible sovereign ran the risk, however, of having his subjects "regard him more in the light of an influential acquaintance, who *ought* to be of the very greatest use to each of them individually, with the inevitable consequence that anyone who does not get *everything* his own way thinks himself personally and particularly aggrieved, and therefore thinks himself entitled to bear a personal *grudge* against the Sovereign!" The King continued:

> The policy of our own King, however, and that of his August and Beloved Predecessor before him, has always been to grant to his subjects free access to his Person; and, in spite of the disadvantages resulting therefrom, as mentioned above, I would not for worlds have it otherwise. I am sure we ought all to be most grateful to our King for granting us the privilege of free access to his Person; for we like to think of him as a Father, who comes freely among his beloved children, interesting himself in their works, and entering into their fun. A Father who thus comes amongst his children ought surely not to lose his dignity thereby, because a few naughty, spoilt children are impolite and unmannerly enough not to behave themselves properly. My friends, it is up to you to ensure the continuance of that privilege which was voluntarily granted to us; I mean the privilege of free access to our King. Shall we lose the privilege because a few "naughty children" do not know how to behave themselves like *gentlemen*? There is no need to cringe and crawl, but we *can* and *should* give our Sovereign the welcome of the children to the father, the friend! ... Surely you could be loyal without being

The Monarchy

slavish, and polite without cringing? Impoliteness is not a sign of independence, but merely a sign of *want of breeding*![36]

But on royal leadership the King insisted. Siam, he said, was fortunate in having had a long history of continuous royal successions. The orderly succession of kings had reduced political discord, had saved the country from foreign threats when Western power began its insistent demands in the nineteenth century:

> In their wisdom, our Kings did not set their faces against the stream of progress. On the contrary, they welcomed civilisation and progress with open doors, and our rulers moved along with the stream and *have been doing so ever since*. Civilisation came to Siam and found no need to knock in any way as insistently as she has had to do in both Japan and China; the stream of progress found no formidable barriers set up purposely in its path, such barriers as were found being merely natural ones, which our wise rulers have always tried to remove as soon as possible.[37]

The image of King Vajiravudh as captain of the ship of state, developed fully in the speech of June 1911, recurs in many speeches and writings and is alternated with similar images. In one speech the King likens himself to one of the three flags of the Thai people—the others being nation and religion.[38] In a poem he looks at the natural world and sees that all things in nature need leaders; even cattle need a leader "to lead the herd where the grass is."[39] And, of course, even the gods have their chief in Indra in the heavens.[40]

The challenges to absolute monarchy that were so evident in 1912, however, could not go without reply. Such challenges were not entirely new in the reign. In fact, King Chulalongkorn in 1887 had been presented with a petition by several of his officials asking that a constitutional monarchy be established in Siam.[41] Chulalongkorn could turn away his polite petitioners with a reasoned reply; Vajiravudh felt he had to go further.

Even before he became king, Vajiravudh showed that he was his father's son on the subject of constitutionalism. In 1905 he penned a short sketch of what it would be like if Siam had a parliament. The parliament session he depicted was marked by interminable and pointless speeches, and it ended in chaos.[42] Another early essay on parliamentary government, written by a courtier for Vajiravudh's own journal, undoubtedly reflected Vajiravudh's views. The essay pointed out that in states with parliaments the law is not fully respected, for laws written by the people cannot be respected by the people in the way that royal law is respected. The essay argued further that parliamentary government was slow and divisive. Government

Royal Leadership in Siam. King Vajiravudh, through his ability and diligence, raises Siam on the ropes of its soldiery and arms, its internal peace and order, its education, and its agriculture and industry above the level of the Burmese, the Cambodians, and the Vietnamese. The faces behind Vajiravudh represent the previous five Chakkri kings. Cartoon from *Dusit samit*.

The Monarchy

tended to polarize into parties and proved the proverb that "Two lions cannot live in the same cave." The essayist admitted that in a monarchical government much depended on the monarch, but he said that in Siam, where the monarch was good, compassionate, and just, the system worked well. Critics of such government in Siam were like those who complained of the soot that emerged from the productive rice mill.[43]

The essential arguments of Vajiravudh against constitutionalism in Siam, aside from those that stressed the value of the monarchy, were that, in fact, the monarchy was already under law, with a degree of constitutionalism already in existence, and that Siam was not ready for any further constitutionalism. The King dismissed the critics of the monarchy as poorly informed young people at best or self-serving ambitious individuals at worst.

The changes in the constitutional position of the monarchy had come about, said Vajiravudh, through the introduction of new laws granted to the people by the king. In effect such laws limited the power of the king, who could not repress the people at will without violating his own laws. The king was not above the law to do whatever he wanted, right or wrong. He had to use his power in righteous and productive ways.[44] Vajiravudh further claimed that democratic methods had long been exercised in the Thai polity; the founder of the dynasty had indeed been "chosen by the people" after his predecessor was deposed for madness.[45]

On the critics of monarchy, first of all the King said they were very few—"not one in a million."[46] Those few were excessively impressed with foreign ideas. He counseled young people in particular to beware of rumormongers, of those given to extravagant talk,[47] of those who looked on all Europeans as "preceptors in the ways of Progress and Civilisation."[48] Students should study European political concepts, but they should judge whether or not such concepts were suitable to the Thai, whether Siam was at the moment ready for such concepts. Further, they should examine their own motives: if they favored certain political changes, did they favor them because these changes would be useful to the majority of the Thai people or because they would suit the purposes of a small minority? Vajiravudh expected that a fair judgment would lead students to reject political change and conclude, with him, that "things of benefit to Europeans might be evils to us."[49] Some critics the King put in the class of people who were merely seeking to avoid their responsibilities to the state by favoring new political orders that would give them personal license to do as they pleased or provide them with new avenues for achieving

The Monarchy

power. These people earned the King's sharpest castigations as "buffoons" and "sinful destroyers" of the nation.[50]

Vajiravudh, who was always well read on foreign affairs, was keenly aware of foreign political changes and their impact on educated Thai. The early years of the twentieth century had seen revolutions in Turkey, Portugal, Persia, and China, and in 1917 czarism yielded to Marxism in Russia. The King wrote many essays and translated numbers of articles on these foreign developments.[51] His theme was consistent: foreign revolutions were no example for Siam. His writings on China were most numerous, probably because he felt that, with the large Chinese minority in Siam, affairs in China had the greatest potential of causing unrest. In one essay, for example, he doubted the possibility of success for the republican government in China. He could not believe that the Chinese would be able to change their character in a blink of an eye, that they could create "a *true* republic in my lifetime."[52] And affairs in China as of the end of 1912 seemed to the King to justify his doubts. The political executions, the absence of law, the prevalence of disorder all demonstrated China's failure to make a foreign polity work. Vajiravudh saw China in chaos, with anarchy, tyranny, and injustice prevailing. He once remarked that Westernizing "politicians" in China had "set back the progress of China by at least a century already!"[53]

In a series of articles on the Chinese Revolution as of the end of 1912,[54] the King explored the details of the Chinese scene so that his people would know the facts and not blindly admire or seek to emulate what they did not understand. Vajiravudh's conclusion was that "*in name* at least, the 'Republic of China' exists. There is certainly a government in Peking, which calls itself the Republic, but is it a real one?... this seems extremely doubtful." The King put the republic through various tests and found it consistently wanting. The president had not been elected. Not even the assembly had been elected; it had rather "Like a glorious God in Hindu mythology ... sprung into being of its own accord." The assembly "in no way represents the people"; it "is not a constitutionally representative body." The King gave the original Chinese revolutionaries credit for good intentions, but he was pessimistic as to how matters would eventually turn out:

> I do not in the least doubt that Sun Yat Sen meant to have a republic when he started the revolution. He undoubtedly felt that China was really having a bad time all round, and probably believed that he could save her from total destruction if he could only turn the Manchus out and turn the country into a republic. He counted upon the sympathetic

The Monarchy

interest of people in Europe and America, and he was right. He got it, with his war-cry of "A republic for China." People in Europe and America have very hazy ideas about China on the whole. They believed the Chinese to be a downtrodden people, and naturally sympathised with them in their struggle for liberty. Then, sure of that sympathy, Sun Yat Sen and his friends went to work with a will, and started preaching revolutionary doctrines and Republicanism to their fellow countrymen. I do not think anyone will contradict me when I say that, to the majority of Chinamen, the revolutionary leaders' preaching conveyed nothing beyond a vague idea, that if the revolution succeeded, they would gain all sorts of wonderful advantages. For example, more wealth would come to them, they would be treated as equals by the Europeans, and so forth; and it cannot be denied that such enthusiasm on their part was infectious, not only to the Chinese themselves, but also to those of other nations, (some Siamese among them), who in point of fact knew but little of Chinese affairs. So Sun Yat Sen started the revolution, and carried it through. He and his friends succeeded in pulling down the Monarchy, but when it came to setting up a republic in its place, they found it not so easy to do as to talk and dream about it. Republics are easy to set up in Dreamland, but it is another thing to do it in China. Sun Yat Sen was no man to build up any sort of government, and he himself knew it. That was why he so kindly left everything to Yuan Shih Kai .... It now only remains for Yuan Shih Kai to carry out his part of the bargain, and establish the Republic of China. For the present, we can not admit that he has done it. Will he ever do it? Will he ever be able to do it in reality? Does he really want to do it?[55]

In a series of articles on the Young Turks and their revolution, also written in 1912, Vajiravudh was equally critical.[56] The principal aim of the young revolutionaries was to bring down Sultan Abdul Hamid, whom they saw as "the one drag upon the progress of Turkey." Sultan Abdul, Vajiravudh admitted, had his faults; he was no saint. But then no ruler could afford to be a saint "except in those ancient times, when saintship seemed to have been easier of attainment than it is now." At least the sultan had "kept his head, and also his Empire," neither of which the Young Turks were able to do.[57]

In his remarks on Turkey Vajiravudh showed considerable empathy for the sultan. In "explaining" the faults of the sultan, he was undoubtedly calling, probably unconsciously, for understanding of his own problems. The King, for example, allowed that corruption had existed among the sultan's officials. But, asked Vajiravudh, what could the sultan have done? If he had dismissed all corrupt officials, he would soon have been without a government, and any replacements

The Monarchy

he might have found would have been just as corruptible as their predecessors. What the sultan needed, and could not get by snapping his fingers, was a new society with a new morality, with new ideals and standards. It is clear, here, that Vajiravudh had very much in mind the propaganda work he was so actively engaged in—his work to establish in Siam those values without which no regime, constitutional or otherwise, could hope to achieve real reforms.

On the subject of constitutionalism, Vajiravudh stated his belief that Sultan Abdul Hamid "did not consider it wise or advantageous for Turkey to have progressive institutions thrust upon the people before they knew how to benefit by such institutions ... that his desire was to go slowly and to gradually introduce such reforms as he felt absolutely sure the people were ready for."[58] The Young Turks, however, a small clique of clever agitators and young officers "who had just enough knowledge in them to make them dangerous,"[59] carried out their revolution and deposed the sultan. Carrying out such a revolution was not difficult, for "destruction is terribly easy,"[60] especially since the Young Turks felt no need to worry about the opinion of the public, "to consult the opinion of a 'thing' like that. Who cares anything as to what the 'thing' may do or say?"[61] The consequences were foreordained. Since the mass of the people knew nothing of the "blessings of popular government" and "had not the vaguest idea of the meaning of the term parliament," the Young Turks "had to teach them, by driving them to the poll at the point of the bayonet!" The King remarked, "Parliament in Turkey has been nothing but a farce."[62]

The final denunciation of the Young Turks, however, was accorded them for their failure to preserve Turkey. By 1912 war had broken out in Turkey's Balkan provinces, the empire was coming apart, and the Turkish army was collapsing. The "warlike Turkish soldier," once moved by an "overwhelming sense of loyalty to the Sultan," had been demoralized by revolutionary propaganda; for this the Young Turks were also held responsible: "... the Young Turks may be said to have killed the ideal Turkish warrior when they killed loyalty and caused the death of discipline."[63] The King summed up his feelings on "the fruits of Turkish constitutionalism" in a scathing denunciation of Turkey's young revolutionaries:

> ... they came before us with a swagger, their mouths full of braggadacio, raising false cries of "Liberty, Equality, and Fraternity," spreading the fever of excitement which reached even as far as these parts of Asia, setting the example for all braggarts in the Orient to raise cries for

"Constitution," a thing which not one in one hundred millions understands the least bit about, except that it is something "civilised"! It is for *this* that I am down on the Young Turks; and I frankly admit I feel no sorrow in their downfall, since it will serve to disillusion such Orientals (including a few of my own countrymen), as may have caught the "Constitution" fever badly.[64]

Experiments with constitutionalism in other Asian states elicited similar royal reactions. With respect to Persia, where revolutionaries had succeeded in forcing the shah to accept a popular assembly in 1906, the King wrote: "The Persian people have been saddled with a parliament that they understand nothing about and do not want, and which has caused the country more trouble than all the most incompetent shahs put together."[65]

The last country to be dealt with by Vajiravudh in his 1912 series of articles was Japan,[66] which he "felt sure" would be brought up "as an example and an argument" to disprove his allegations that Asian states were not ready for constitutional government. Vajiravudh maintained his ground; he readily admitted the successes Japan had achieved but held "that Japan does not owe her present greatness to constitutionalism; on the contrary, Japan has attained her present position, not on account of constitutionalism, but rather *in spite of it*."[67] And the King strongly substantiated his argument with abundant evidence that the crucial decisions and fundamental policies that led to Japan's progress had been taken long before the adoption of the 1890 Constitution. Further, the Japanese government since 1890, wrote the King, could not be called a pure parliamentary regime; it was rather "a bureaucratic monarchy, not to say oligarchic"[68] government with at best a constitutional instrumentality in "the experimental stage."[69]

The lessons for Siam were clear. A small group of young people with "the wrong kind of education, and an insufficiency thereof" had picked up ideas of Western political institutions and sought to apply them in Asia with catastrophic results.[70] Where their revolutions had succeeded, they had merely instituted "synthetic constitutions" without affecting basic problems or traditional political points of view. The revolutionaries had proved that they could stir things up, could destroy; they had yet to show that they could build anew. Using a dramatic example, the King pointed to the success of Chinese agitators in getting their followers to cut their pigtails. What, asked the King, had this to do with "the inner consciousness of a man"? How would any tonsorial technique enable a person to pass, at a stroke, "from

The Monarchy

the darkness of political ignorance to the brilliant light of political understanding"?[71]

Vajiravudh obviously had men such as those involved in the abortive 1912 coup in mind when he advised his people to learn from mistakes made elsewhere and to beware of "that insidious foe, who comes in the guise of a friend, a self-styled 'patriot' with his mouth cram full of dead theories specially dug up and dressed in attractive garments to catch your fancies!"[72]

The show of constitutionalism without the substance was worse than useless; in the King's trenchant English, "...the glory of a nation who assumes the cloak of Constitutionalism ... [is] like the glory of the ass who wore the lion's skin! If only the ass had not started braying, he would not have been found out so soon; but what ass could ever help braying?"[73]

Siam had its own national "traditions and fundamental principles" that could not be swept away "with one magnificent wave of a magic wand." The King denied that he was a reactionary; he was a conservative, perhaps, but not a reactionary. He favored reforms, he said, when they were needed; he favored real liberty and real equality and not artificial representations of these virtues. But, the King concluded, Siam not only was not ready for democratic government but would be ruined by such government. He stated that "any precipitate movement in the direction of constitutionalism would cost us dear." It would cause confusion that would lead to results "too appalling" to mention.[74] The Young Turks, he said, had succeeded in destroying Turkey in three short years, "but Siam will not take so long to destroy. A year, at most two will be enough."[75] Revolutionary confusion in some states was damaging, but in Siam's case it would be the end; China might lose territory, Turkey might lose its imperial lands, but tiny Siam would simply cease to exist.

The King did not argue publicly against the theory of constitutional government on general principles. He admitted that progressive states in Europe and America had such governments. But Europe and America were not Asia. And, he pointed out: "Where a nation has not gradually grown up in the understanding and practice of self-government, it is sheer absurdity to talk sentimental nonsense about setting up a parliamentary regime." Democratic political systems took centuries to bring about; they came slowly and only at the price of the blood and tears of countless people. England, for example, had taken several centuries to "grow" its parliamentary practice. And although the United States had started off its history as a constitutional

The Monarchy

republic, it had been able to do so because it was founded by Englishmen who were "already well-used to the representative method of government."[76]

But privately the King freely criticized the basis of constitutionalism. Several pages in his diary, written for his own benefit and the education of his closest courtiers, are devoted to a hard look at the constitutional system of government. First of all, he admitted that absolute monarchy had its weaknesses; the overriding one was the danger of the ascent of an incapable monarch. An unwise, selfish, or cruel king could do incalculable harm to the nation. Constitutional governments sought to remove that danger by placing power in the hands of the people. A government responsible to the people that could be changed whenever the people chose was, he said, an excellent system—on paper! But in practice the system had many imperfections. The citizenry by and large lacked enough knowledge to govern themselves. And the necessity for the people to govern themselves through elected representatives led to all sorts of aberrations of the democratic ideal, such as party politics, bribery, vote-buying, and the spoils system. The King's criticisms were reasoned. He did not stand as an unalterable opponent. He wrote, "If any responsible and well intentioned groups should petition me to grant a constitution . . . I would be glad to consider it." More significantly he said that the people of Siam would determine their own future. Whenever the great mass of citizens made clear they wanted constitutional government, whatever its imperfections, "there'd be no one able to oppose them." But clearly that day had not yet arrived.[77]

Even though Vajiravudh professed admiration for progressive European states with parliaments, he could not suppress, privately at least, a certain satisfaction in a minor "setback" to British constitutionalism that occurred in 1917. The King had learned that the new prime minister, Lloyd George, had made bold changes in the cabinet to make it "less unwieldy and unpractical as an instrument of government in these critical times." Vajiravudh wrote in a letter to his minister to France:

> This change will have the effect of causing some chagrin to "politicians" all over the world, whose theory of constitutional government has thereby received a direct blow to its prestige, since it has been examined and found wanting in times of national crisis. It is surprising—and also very refreshing—to find how silent our own "nationalists" and "Constitutionalists" have become! Well, well, "It is an ill wind that blows nobody any good," and this dreadful war has been a blessing in disguise to those who are lucky enough to be able to stay out of it![78]

The Monarchy

The King's reactions to republicanism and constitutionalism were by no means peculiar to him; they were echoed by other leaders in government and the royal family. Prince Devawongse, for example, shared Vajiravudh's view that Siam was already, in effect, a constitutional monarchy and strongly rejected the idea of a parliament for Siam. Writing to the King in 1919, he pointed to the danger of rushing "half-ripe" to parliamentarianism, which in Russia had led only to the tyrannies of Bolshevik enslavement of the people. And he specifically mentioned the danger that members of parliament might easily succumb to pressure groups in the community and enact self-serving legislation such as reinstitution of the gambling houses that Vajiravudh had taken action against in 1916.[79]

Prince Paribatra, in a letter written to the King shortly after the abortive coup of 1912, defended the monarchy and strongly supported Vajiravudh personally. He attributed the growing political consciousness of some people to the spread of education; to the influx of foreign peoples, that is, the Chinese, who were accustomed to antimonarchic views; to the growth in the number of officials, many of whom tended to forget their obligations to the king; to the increasing influence of an irresponsible press; and to the operations of lawyers whose search for legal loopholes tended to reduce respect for royal decrees. The Prince came up with solutions. The first was to make clear "that there is but one king who has the power to govern the country." All government officials, from cabinet ministers on down, should recognize that they were but the servants of the king and executors of his policy. A second solution was to make certain that the welfare of the people was paramount, that government did not exist for the welfare of officialdom. Thirdly, the government should make its purposes and plans better known to the public; it should explain its actions, preferably through its own press organ. Lastly, a law regulating the press should be enacted.[80]

After reading some press criticisms, Vajiravudh's brother, Prince Chakrabongs, wrote a memorandum to the King to the effect that the absolute monarchy could use an escape valve for attacks in the form of a revival of the long-defunct Legislative Council established in 1874 by King Chulalongkorn. The King replied that, although he was a constitutionalist at heart, he did not believe that Siam was ready for a proper legislature; as for the halfway house of an appointed council, that would not still criticism, for it would be sure to be attacked as but a rubber-stamp institution.[81]

The King summed up many of his ideas on politics in a short play written the year before he died.[82] Called *Coup d'état* and set in a

The Monarchy

mythical kingdom, the play recalled many of the events of 1912. The play deals with an attempt by some revolutionaries to overthrow a king who is unjustly blamed for all the ills of the country; the coup fails, and the king is discovered to be a man of great worth whose "desire has always been to govern his people so that they should obtain as much happiness as possible"[83] but who has been prevented from putting his progressive policies into effect because of the obstruction of the government's all-powerful ministers and parliament.

Through the speeches of characters in the play, the King gave vent to many of his own ideas. Monarchy is praised. Republicans are damned. Revolutionaries who desire the removal of the king are made out to be selfish men, traitors, or people "too enamoured of theories."[84] One character looks at China and comments: "China has been a Republic for several years, but has it become any better than it was before?"[85] Another looks at Russia and concludes that the Russian people are suffering more than ever: thousands have died; many must eat "the flesh of dead and putrid horses"; and "instead of having freedom they are being oppressed a thousand times worse than before."[86] These various views are summed up in one remarkable speech:

> I will say briefly, that every one of those who have expressed the desire for changing the form of Government from a Monarchy to a Republic have no reason for their desire except a personal one and from want of judgement, believing the words of demagogues and of newspapers owned by aliens or by people with personal grievances, who are endeavouring by specious words to foster sedition and rebellion. Comrades! We are true-born Coronians, so why do you want to listen to the words of aliens? We have received from our ancestors a noble heritage, namely birth in the Coronian Nation which we all love and want to cherish; shall we sell our birth-right to the Jews and the aliens? Let us not do it, comrades! Be patient. It is true that we are at present passing through some hard times, but it is nothing so bad as we shall see as slaves of the Bolsheviks. Do you want a Republic, comrades. *That* will be the first step leading us into slavery under the Bolsheviks! *That* will be the first step towards an inferno that is hotter than the nether most hell![87]

On democracy in general, one character in the play notes that such governments do work where historical traditions have favored them; the American government, for example, is a success, but the United States, after all, was founded by Englishmen "and no people understand the principles of constitutional government better than the

English."[88] But the applications of democracy are like doses of medicine:

> If the medicine we choose is too strong it may do more harm than good, as for instance a purgative if taken in excess may make us so ill that we may even die of it. Strong purgatives are useful in that they cleanse the system of undesirable elements, but they also weaken our system for a time so that we become less able to resist the invasion of disease germs from without, and if the new disease should get a firm hold the result might be fatal.[89]

Dusit Thani

What has to be one of the world's most unusual expressions of political thought was the miniature city called Dusit Thani that King Vajiravudh had built in 1918. Dusit Thani is still the subject of controversy. Courtiers who were once close to the King have written of it as an experiment in democracy, as evidence of the King's intention to establish parliamentary government in Siam, as the first planting of the seeds of democratic thought in Siam.[90] Detractors have called Dusit Thani mere fun and games, playacting or puppeteering.

Dusit Thani was indeed a play: the setting was a beguiling miniature town; the owner, director, and principal actor was the King; and there was a cast of hundreds, the King's closest courtiers. The substance of the play enacted, or at least some scenes of it, were indeed political.[91]

Dusit Thani, however, was first and foremost a model city, built in Dusit Gardens behind the royal palace and later moved to more spacious quarters behind Phya Thai Palace.[92] The city was elaborate, complete with houses, palaces, temples, roads, rivers and canals, trees and parks, fountains, waterfalls, and electric lights—an enchanted fairyland by more than one account. The King was chief planner and chief architect. The city had two daily newspapers and one weekly journal.[93] It had a fire department, electric company, sewage department, and health department. Parties and ceremonies were held on its grounds. And boat races of miniature boats on its miniature river were held almost nightly "for relaxation after work" under rules established by the Dusit Naval Association.[94]

The political life at Dusit Thani started in 1918 with the election of a mayor in October and was formalized with a constitution granted by the King in November, amended slightly in December.[95] The preamble to the constitution stated that Vajiravudh's purpose was to offer "residents" of Dusit Thani (i.e., his courtiers) the opportunity to study self-government. The government's purview was, of course,

The Monarchy

restricted to the miniature affairs of the miniature city. Ultimate power was retained by the King, who might at any time revoke any action at Dusit Thani that he disapproved of.

The constitution of Dusit Thani called for popular elections, with suffrage extended to all "residents," who numbered about 200. The elected mayor and his appointed cabinet were to serve for one year. An assembly of representatives from each district was provided for in the amended constitution. In order to stimulate interest in the political process, the King created two political parties, a Blue Ribbon Party led by himself and a Red Ribbon Party led by his closest courtier, Čhaophraya Ram. Some seven elections for mayor were held in the first two years, with at least one mayor's career ended abruptly by the successful politicking of the King's party.[96]

In terms of its real effect on the world outside the palace, Dusit Thani had no influence at all. In fact, very little news of the existence of Dusit Thani appeared in the public press.[97] Some writers have suggested, however, that the ultimate plan was to extend the Dusit Thani idea into the regular government, starting with the provincial government at Samut Sakhon, a province close to Bangkok.[98] The Deputy Minister of the Interior apparently talked to the King about conducting such an experiment on the provincial level.[99] The closest the King came in an official document to declaring Dusit Thani a real model for the real world was in his dedicatory comments on the opening of Dusit Thani's municipal hall on July 9, 1919: "Our method of proceeding in this little country of ours will I trust be an example for Siam, but to achieve such rapid success as has this little country is not possible, for there are obstacles."[100]

A final assessment of Dusit Thani's significance as a representation of Vajiravudh's thoughts is hard to make. Certainly much of the miniature city was for fun. And firm evidence of an underlying serious intent is scanty. Yet serious purposes cannot be ruled out; the King was fond of thinking in utopian terms, of setting forth models and ideal types which would spread their message as a pebble spreads ripples in a pond. Serious or not, Dusit Thani gives us yet another instance of the King's mode of thought, for Dusit Thani, the model of democracy, was entirely a monarchic creation. It was conceived by the King, was managed by the King, and was expanded or curtailed depending only on the monarchic perception of need.

A Democratic King

Despite the abundant proofs that Vajiravudh was fully aware of his absolute powers as a Siamese monarch and was anxious, in fact, to

The Monarchy

focus more attention on the monarchy than ever in order to build national unity, the image of him among the Thai is that he was a democratic king. One author entitles a chapter on Vajiravudh "The Liberal";[101] others refer to him variously as "an expert in democracy," "a true believer in the principles of democracy in its true sense," and "a very democratic king."[102]

In part this image of Vajiravudh may have derived from his efforts to endear himself to his people, to move among them more freely than was customary, and to include the public in various festivals. From the very start of the reign, elements of the general population were included for the first time in such events as the cremation rites for Chulalongkorn and the coronation ceremonies for Vajiravudh.[103] There were, of course, countless other official ceremonies that had to be performed, age-old obligations of a monarch who was supposed to have inherent magic powers. These ceremonies were traditionally performed by the king *for* the public, but not *with* the public, and it would appear that Vajiravudh performed many of them perfunctorily. But not all of them. One such ceremony was the royal *kathin*, the rite of presentation of robes to Buddhist monks. In 1913 the King, breaking custom, decided to go on an unofficial *kathin* by boat to a small temple and soon found himself the "object of a warm popular demonstration."[104] A newspaper writer commented on the event as follows:

> In their enthusiasm the people afloat hemmed the King's boat all round. The officials would have liked to keep the distance a little bigger, but His Majesty enjoyed the unaccustomed nearness of the people. The Royal acknowledgement, oft repeated, of the people's greetings, was one of the ways of fulfilment of the Coronation promise to extend his favour to all his people. The occasion does not arise often as regards the great bulk of the people, but this was one, and the opportunity was taken advantage of.[105]

Another impromptu *kathin* occurred a few days later. The King noted in his diary that while on a pleasure jaunt he happened on a rural *kathin*. He was invited to take part, and he did—joining in on the prayers, the gift-giving, the noodle repast ("it was delicious"), and play-watching.[106] The unexpected success of these events led Vajiravudh to try to repeat them, and "people's *kathin*" followed in 1914, 1915, and 1916. The later affairs, however, lacked spontaneity, and one feels that the real desire of the King to come into closer rapport with his people was thwarted by the elaborate preparations of his courtiers to give him a good show, with safe official floats substituted for the lively enthusiasm of an unpredictable crowd.

Probably more important, however, in giving Vajiravudh the "democratic" image was his practice of surrounding himself with courtiers of less than princely rank, with whom he spent much time. The Thai definition of "democratic" here really means egalitarian rather than democratic in a political sense. Although the highest levels of government continued to be occupied by senior nobles and princes of elevated rank, the relations between these nobles and princes and the King were not close[107]—a fact that accounted for many of the charges of government inefficiency that were made against Vajiravudh's reign. However the King's habits affected the administration, it is true that the guests at Vajiravudh's dinner parties, his social companions, his "neighbors" at Dusit Thani, his most trusted Wild Tigers, the actors in his dramas all came from a relatively small circle of *mahatlek* (court pages) and others in the inner circle of the Ministry of the Palace. And these men represented various classes. Many were commoners. Some were of Chinese descent. Those whose ancestors were royal were of lower royal ranks. It was because of this choice of associates that Vajiravudh was awarded a reputation for favoring sycophants by those who criticized him and the name of democrat by those who admired him. In any case, it does not appear that the King chose his associates for political purposes; rather, he seemed simply to prefer to spend time with men of humble origin, whom he treated with remarkable freedom and familiarity.[108]

5

National Survival and Militarism

The stress on military preparedness and military values that led to the creation of the Wild Tiger Corps was also evident in many other aspects of King Vajiravudh's national policy and nationalistic program. The justification for this stress was Vajiravudh's oft-repeated assertion that Siamese freedom was in real danger.

Was it? With the advantage of hindsight it is tempting to say no. For no new demands for Siamese territory or other concessions were made by the powers during Vajiravudh's reign. But from the perspective of 1910, it was by no means clear that new demands might not be forthcoming at any time. A loss of territory, after all, had occurred just the year before Vajiravudh came to the throne; another, two years before that; yet another, three years before that—and so back through the nineteenth century. The new king who came to the throne in 1910 had no reason at all to assume that the 1909 loss was to be the last.

National Survival and Militarism

Nor were foreigners very sanguine about Siam's chances for survival. One writer saw for Siam the inevitable doom of the "small and feeble" nation that formed "a barrier between two portions of a powerful and aggressive empire."[1] He added that Siam "occupies the uncomfortable and precarious position of a fat walnut clinched firmly between the jaws of a nut-cracker, the jaws being formed by British Burmah and French Indo-china. And for the past thirty years those jaws have been slowly but remorselessly closing."[2] Prince William of Sweden, although more hopeful, still found it "difficult to say" what "the future destiny of the country may be."[3] An American educator termed Siam's liberty "precarious, unquiet, and charged with responsibility."[4] And, representing at least one official view, the Russian minister to Siam claimed, in a private letter to his foreign minister, that the British in the 1910s had said "quite openly that the fate of Siam was predestined, that sooner or later this country would be either a British colony or it would be divided between England and France."[5]

Even as late as the years following World War I, rumors periodically cropped up that the British were about to make new territorial demands of Siam in the Malay Peninsula;[6] such rumors were undoubtedly responsible for the advice given the King in 1919 by his minister to France that Vajiravudh should not proceed with plans to visit Europe. Such a visit, said the minister,

> may be made a lever to obtain some advantage from us. This danger is very persistent in my mind, for there has already been a precedent in the case of His late Majesty. On the eve of his departure a demand was made to Him for the secret treaty in the Malay Peninsula. I have a feeling that only an opportunity is sought to present the same demand again.[7]

A missionary concluded in 1923: "The encroachments of foreign nations make it uncertain how long there will be an independent Siam."[8]

Not all observers were as gloomy as these about Siam's future. But no wise monarch would ever take only the most encouraging prophecies of his country's future as his guide.

Within government circles in Bangkok, the dangers to the country's independence seemed manifold. It was apparent that some British colonials in Malaya were not satisfied with the borders that had been established in 1909; one pamphlet published privately in 1923, for example, pleaded passionately for the British to take over Pattani.[9] Although there is no evidence of official British interest in further border rectifications, King Vajiravudh was aware of the

National Survival and Militarism

attractiveness of his remote southern provinces and made several journeys to the South to let his Muslim and Malay-speaking subjects see him and to demonstrate to them that he was their king too. He wrote that the southern provinces were beautiful, were underpopulated, and had much untapped wealth, and he encouraged Thai of the Bangkok area to invest in the South. For, he pointed out, things of value could not be kept secret long, and the South, if not exploited by the Thai, would be taken over "by other people" who would recognize its value.[10]

Fear of French acquisitiveness was particularly strong. The vituperative comments by French colonialists about Siam before Vajiravudh came to the throne are too numerous to quote. One will suffice, that of a French columnist who was quoted in the *Bangkok Times* of February 24, 1904, as saying:

> *Carthago delende est*—for the honour, for the prestige, for the peace of France and of French Indochina, Siam must be destroyed, it being impossible for her to play an imperial role at the same time as ourselves. Inevitably the day will come when this people—brigands, robbers of men and holders of slaves—will tire the patience of the English as well as our own.

No doubt this remark (as well as other similar ones) was read by the 23-year-old Prince Vajiravudh. Although the treaty of 1907 labeled the Thai cession of three provinces to French Cambodia at that time as the "final settlement" of all border questions,[11] history had shown the inadvisability of absolute reliance on treaty verbiage. The caution with which the Thai approached the economic development of their own northeastern provinces was undoubtedly in part a result of fear of French reactions. A railroad line built into the Northeast would, it was clear, prove a boon to this perennially impoverished region, and it was repeatedly favored by Thai officials. But, in addition to the problem of financing such an enterprise, the view prevailed that building a railroad would "stir into activity certain political elements in France and Indo-China which are now dormant."[12] One French reporter even ventured the view that the Thai would not spend any money "developing territory that to-morrow may cease to be Siamese"; he said that "dread of a French occupation of the right bank of the Mekong" and of the valley of the Mun River would prevent the Thai from building any railroads in the area "for fear of France taking possession of those lines on short notice."[13] Stories continually reached Bangkok of French intentions of building a road or railway opening up French Laos and Siam's adjacent northeastern provinces

81

to French economic penetration; the existing pattern of trade of this region, flowing westward, was obviously a matter of some annoyance to the French.[14] The Thai kept close watch on the Northeast, and reports that Northeasterners resented the French and loved the Thai, that the French were having continual trouble with dacoits and were barely able to govern their Lao territories,[15] undoubtedly heartened the Thai. The policy with regard to the problems of the French in their territory, however, was not to interfere and in fact to aid the French by refusing to allow anti-French political activists to enter Siam and deporting any who managed to skip over the border.[16]

Another source of worry with respect to Westerners was the Western community in Siam itself. There was continual rivalry among the Western diplomats; each contended for special influence, particularly by trying to manipulate the system of foreign advisers to his country's advantage. In this situation, the Siamese government attempted to play the role of special friend to all. It was not an easy role to play because of "the rabid competition between foreigners in outbidding one another whenever there is anything to be obtained."[17] The prizes most bitterly competed for were posts in the ranks of foreign advisers. The system of appointing foreign advisers to the various ministries and departments had started during the reign of King Chulalongkorn as a temporary expedient to forward the work of governmental modernization until such time as sufficient numbers of Thai could be trained to manage government affairs on modern lines.[18] Foreign governments were aware of the leverage gained by having their own nationals in the ranks of the Siamese government service; a rough index of a foreign government's political influence was the number of posts that the government had been able to win for its nationals. From the start, Britain had the largest group of advisers and technical experts. The Thai, however, attempted to keep some balance by apportioning the key advisory posts among several foreign nationals: that for finance to a Briton, justice to a Frenchman, foreign affairs to an American.

Whenever an advisory post became vacant, the scramble for preference began. No prize was beneath contempt. In 1910–1911 there was a long series of exchanges between the British minister and Siamese government officials over the Siamese intention of appointing a Dane rather than a Briton in the Royal Survey Department. The British, stating that they were reluctant to conclude that the Siamese "desire to put a slight on His Majesty's Government," asked that the Siamese government "consult" with the British before taking a step "which seriously affects the interests of His Majesty's Government in Siam." British pressure in this instance was particularly heavy-handed, and the Siamese government let it be known that it "did not feel itself obliged to consult another Government about its employment of officials." After several months' delay, the Danish appointment was made.[19] A similar pressure was put on the Thai by the French in 1917 to appoint Frenchmen to managerial posts vacated by Germans in the Siam Commercial Bank. The French minister stated that he would regard such appointments as "testimony of confidence."[20] French persistence in this matter brought the affair to the attention of the King, who in a long letter to the French minister pointed out that, although he was anxious to accommodate the minister, other appointments had already been made and that for the King to revoke them now would be "awkward," would lay the King "open to serious criticism of arbitrariness, an accusation which even I cannot afford to ignore."[21] The French minister had charged the Thai with giving preference to the British and had implied that His Majesty was strongly influenced by the British minister. The King went to some lengths to point out that the British minister and he never met privately, but that the British minister sometimes wrote the King "to present his own personal views in certain matters"; he invited the French minister to do likewise.[22] The Siamese government in general maintained its essential freedom in appointment of foreign advisers; it realized that yielding too readily to foreign pressures would be even more dangerous than never yielding at all. In response to German pressures in 1911 for more power than their Thai counterparts in one enterprise, the King advised his officials that

> we cannot forget that the government is a Thai government, we are Thai, I am a Thai king who, if I were to use my power to oppress my own Thai people for the benefit of foreigners, would be going too far. If I did so even once it would not be long before respect and trust of the government would come to an end and I would be unable to do anything in the future. It would be like putting a rope around my own neck.[23]

There are indications that the influence of foreign advisers diminished during Vajiravudh's reign. For example, the new appointee to the post of "General Adviser" in 1916 was demoted to the rank of "Adviser in Foreign Affairs." The King made his reason clear. In a private letter he explained that, since the new appointee was "not only my junior in age, but also in education and experience, I could not see why I should have adopted him as my mentor in all affairs."[24] By the end of the reign one foreign adviser wrote that in the last few

National Survival and Militarism

years foreign advisers had been eliminated from positions of actual control of government affairs; he accounted for this trend by the growth of Thai expertise, courage, and ambition.[25]

Thai suspicions and fears of foreign diplomats were not occasioned only by disputes over foreign advisory posts. Foreigners in general were not trusted. The background of the French minister to Siam as a colonial administrator in Indochina was resented, and this resentment was not kept secret. In a letter to the King, the Thai minister in Paris wrote that the French Foreign Office knew "very well our objection to men of such experience."[26] The recall of the French minister in 1918 under a cloud was a matter for considerable royal rejoicing.[27] There were even suspicions that foreign legations were not above meddling in local affairs. Here again the French seem to have been most suspect. For example, when the head of a Chinese secret society which was rumored to be planning a revolt against the government was elevated to be headman of those Chinese who were French subjects, Prince Chakrabongs wondered whether the French did not favor "these arrangements" because they knew the Siamese were gaining in strength and so favored "some disorder to cut-down our strength."[28] In 1912 the French urged that a Chinese labeled an "undesirable alien" by the Thai be allowed to return to Siam. The Siamese Minister of Foreign Affairs confided to the General Adviser: "I cannot help thinking that it must be with a sinister purpose if the French Government will insist upon the return of this man to Siam."[29] The French did insist, and the government yielded.

All in all, it is impossible at this point to tell how real the threats to Siamese independence were during the reign of King Vajiravudh. Certainly there were danger signs, especially during the earliest years of the reign. And, whatever the realities may have been, whether or not any designs on Siam's future were actually being drawn in Paris, London, Berlin, or even Tokyo, the Siamese felt they could not be complacent.[30]

Complacency with regard to outside threats had indeed never been the keynote of Thai foreign policy. From the early nineteenth century on, the Siamese government had been particularly sensitive to the realities of growing Western power. The concessionistic foreign policy pursued by Kings Mongkut and Chulalongkorn originated out of their appreciation of Western power. And the vast program of reform and modernization of government conducted by King Chulalongkorn was meant to strengthen Siam internally so that it would be better able to meet outside threats.

Part of King Chulalongkorn's program of internal reform had been

National Survival and Militarism

to build Thai military might. Even before a Ministry of War was organized, Western drilling techniques, uniforms, and armaments had been adopted. The organization of the military administration—a complicated task because the traditional administration drew no sharp lines between military and civil affairs—occupied much of Chulalongkorn's attention. By 1892, however, a Ministry of War had been created, and in 1894 the first conscription law was passed, a law that laid the foundations for a modern military force.

A mark of the great importance Chulalongkorn attached to the military is the fact that over half of all the sons he sent abroad to study were required to receive military training.[31] And these sons, on their return home, were in a very short time awarded the premier positions in the armed forces. For example, by 1910 Prince Chira had become Commander in Chief of the Army; Prince Paribatra, Commander in Chief of the Navy; Prince Abhakara, Deputy Commander in Chief of the Navy; Prince Chakrabongs, Army Chief of Staff; and Prince Purachatra, Inspector General of Army Engineers.

This policy of adding to the real strength of the military was continued by Vajiravudh. One of the King's earliest acts was to further the work of his father in streamlining the military establishment by combining all army leadership posts under the Minister of War and separating out the navy under a newly created Ministry of Marine.[32] The favor to be awarded the military forces was also shown at the coronation celebrations. One whole day was given over to military programs. Some 30,000 troops participated, the largest force ever assembled in the capital.[33] Practical measures for improving military strength were taken throughout the reign, following much the same pattern as that established by King Chulalongkorn. Ships were bought for the navy. Army maneuvers were held annually—and usually attended by the King. New weapons were bought even when these led to budget overruns.[34] Vajiravudh gave every sign that he intended to make sure that Siam would stay abreast of modern military developments.

The establishment of an army aviation corps was one outstanding example of royal emphasis on military modernity. In 1912, three Thai officers were sent to a French flying school. By the end of 1913 the three had received their flying certificates and returned to Siam. Airplanes were bought. An army airport was started at Don Muang. And new pilots were trained. Aerial displays were given for the benefit, and delight, of the King, the princes, and the people.[35] After watching the first such display, Vajiravudh in his diary entry for January 13, 1914, drew a broad conclusion: "I am delighted that we

National Survival and Militarism

Thai are not bested by the Westerner; truly we can do whatever they can do."[36] By 1920 Siam had over 100 pilots, airmail service had begun, and the airport at Don Muang was called "one of the finest aviation camps in the world."[37] The French in Indochina and the Australians both commented on their "humiliation" because of the leadership of "a little country like Siam" in the aviation field.[38] Aviation seems to have caught the Thai public's imagination as it had caught the interest very early of Prince Chakrabongs, the Army Chief of Staff. Although no national drive for public financial support was ever officially launched, voluntary contributions continually poured in to the Ministry of War for the purchase of new planes. Interest seemed heaviest, logically enough, in the more remote provinces, and the army paid tribute to this interest by naming new planes for provinces which had subscribed money.[39] An American pilot who stopped in Siam on a round-the-world flight in 1920, on his return to New York talked first about Siam and remarked that "Siam is leading most of the countries of the world in aeronautical development."[40]

Still another demonstration of Vajiravudh's attention to the practical strengthening of the military is a volume he wrote on trench warfare in 1916, obviously in response to the trench war then being waged on the Western front in Europe.[41] In addition, the King wrote countless articles on various aspects of warfare by land, sea, and air.

There is no doubt that Vajiravudh believed in military power. Perhaps his clearest statement in this regard is preserved in the lines of one of his plays:

> Those with power usually get what they want.
> A fist is justice; the larger the better.
> The small-fisted must stoop and crawl,
> Waiting in doubt and fear, not daring to rise.
> What the powerful say is never wrong,
> Or, even if wrong, the fist makes it right.
> Even children contradict the small fist that cannot prevail;
> It needs the loan of a big fist to put things right.[42]

Yet the King was fully aware that it would be impossible for Siam to build the sort of power that could stand against a determined European enemy. His thought was to build as strong a force and as independent a force as the country could afford in order to act as a deterrent to foreign cupidity. In a government liberally sprinkled with foreign advisers in virtually all departments, the King was proud that Siamese policy with regard to the army and navy had "always been

National Survival and Militarism

to run them ourselves as much as possible."[43] Although the military was one of the first branches of government to use Western expertise, it was, for reasons of pride and security, the first to abandon reliance on Westerners.

Vajiravudh was firmly convinced that Siam must build its own independent force and rely on its own military strength; it must not rely for its defenses on the expressed good intentions of any other state. In an essay published early in the reign, he summarized his position succinctly:

> Every small nation must place its trust equally in its courage and its utmost efforts for its own people. Trusting or hoping for help from others is the best guarantee of failure.... Thailand must find its strength in its own Thai people. Thai weapons must protect Thai borders. And if the Thai nation hopes to survive, it must rely on its own strength and on the true patriotic feelings of those who are truly Thai.[44]

Nationalistic Militarism

There was a crucial difference between the military outlook of King Vajiravudh and that of his predecessors, and that difference is revealed in the above quotation. The difference is Vajiravudh's view of the military as a means for building national esprit, for welding together a unified and patriotic people, for creating a symbol of national pride.

One target of the King's program of militaristic nationalism, or nationalistic militarism, was the military itself. The same kinds of appeals the King made to the Wild Tigers he made to the military; in fact, the "Wild Tiger spirit," the spirit of self-sacrifice for love of country, the spirit the King hoped would animate the whole of the Thai nation, was, he said, essentially a warrior spirit that should find its purest expression in the soldierly ranks. In a speech on the responsibilities of the people to the nation, Vajiravudh pointed out that it was the particular responsibility of young men to serve in the armed forces and do the essential job of defending the country. It was impossible, he said, for a society to operate with each individual defending himself from internal and external dangers. The society needed armed forces, police, and gendarmerie in order to ensure peace and make it possible for people to pursue their livelihoods. And these protective agencies needed to be staffed by young men, men who were both strong in their youth and still free from family responsibilities. This obligation of all young men was a kind of "expression of gratitude to their elders."[45] And the "elders" in the society, the parents of the young men, should help instill in their offspring soldierly values, the desire to serve the nation as fighters for its freedom. Parents should

National Survival and Militarism

willingly sacrifice their personal comfort by urging their sons to serve—for the welfare both of the sons and of the nation. To encourage or aid a son to avoid military service was not an expression of love, for it denied the son the good training he would receive and it encouraged the son to spend his time in wasteful ways. Vajiravudh told the parents that boys naturally "like being soldiers"; it should not be difficult for parents to abet that natural inclination.[46]

In speeches to the military forces, the King consistently placed himself in their ranks as a fellow soldier and friend. All deserved the special honor and respect that devolved on Thai men who defended their ancestral bequest of freedom. And this honor was shared equally by officers, noncommissioned officers, and foot soldiers. On the occasion of presenting to an army troop a "flag of victory" similar to those he gave Wild Tiger units, the King stated that his gift was "proof that my heart, that of your general, is with every one of you soldiers, every day, every hour, both at midday and at midnight."[47]

Among the many patriotic songs, poems, and plays written by the King, several are meant particularly to inspire the soldier. In a play written in 1912 appear the lines:

> When you are about to die, don't deplore the life you are losing;
> Think only that you are giving your life for your country.[48]

In a later play occurs the thought: "Dying on the field of battle is the most splendid way of all for men to die."[49] In still another play appear in Thai translation the well-known lines of Macaulay:

> How can man die better
> Than facing fearful odds,
> For the ashes of his fathers
> And the temples of his gods?[50]

And in a poem extolling bravery in battle one stanza reads:

> When the hour of death draws nigh,
> Show you are men of a brave race.
> Man leaves but a trace in history,
> So valiantly face your foe to die.[51]

The kind of esprit he hoped to build in the armed forces would, the King felt, make a vital difference in Thai military effectiveness. Two illustrations used by the King make his point. One, developed in a speech of January 28, 1914, before an audience of soldiers and Wild Tigers, told the story of a ruler of Afghanistan who was planning a war against the British. The ruler was informed that British soldiers

National Survival and Militarism

were of low class and were unpopular in India. The British viceroy in India, hearing of the war plans, invited the Afghan and his army of 8,000 men to see a review of British troops. The ruler came and spent a week—a restless week, for he did not trust the loyalty of his men. All the British, however, slept well, and they paraded smartly and put on a fine martial show. The Afghan ruler was astonished at British efficiency and asked the viceroy how he managed to shape a randomly chosen rabble into a cohesive body of loyal fighting men, a feat he could not match even by handpicking his army. The viceroy asked his guest what Afghan soldiers fought for. He was told they fought for rewards, men to enslave, and booty. "That is my answer," said the viceroy, for, in contrast to these selfish goals, each British soldier "thinks only of the honour of his company, each company is for the regiment, each regiment for the army, and the army is for the Sovereign. Thus everybody's ideal becomes one ... every man is imbued with the same desire to uphold the power and dignity of his Sovereign." The Afghan ruler saluted his host and avowed that "nothing in the world can contend" against men so dedicated.[52] Having told his story, Vajiravudh pointed to the obvious moral that the spirit of patriotism that animated the British, and that had saved Siam in its perilous moments in past history, would also save Siam in the future. A second illustration used by Vajiravudh to show the real military strength of patriotism and loyalty was drawn from the modern history of Japan. Japan's victory in the Russo-Japanese War, truly a David-versus-Goliath battle, came about chiefly, said Vajiravudh, because the Russian soldier did not know what he was fighting for.[53] The spirit of the Japanese soldier, on the other hand, had been raised to fever pitch. It was the fusing of the ancient martial values of *bushido* with the modern military techniques of the West, both brought into service in the single cause of the emperor, that had produced the "extraordinary signs of loyalty and patriotism" that had made Japan's record in two modern wars the cause of "a great deal of wonder and admiration."[54] Again the moral was clear: a little state whose soldiers were united and fearless had little to fear.

To illustrate his point that a little state could indeed defend itself, Vajiravudh in one speech drew a parallel between men and ants:

> If you see an anthill, although you are much larger than the hill, do you go trample on it? It doesn't take much thought for you to decide that you dare not. You get a stick to destroy it or burn it. You find a hoe or a spade to dig it out. Perhaps the ants will move away before you do anything. I'm not suggesting here that you go fight giants. I

National Survival and Militarism

ask you only to put yourselves in the position of the ant whose nest is about to be stamped on by an enemy. If such an enemy comes to bother us we can give him some nasty bites.[55]

Among the practical steps taken by Vajiravudh to enhance morale in the armed forces were revisions of the law on conscription. The Military Service Law in effect when Vajiravudh came to the throne had been enacted in 1905. Under its provisions all men between the ages of eighteen and forty were liable to two years of compulsory service. By 1910 the law had received much criticism because there were various loopholes in it that made it possible for many men, especially those of the upper classes, to avoid service. Prince Chakrabongs commented that, because of the loopholes, "the army could only get men who could do absolutely nothing, and who had no pretensions as to their capability of doing anything."[56]

A series of steps was taken from 1910 to 1917 to reduce the number of exempt categories. First, students in secondary schools who were over the age of eighteen were made liable to conscription.[57] Second, the exemption of government employees was ended.[58] The final step eliminated all other exempt categories except those of the medically unfit, monks with ecclesiastical rank, and hill tribesmen.[59] The "escape" categories that had been available particularly to the wealthy and elite classes were deliberately removed in a campaign to make military service more democratic, to reduce the stigma that had become attached to military service, to stem the flood of young men into minor clerical positions in the government in order to avoid service—in short, to "bring home to every one that the life of a private is an honourable calling."[60] This last point was made often, for the government realized that until the principle was accepted that "there is nothing dreadful in the sons of gentlemen serving in the ranks"[61] Siam was not likely to get a patriotic army in which every young man would be willing to serve "in order to defend his Fatherland in time of stress."[62]

But the King's message of military values went far beyond the military itself—and even beyond the Wild Tigers and Boy Scouts. It went to the nation at large. The values of discipline, loyalty, and unity inculcated in the army, navy, police, Wild Tiger Corps, and Boy Scouts were, in the King's view, necessary values for the total population. And the rallying cry of defense for the nation's freedom was one that he wanted to be picked up not just by the thousands in uniform but by the millions in the towns and fields.

The theme of the need for every man to defend the nation was

National Survival and Militarism

developed by the King in countless essays, speeches, poems, and plays. In an essay of 1911, typical of many striking the same note, Vajiravudh started by pointing to the great Thai inheritance bequeathed by Thai warrior heroes of the past. We are glad, said the King, to have been born of a race so brave, whose men—and women—loved their king, nation, and religion so much that they were not afraid of dying to maintain Thai freedom. "We who have received such an inheritance, can we let this inheritance be destroyed?" Are Thai today to be the profligate sons of hard-working fathers? No, we cannot waste what our ancestors worked so hard to give us. At this point in the essay the King began to use a rhetorical device that he turned to very often; he used the word "Thai" in its two meanings, one referring to the race or nation, the other meaning free:[63] "We were born in the Thai race, we were born free [Thai], we must die free [Thai]; if we become slaves, we will no longer be Thai [free]." So the Thai today must face up to whatever dangers may come to the country. Whoever is not willing to sacrifice his life for the country, said the King, "let him give up being a Thai, let him not call himself a Thai and so shame his fellow countrymen. Anyone who is not completely willing to sacrifice his life to preserve his king, his country, and his religion should abandon his motherland and go live alone, for he loves himself more than his nation."[64]

Typical of the King's poems dealing with this theme is the following, which was composed by Vajiravudh while he was still Crown Prince and was sung on many occasions during the reign:

> Free-born men
> Let us not forget our race and our faith;
> Let us not have been born in vain
> Of a free nation.
> How could a man who respects himself
> Remain idle?
> Each one ought to work,
> That all may be ready!
> In a country without love and union
> The best work cannot bear fruit;
> And if a nation is breaking up and near its ruin,
> How can the private individual hope for prosperity?
> If foreigners should rule over us,
> We should be slain and ill-treated;
> They would oppress us from morning till night,
> As is the way of conquerors.
> Do not imagine that they would respect our position and name,

National Survival and Militarism

> Or that they would consider our birth;
> We ourselves should suffer
> And be put to shame before the rest of the world.
>
> Therefore, comrades, may we be loyal to the King
> And true to our country and our faith:
> May we offer our lives without regret
> That the freedom of "the Free" be not lost!
> Let us stand united,
> And certain victory is ours!
> Let us be brave and firmly determined
> To protect our liberty till heaven and earth pass away![65]

The civilian no less than the soldier, said Vajiravudh, must be willing to defend the nation. For, he asked in a speech, are not civilians also Thai? "What language do civilians speak so that they need not perform the duty of defending their nation and their land? Even wild animals know how to protect their nests and lairs. If we do not defend our homeland, are we not worse than they?"[66] And in another speech the King stated: "If we love the nation, we must protect the nation." If the Thai lose their freedom, there will no longer be a Thai race. Whatever the cost in lives to preserve freedom, that cost must be paid. For the survivors in a free Thai state, no matter how few, will be Thai and the Thai race will go on. But if the nation is destroyed, it will not matter how many people live. In effect they will be dead, for they will no longer be Thai; "wherever they go they will be sorrowing like fatherless children."[67]

The theme of total national commitment to defense is also an important element in several of the King's plays. It is central to the plot of one play, whose title in English would be *The Soul of a Warrior*. The play concerns an older man who has little respect for the military or military values. Siam is invaded, and the hero discovers the values of self-defense. In a speech after his enlightenment, he tells his daughter:

> In times to come when you have children at breast, teach them never to abandon their race, teach them to be willing to sacrifice their lives rather than abandon their leaders, teach them to be steadfast in love of our king. Have them love our country and hold firmly to Buddhism, more willing to die than to be lacking in any of these duties.[68]

Beginning of World War I; Siamese Neutrality

Just four years after King Vajiravudh mounted the throne, World War I broke out in Europe. The rumblings of war, of course, had been

National Survival and Militarism

heard much earlier. The growing political and economic rivalries of the major European powers, the fierce competition that had been so manifest in the imperial contests for power throughout the "unclaimed" world in the late nineteenth century, had come more and more to focus on the gray zones of political claims on the European continent itself. This narrowing of the target, which had started some time before Vajiravudh became king, had, indeed, helped save Siam. World War I was, then, seen by the Thai as a breathing space in time, a respite, a new and probably brief chance to accrue strength and rally the people before the day of peace in Europe, which, by all logic, would coincide with the day of resumption of power plays in the weak world outside. Vajiravudh summed up this feeling dramatically in a speech to the Wild Tiger Corps:

> Foreigners already have their eyes on our rich country. Even if they do not grab our land but only send off many of their people to live here, to eat our food, to suck our blood, what do we do? Let them come and then prepare ourselves? But then there would be no time to prepare! We must be prepared before they come. We must be prepared before anyone makes plans to come. We've talked about it, so now let's truly prepare. We must prepare now while they are fighting and have no time to think of us. We must be prepared! The time is now.[69]

World War I presented Siam with a whole new range of policy options and propaganda opportunities. And Vajiravudh was determined to make the best use of such options and opportunities. On the policy level he was determined that Siam should follow a course that would yield the greatest advantages in terms of international standing. On the propaganda level he was stimulated to use the war to lead his people further along the path toward the nationalism that he had already charted as his primary goal.

The first order of business as declarations of war multiplied with each new day in early August 1914 was for Siam to clarify its international position. This was done on August 6 with a royal proclamation for the observance of "a strict and impartial neutrality."[70] This policy was in full accord with the King's private views.[71] Neutrality, indeed, was the only course possible for Siam at the time. The King and his highest officials were thoroughly acquainted with affairs in Europe, with the political and economic rivalries that had led to the outbreak of war, with the delicate balance of power in Europe that made guesses as to the final outcome extremely difficult. The profundity of Siam's knowledge is well illustrated by a series of talks given to the Wild Tigers by Čhaophraya Yommarat in August, Sep-

National Survival and Militarism

tember, and November of 1914.[72] Chaophraya Yommarat described in great detail the history of German unification under Bismarck, the Franco-Prussian War, the growing alliance between France and Russia, the German advances in military and economic strength, the British concerns over German naval and economic competition, the involvement of whole populations in xenophobic nationalism. He spoke realistically about the impossibility of determining who the eventual victor would be, especially since Siam had to rely on English and French sources for news. Again he was the realist when he pointed out that international law was not like national law in that there was no supernational court of justice; justice was whatever the strongest power determined it should be. At least some of these comments were made in the presence of the King. All of these views were undoubtedly shared by the King, and the King may even have "suggested" beforehand the topics his minister should speak on. The King himself, however, said little about the war, at least not publicly or in his own name.

For Vajiravudh, a keen student of international law himself, was determined to observe the strictures of neutrality with the utmost circumspection. In a speech to the Wild Tigers on August 9, he set forth his concept of neutrality—"neither rejoicing nor sorrowing on account of the victory or defeat of one side or the other"—and the proper behavior of a neutral: "... it is best for us Siamese not to speak too much. With regard to the war, the more words spoken, the greater the difficulty to recall them; if less were spoken, less would remain to be recalled, while if none were spoken at all, that would be the easiest of all."[73] And the King followed his own advice scrupulously. The King's public pronouncements on the war were meager indeed. In his annual addresses of 1915, 1916, and 1917 Vajiravudh spoke of the war only in terms of Siam's impeccable neutrality; even the speech of 1917—the year that Siam entered the war—contained only the laconic remark "It gives Me much satisfaction to state that the friendly relations between the Kingdom of Siam and all Foreign Powers continue to be cordial and firmly maintained."[74] And one of Vajiravudh's first acts after the war broke out was to compel all Siamese princes in military training in European states to resign their foreign commissions "in order to prevent any possible breach of neutrality on the part of Siam."[75] High princes and officials in Bangkok of varying political biases continued, apparently, to attend parties and affairs given by the German community,[76] as well as by nationals of the Allied Powers, with the King's approval. And each new declaration of war by a major power, including that by the United States on

National Survival and Militarism

April 6, 1917, was followed by a new Siamese declaration of neutrality.[77]

Yet the formal course of neutrality Siam pursued did not mean that the war was ignored or that Siam was not constantly reevaluating its policies. The war, rather, was used as justification for a new nationalistic campaign, and the policy of neutrality itself was eventually abandoned, after adequate unofficial preparation by the King, when events in Europe seemed to show that neutrality was no longer advantageous for Siam.

The direction the new propaganda campaign was to take was indicated in a speech by the King on August 9, 1914, in which he urged Wild Tigers and soldiers "to learn a good lesson from this war, and profit by its examples." The lesson was not how to fight, but how to unite to meet the common peril. In England, France, Russia, and Germany internal factionalism had come to an end as parties and classes submerged their differences in order to fight their common enemy. The King asked his listeners if they would "be ready to drop all personal quarrels in order to turn and face our common foe together."[78] Obviously, to Vajiravudh the war gave new meaning and urgency to his nationalistic messages.

All the familiar programs of the years before 1914 were maintained in 1915, 1916, and 1917. Wild Tiger speeches, drills, and maneuvers continued. Military exercises continued. In some cases old efforts were intensified; for example, the army in 1916 for the first time called up reserves to take part in the war games.[79]

Creation of the Royal Navy League

In late 1914 one new campaign was started that became the King's prime interest, the beneficiary of countless writings and organizational efforts; it was given attention comparable only to the attention the Wild Tiger Corps had received in its earliest years. This new pet project of the King was the national subscription of money from the general public to buy the Thai navy a new warship, a light cruiser, to be called *Phra Ruang* after the legendary heroic founder of Thai independence.[80] In support of this project the King wrote two plays, countless essays, and several poems on the importance of navies, on naval warfare, and on the importance of making contributions to Siam's defense;[81] he sponsored or encouraged various benefits, including some twenty-six theater performances, to raise money for the cruiser fund; and he gave lavishly out of the privy purse to swell the coffers of contributions.

The campaign for the cruiser fund started in late October, less

Appeal for Contributions to Cruiser Fund (Advertisement in *Dusit samit*). The drawing is by the King; the text was originally in Thai.

National Survival and Militarism

than three months after the war began in Europe. Presumably it originated with a group of officials who, seeing Siam's weakness by sea, decided that Siam needed a new warship to protect its coasts and river banks. Recognizing that the government could not afford to buy such a vessel, the officials decided to lead a drive to enlist funds from the general public. The officials presented their plan to the King, who accepted it, named the sponsoring group the Royal Navy League of Siam, consented to be the patron of the league, and gave the name *Phra Ruang* to the vessel to be obtained.[82] In fact, however, the cruiser fund idea was the King's from the very start; the official story that the idea originated with a group of government servants was undoubtedly put forth to avoid the awkwardness of having His Majesty initiate a drive to give himself a warship.[83]

Without doubt the King believed in the military benefits of the campaign he launched. In his view the Siamese army was well advanced; the navy, however, was still relatively weak. Although an enemy invader could be met by land forces, an invader by sea would find Siam vulnerable. Vajiravudh likened Siam's defenses to a wall that was complete on only three sides, leaving the country wide open on the fourth. A householder who built a fence to keep out wild animals and robbers could hardly feel secure with fences on only three sides of his home; similarly, Siam could not be secure so long as its defenses by sea remained inadequate.[84] The King summed up these ideas in several poems. One of these poems was printed in the second issue of a journal entitled *Samutthasan* published by the Navy League; it reads:

> Come let us help, without delay,
> To rouse popular enthusiasm
> For the Navy League and invite
> Thai everywhere to build the barrier to protect Siam.
>
> . . . .
>
> On land we have soldiers ready to fight the invaders;
> The glorious Wild Tigers wait to help in the fighting.
> The gap that remains in our defense is by sea.
> We lack the ships and power to protect us.
>
> To ignore this is like leaving an open door.
> If the enemy bursts in, how can we contend?
> Don't be indifferent; we urge you to be concerned.
> To be unconcerned too long will lead to great difficulties.
>
> The enemy can attack and set our homes on fire,
> Reducing our homes to ashes and scattering our goods.

National Survival and Militarism

Our families will be lost, our positions ruined.
Those remaining will be shamed and will prefer death to lost honor.

Wake up! We are born Thai [free]; let us not lose the chance
To help our Navy gain the strength to defend our country.[85]

The equation of national power and naval strength was, in Vajiravudh's view, demonstrated conclusively by Britain: "Any nation that has a navy it can send to battle on the sea has the power to protect its race, religion, and king."[86] The King assiduously studied naval matters, naval strategy, and naval vessels and came to the conclusion that a light cruiser, with a draft shallow enough to cross the sand bar at the mouth of the Čhaophraya River, would best suit the Siamese navy's needs.[87] The vessel he had in mind should be fast, capable of outmaneuvering larger, more powerfully armed vessels. The German ship *Emden* and its dramatic career early in the war much impressed the King.[88] Even one vessel, as the *Emden* had proved, could be enormously valuable. A cruiser patrolling the waters of the Gulf of Siam would be able to gain intelligence on naval movements in the gulf and could be a respectable adversary in fighting quick campaigns.

Far more important than the military benefits of the cruiser campaign, however, were the benefits to be expected from the campaign itself in stirring Thai nationalism. Stimulating Thai nationalism was clearly the primary objective, for the King certainly would have been able, if he had thought the need pressing enough, to purchase a naval vessel out of government funds. In his birthday speech of January 1, 1915, Vajiravudh spoke of the subscription drive as "an evidence that the Siamese people are determined, like their ancestors, to show their affection and loyalty to their Sovereign, to preserve the independence of the nation, and to uphold our Holy Religion."[89] In its editorial comments on this speech, the *Bangkok Times* perceived the King's intent, that the "actual object" of the cruiser fund campaign was "after all a small thing compared with the spirit that animates the movement, the spirit of sacrifice for national security, which marks the growth of national consciousness."[90]

To achieve the kind of national consciousness he desired, it was necessary that everyone give, that the gift be voluntary, that the gift represent an outpouring of the hearts of true Thai for the welfare of their country. And it was in such terms that the King and his officials spoke of the cruiser fund. The remarks made in a speech by the High Commissioner of Phuket were much to the point:

National Survival and Militarism

> His Majesty could easily have raised the money by taxation or otherwise, but it is better for it [the cruiser] to be bought by voluntary subscriptions. So all must help, women as well as men, for they are the chief sufferers in case of war. If we pay for it we shall have an interest in it, and more regard for our country. Why do we love our children? Because of what they have cost us.[91]

To bring the costs, and so the love, to all, the campaign was extended into the provinces, and officials high and low were urged to give speeches to promote public understanding and rally public support. In a report on the successes of the High Commissioner of Nakhọn Sawan, the generosity of a boatman, a blind man, and a farm wife were particularly noted.[92] And in Phuket, particular pride was taken in the large number of contributions from women, which was interpreted as showing the truly voluntary nature of the donations, and in the success of the campaign in reaching Chinese coolies in the tin mines. The coolies were addressed in the Chinese language by their bosses, who urged them to make donations to the cruiser fund to show their gratitude for the many favors the Siamese government had shown Chinese immigrants. In the speeches to the miners, it was particularly stressed that the size of the gift was less important than the act of giving itself; the important thing was that everyone should give.[93] This point was often made; as one official put it, no gift would so please the King as a ten-satang (about four cents) contribution to the cruiser fund.[94]

In his own writings the King on occasion played on the theme of pride and shame. Writing under the pseudonym Asvabahu, the King said that he had been asked if he would make a contribution; there was but one answer for a "true Thai" to give, and for Asvabahu in particular, well known for his patriotic writings, "I could look no one in the face if I didn't contribute." Vajiravudh went on to classify Thai who were not moved by the national appeal as sick, mentally retarded, thickskulled, addlebrained, doperidden, ignorant, misled, or selfish. Everyone, he said, could afford to give a little, and little by little the fund would grow. Everyone could make some small sacrifice for the nation's welfare. And in an obvious dig at the Bangkok elite, he specified: men with many concubines could give up one; men who ate out often could eat at home for a month; men who played billiards every night could sacrifice games three nights a week; men who liked loose women could sleep at home for a while; those who liked the movies and an after-movie supper could give these up for a week or two; those who liked fancy clothes could dress in homespun

National Survival and Militarism

for a change. Through such deprivations the drive would succeed and the day would arrive when the *Phra Ruang* would steam up the river for all to see. On that day of fulfillment, those who had given, who would be part owners of Siam's pride, would rejoice. And those who had not given would be filled with shame. In fact, said the King, the entire prestige of the nation was bound up in the cruiser-fund campaign. Failure of the campaign would earn the Thai the reputation of giving only lip service to national love, of not being "civilized" enough to see the benefits of naval defense. So, concluded the King, "we *must* help each other succeed" and on the day of success all Thai subscribers would be able to greet "our ship" with "full hearts and full voices shouting 'Chaiyo! Chaiyo! Chaiyo!'"[95]

This same vein of pride and shame is developed in a play, *Mahatama* (The Mahatma), that Vajiravudh wrote specifically to support the cruiser campaign. The chief character, Son Setthi, opposes giving contributions to a warship fund. He falls asleep and, in a dream, learns that the fund drive has failed and that enemy warships, meeting no opposition, have easily conquered the country. An enemy soldier sarcastically praises Son: "You did a good job in destroying the Thai nation; I thank you heartily."[96] Near the end of the dream, as the shamed Son is led out to be shot, he says:

> Before I die I want to say one thing. I am sorry I have been the worst citizen possible. It is not right for me to be called a Thai. I am not at all sorry to lose my life now, for if I went on living I couldn't face anyone. If I have any regrets it is that I won't get another chance to help my nation. If I had only known that this was the way it would come out, I would have contributed 5,000 baht to the warship fund. If I had done that, I would have no regrets now about dying.[97]

At the end of the play Son wakes from his dream and gets the second chance his nightmare denied him.

Other techniques the King used in his cruiser campaign propaganda were designed to work upon the Thai "natural traits" of apathy and generosity and the Thai love of fun and a good show. The apathy or even-temperedness of the Thai, Vajiravudh said, made it difficult for them to be readily roused to action. The Thai people tended to postpone action, to fail to appreciate urgent needs; they had to be reminded again and again of their obligations.[98] And so the reminders came, in lighted street signs, for example, that spelled out "Have you contributed to the cruiser fund?"[99] and in newspaper advertisements that read:

National Survival and Militarism

HAVE YOU GIVEN YOUR DONATION YET?

IF NOT,

WHAT ARE YOU WAITING FOR?

WHY DO YOU TARRY?

SIAM HAS NO TIME TO LOSE![100]

As for Thai generosity, the King said simply that the Thai were not stingy; they had only to be affected and they would give freely. Their liberal donations to Buddhist temples proved their unselfishness. The Thai, he said, should see donations to the cruiser fund as meritorious acts showing unselfish concern for all Thai citizens, loyalty and gratitude to the sovereign, and, in the end, understanding that the temples built by merit would be protected by a meritorious navy.[101] The appeals to the Thai love of fun in the cruiser subscription drive took many forms—concerts, performances of plays, publishing of stories—but none was more popular than the miniature naval engagement staged for a temple fair in January 1916. Models of naval vessels, three battleships, one cruiser, and four destroyers, propelled by gasoline or electricity, sailed across a small pond, saluted the King, and then took part in a naval engagement, which a newspaper described as "a most realistic affair" in which "mines explode, a village is wrecked and the effect of gun fire on shore defences is plainly visible to spectators."[102] The elaborate show, which involved much detailed planning and took 200 men to stage, was meant to be fun, but it was also meant to illustrate the usefulness of cruisers and to convey the message that appeared at the end of the 26-page program of the spectacle: "Help Thailand—our country."[103]

The cruiser fund campaign, in monetary terms, got off to a grand start. Aided by donations of the King, from various sources, that amounted to 200,000 baht, by April of 1915 the fund had reached the figure of 1,000,000 baht. In another year, the 2,000,000 baht figure had been reached. Although the campaign had lost some glamor and the rate of contributions had slowed down, it was clear by 1917 that the Siamese people would one day be able to buy their king the warship he could then bestow on the royal navy.

Entry of Siam into the War

The policy of neutrality that Vajiravudh had adopted in August 1914 had met general acceptance in educated Siamese circles. Although some German-educated princes and nobles were undoubtedly pro-German, and some English-educated princes and nobles were

National Survival and Militarism

pro-British, the sympathies of neither side were so strong as to create a party in favor of Siam's direct involvement in the war.

Insofar as a general sentiment can be identified, it was rather more pro-German than pro-Allied. The reasons for such sentiment are clear. The Germans had no imperial record in Siam, in great contrast to the flagrant records of both the British and the French, whose empires in Malaysia and Indochina had been augmented at Siam's expense. Further, the German community in Siam was well liked. The Germans had a better reputation than any other foreign group for learning the Thai language (few Thai spoke German) and for mixing with the Thai socially—to such an extent that many Germans intermarried with the Thai and some even became naturalized Thai. German trade with Siam had expanded greatly in the years immediately preceding the war, and German products were regarded as top quality.[104] German technicians and experts employed in the Railway Department, the Department of Communications, and the Siam Commercial Bank were favorably regarded for their skill and efficiency.

From the very start of the war, however, Siam, because of its geographic position, had to be much more cautious of provoking British or French suspicions of unneutrality than of provoking German suspicions.[105] And the British and French were extremely sensitive to possibly unsympathetic views and much more likely to apply pressure on the Thai than were the Germans. Even before the end of 1914 the Thai, having learned that the French in Indochina were accusing them of partiality toward the Germans, planted a story in the Saigon press to the effect that, despite the "strict neutrality" of the Siamese government, the Thai citizenry, far from being pro-German, was horrified at German "acts of sacrilege and vandalism" in Belgium and French territories.[106] The Bangkok Western-language press in 1914 consisted of three English-language newpapers, the *Bangkok Times*, the *Daily Mail*, and the *Siam Observer*, and all leaned toward the Allies. The local Germans, after lodging an unproductive objection to this state of affairs with the Siamese government, began to issue their own paper, the *Umschau*. The British minister in August 1916 objected to the *Umschau*. In a fine instance of diplomatic tightrope walking, the Thai Minister of Foreign Affairs pointed out to the British minister that any objection that he might make to the Germans would only occasion a countercomplaint by the Germans against "certain of the other local papers, which ... are distinctly favorable to Great Britain and its allies."[107]

One area in which the Thai did cooperate fully with the British

National Survival and Militarism

was action against the supposed activities of Germans in abetting the conspiracies of Indians in Siam aimed at undercutting British power in Burma and India. The British were extremely sensitive on this subject. They brought some seventeen Indians to trial for sedition in Burma in 1916. During the trial proceedings, which started in March and ended in August with guilty sentences for most of those accused, some testimony indicated that seditious activities had also been conducted in Siam.[108] The British kept the Thai alerted to the Burma evidence and also to news and rumors of similar activities. They asked the Thai in March 1915 to take action against supposed Indian agitators on the Siamese southern railway and in August 1916 to patrol the west coast of Siam to watch for a possible shipment of arms from Siam to Burma through "unscrupulous" Japanese agents of the Germans. The Thai complied with both requests.[109] Wildly extravagant newspaper stories, starting with one in 1915 about thousands of Indians being trained in Siam by Germans to invade Burma and ending with one in 1917 that linked the German conspiracies in Burma and Siam to the Zimmerman Plot to get Mexico and Japan to dismember the United States, were featured in the *Bangkok Times* as well as in the *New York Times* and the London *Times*.[110] The Thai, while denying the truth of the exaggerated accounts, took all British official requests seriously and were commended by the British for "the services they have rendered."[111]

By the end of 1915 and through 1916, however, the Siamese King and many Siamese officials began to display a friendliness to the French and British that, although it did not constitute a withdrawal from neutrality, seemed to be greater than the geographic and political realities required. Late in 1915, for example, the King sent money to the widows and orphans of the Durham Light Infantry Company, the unit in England in which he had once served. The King justified this action on the grounds that it would still British suspicions that the Thai were pro-German.[112] And when, in September 1915, Vajiravudh was offered an honorary generalship in the British army—a favor he returned by conferring an honorary generalship in the Siamese army on George V—he accepted, according to a statement he later gave his ministers, for the same reason.[113] Other public acts friendly to the Allies sprinkled the calendar of events in 1916—for example, royal presences (and presentations of gifts) at fairs, parties, and plays for the French Red Cross, the Russian Red Cross, the British Red Cross, and the Allied Red Cross.

More subtle indications of a pro-Allied bias can be perceived in the pages of the journal of the Royal Navy League, *Samutthasan*. The

National Survival and Militarism

sinking of the *Lusitania* in May 1915 evoked a long article in the August issue by the King, writing under the pseudonym Ramachitti, who deplored the act as a violation of international law.[114] In the September issue Ramachitti translated a series of American notes protesting German practices of submarine warfare. In a commentary appended to the translation, he labeled the United States as the only major power not in the war and the outstanding protector of the rights of neutral states; supported the American protests, stating that, indeed, nothing in war could justify the abandonment of morality and the killing of innocent people; and said that the Thai, as Buddhists, could not help but agree with this moral stance.[115] Subsequent issues of *Samutthasan*, and occasionally the newspapers, contained other articles by the King, always writing under a pseudonym, that were distinctly critical of and uncomplimentary to the Germans. None were violently anti-German, however. And certainly none called for a declaration of war. In fact, even if the King had not used the stratagem of a pseudonym, none could be regarded as a real departure from neutrality.

One of the King's young courtiers, recalling this period of time decades later, has noted that Vajiravudh consistently maintained a public position of neutrality and kept silent about whatever personal opinions he may have held. The courtier says that he later discovered, however, that the King had been conducting an extensive personal correspondence with various European friends during this period, asking for their opinions and adding the intelligence from these replies to what he already knew in order to help him make up his mind on future Siamese courses of action.[116]

Early in 1917 the signs that a change in policy was being considered became unmistakable. Precipitating the change was the altered position of the United States. The Germans resumed unrestricted submarine warfare on February 1, 1917, and two days later the United States severed its relations with Germany. Barely had the news of this American action reached Siam than Prince Devawongse, the Minister of Foreign Affairs, wrote to Vajiravudh's private secretary for foreign correspondence, Phraya Buri, raising questions about the effect this American move toward a declaration of war would have on Siam's position. In his letter of February 9, Prince Devawongse set forth his opinions on what a Siamese declaration of war might mean. For one thing, it would allow the Siamese to seize the German merchant vessels that had taken refuge in the port of Bangkok; if they could be seized before the Germans damaged them, this would be a gain that would be about equal to the loss Siam would incur by

National Survival and Militarism

German confiscation of Siam's considerable bank assets in Germany. A declaration of war against Germany would have distinct dangers, however. First, the Germans had done nothing specific against the Thai to justify such a declaration. And the members of the German colony in Siam, who, the Prince said, numbered about 300 (in fact the total was closer to 200) and would become enemy aliens if war were declared, would pose a threat. Some might fight the Thai and destroy property; particularly to be feared were those who were in charge of the railroad line then under construction in northern Siam. Others might foment trouble among sympathetic Siamese military officers or among those Chinese merchants who had had close business connections with the Germans. Siam might find itself with a civil war on its hands. An alternate course of action would be to follow America's lead and simply break off relations. Such a step would free Siam from obnoxious treaty provisions with at least one major European power. Even such a limited step, however, was dangerous and ought not be undertaken until the Siamese military forces had signified that they were fully prepared to meet any emergency. The minister throughout his note, with all his words of caution, sounded as if he were arguing for a more conservative approach than he imagined the King would favor. He ended by pointing out two facts: first, that Britain, whose views the Prince regarded as vital in such matters, was not encouraging Siam to follow America's lead; second, that America's call for neutral states to follow its example had not led to a clatter of scissors snipping diplomatic ties. Each state, he said, was deciding its own policy on the basis of its own advantages, as indeed it should.[117]

The Prince's recommendations undoubtedly had weight, and Siam confined its reaction to the American move to protests against the violations of international law implicit in the German submarine campaign. These protests were communicated in March to the German government and to the Austro-Hungarian government by the Siamese minister in Berlin. A further protest against a German policy of making subjects of neutral countries who were serving on Allied merchant vessels liable to seizure as prisoners of war was sent to the Germans in mid-April. None of these communications were made public, however, until the end of April 1917.[118]

On April 6, 1917, the United States finally declared war against Germany. The United States, depicting its role as that of champion of "the rights of nations great and small" and defender of neutral rights in general, urged other neutrals to join in the crusade. The American declaration led to still another reexamination of Siam's position—

both because of America's moral leadership and, even more important, because of the great material strength that the entry of the United States would necessarily contribute to the Allies. The first Siamese act following the American declaration, however, was a restatement on April 12 of Siam's neutrality in the enlarged conflict.[119]

No new foreign policy decisions were made, or even discussed, by the King through the rest of April and most of May. For during the period from April 10 to May 22 Vajiravudh was busy on a trip to Siam's southern provinces. During the King's preparations for his journey and his absence from the capital, two members of his government, Prince Chakrabongs and Prince Devawongse, became deeply involved in the war problem. Both princes had engaged in conversations with the diplomatic representatives of England, France, and Russia in Siam and, as a result of these conversations, had taken up divergent positions on foreign policy. Prince Devawongse, seconded by the British, favored continued neutrality; Prince Chakrabongs, urged on by the French and Russians, favored active Siamese involvement on the side of the Allies. It was up to the King at the end of May to resolve the dispute and chart Siam's future course of action.

The only real concern in the deliberations on the war at the end of May was Siam's advantage. Was it in Siam's interest to remain neutral? Was it in Siam's interest to join the Allies? What would be the reaction of the major Allied powers to Siam's decision? If Siam were to join, what reasons should be given for the action? What rewards might Siam, as an ally, expect at the war's end?

In a secret memorandum of May 25 concerning Siam's possible entry into the war, Prince Devawongse gave his views on some of these questions. The memorandum was probably prepared to bring His Majesty up to date on the subject of the war after his trip to the South. The Prince's prime concern was how to respond to the representations the British, French, and Russian ministers in Bangkok had made to him at various dates in April and May. The French and Russian ministers had urged the Siamese to declare war. They had pointed out that the failure of Siam to publish its objections to German submarine warfare and Siam's continued neutrality after the American appeal to neutrals were tantamount to being pro-German. And they had promised that, if Siam joined the Allies, they would help Siam gain beneficial treaty revisions, revisions that would remove restrictions on customs duties. The British minister, in his talks with Prince Devawongse, had deplored these actions of his diplomatic colleagues and had stated that his view—and that of his government—was that Siam's decision on the war should be made by Siam alone and not in response to promises or pressures. Insofar as Britain was concerned, he had said, no treaty revision could be contemplated, for Britain, unlike France or Russia, had a considerable stake in Siamese trade and so could not lightly abandon its treaty rights. He had also stated that revision of customs duties might well create difficulties for trade, which would be a disadvantage for both England and Siam. The British minister had mentioned, however, that, as a measure to placate the French and Russians, Siam might publish its notes to the Germans objecting to submarine warfare, and this Prince Devawongse, with the King's approval, proceeded to do on April 30. With regard to his own opinions on future policy, Prince Devawongse stated: "I have believed from the start the Allies would win, but see no good reason for Siam to join in; remaining neutral is our best course."[120]

Prince Chakrabongs, who did not agree with the Minister of Foreign Affairs, presumably also told the King his views.[121] He probably also wrote to him during this period, for Vajiravudh sometime later complained of the "many violent memoranda submitted to me by my brother concerning our foreign policy," memoranda that supported the French and Russian position and depicted Prince Devawongse as overly reluctant to take any action that might provoke British resentment.[122]

On May 28, 1917, King Vajiravudh read to his Council of Ministers a long and critical statement on the war that was meant to clarify issues and serve as the text for a definitive decision on Siamese policy.[123] After a brief historical background on Siam's neutrality, the King analyzed in hard terms the realities of Siam's position. First of all, he asked—and then answered—the question "What is the true position of Siam?" Siam, he said, lay between the colonial territories of England and France. This central fact had determined, from the start, that Siam could never dare to show the slightest partiality toward Germany; to do so would have meant Siam's immediate annihilation. And, further, Siam had been able to declare itself neutral only because it had suited the purposes of its powerful neighbors: "If at any time they had felt our neutrality to be an obstacle, there is no need to doubt that they would have ceased to allow it to continue." Those who would argue against this reasoning and cite the inviolability of Siam's sovereign rights should take a look at Greece. Siam, however, had two choices: to join the Allies or to remain neutral.

Siam's choice, said the King, should always be based on what would serve its interests best. At the start of the war, when it could not be clear which side would win, Siam, as a small country that could

National Survival and Militarism

not afford any vengeful enemy, had had to decide on neutrality. But now that Germany was clearly losing, it was time for advantages and disadvantages to be weighed anew.

In a future that would be dominated by the victorious Allies, Siam's interests no longer lay in neutrality; they lay in joining the victors. As a neutral, Siam could hope, at best, to retain what it had, but it would run a large risk of losing a great deal. As a member of the Allies, Siam could hope, at least, to retain what it had, and it would stand a good chance of making real gains. As a neutral, Siam would be at the mercy of the Allies. If Britain and France decided to take over German assets and privileges in Siam—and France, said the King, already had such intentions—Siam could do nothing but yield. Siam would have to yield not only rights but honor and part of its freedom. If, however, Siam joined in the war, Siam almost had to come out better than even. The undesirable treaties with Germany, at least, would be terminated. And there was a possibility that some treaty concessions could be won from the Allied powers.

Although cool logic showed the advisability of joining the Allies, a declaration of war, said the King, could not be made in a vacuum. Reasons had to be given for a declaration. And Germany had done nothing antagonistic to Siam: no Thai nationals had been killed; no Thai ships had been torpedoed; no Thai sailors had been taken prisoner. If Germany had committed some injury, even a slight one, the King said almost ruefully, then "I would not hesitate in advancing the view most strongly that we had just cause to rid ourselves of our neutral position." Any declaration of war without proper reason would be understood as a "policy" decision, one made to pursue advantages. Such a declaration would from the outset, then, fail in its intended effect; Britain was already wary of the new additions to the Allied roll of nations, such as China, which expected rewards or expected to share in the ultimate victory. Further, if Siam hoped to allay suspicions of its motives, it could declare war only if it could offer real services to the Allies, and the King could not imagine at this point what those services might be.

Under these circumstances, the King suggested, Siam should wait for an opportunity to declare war to present itself and, in the meanwhile, do its best to prepare for the peace by making pro-Allied statements and by taking steps to remove German nationals from posts in Siamese government departments, an action that it would be better for Siam to take on its own than be forced to take by the Allied Powers.

King Vajiravudh ended his statement with a plea to his ministers

National Survival and Militarism

to discuss it freely; he said that, if they had criticisms of his suggestions, they should make them right away and "not suppress them and then grumble later that you had no chance to present your views."

The Council of Ministers on May 28 essentially agreed with the King's policy statement. Some of the ministers whose ministries had German employees spoke of the difficulties of finding replacements, but none spoke against the policy of replacement. The consensus was that a policy of neutralism friendly to the Allies should be pursued and that eventually Siam should find an honorable way to enter the war. The ministers also agreed that if the Allied Powers officially invited Siam to enter, the government would then be able to enter with honor.[124]

Although he was out of town for the May 28 meeting, Prince Chakrabongs sent a strong letter of support to the King. He urged the King to put into effect immediately the policy of dismissing the Germans; suggested that Siam should not be unduly influenced by the negative feelings of the British, whom he described as a people who were always interested in "practical politics" and their own interests; and proposed that a *note verbale* be issued deploring the "inhuman manner" of warfare of the Central Powers and denouncing this evil in the interest of upholding "the sanctity of international right." If the Germans objected to the *note*, so much the better, since that would provide Siam the desired opportunity to sever diplomatic relations. The Prince's letter was much more aggressively prowar than the King's May 28 statement had been. Chakrabongs criticized various ministers at length for dillydallying and for excessive caution. He advised that Siam "must find a way" to enter the war, that to "sit idly by while luck passes" would give England "a free hand" to do as it liked in Siam after the war, that Siam would be like someone "blindfolded in the center of the room" with respect to the trade arrangements that would be made at the war's end.[125]

The King was obviously impressed by Prince Chakrabongs's arguments, which corresponded so closely to his own.[126] In a council meeting on June 1, he proceeded to announce as firm policy: (1) the dismissal of all Germans; (2) a search for a good reason to enter the war without waiting for an invitation from the Allies (the powers who were unenthusiastic about Siam's entry had grown to two; Japan had joined Britain by June 1);[127] (3) the issuance of a private "verbal note" to the foreign ministries deploring the German methods of warfare (with hope of a German objection that would allow Siam to sever relations); (4) the avoidance of any mention of hoped-for concessions from the Allies in the form of tariff concessions—Siam's new policy must assume the form of a solely moral protest. Even the firmness Prince Chakrabongs recommended appeared in the wording throughout; the statement closed: "And let me remind you, no further wavering is allowed."[128]

On this vital subject of Siam's decision to enter the war, the common view in Thailand today is that Vajiravudh led the country to war because of prejudice and passion and pro-British sentiments acquired during his long residence in England. The record does not substantiate this view. Although the King may have had his private biases,[129] the reports of the secret ministerial meetings clearly reveal a king who was committed to pragmatism and realism and was willing, indeed, to resist British pressures toward neutralism in order to promote his country's welfare.

After June 1, the diplomatic and practical preparations for war proceeded apace. The heads of various ministries were asked to complete detailed plans for replacement of Germans, for capture of German ships, for imprisonment of enemy aliens, and for other such actions. Allied diplomats were informed of Siam's intentions; Siamese legations abroad were also informed. The reception by June 18 of a cordial reply from London welcoming Siam's imminent entry into the war resolved the last doubts as to the policy decision.[130]

Only one important matter remained: to prepare the population for the policy change. And here the King stepped forward to perform the role he enjoyed most; he became chief propagandist for the new cause. But since Siam was still technically neutral and since the government was anxious not to alert the local Germans before all was ready, the King issued the propaganda under his pseudonym Ramachitti. Using this thin disguise,[131] Vajiravudh published in the newspaper *Nangsǔphim thai* from July 7 to July 21 a series of articles that were bitterly anti-German.[132] The Germans were characterized as a people who believed that "might is right," and their history was surveyed to show their aggressiveness, their disregard for the rights of other peoples. German transgressions in World War I, said Ramachitti, finally compelled America, which had "for so long remained steadfast in her neutrality," to declare war "to defend the Rights and Liberty of all mankind." Siam could do no less than follow America's lead. The arguments for continued neutrality were all bankrupt: even if Germany won the war, a Siamese record of neutrality would not save the country from German aggressiveness; the German "intrigues" with "Indian seditionists" in Siam had already proved how little respect the Germans had for the neutral rights of the Siamese. And, most important of all, Siam as a Buddhist nation that believed

National Survival and Militarism

in the right could not remain aloof while members of the family of civilized nations were "suffering injuries and atrocities at the hands of a ferocious giant." The Germans, he concluded, "have shown themselves to be monsters of depravity before the whole world, utterly without shame or fear of sin"; for Siam not to act against such evil would be "tantamount to aiding and abetting the wicked bandit."[133] And so, for the highest moral reasons and in keeping with Siam's finest traditions, "Siam must break with Germany who is the enemy of the world."[134]

On July 22, 1917, the day after these last ringing words by Ramachitti were published, Siam declared war on the Central Powers. The wait for a provocative incident had been abandoned, and the declaration of war, drafted personally by the King, who deliberately borrowed from lofty phrases of Woodrow Wilson and others, was based on the need to help defend "the peace of the world," "respect for small States," and "the sanctity of International Rights."[135]

To solemnify the declaration of war and put the power of traditional royal magic behind it, the King performed a "First Action" rite. Wearing a "victory dress" all of red (the proper color for Sunday wear), carrying the sword of the sixteenth-century warrior king Naresuan, and bearing auspicious leaves in his right hand and tucked behind his left ear, the King proceeded at 7:00 A.M. to the Chapel Royal at Wat Phra Kaeo, where he offered candles and prayers to the Emerald Buddha. He then proceeded to the hall that housed statues of his royal predecessors and asked that the merit of their transcendent virtues might help bring victory in war to Siam and its allies. After this he went to a hall of audience and gave a short address announcing Siam's declaration of war before the royal ministers, foreign diplomats, and members of the press. Last came the "First Action" rite proper. This symbolic act was performed on a special stage built at the Royal Plaza. Before the dais stood a newly planted tree representing the enemy. In the ceremony the tree was first "disgraced" by being doused with wash-water from a royal footbath; then, on the King's direct order, it was chopped down. The meaning of the rite was clear enough; Siam had taken its first action to destroy the enemy.[136]

In fact, however, some very practical steps had been taken several hours earlier. In the early morning hours of July 22 the declarations of war had been delivered to the German and the Austro-Hungarian legations; all male enemy aliens had been arrested; the German merchant ships in the port of Bangkok had been seized; and various strategic places—particularly along the route of the railway line to the north, then being constructed under the supervision of German technicians—had been put under elaborate guard.

Plans for these actions had been extremely well laid. For weeks military, police, and civilian units had been secretly preparing for the great day. All Germans and Austrians had been placed under constant surveillance. Navy construction crews had been feverishly building ladders specially designed for scaling the large German merchantmen from the small Thai navy launches.

And all had gone extremely well. Aside from some minor damage the German crews had managed to inflict on their own vessels, nothing untoward had happened. No sabotage had occurred. The railways, despite the loss of German technical help, continued to run without any delay in schedules. The King was pleased. The navy, army, and police were pleased. And foreign observers in Bangkok and elsewhere were lavish in their praise of the thoroughness and efficiency of the Thai operation. *The Far East*, published in Tokyo, commented on Siamese "businesslike efficiency" in executing a task "that has simply been bungled by other nations."[137] In a later birthday message to the King, the Siamese princes remarked on the submission of the enemy aliens, who were "awed by Your Majesty's powers and greatness." The message went on: "Everything was accomplished without necessitating the shedding of a single drop of blood and without causing the least trouble or inconvenience to the general public, who simply woke up from their sleep and saw victory already attained."[138]

The follow-up actions with respect to the captured German ships and the prisoners of war were also handled in an orderly fashion. Thai claims to the ships were legally cleared in a prize court, and the ships were then repaired, renamed with Thai names, and put to use, some by the Thai and some by their allies, under charter terms favorable to the Westerners.[139] The prisoners of war, who by August 8 included German women and children, were eventually transported by the Thai to British prisoner camps in India. This last action was insisted on by the British, and, although some Thai suspected the British of racial motives (not wanting white people to be held prisoner by Asians), King Vajiravudh, who was "elated that we have been able to intern Europeans which has undoubtedly increased our prestige a great deal," decided that continuous imprisonment of the Germans was not necessary or politic.[140]

Although Siam's major objective in joining the war was to further foreign policy aims, a secondary objective was to use the war to further internal policy aims of stimulating nationalism. Joining in the battle, the King undoubtedly thought, would shake the Thai loose of the

National Survival and Militarism

lethargy and selfishness that were characteristic of a people long used to peace. Vajiravudh had expressed such sentiments in an essay of 1915:

> Where there has been a long period of peace, people have had time to think of the pursuit of pleasure and the gratification of self, so that they have grown selfish; their outlook on life and things in general have become narrower and narrower, until nothing becomes so important to them as their own selves. In a way, I agree with some of the German writers who say that war is actually a blessing in disguise, because war compels one to think of something bigger and greater than one's own self. War certainly rouses people from that dream of self-interest, from which it is extremely difficult to wake, except with the thunder of guns or the points of bayonets.[141]

The primary objective, it was decided, was best promoted by quiet means: Siam should not make a point of what it hoped to achieve from its allies at the war's end. Private though this objective may have been, it was guessed at and hinted at on occasion. The prescient editor of the *Bangkok Times* on the day after the declaration of war, while lauding Siam for its moral stance, pointed out that essentially Siam's action was "a matter of practical politics" and that, while the question of duties revision had not yet been raised, it was sure to be raised "when the time comes."[142] Prince Mahidol, half a world away in the United States at the time of Siam's entry, was caught off guard and spoke freely about the benefits Siam hoped for:

> First she will secure her place as an independent nation, free to work out her own destiny without fear of more powerful neighbors. Again, she will get rid of the extra territorial rights which now brand her as a nation of inferior civilization. She will be recognized as she ought to be in the great family of nations. She will, I hope, obtain a readjustment of her internal relations which will relieve her of the unequal and unfair tariff agreements under which she now suffers.[143]

By the beginning of 1918 King Vajiravudh was willing to state publicly that Siam's entry into the war "enables us to hope that we may be able in the future to enjoy every right and privilege on an equality with all the other nations."[144]

The Siamese Expeditionary Force

One wartime activity of Siam that served both foreign policy objectives and the domestic policy of nationalism was the organization of a Siamese Expeditionary Force. The original Siamese intention was not to participate directly in the war in Europe,[145] but pressures

National Survival and Militarism

chiefly from the French, supported by Prince Charoon, the Siamese minister to France, and by Prince Chakrabongs, led to a new decision to outfit and dispatch expeditionary units. Prince Charoon not only suggested to the King that Siam should "take some active part or make a bit of a show" but also specified that aviation and ambulance units would be the best bargains, since they would give even small Siamese forces great visibility and prestige.[146] Some of the King's ministers seemed primarily interested in keeping costs for the force as low as possible, but others, such as Prince Charoon, argued that "Siam should give as much as possible without counting the cost NOW. It will pay in the long run to do all one can and to show the other Allies that one is doing so." Prince Charoon's view was that some expenses "will pay in the long run. I do not say in money but in other ways."[147] The ultimate decision, made in September, was a compromise: there was to be a Siamese contingent of around 1,300 men (though the number was to be kept secret so as not to lead to disparaging comparisons); the contingent was to consist of an ambulance section, a flying squadron, and a detachment of automobile drivers and mechanics.[148] The units sailed for France in June 1918 and served through the end of the war.

As an instrument of foreign policy, the Siamese Expeditionary Force was expected to demonstrate the sincerity of Siam's intentions of aiding its allies and to bring the name of Siam before the world. Siamese participation as an active partner in the war effort, it was felt, could not help but increase the country's chances of improving its treaty conditions at the war's end. A further practical result of sending the expeditionary force would be that Siamese military units would gain invaluable field experience.

As an instrument of national policy, the Siamese Expeditionary Force was seen as a means for rallying the Thai people. The method of selecting the members of the force was itself a means of promoting patriotic feelings. Service in the force was described as a special honor; therefore, enlistment was made voluntary and opened not only to men in the armed forces but also to civilians. The call for volunteers was issued late in September. Three weeks later the King expressed his great gratification at the response, thanking all who had volunteered —many more than could be used—for their loyalty and patriotism. Further, during its months of preparation in Siam the expeditionary force received special attention from the King and considerable publicity.

Late in December 1917, the Ministry of War took the occasion of the annual "Swinging Ceremony," a traditional Hinduist rite, to

National Survival and Militarism

stage an elaborate military procession and "a splendid popular advertisement" for the armed forces, including, of course, the Siamese Expeditionary Force. The purpose of the procession was to show the antiquity of the military tradition in Siam and to increase the pride of the Siamese in their existing military might. The military procession, complete with floats, bands, and even a large model airplane, was staged on two days and attracted large crowds.[149]

On January 8, 1918, the King gave a dinner party for a group of Thai officers who had been selected to constitute a military mission to go to Europe to act in liaison with the Allies in the prosecution of the war. After the dinner Vajiravudh addressed the group on their responsibility "to show to the nations whose prowess, we must confess, we have known in the past, how much we have advanced." The members of the mission, he stated, "will be the first persons to carry with them the dignity and fame of my Army to be made known before the world, and will be the first to unfurl the Siamese flag on the continent of Europe." These men were in effect the King's representatives, he said, and they were chosen because they possessed the "high patriotic qualities" that are the measure of a nation's greatness. He described the sending of this mission, and of the full Siamese Expeditionary Force later, as of the "utmost importance" not only for the King and the individuals involved, but for the entire Siamese nation. Posterity, he said, would one day be able to turn back the pages of history and "exclaim with pride: 'Ah! they are not cowards! They enhanced the dignity and honour of the nation, did things befitting the name of Thai, and, loving freedom, were ready for every sacrifice....'"[150]

To promote public awareness of the military and the war, on April 6 King Vajiravudh instituted a new order of chivalry, named the Honourable Order of Rama. The order was created particularly for individuals who distinguished themselves in military service, especially those who proved themselves ready "to sacrifice their lives in defence of the independence and prosperity of the Nation and Country." Many members of the Siamese Expeditionary Force were eventually to receive this coveted new mark of royal favor.[151]

On May 26 the Siamese Expeditionary Force itself was hosted by the King at dinner. His remarks on this occasion were similar to those he had made to the military mission in January. He spoke of the long time that the Thai people had been forced to feel "slighted and hurt because others looked on us as a small and inferior nation." Now, he said, the chance had presented itself for the Thai to show the world that they had been accepted by the powers as an equal. This chance could be seized because the government, despite the criticisms of many, had gone ahead and developed an army. On the troops now going to Europe would rest the reputation of Siam; Siam would be judged according to how its troops behaved, on the field of battle and elsewhere. And so these troops must be on constant guard to earn for Siam nothing but praise. But, said the King, in this respect he had full confidence in each and every member of the expeditionary force.[152]

The dinner on May 26 had one interesting nationalistic byproduct. After the dinner, English films were shown; at the end of one film there flashed on the screen the Kipling lines "What stands if Freedom fall? / Who dies if England live?" Prince Chakrabongs told the King how moving he found these lines. And the King, when he awoke the next morning, penned the words of the reign's most famous patriotic poem:

> Love the king with complete loyalty.
> Love the nation with unswerving duty.
> Love the Buddhist Trinity faithfully.
> Love honor to merit the world's praise.
>
> On all occasions show respect
> And think of your land
> As the state where Thai live in peace.
> We must cherish it so it endures forever.
>
> Whoever invades the land of the Thai
> We will fight to the last man, to the last mile,
> Sacrificing life's blood and life itself
> Rather than lose our honorable name.
>
> If Siam endures, survives,
> Then, secure, our lives go on.
> But if Siam's doom arrives, can Thai endure?
> Our family line is gone; the Thai are done.[153]

Popular involvement in the Siamese Expeditionary Force was promoted by the organization of a fund drive. Private individuals who wished to make contributions were encouraged to do so. This money was to be used to buy cigarettes, socks, and chocolate bars and in other ways contribute to the personal comfort of the Thai soldiers. The drive started in October 1917. It was nationwide in scope. Various benefit affairs, including motor races and performances of plays, were also organized to add to the public contributions. By the time the drive ended, about $100,000 had been collected.[154]

That the measures taken to make the Siamese Expeditionary Force

National Survival and Militarism

a national symbol had been successful was demonstrated on June 19, 1918, when the force left Siam. After various ceremonies and departing speeches, the soldiers boarded the troop transports.[155] It was very early in the morning, and for "security" reasons the departure of the force had not been made public; so, as the ships went up the river to turn at the Samsen bend, "there was practically no one to be seen along the river banks." But the soldiers "cheered lustily the whole time while going along the river," and their cheers woke up the people along the banks. By the time the ships came back down the river the "banks were absolutely full with people, all jetties and landings were crowded to a dangerous point, everybody desired to see and wish 'bon voyage' to the brave soldiers, who were going away to take part as representatives of the Siamese Nation in the great war."[156]

To mark the first anniversary of Siam's entry into the war, Vajiravudh on July 22, 1918, issued a royal proclamation repeating many of the lofty phrases he had previously used about the great cause in which all the Siamese people were involved. He praised his people for their spirit of unity, their loyalty, their patriotic love of country; these, he said, had been manifested by the troops who had volunteered their lives, by the support everyone was giving to fund drives, and by the devotion of all to the performance of their duties and the maintenance of peace and tranquillity.[157]

After the arrival of the Siamese Expeditionary Force in France at the end of July 1918, there were periodic favorable reports on the group's activities. Such news as "... the French general public express much admiration for our soldiers for their smart military bearing and for their discipline"[158] was bound to swell the national pride of Thai at home. In Europe, the Siamese minister in Paris made special efforts to ensure that Thai troops were given all due courtesies as full partners in the war effort, were not treated in any way as inferiors, and particularly were not confused with colonial contingents, such as, for example, the Vietnamese labor battalions.[159] The arrival of the Siamese motor unit at the front in September was noted in the Thai press, and the French recommendation of the Croix de Guerre for two Thai officers in November was well publicized. On December 17 the King received telegraphic news that Siamese contingents had advanced with the Allied army of occupation into Germany. Vajiravudh's reply, printed in the local press, said in part: "It was the proudest day in my life when I learnt that my troops had advanced into enemy territory, and the memory of this glorious event will ever live in mind as an incentive to further sacrifice on behalf of my beloved nation and motherland."[160]

National Survival and Militarism

Postwar Celebrations

The end of the war with the proclamation of an armistice on November 11, 1918, occasioned a long series of nationalist outpourings in Siam.

On November 19, 1918, King Vajiravudh issued a Proclamation of Victory. In this proclamation he set aside December 2, the anniversary of his coronation, as a day of national thanksgiving for the victory that had come in part, at least, as a result of Thai invocation of the Holy Buddhist Trinity and the virtues of Siam's previous monarchs.[161]

The December 2 holiday started in the afternoon on the palace grounds with ceremonies in the traditional style: a "First Action" rite was again performed, this time to signify achievement of victory; reverential prayers and invocations for continued aid were offered to the spirits of the departed royal ancestors and to the Buddha.[162] After the close of the private ceremonies, the royal party proceeded to the Royal Plaza. There, in a specially constructed pavilion, the King led his people in ceremonies of public thanksgiving. These ceremonies were completely without precedent in Thai history. Thai kings were expected to conduct countless ceremonies *for* the public; never before, however, had such ceremonies been conducted with the public as participants. On the broad open grounds of the Royal Plaza there gathered government officials, military units, foreign diplomats, "a dense mass of the cosmopolitan people of Bangkok." At an altar facing this assemblage of thousands Vajiravudh led the thanksgiving rites. A foreign reporter present was deeply moved by the spectacle:

> At the outset all knelt—the King, the Princes, the officers of state, the assembled troops, the school children, the people on the plain. It was the greatest moment of the day—a people kneeling in prayer. None could fail to be thrilled by the spectacle. It was where the bare plain held possibilities above the temple . . . . The people were on their knees some few minutes, and then rose together and proceeded with the service. The chanting of the prayers of thanksgiving . . . by the great body of the assembled troops was most impressive. The great volume of sound seemed to come in waves . . . .[163]

The ceremony closed with the playing of the national anthem, followed by enthusiastic cheers for the King. As His Majesty left the plaza in his carriage, there were more "hearty cheers of the great multitude, cheers which were taken up and continued along a good part of the road round the Royal Plaza."[164]

The success of the day and the public participation were not

National Survival and Militarism

simply happy accidents. The government had wanted a display of unity, and government offices had been given a holiday, people had been urged to decorate their houses with flags, public transportation fares had been reduced by half, free refreshments had been provided —all in an effort to give sign of and substance to national spirit.[165]

The celebration of the day of national thanksgiving was not confined to Bangkok. Provinces were instructed to take part by closing government offices, distributing copies of the King's royal proclamation, displaying flags, and holding their own public ceremonies.[166] In the ceremonies at Ayutthaya, closely patterned after those in Bangkok, the King's portrait was substituted for His Majesty's person. A "beautifully bedecked boat" carrying signs about the victory plied the waterways to bring the thanksgiving message to villagers. About 10,000 people in the city, and many more thousands on the waterways, joined in the festivities.[167] Reports from Nakhǫn Pathom, Lampang, and Lopburi indicate that provincial cooperation was widespread.

The next wave of celebrations, those associated with the return of the Siamese Expeditionary Force units, was prepared for by the screening of films of the force. The films arrived in Bangkok in January 1919, and by March they were being shown to large crowds in the provinces.[168]

On May 1, 1919, the first returning contingent, consisting of some 340 members of the aviation corps, arrived in Siam. The welcoming arrangements were elaborate: buildings along the Čhaophraya River were decorated; fireworks were set off; the King, officials, troops, and families all greeted the returning soldiers at appointed places. The King gave each of the soldiers a medal commemorating his service in the war. And he addressed the returning members of the expeditionary force as comrades and as sons who had brought honor and fame to Siam, its monarch, and its people. During the following three days many other functions were held to welcome the soldiers home.[169]

Shortly before leaving Europe, the remainder of the Siamese Expeditionary Force took part in three gala victory parades: in Paris on July 14, in London on July 19, and in Brussels on July 22. Communiques from the Siamese general staff given to the press mentioned how well the Thai troops marched, how proudly the Siamese colors were carried in the streets of Paris, how cordially the Siamese were greeted everywhere.[170]

In Bangkok it was decided that Siam should time its formal victory celebration to coincide with the arrival of the 800 returning members of the expeditionary force. The celebration started on September 21, 1919, a Sunday, and lasted for three days; September 22 and 23 were

National Survival and Militarism

declared national holidays.[171] On the first day the returning members of the expeditionary force were formally received at the Royal Plaza. The ceremonies were led by the King, who, "filled with emotion," praised the soldiers for their sacrifices to show all the world that Siam was a nation devoted to righteousness. He added that, indeed, it was Siam's "respect for right which has made us into a Nation, a compact Nation," composed of people loyal to their sovereign, loyal to the nation, and steadfast in their noble faith. The King proceeded to bestow decorations on fifty-four men; five received medals of the new Order of Rama. The colors of the Motor Transport Company were also given the Order of Rama.[172] Among the other highlights of the three days of events were a torchlight procession, parties at the British and French legations, a royal banquet, nightly illuminations, a gymkhana at the Royal Bangkok Sports Club, and performances of plays in pavilions put up by various government ministries. Popular enthusiasm ran high; even before the troops landed, people came down the river in small boats to see them and to cheer them with shouts of victory.[173] A newspaper reported that "there was no mistaking the heartiness of the popular welcome."[174] The final day was given over to more somber rites, the interment of the ashes of the nineteen war dead in the base of a special monument then under construction. (Though none of the nineteen had actually died in battle, they were nonetheless regarded as casualties of war.)

Like the day of national thanksgiving, the victory celebration in September was nationwide in scope. The ceremonies and festivities were, however, even more elaborate and apparently involved even more provincial centers.

Another national celebration, which was similar in scope and purpose to those commemorating the end of the war, took place in October 1920 to herald the arrival of the *Phra Ruang*, the naval vessel purchased in England with the money that had been contributed by the people to the Royal Navy League fund drive. The reception of the *Phra Ruang* was declared an affair of state. Prince Abhakara had purchased the vessel, a destroyer (at the last moment the British Admiralty had refused to allow the Siamese to purchase the scout cruiser they wanted[175]), and had captained it back to Siam. On its arrival at Paknam at the mouth of the Chaophraya River on October 7, the vessel was welcomed by various officials. The vessel, moored in the river, was outlined with electric lights and "made a fine display"; on shore, government buildings were lit up, and each department hosted night-long performances of plays and other entertainments.[176]

National Survival and Militarism

The *Phra Ruang* came up to Bangkok on Friday, October 8; its arrival at the capital was the occasion for three days of ceremonies and festivities, including formal reception by the King and a ride by the King on the vessel up and down the river. Sunday, October 10, was the public day, and the throngs of people from Bangkok and the provinces who had made their contributions were allowed to come on board and inspect their purchase. People came by the thousands and demonstrated their delight: "The ship was crowded all day, and any handle that could be turned, or gun made to move, was operated by enthusiastic sightseers. The vessel was garlanded wherever it was possible to hang flowers...."[177] To those who made a further contribution to the Navy League, a souvenir picture of the *Phra Ruang* was presented.[178]

The campaign to enlist popular interest obviously seems to have succeeded. One writer, answering a foreign critic who questioned Siam's need for a navy at all, commented:

> ... man does not live by bread alone, nor is any nation made a reality by a cash nexus. One of the aims of this reign has been to bring home to the people that their claim to self-determination involves on their part the duty of self-defence. The gift of the *Phra Ruang* is one response of the people to that teaching. From that point of view it is surely worth the money paid, and all the significance that is being attached to its arrival.[179]

As the fitting close to Siam's involvement in World War I, on July 22, 1921, the fourth anniversary of Siam's declaration of war, a permanent monument to Siam's war dead was dedicated. The monument, located in a prominent place near the Royal Plaza, was beflagged with colors of the Allied Powers. All day long, wreaths were placed at the memorial by various sections of the population. The King, foreign diplomats, and some French aviators who were on a formal visit from Indochina also presented wreaths and took part in an official ceremony.[180] With the ceremony of 1921, July 22 became a day of national commemoration in Siam.

Celebrations of the military that were not exclusively associated with the war and Siam's role in it were also held in the postwar years. The King continually made the point that the war had helped secure Siam's future, but the future was not without threat; Siam must stay on guard and maintain its military establishment. The King seized every opportunity to dramatize the importance of the armed forces. For example, in November 1921, on the eleventh anniversary of the King's first coronation, a great two-day military tournament

National Survival and Militarism

was staged featuring displays of the skills of "every branch of the Service" from ancient hand-to-hand (and foot-to-foot) combat to the building of a bridge under battle conditions by the army engineers. The tournament even included a mock engagement featuring the "bombing" of a village by the air corps and the dousing of the flames by the fire brigade, whose arrival was greeted with loud cheers by the enthusiastic audience.[181] In December 1921, on the occasion of the visit to Siam of Marshal Joffre, who was received with extraordinary displays of courtesy and honor, the Siamese military was again shown off "at its best." Some four thousand troops were assembled for a general inspection, and other activities were scheduled that were calculated to impress the French general with Siamese military strength and proficiency.[182]

Products of Participation

In the area of foreign relations, there is no question that Siam's participation in World War I yielded practical results. Since these results were primarily the consequence of diplomacy and only indirectly related to the rising spirit of nationalism, they need not be related in detail here; a brief summary will suffice.

A large step was taken at Versailles. One objective, the formal abrogation of all German treaty rights in Siam, was easily accomplished. Although Siam had expected no difficulty in gaining "full satisfaction" from the Germans, nonetheless Prince Charoon, the head of Siam's delegation to Versailles, expressed the belief that the recognition by the powers of Siam's "full jurisdiction over one of the great European states" augured well for the future: "To have this in black and white signed by all the Allied nations as well as the enemy, is indeed important for the future."[183]

With regard to the more difficult goal of revising treaties with other nations in order to rid Siam of the limitations on its fiscal and juridical autonomy, the King's advice to his delegates at Versailles was to pursue these goals astutely and delicately, "being careful not to make other delegates annoyed or angry, which would lose us our advantage."[184]

The Siamese delegates followed Vajiravudh's instructions, but found only one responsive listener, the American president Woodrow Wilson. After his conference with the Siamese, Wilson wrote the Department of State that he felt "there is a great deal of force in their contentions" and indicated his desire "to go as far as it is prudent and possible . . . in conforming to their suggestions."[185] The negotiations with the United States proceeded rapidly and successfully, and by the end of 1920 a new treaty had been negotiated whereby the Americans surrendered all fiscal rights (subject only to most-favored-nation treatment) and all extraterritorial rights (subject only to a five-year option to withdraw cases from Siamese jurisdiction).

The American concessions were real and significant, but there still remained the large task of convincing other nations to follow the same route. And Great Britain, the most powerful Western power in Asia and in Siam, was the power to convince. The British were generous in their praise of Siam and Siam's war role. And the British minister in Siam assured Vajiravudh that the British delegates at Versailles would be "wholehearted" in their support of Siam. Since the minister was not specific as to what would be supported, the King in his reply came closer to the point: "Siam's desires will not be really very ambitious and will be confined merely to things that really matter in order to ensure our national freedom and right to live!"[186] In an effort to persuade the minister to help, the King added: "I have been called an incorrigible optimist, but somehow I have faith in the honesty of my Allies, especially in my immediate neighbours, who in my opinion must surely have already become convinced of the sincerity of Siam's desire to live at peace and absolute amity with them."[187]

The British seemed willing enough to consider tariff revision favorably, but they were reluctant to renounce extraterritorial rights.[188] The British minister to Siam, and British individuals, were critical of Thai courts and opposed to placing British subjects unconditionally under Thai law. A veritable campaign had been waged in the English-language press since at least mid-1918 about Siamese judicial shortcomings and the continual "poor advertisements of the state of the administration of justice in Siam."[189] In the spring of 1919, while the Versailles meetings were going on, the chief justice of Siam's highest court, Prince Svasti, was involved in a scandal that resulted finally in his dismissal from the government. Prince Charoon was convinced that the Svasti case constituted a real "handicap" in negotiations with the British.[190] One of the Siamese delegates to Versailles, in his conversations with an official of the British Foreign Office on Siam's hopes for treaty revision, assured the official that Siam would do nothing drastic with its autonomy; he said, also, that the British claim that Siamese courts "do not quite work in good order" represented merely one opinion—an opinion with which he certainly could not concur. The Siamese delegate, in what would appear to have been a considerable departure from the royal instructions calling for extreme care, made an indirect threat to the

National Survival and Militarism

British by bringing up the Japanese idea of a Monroe Doctrine for Asia, but added: "Siam prefers her old friends and neighbours."[191]

In Siam the policy of doing all that was possible to please the British, to win them over with favors, was continued. One remarkable evidence of this policy was the proclamation early in January 1920 of a decree barring all former enemy aliens from reentry into Siam for three years.[192] By way of preparing for this policy, which may have reflected the King's own anti-German bias, Vajiravudh, again using the alias Ramachitti, wrote a bitterly anti-German article entitled "We Don't Need Lizards." The article, repeating much of the atrocity propaganda of the Allies, compared the "Huns" to water lizards and declared that Siam already had a surfeit of vile creatures of that sort.[193]

Despite the blandishments of the Siamese, little progress was made in treaty negotiations for some time. Only two powers, Japan and France, seemed willing to follow the American lead. By 1923 a new treaty on the American model had been negotiated with Japan, and discussions with France along the same lines were well advanced. No progress at all, however, had been made with the British.

The log jam was finally broken in 1924 with the appointment of Francis Bowes Sayre of the Harvard Law School as Adviser in Foreign Affairs. Sayre took the Siamese case directly to the centers of power and decision in Europe, and in a period of nine months succeeded in persuading the ten European states with special rights in Siam to assent to new treaties.[194] By August of 1925 he was able to cable King Vajiravudh that "Siam's complete autonomy is now regained."[195]

The achievements of the war in the area of the mind, in stimulating the national unity the King hoped for, are much more difficult to estimate than the achievements in the area of foreign relations. Vajiravudh apparently thought that the results were good. In his birthday speech in 1921, in commenting on the general state of Thai nationalism, he observed that there had been "a progressive realization" of the consciousness of the Thai people "of the love for their country, of the duties that the individual owes to the State, and of the notion of right and justice for nations," all of which were tokens of a people "being truly civilized." He added "... it has become more and more apparent that our people are realizing the importance of the defence of their country."[196]

Some foreign observers also noted real effects of the militarist campaigns and of involvement in the war itself in stimulating nationalism in Siam. Most conscious of change were the French in Indochina, who consistently throughout the reign were most sensitive to Thai

National Survival and Militarism

nationalism as the source of a possible threat to the French colony. The Saigon *Opinion* in early 1921 commented:

> The Siamese nation is at an interesting stage of its evolution. In it, as in many others, the great War has infused a new ardour, a powerful breath of national feeling, a certain degree of combativeness in order to reach the level of civilisation of the great Western Powers.

The article went on to speak of the "awakening of this small nation" and "the fever which now burns the Siamese people," who had come to realize "that a people cannot escape defeat and humiliation unless it has the energy indispensable for the defence of its own interests."[197]

The French writer in Indochina may have somewhat exaggerated the strength of Siamese national spirit; but it can hardly be doubted that some change along the lines of his observations occurred as a result of Siam's participation in World War I.

6

The West as Model

Nationalism in Siam under King Vajiravudh was riddled with paradoxes—as it probably has been in all places and in all times, for nationalism is essentially a phenomenon of the emotions rather than of reason. A population stirred to loyalty to the state is the goal, and the ways to that goal are various and often seemingly incompatible. A nationalistic people needs to be proud of its nation. And the elements of that pride must, in large part at least, be universals, that is to say, elements widely agreed upon as desirable throughout the world. A nationalistic people must feel that it excels in significant ways, that what it excels in—an empire on which the sun never sets, an ability to tame and populate a wilderness, a refinement in the arts and culture—elicits the praise and envy of other peoples. In addition to universals, a nationalistic people may focus its pride on qualities that are unique, that no other people considers noteworthy or worthwhile. But an exclusive diet of the special is an austere diet little apt to satisfy nationalistic appetites. Nationalism characteristically has fed on both the universal and the particular.

The West as Model

And so with the new and the old. Since nationalism is a modern phenomenon, its tokens have taken modern forms. Excellence or preeminence in the desiderata of the industrial age has been the goal. Miles of railroad lines, gross production of coal and iron, numbers of cotton mills, total tonnage of merchant ships, firepower of armies are the criteria for pride. But nationalism need not consist entirely of the new. The old also has its place. The new tends to equate with the universal; the old, with the unique.

In developing a nationalistic program for Siam, King Vajiravudh had to include the universal and the new, to which he could also add the unique and the old. The former will be considered in this chapter; the latter, in chapter 8.

In the fields of the widely acknowledged new sources of national pride, Siam could hardly hope for preeminence. For these fields were virtually all pioneered by Western nations; the standards of value of the modern world were Western values, arising out of the context of centuries-long development in Western culture. They were values that had been forged in the blast furnaces of the Industrial Revolution into the constituents of unprecedented wealth and power. The best that Siam could hope for in these fields was some progress, some significant advances that would win the nation respect.

And so Siam under Vajiravudh built railroad lines and telegraph lines, constructed roads and bridges, improved ports, established military and civil aviation. The modest program of technological advance started by King Chulalongkorn was continued and expanded by Vajiravudh. Whenever possible—as, for example, in the field of aviation—maximum capital was made of modern advances for nationalistic purposes.

The use of the modern Thai military as a point for new pride is clear. Above and beyond the belief in the practical utility of the armed forces as armed forces, King Vajiravudh obviously saw the army, the navy, and, indeed, the Wild Tigers and Boy Scouts as proud emblems of Siam's growing modernity. With due allowance made for Siam's size, its military might, said Vajiravudh, was approaching equality with the West.

The ultimate in national pride, the King implied, would come from real power defined in Western terms of economic and military strength. Power produced pride. But it was also true—and here the King spoke unequivocally—that pride produced power. The road to power for a small, underdeveloped, and ununified country such as Siam was extremely long and lonely. Such a road could not be traversed without stamina and spirit. It could not be traversed without

The West as Model

a national will. So, while power should be pursued in a practical way with whatever means were at hand, the national will also needed development. Development of a national will would bring real power much faster. And development of a national will, further, would be easier to accomplish, would require at least less capital if not less energy. Such seems to have been the pattern of Vajiravudh's conscious and unconscious thought.

The outstanding instances of the Westernization programs initiated by Vajiravudh, outside of the military, belong predominantly to the category of the accomplishable, the attainable. They were often programs for introducing symbols of Westernization. Even though the new elements were little more than symbols, they could win foreign praise, they could raise internal morale, and they could lead to equation—in a limited way—with the West. Perhaps even, miracle of miracles, the "symbol" might prove in the end to be the "secret." The unknown wellsprings of the mysterious West might serendipitously be found to lie, for example, in the Western predilection for surnames.

Surnames

In traditional Siam, as in the rest of South and Southeast Asia, surnames were unknown. For most people the only appellation was the given name. There was a wealth of such names.[1] Some were pure Thai words for various fruits and flowers,[2] personal characteristics, and the like. Less frequently, Sanskrit or Pali words were used. Many of the latter had grandiloquent or religious meanings—for example, "peerless," "merit," "superb."

It can be assumed that, for purposes of personal identification, the Thai in traditional times were well served by given names. Society in those times was village oriented, and there was little population movement. Further, Siam lacked social organizations such as the clan, for which in many societies special means of organizational identification have been devised. The preponderance of outside cultural influences from India, where surnames are not used, rather than from China, where the names of ancient progenitors have long been passed on from generation to generation,[3] reinforced the habit of reliance on given names and enriched the vocabulary from which such names could be chosen.

Not for all individuals in traditional Siam, however, did identification rest on personal names alone. People who "counted" in traditional society—that is, the elite, who were either members of the royal

The West as Model

family or appointed nobles—were identified by an elaborate system of titles made up of ranks and conferred names. These titles functioned in much the same way as personal names. A commoner born as Sing ("Lion") could rise in the bureaucracy to the appointed rank of *čhaophraya* with the specific conferred name Bǫdintharadecha. His rank and conferred name (Čhaophraya Bǫdintharadecha), rather than his given personal name, would be the name used for him. Similar ranks and conferred names existed for members of the royal family. The conferred name usually indicated in some way the individual's duties or functions, and when a person was promoted to a new rank, he was usually given a new conferred name as well. At any given time no two individuals would ever bear the same title; identification of members of the elite, from lesser clerks to high ministers of government, was thus precise and unequivocal. The use of such a system of titles deemphasized the individual, since an individual, as he rose in the bureaucracy, would be known by different names at different stages of his career.

A clue to Vajiravudh's interest in the subject of name reform was provided by an essay he wrote in 1906. The then Prince, writing under a pen name, gave essentially practical reasons for favoring surnames: surnames would be a great convenience in precisely identifying people and showing their family background.[4]

This early trial balloon was followed in later years by some favorable editorials in the press on the subject of surnames. There is no doubt that the English-language press, at least, favored reform in the Siamese name system. It even gave nationalistic reasons for such a reform. One correspondent in 1910 suggested that surnames indeed constituted "one of the signs by which one may judge of the progress of civilization in a people" and that in this area Siamese civilization could stand improvement.[5] A year after Vajiravudh came to the throne an editorial in the *Bangkok Times* recommended adoption of family names as a means for placing more emphasis on the individual and his family connection and thus advancing "the patriotic spirit which is moving the country today."[6]

The decree announcing the awarding of surnames was issued—with very little prior notice of its coming—on March 22, 1913.[7] It thus was an early act of the King, coming only two years and four months after the start of the reign. The preamble of the decree gave only a brief statement of the reasons for its enactment. It said that the King wished to ensure that government records of births, marriages, and deaths would be clear and reliable and that identification of individuals and their line of descent would be free from possible error. These goals he believed would be achieved by the universal adoption of surnames in the state.

The obvious benefit of surnames, cited by various Thai authors,[8] was their great utility in personal identification. The growth in population had led to a great multiplication of repetitions of given names. One commune might have ten people named Di; how could the good Di be told from the bad one?[9] Clearly this was a problem for society as a whole, and most particularly for government. A government that was anxious to build its central power needed to establish a close connection with its people, and a close connection required precise identification of individuals.

A fuller explanation of the social utility of surnames has been given by a former royal official. He cites three main functions of surnames. First, surnames are the basis for the continuation of a paternal line of descent. Second, surnames promote family identity, a love and friendship that extends from family members of high rank down to those of low position. And, third, surnames are a good attribute of people no matter what their race or lineage because the family name is "like a flag of victory promoting the pride of people who are members of the family." The family name is something family members are spurred on to protect, to keep unblemished, to glorify by individual achievements and beneficial intrafamilial contacts.[10]

The social value of surnames was clearly spelled out by King Vajiravudh himself. In his birthday speech of January 1914, he succinctly summed up the specific social aims of the new law: "It is hoped that this law will prove a social benefit and an aid in the maintenance of family tradition. It will also serve as an incentive to every one to uphold not only personal honour but the honour of the family as well."[11] In an essay, he explained the more far-reaching results that he hoped for. The cohesion of the family, the growth of love and respect along family lines, the proper governance of a family —all of which, he said, would be promoted by the use of surnames— would be means for instilling respect for government. A family, the King stated, is bound together by love. Younger members of the family respect their elders because they know that their elders act only for the benefit of the family as a whole. The strengthening of such attitudes on the family level could not help but find expression in attitudes toward government. Inculcation of love in the family would inevitably promote inculcation of love toward the head of the government of the nation.[12]

Administrative and social usefulness were arguments for the

The West as Model

surname decree, but, as with so many of the King's actions, international prestige was never far from the King's mind. Vajiravudh's syllogistic reasoning is clear: Western countries were progressive; Western countries had surnames; Thailand, to be progressive, must also have surnames. The King came closest to stating the equation that surnames equal progress in an essay comparing surnames with clan names.[13] He wrote: "Now we have surnames and it can be said that we have caught up with people who are regarded as civilized."

The King's essay comparing surnames with clan names demonstrated two important aspects of the King's nationalism: first, his desire to equate the Thai with Westerners; second, his desire to distinguish the Thai from the Chinese and to prove that the Thai were ahead of their one-time-superior neighbors in the march toward progress. Clans, the King stated, marked an early stage in human progress and arose out of the need for primitive groups in a Hobbesian world to protect themselves. Such was the nature of the Scottish clan, the Chinese *sae*,[14] the American Indian totem. But the march of progress had moved beyond the clan to the larger unit of the nation. And in the nation clans were a disruptive force that had to be eliminated. "Nations," the King stated, "that have become civilized in the modern sense, even if they traditionally used clan names from ancient times, have changed to the use of surnames."[15] Only the Chinese, as a nation in the modern world, still clung to the use of "the old-fashioned clan names." The King admitted that in earlier times the Chinese had been more advanced than the Thai and that the Thai, for this reason, had looked up to the Chinese, had been glad to learn from the Chinese.[16] But times had changed. The Chinese had grown self-satisfied, had fallen behind in the advance of civilization, were determinedly holding on to customs now out of date. The Thai, the King implied, must turn to new leaders. And, in the matter of surnames, by so doing Siam had "succeeded in surpassing its neighbor which still has no surnames but only the clan names that were their ancient custom."[17] The Thai surnames, then, had nothing to do with Chinese clan names, and the King showed considerable irritation with those whose ignorance or superficial knowledge or sympathy with the Chinese led them to suppose that the royal decree on surnames was inspired by the outmoded Chinese custom.[18] Such people should certainly realize that the King was perceptive enough to know better.[19]

The decree of March 22, 1913, was a clear document of twenty articles that set forth the details of the law. Its main provisions were as follows: Surnames were to be adopted by all Thai. The surname was to be the permanent name of the family and was to be handed

The West as Model

down in the male line. A married woman was to bear her husband's surname. Neither given name nor surname was to be changed without securing prior permission from the district (*amphoe*) official. The family head, that is, the oldest living male of a family, was to choose the family name. This name had to be a suitable one: it must be in keeping with the person's position (certain names were to be restricted to royalty or to the nobility and were not to be used by commoners); it should not have coarse connotations; it must not require more than ten letters to write; it must not duplicate any other surname in a district or neighboring district. District officials were to help the people choose surnames, and, to this end, circulars were to be issued listing possible names. Names were to be registered in the district office, and a certificate of registration was to be awarded the family head. There was to be no charge for this registration. The decree was to become law on July 1, 1913, and six months thereafter all heads of families were to have complied by registering a name with the district office. At the end of the six-month period no official document was to be prepared that did not set down the surname as well as the given name of individuals mentioned in the document.

The decree of March 1913 constituted the basic law, but there were elaborations in the writings and actions of the King. The surname idea was Vajiravudh's; it became one of his pet projects. He could not restrain himself—as in so many other of his favorite projects—from getting personally involved in the detailed working out of the idea. He developed systems for differentiating social classes by means of the surnames. He decided how names should be transliterated into Roman letters. He personally devised and awarded many names for members of his court.

Surnames, the King had early decided, were not to be chosen at random or haphazardly. The family name should be a token of family pride, and every effort should be made to find as root for the name some distinguished or noteworthy progenitor. Certain names were reserved for high princes. These names were composed of elements derived from an ancestor's name to which was added na Krungthep ("of Bangkok").[20] High provincial officials who stemmed from regional hereditary princely families were surnamed na plus the name of the locality—for example, na Chiangmai and na Songkhla. Members of the nobility were frequently given names pointing to the official position the family held.

The King freely offered his services to members of the court who wanted personal royal attention in devising a proper surname. The

The West as Model

petitioner was urged to supply the King with information on his parentage, his family's usual occupation, and the like. Vajiravudh then meticulously set to work. Often he chose an ancestor's given name, a place name, or an occupation as the base for the surname. If the King thought the root word he had settled on was too homely, he drew on his fund of knowledge of Pali and Sanskrit and brought forth the name in more resplendent form. Someone whose family had been associated with horses or the cavalry would find the simple Thai word *ma* rendered as Atsawa. If someone's ancestor had been called Lek ("little"), the substitution would be apt to be Chula. Foreigners who wished to be naturalized as Thai could also petition for Thai surnames. The names awarded usually had some connection in meaning or sound with the original foreign names. For example, a Chinese named Tan was renamed Tantha; a Westerner named Lawson was renamed Lawasan.[21]

When the King personally devised a surname, he prepared a document setting forth the name, the reasons for his choice, and the way in which the name should be transcribed in Roman letters. One petitioner, a noble with the title Chaophraya Thewetsarawongwiwat, was advised to take the name of a royal progenitor, Prince Kunchon, spelled Kunjara in Western letters.[22] Such documents are still preserved by many Bangkok families. And the spellings devised by the King, which are transliterations of Thai writing rather than phonetic renderings, are also usually adhered to.[23]

When the decree was announced, the *Bangkok Times* hailed the news and opined that "the change can be brought about without great difficulty."[24] This optimism was unwarranted. As it turned out, numerous difficulties arose. The deadline in the original decree was not met. Other deadlines were set: April 1, 1914; April 1, 1915; April 1, 1918.[25] All proved to be too optimistic. By the end of the reign in 1925, it appeared that enforcement of the decree had been indefinitely postponed.[26]

The main difficulties in enforcement arose in rural areas. Urban Thai, Bangkok Thai, especially those associated with the government, seem to have taken to surnames readily enough. Educated Thai could understand the reasoning behind the decree and, further, were the element in the population most anxious to please the King. The King's personal interest was a powerful stimulus; apparently King Vajiravudh himself devised or awarded more than 3,000 names.[27] In the countryside, however, among the farmers who comprised some 90 percent of the population, the decree was more difficult to enforce. The majority of the farmers were illiterate, and surnames meant

The West as Model

nothing to them. Apparently there were breaks also in the administrative machinery leading from Bangkok to the villages. At the top of the administrative ladder the law was effective, but as it was passed down from ministerial office to province to district to commune to village, enforcement became progressively laxer and laxer. As late as 1924 the Ministry of Interior was still having trouble in getting its own officials to comply with the law. By this date the ministry had made possession of a family name a prerequisite for all new appointments to the positions of commune head and village chief.[28] But it seems clear that many of these lowest officials in the hierarchy, the officials who maintained the closest relations with the general population, were themselves unappreciative of the surname decree. A newspaper report of 1924, which complained of the lack of effort in urging people to adopt surnames, stated: "The average kamnan [commune head] and phu-yai-ban [village chief] say frankly that they have neither duty nor responsibility in the matter...."[29] Given these circumstances, it is not surprising that the average farmer did nothing to acquire a second name.

For those in the general population who did attempt to comply with the decree, there were also problems. A newspaper report illustrates the dilemma faced by many:

> If the average farang [Westerner] was suddenly fronted with the problem of selecting a surname for himself and his family, with a world of names to choose from, he would naturally be somewhat bewildered, and one may be sure a deal of human nature would be displayed in the choice. How many of us would after due deliberation select the ordinary names we now bear? Who among us would expect his wife to be content with a plebeian patronymic when there is a bookful of high-sounding possibilities?[30]

Some Thai commoners chose their names well, too well from the government's point of view, by seizing on names with royal or noble connotations. To check this tendency, lists of forbidden names had to be compiled and disseminated.[31]

As far as is known, there was only one objection to names on principle. An article in a Thai publication late in 1925 raised the question of whether the possession of surnames might not lead to favoritism: a high official might tend to be prejudiced in favor of a job applicant or a legal suppliant who bore the same family name. This objection was dismissed in the English-language press with the statement that "With or without surnames there are ways of pressing the claims of relationship on those in place and power...." In fact,

The West as Model

the argument continued, the possession of surnames should discourage favoritism, for the name advertised the relationship for all to see.[32]

Problems of surnames in the countryside did not cease even among those who had chosen and registered names and acquired the legal documents recording the new possession. For the whole process was still meaningless to the average peasant. The surname did not answer any need of his; it did not fill a vacuum in his cabinet of desires. It was tolerable; it, at least, did not cost anything.[33] But it was no more loved or even remembered than Americans love or remember their social security numbers. The ordinary villager who got a paper with his surname on it, said one newspaper account, brought it home and stuck it into the bamboo-plaited wall or in the thatched roof, and in no time at all the document was gone—eaten by rats or termites. If the villager should be asked what his surname was, he would not know.[34]

In the years since the first proclamation of surnames in 1913, surnames have become universal in Thailand. The law on surnames is enforced; government records include surnames. Characters in novels and short stories are supplied with surnames. Newspaper accounts give surnames. And individuals, even in villages, apparently know their surnames. There is no doubt that the family name has become a permanent feature in Thai life, so much so that many Thai are probably unaware that there was ever a time when surnames did not exist. Yet it would be inaccurate to assume that surnames perform the same function in Thai society that they do in Western society. For the most immediately recognizable part of a Thai name remains the first name. And this is the name that is most frequently used. A newspaper article may begin by referring to Mr. Sanya Dharmasakti, but later references will always be to Mr. Sanya. The predominance of the first name extends even to Western writings on the Thai: Pridi, Thanom, Seni are all more familiar than Phanomyong, Kittikachorn, or Pramoj. In the village, adults are apt to know their own family name and those of a few close neighbors, but school-age children often do not.[35] The surname functions as a means of making government records accurate; it functions to identify individuals precisely. On the personal level, it may be felt to be a kind of royal ornament, perhaps a kind of honorable title, in the tradition of the titles once granted by the king to government officials.[36]

The larger social purposes that King Vajiravudh hoped would be served by family names seem not to have been served. The Thai traditionally have felt no strong familial ties in time; there has been little or no interest in genealogy. Nor is there now. King Vajiravudh

The West as Model

hoped that Thai bearing the same name, a name derived from an honored progenitor, would develop a kind of family pride. This sense of lineage ties and lineage responsibilities might then serve as a stimulus to national drives and national unity. No such sense of lineage seems to have resulted from the adoption of surnames. No perceptible change in attitudes toward the past or the future has been noticed.

The success of Vajiravudh's reform lay in the acceptance of a Western model by domesticating it. A foreign concept was transformed and made Thai. By providing surnames with high-sounding Sanskrit roots, Vajiravudh gave the reform the familiar ring of traditional conferred names; in a sense he was elevating the entire population to the prestige of royal position.

The failure of the reform lay, it would seem, principally in Vajiravudh's own definition of success. It is difficult to imagine that the unity, power, and devotion to the nation that Vajiravudh admired in the West could have been achieved in any appreciable degree by adopting the Western custom of surnames. Hardly so much could be expected from what was essentially a convenient habit.

"King Rama"

The system of names, ranks, and titles in traditional Siam was enormously complex. It was difficult even for Thai to understand; most Westerners despaired of understanding it.[37]

Siamese leaders were well aware of the difficulty Westerners had with princely and noble names, ranks, and titles, and from the time of King Mongkut attempts were made to explain the system and even to simplify it. For the kings and officials knew that what the West could not understand, it would be sure to deprecate.

It was primarily to win Western approbation that several changes in the system were made in the Sixth Reign. One was to provide translations for princely ranks whereby the three highest such ranks would be termed His (or Her) Royal Highness, His (or Her) Highness, and His (or Her) Serene Highness.[38] Some thought seems to have been given to reformation of the names and titles of appointed nobles throughout the bureaucracy; at least Prince Damrong was charged with the task of preparing a "rationalization" scheme for such official designations. Prince Damrong submitted a huge draft along with a note saying that true rationalization embracing all ministries of government would be impossible to achieve.[39]

The most important change in the area of official appellations was the adoption by the King of a new "dynastic" name on November

The West as Model

11, 1916, the sixth anniversary of his first coronation.[40] The name Ramathibǫdi in Thai, to be translated King Rama in English, followed by the proper reign number, was to be used as a simple means for designating the kings of the Chakkri dynasty. The dynastic founder, formerly termed Phra Phutthayǫtfačhulalok, became Rama I; his successors became Ramas II, III, IV, V. King Vajiravudh was to be known as King Rama VI. Older name systems were not to be abandoned: the use of the very long official "royal style and title" was to continue; so was the use of personal names, which had been instituted by King Mongkut. But preference was to be given to the new scheme. Although no clue as to the origin of this name scheme appears in the available literature, it seems clear that it was inspired by European custom. England had its succession of Georges; now Siam had its succession of Ramas.

After the adoption of the Rama name, all medals that bore abbreviations for King Vajiravudh were changed so that the abbreviations would stand for King Rama VI. By 1919 the King had even come to use Rama R. (a shortened version of Rama Rex) as his personal signature.[41]

Some changes, apparently inspired by the European model, were instituted in modes of address. The terms *nangsao* for "Miss," *nang* for "Mrs.," and *khunying* for "Lady" (the wife of a high-ranking noble) were prescribed by royal rescript in 1917.[42] A similar system for children was instituted in 1921, but the distinctions it made between the offspring of government officials and those of commoners raised an outcry in the local press and the system was quickly abandoned.[43]

The Flag

Symbols. Lions and unicorns rampant. Black eagles with feathers unfurled. Stars and stripes. What is a nation without its emblems, its immediately recognizable symbols? Vajiravudh was well aware of their importance. In one speech he stated it very clearly: "Whatever the task undertaken, there must be something to symbolize its meaning so that the spirit will be involved."[44]

A country's primary symbol is its national flag. Siam had one, a white elephant on a red field, the design from King Mongkut's days. But to King Vajiravudh it seemed not dignified enough. And shame of shames could and did result when out of inadvertence or ignorance the flag was raised upside down. Such a misadventure occurred in September 1916.

The misadventure was associated with the King's trip up river

The West as Model

to the northern provinces. It had long been customary for Bangkok kings to make a royal progress by boat to the palace retreat at Bang Pa-in, near Ayutthaya, during the lull in government business in September. In 1916, however, rains had been particularly heavy and there was fear of destructive floods. The King decided to journey farther to the north than was usual in order to appraise the flood dangers for himself. The boat trip would also constitute a holiday, and the visit to new places would give him a chance to see some of his up-country subjects, and be seen by them, for the first time.

The royal party reached the town of Utthaithani on September 15. The local people, whose opportunities to welcome a royal guest were rare indeed, outdid themselves in preparation. A royal pavilion had been specially built. Everywhere there were banners and flowers. And flags. The national white elephant flag. Or, more commonly, since elephant flags were expensive and hard to come by, simple streamers of cloth of the colors of the elephant flag, red and white.

On the following day the King and his party proceeded by land to visit a local temple and to give the people of Utthaithani a chance to pay their respects to their monarch. On the way Vajiravudh noticed that there were relatively few national flags; he also had misgivings about the use of strips of red and white cloth in lieu of a flag, feeling that these partook too much of "Chinese custom." But the genuine displays of popular affection stilled his misgivings.

Along the route lay a small peasant house whose owner, somehow, had found a small flag. The King stared in disbelief. The flag was flying upside down, with the elephant supine, all four feet pointing heavenward. The King quickly turned away and made no remark then or later. But, according to a member of his party who remembers this incident at Utthaithani and whose description is relied on here, the incident was the crisis that ended in the adoption of a new national flag shortly thereafter.[45]

Whatever the importance of the incident at Utthaithani, there were other reasons for Vajiravudh's interest in changing the flag design. For one thing, the King had always taken a special interest in such symbols as medals, decorations, and uniforms, and the flag fit into this category. All flags, even those of ministries or departments, had to be submitted for the King's approval, which was by no means automatic.[46] Flags were given great prominence. The theme of many of the King's addresses was the flag as the symbol of national spirit. One could look on a flag, he said, as merely "a piece of cloth" or as "a rag on a pole." But in fact, because of the association of ideas, a

The West as Model

flag was transformed in men's eyes into a rallying point for the entire nation.[47] The King made clear that the flags that he presented as colors to military and Wild Tiger units were to be regarded as betokening the King's own presence. In one typical address Vajiravudh told a story about the god Indra's instructions to his soldiers in a battle: when they became exhausted, they were to look at the flag of their general, for that would make them recover their strength. Siam, the King said, had three flags—the king, the nation, and Buddhism. Of the flag that symbolized the nation he said:

> The Thai flag is no one's slave! It has never been anyone's slave! We'll never let it become anyone's slave. We will never let this flag be dirtied in the dust, be besmirched in the mud. We may stain it with our blood, but it is impossible for us to let it be soiled by dust or mud![48]

The national flag was, of course, especially important. It was, or ought to be, the symbol *par excellence* of national glory. But Siam had a flag that was termed by one Westerner a "distinctive emblem"[49] and described by another as "picturesque."[50] Perhaps it was the picturesque that bothered the King. The elephant flag may have been seen as too exotic, too quaint for a young nation that wanted respect, honor, and esteem for its progressiveness.

Further, the elephant flag had some practical disadvantages. The flags were printed, and printed materials had to be bought from abroad. Importation made them relatively expensive. The design was often poorly executed, frequently making the elephant an undefinable species of quadruped. If a simpler design were adopted, one that could be made locally, one that it would be impossible to hang improperly, the national flag, rightly displayed, could become common and universally known throughout the country.

The matter of changing the flag design was broached to government ministers. On May 27, 1916, the Minister of Marine, Prince Paribatra, and the Minister of Foreign Affairs, Prince Devawongse, collaborated on a report that advised against any flag change, at least for the moment. Their argument was based on tradition: the old flag was well known all over the world; it was highly respected by the Thai people; it was associated with the prosperity of the kingdom and the dynasty. As to the King's dissatisfaction with the execution of the elephant design, the navy could either release an approved design to foreign manufacturers or else see to the local manufacture of a suitable product.[51]

The West as Model

The matter rested for a time. The King experimented with various designs, including a pattern of red and white stripes that he ultimately rejected as too plain.

Siam's entry into World War I seems to have decided the flag matter once and for all. At a meeting of the Council of Ministers on August 18, 1917, Prince Chakrabongs announced the King's resolve to adopt a new flag and the council went along.[52] The new design, decreed on September 28, was the striped tricolor that remains the national flag of Thailand today.[53]

Vajiravudh produced the design. He found it beautiful. He found it practical. He noted that the colors—red, white, and blue—put Siam more fully in harmony with the Allied nations, Siam's brothers in arms, most of whom had standards of red, white, and blue.

The King expanded on the symbology. The colors had meaning: they represented the triumvirate of nation, faith, and king (the Thai version of "god, king, and country"), the mainstays of the united and strong Thai people. And to express his satisfaction with a deed well done, Vajiravudh wrote a poem:

> Let me speak of the meaning
> Behind the three colors.
>
> White is for purity and betokens the three gems
> And the law that guard the Thai heart.
>
> Red is for our blood, which we willingly give up
> To protect our nation and faith.
>
> Blue is the beautiful hue of the people's leader
> And is liked because of him.[54]
>
> Arranged in stripes, these three colors form the flag
> That we Thai love.
>
> Our soldiers carrying it forth to victory
> Raise up the honor of Siam.[55]

Patriotic Holidays

The court calendar of traditional Siam was replete with rites and ceremonies. Most of these ceremonies were Brahmanic in origin and were conducted within the palace; they were derived from Indian practices based on the belief that the conduct of proper rituals by the king or through his auspices would ensure prosperity.

Significant changes in the court ceremonies were brought about by King Mongkut in the mid-nineteenth century. The changes were in two main directions: first, to add Buddhist ceremonies or provide for Buddhist participation in Brahmanic ceremonies; and, second, to

The West as Model

add ceremonies giving prominence to Siam's royal house. The latter ceremonies had the effect of adding a patriotic element to what had once been exclusively magico-religious court affairs. Thus, for the first time, ceremonies were inaugurated to honor the previous monarchs of the Chakkri dynasty and to celebrate both the king's birthday and the anniversary of the king's accession. In bringing into being ceremonies of this patriotic sort, Mongkut was inspired by the practices of nations of the "progressive" West.

The changes in royal ceremony introduced by King Mongkut were continued in effect, with only periodic modifications, by Kings Chulalongkorn and Vajiravudh. Vajiravudh modified the accession anniversary program on occasion by adding to it the simultaneous celebration of other events—the opening of the Bangkok water works in 1914, the introduction of the "Rama" name in 1916, the commemoration of the armistice and League of Nations in 1919, and the honoring of Siam's military forces in 1921. And he made his birthday celebrations more elaborate than those of his predecessors, with more events scheduled and wider participation, particularly of the population in the provinces.

Vajiravudh's main contribution to the ceremonial schedule was to add two new patriotic days: Chulalongkorn Day and Chakkri Day.

Chulalongkorn Day, October 23, the anniversary of the King's death, grew out of the public festivities during his reign on his day of accession, November 16. These festivities were celebrated on an unprecedented scale in 1908, the year commemorating the fortieth anniversary of the reign, and an equestrian statue of Chulalongkorn, paid for by voluntary public subscription, was unveiled in that year. In 1910, the year of his death, November 16 continued to be celebrated, but as a day of mourning. In 1911 attention to Chulalongkorn was, of course, centered around the day of his cremation, March 16; in the fall, preparations for Vajiravudh's second coronation took precedence over everything else. By 1912 Vajiravudh had decided to preserve a special day for his father, but he chose to move the date from November to October 23, the date of Chulalongkorn's death. Chulalongkorn Day thus originated. In Bangkok the rites centered around the equestrian statue of the King, in front of which King Vajiravudh, and others, presented memorial wreaths. The tribute to Chulalongkorn was in large measure a popular and spontaneous outpouring of public sentiment, but the government supported the occasion by providing entertainments and by closing public schools for the day. The significance of the day was made clear to the school children; the *Bangkok Times* editorialized:

The West as Model

... the pupils have explained to them why the occasion is observed. It is well that youth should be taught to praise and honour the great dead; and just as Victoria Day is largely an opportunity for bringing home to youth at school something of the meaning of the British Empire, so Chulalongkorn Day may well survive to a later generation as an aid to inspire youth with the spirit which the Rulers of Siam in our time have done their utmost to foster.[56]

Special rites and festivities for Chulalongkorn Day continued throughout the Sixth Reign, and the day continues as one of Thailand's national holidays.

Chakkri Day, Vajiravudh's second contribution to the ceremonial schedule, was deliberately fostered as Siam's "National Day." The essential purpose of Chakkri Day is to pay obeisance to the deceased monarchs of the Chakkri dynasty. The practice of paying such obeisance, before statues of earlier Chakkri kings, started during the reign of King Mongkut; ceremonies of obeisance were conducted on several occasions during the year. King Vajiravudh singled out April 6, the date of the accession of the first Chakkri king, as the day on which the honoring of his predecessors was to be the central event. In 1918 the statues of the preceding five kings were moved from a building within the confines of the palace grounds, an area forbidden to the general public, to another building in the accessible precincts of the royal temple, Wat Phra Kaeo. The new site was suitably renamed Prasat Phra Thepbidon ("Palace of the Holy Ancestors"), usually called the Royal Pantheon in English.[57] On April 6, an elaborate ceremony was performed in the pantheon and the day was declared an auspicious day "both for the Chakkri Dynasty, and also for Siam as a Nation."[58] On April 7 the pantheon was opened to the public for general devotions.

In 1919 the ceremonies were repeated, and April 6 was for the first time termed Chakkri Day and observed as a national holiday.[59] The observance of Chakkri Day was thus established.

The final elevation of Chakkri Day occurred almost as an afterthought. In June 1920 the Spanish Minister for Foreign Affairs, wanting to make a list of the national days of various countries, asked Prince Charoon, the Thai minister in Paris, what day Siam celebrated as its national day. Prince Charoon could not decide whether the proper answer should be the King's Birthday (January 1), New Year's Day (April 1), or the Day of the King's Accession (November 11), so he put the question to Prince Devawongse in Bangkok.[60] Prince Devawongse proceeded to ask Vajiravudh, and the King's reply was that Charoon's three guesses were all wrong; the Thai day

The West as Model

comparable to the French July 14 or the American July 4 was April 6—Chakkri Day.[61] Perhaps because of Prince Charoon's ignorance, Chakkri Day in 1921 was preceded by an announcement from the Ministry of the Palace on the significance of the day. Also, to make the day more popular, the festivities on April 6, 1921, were made more elaborate than in prior years; they included continuous performances by military brass bands from 4:00 P.M. to sunset.[62]

"Chaiyo!"

"Hooray!" "Viva!" "Sieg Heil!" "Bravo!" "Olé!" A comparable term for expressing enthusiasm for a football team, a political leader, or a king was unknown in old Siam. There was little room in the traditional culture for such terms. Kings and other great persons were revered, not cheered.

The few occasions when popular enthusiasm could be given voice were affairs associated with religion. At the ordination rites for a young monk or at temple circumambulatory rites (*wian thian*), the mass of people might express their joy by shouting "Ho hiw!" or, to show more joy, a lengthened "Ho-o-o-o-o hiw!"

With the increase of public exposure for kings in the Western style, and the desire by kings for more "public spirit" and expressions of patriotism, the need arose for a more appropriate cheer.

If only because of his Wild Tiger appearances and speeches, Vajiravudh quickly outdistanced his father in frequency of public appearances. And in the first years of the reign, the "Ho hiw" cheer was apparently used before the King. But in January 1914, after a very important nationalistic speech to a Wild Tiger audience on the valor of the Thai ancestors, Vajiravudh instructed the Tigers in how to give a new yell, "Chaiyo!" It is probable that some experiments with the yell had already been conducted,[63] but the performance of the unfamiliar cheer was still deficient. Vajiravudh taught the Tigers how to space out the syllables, *chai—yo*, and how to deliver the cheer in unison. The Tigers ended up with a loud and clear "Chaiyo," delivered three times, that was completely to the King's satisfaction. From that time forward "Chaiyo!" became the Siamese equivalent of "Hurrah!" and was used repeatedly after the King's addresses and at his various other appearances before Wild Tigers and other groups.[64]

According to one Thai commentator, the King preferred "Chaiyo" to "Ho hiw" because the latter cheer was so closely associated with Buddhism that it did not seem proper for purely secular occasions. Other reasons may easily be imagined. For one, *chaiyo* means victory;

The West as Model

it thus had connotations well suited to the nationalistic and militaristic purposes of the King. For another, Westerners found the sounds and tonal pattern of the old yell exotic—eerie or funny rather than inspiring.[65] Vajiravudh most certainly would have been sensitive to such Western reactions, would have been anxious to adopt a yell more acceptable to Western ears.

Sports

In his search for the Western key to unlock nationalistic outpourings, King Vajiravudh came close to success in his stress on sports.

When Vajiravudh came to the throne, the status of sports in Siam contrasted sharply with that of sports in the England that the King had known as a prince. English schools, clubs, and military units all had their cricket and football teams and countless other athletic groups that vied with each other in seemingly endless matches. Final events attracted national attention and enthusiastic crowds; in 1897 a crowd of 65,000 witnessed the football contest for the English Cup played at the Crystal Palace in London. In Siam the scene was totally different. Team sports were virtually unknown. Traditional athletic events, such as *takrọ*, boxing (Thai-style), and swordplay competitions, were contests between individuals rather than groups. Individuals played as individuals and not as representatives of schools or other such social units. Although Western team sports, as well as other foreign sports such as gymnastics and jujitsu, had entered Siam by 1910, they were not widely played and attracted little attention.

Very early in the reign Vajiravudh adopted the policy of sponsoring sports and athletics as part of national policy. The training of both the Wild Tigers and the Boy Scouts included athletic events of various sorts. The English-language press commented in 1911: "At the moment physical culture seems to be becoming a matter of national interest."[66]

The reasons for the King's interest are apparent. The King strongly believed in physical fitness, hardiness, and stamina; he equated these with manliness and the "warrior" spirit that Thai men were not demonstrating to their fullest potential. Further, he believed that Thai men wasted much of their leisure—and their strength—in gambling, drinking, and even opium smoking. The government took steps to limit the accessibility of these harmful attractions; gambling dens were finally outlawed completely by 1917. But removal of corrupting and wasteful temptations was not enough; attractive and worthwhile substitutes had to be supplied. Sports and athletics were

The West as Model

decided on as those substitutes. The King pointed out that Thai soldiers, for example, had had few forms of relaxation in the past. Military training did require men to expend energy, but this was work, not fun. Drinking was one resort, but it was expensive, and it led to troubles for civilians (whose heads got broken), for the police, and for officers. The army's sponsorship of sports was providing soldiers with a new form of relaxation that was fun and not criminal.[67] Sports had advantages, furthermore, that went beyond the physical. Creation of a team of players meant greater unity for the group: it tied a school together; it made army men, or navy men, or a Wild Tiger unit, or any group represented by a team, into a unified, loyal whole. And for rival teams competing in a sportsmanlike way, it brought increased knowledge, mutual respect, and a feeling of camaraderie. After team matches had been introduced, the King commented: "The feeling of being friends and companions between soldiers and Wild Tigers arose primarily from their playing football together."[68] A final product of inculcating enthusiasm for sports, it was hoped, would be to weld the entire nation together; as the Thai interest in and proficiency in sports grew, a welling up of confidence and pride, national pride, would result. To the extent that sports could further nationalism, Vajiravudh's prime goal, it was worth a serious effort.

The first actions to promote sports were taken in the schools. On his annual visits to the Royal Pages College and to Suan Kulap School, and on his periodic visits to the War College and other Bangkok schools, the King viewed various athletic events and awarded prizes to outstanding players. The Suan Kulap visits began in January 1913,[69] and every January thereafter the King came to the school, devoting a major segment of his time there to viewing various athletic events. These events, in which athletes and teams from other schools also participated, had by 1917 grown to include three cup prizes for track contests and three for football championships.[70] On December 27 and 28, 1913, Vajiravudh spent an entire day at the Royal Pages School, arriving at 3:00 P.M. and leaving at 4:00 P.M. the following day. Much of this time was occupied in viewing athletic events. For the first time at the school a sports match was scheduled—between the Royal Pages School and King's College. While there is no proof that the King had promoted the match, he was openly pleased at seeing his two schools come together in sport and fellowship and he exhorted the students to uphold the reputations of their schools, for by so doing they would be upholding the honor of the country.[71]

Another early approach in expanding interest in sports was devel-

The West as Model

oped through the Ministry of the Interior. This approach was aimed at the provinces and was directly linked to the desire to discourage gambling. On October 28, 1913, the minister called together the lord lieutenants of the six provinces closest to Bangkok. A proclamation had been issued shortly before the meeting prohibiting "free gambling," that is to say, open public card playing, which had theretofore been allowed on the three great national holidays. The minister urged the lord lieutenants to do their utmost to "revive the national sports as a popular institution at holiday time."[72] The advice was quickly taken up. A few days after the conference, news from Nakhọn Pathom announced that a "great feature" of the celebration of the King's Accession (November 9 through 13) would be a series of athletic events. At the New Year's festivals in Ayutthaya and Phitsanulok in April 1914 similar efforts were made. The Lord Lieutenant of Ayutthaya made the new policy explicit by delivering a speech against gambling.[73] Reports from other provinces, including some concerning the third great holiday, the King's Birthday, indicate that the policy was generally and immediately put into effect.

The pro-sports policy, pursued in only moderate measures through the first five years of the reign, came flamboyantly alive in 1915. In the fall of 1915 the King became a football enthusiast. And, in immediate consequence, all of Siam was gripped by football fever.

The source of the King's sudden enthusiasm for football can only be speculated on. In the summer of 1915 he made a journey to the southern provinces. While in the South he attended a number of functions in which sports contests, including football games, were featured. Football seems to have gained, by this time, a fair amount of popularity in the South, perhaps because of the influence of the more football-conscious British colony of Malaya nearby. In any event, in late July during the later part of the King's tour, the King's attendants arranged a series of football games between teams made up of members of the royal retinue matched against teams from Nakhọn Sithammarat. The King obviously enjoyed the matches, and his ideas of utilizing sports on a national basis seem to have crystallized at this time. After seeing the football games in Nakhọn Sithammarat the King wrote:

> I am happy with this English game and wish it would spread widely. Perhaps this is because I was educated in England, but I hope you won't think this is the only reason. I hope you who are of the same race and generation as myself will agree that football will be useful to the Thai

The West as Model

people. We should help each other to make this game that the British have demonstrated the utility of endure long in Siam.[74]

Within four days after his return from the southern tour the King had arranged for a series of eight matches between various units of the Wild Tigers, the army, and the police.[75] These appear to have been test-out and practice games. By the end of the month the King, obviously feeling that his Thai boys were ready, challenged the most avid "footballers" in Siam, the British, to a match. The Thai players were to be the team of the Royal Hunters Company of Wild Tigers; the adversaries, a team of the Royal Bangkok Sports Club.[76] While the Sports Club legally and officially was not a foreign club (the King, indeed, was the club's honorary president, and Thai were free to become members), in fact the club and, in particular, its athletic activities were dominated by the British. Thus football mania in Siam was to be kicked off by a competition with a distinctly nationalistic coloration, the Thai opposed to the British.

The match took place on September 5 and resulted in a Sports Club win. But the disappointment of the Thai in the results of the match did not cool their ardor for the game. Royal high favor for football led to organization of many new teams—by the palace guards, by the police school, by teachers, by Wild Tiger units. In early September newspapers reported that "there is not a football to be bought for love or money in Bangkok."[77]

The next move by King Vajiravudh was to institute a gold cup competition for Thai teams. The competition began on September 11, 1915, and ended, three rounds and twenty-eight games later, on October 27 with the Royal Naval College team the winner of the cup. This series of matches became an annual affair; the cup was later to be named the Warrior Cup. The organization of the Warrior Cup competition brought into being a King's Cup Committee to supervise the event. The committee also issued a brochure that spoke of Vajiravudh's "aim in giving special encouragement to the game of football. The King wisely desires to promote in every way opportunities for healthy open-air exercise, and considers football to be a game suitable for the development of the nation's manhood and warrior spirit."[78]

In November yet another organization was created, the Football Association of Siam, which was to serve as the general governing body for football affairs. Vajiravudh became patron of the association, and his favorite courtier, Phraya Prasit (later to become Čhaophraya Ram), its president. The Football Association of Siam, as its first task,

The West as Model

organized yet another cup competition, the King's Gold Cup, to be played for by a team representing the association and a team of the Royal Bangkok Sports Club. This game was to be preceded by still another match between Thai and Westerners organized by the Sports Club for the Sports Club's own cup. In 1915 the King's Cup contest ended in a draw and the Sports Club cup went to the Siamese team. On the Siamese victory the English-language press commented: "His Majesty was really delighted with the result.... There was no mistaking the popularity of yesterday's win.... The big crowd went away thoroughly happy."[79] The final match of 1915, also sponsored by the Sports Club, was for the club's Pollard Cup. The round of games started on December 24 and ended on January 6, 1916. The Siamese team also won this contest, handily and gratifyingly.

The King played a prominent role in the actual work of promoting football—the organizing of teams, arranging of matches, and awarding of cups. And a very significant part of the popular enthusiasm came from the King's display of direct interest by his constant attendance at games. In the Warrior Cup series of twenty-eight games scheduled almost daily from September 11 to October 27, the King went to every game but the last, and that game was played on the day after the championship had been won.[80] On more than one occasion Vajiravudh watched in pouring rain, staying until the last whistle. In 1915 he personally presented the winning prize at all cup events and gave special medals to players of the winning teams. There is little doubt that he considered football not only good for Siam but also good fun for himself. The King's interest drew other high dignitaries, princes and nobles, to the games. Even the Queen Mother came to one match, to have "a look at the game which is now rousing so much enthusiasm."[81]

The character of the football season in Siam was fairly well set in the first year of play in 1915. The essential matches were the Warrior Cup competition to determine the Siamese champions, and the two "international" competitions, the Sports Club cup and the King's Gold Cup. Other all-Thai matches, for a junior cup and a senior cup, were added. There was some desire to internationalize the game further by engaging in matches with foreign teams. When a British warship, the *Whiting*, came on a visit to Bangkok in September 1918, a match was quickly arranged between the British navy team and a team representing the Siamese navy. The match, held on September 12, was attended by "a huge crowd." The game, after "a hard, ding dong struggle," ended in a tie; the crowd was not displeased, and

The West as Model

the match was called "one of the happiest and most successful events in the present naval visit."[82] There was some discussion periodically of arranging matches with teams in British Malaya. In 1917 a Penang team, saying it had heard of "the ability the Siamese have shown in the game since His Majesty the King showed his personal interest in it," suggested the visit of a "Siamese eleven" to Malaya and the Straits Settlements.[83] The Thai did not follow up on this suggestion. A more precise suggestion was made in 1919 by a Bangkok businessman who proposed to the King's secretary that a Siamese team play a Chinese team from the Straits Settlements.[84] The proposal was put to the Football Association, which decided against the match on political grounds. Playing a "Chinese" team, the association concluded, would tend to crystallize racial feelings in Bangkok; local Chinese, who were coming to feel more and more "Thai," might be impelled to sympathize with the foreigners. A truly representative foreign team, including Westerners, Chinese, and Indians, would be an entirely different matter.[85] The proposal thus was politely declined as "too premature."[86]

Royal promotion of football continued unabated in 1916. For example, of a series of games played on October 18, 22, 24, 25, 27, 28, and 31 and November 1, 3, and 6, the King missed only two games.[87] He was present at all cup games. By 1917 royal attendance began to drop off, but by this time football had definitely caught the public fancy, and games continued to attract large and enthusiastic crowds through the remainder of the reign.

The aim of using football to counteract public apathy was certainly achieved. But not always in the manner intended. On one occasion in 1915 the King had stated:

> In my opinion, there is nothing that helps the formation of friendship more than taking part in or watching of sports and games, since there is that absence of formality which characterizes more serious functions, and people who meet in the field of sport become friends more readily than at more formal gatherings. Friendship thus begun without the feeling of constraint is more likely to be lasting than otherwise.... [88]

And in a government booklet on football appeared the words:

> Football is a clean and open fight, not an occasion for taking unfair or secret advantage which is the essence of meanness. Neither in victory nor in defeat ought there to be any thought of revenge on the one side or of jeering at the vanquished on the other. That is to say, Football is a game which steadies a man and makes him a sportsman.[89]

The West as Model

Such ideals proved easier to proclaim than to realize. In Siam's first football year the competition for the King's Gold Cup between the Thai and the British saw displays of temper and "a determination to win anyhow" that went beyond sportsmanship.[90] Said one paper of the game, "the less said the better."[91] One columnist, less reluctant to comment, wrote of spectator involvement, strained relations, "good fellowship" turned sour, and "very ugly remarks" against both sides, and recommended that games between the nationalities be abandoned.[92] It is noteworthy that the next game the Thai played against a Sports Club team was noted for its excessive gentleness, leading the press to wonder if "some one" had "whispered" to the Thai players.[93]

In succeeding years there were periodic reports of excessive zeal and partisanship, particularly in games between rival Thai teams. While overexuberance between Thai and Westerners could be looked on as contributing to a nationalistic arousal, bitter rivalries and divisions among Thai teams could hardly be seen in the same light. Most games seem to have been fairly played, but on occasion there were ugly displays and even violence. The most violent outburst occurred on August 17, 1919, on the occasion of a playoff for the senior cup between the Royal Pages and the Naval Cadets. The press called the game a disgrace, with fouls occurring every minute of the game; it reported that the Cadets, urged on by the crowd, played liked "a band of hooligans." When the crowd began to encroach on the field in support of their losing favorites, the referee called the game. The crowd then got ugly, throwing bricks and stones and injuring several people, including the referee.[94]

The August 17 game marked the nadir of football in Siam and revealed several problems aside from that of inculcating the British kind of sportsmanship ethics. The main problem seems to have derived from partisanship of the King himself. The King, forgetting his nationalistic objective, identified himself with certain teams. One was the team of the Royal Pages, directed by Phraya Prasit, who was also President of the Football Association of Siam. The Pages team was very good. Two years earlier, after winning a crucial game, it had had its win disqualified on the basis of an infraction of the rules. Vajiravudh was privately incensed at the decision. The Pages, in a pique, even left the Football Association for a time.[95] The influential backing the Royal Pages received permitted them to organize an expert team, and good football players were deliberately recruited to join the Pages so they could add to the strength of the team.[96] The end product of this favoritism—and favoritism for the Pages, as one Thai pointed out, had been the cause of trouble in Siam earlier in the reign[97]—was to arouse strong antagonism to the Royal Pages team.

Several changes followed the episode of August 17: Phraya Prasit resigned as president of the Football Association; navy teams were royally reprimanded. Eventually, much of the bad feeling wore away.

All in all, it appears that encouragement of football and other sports did succeed to a degree in furthering Vajiravudh's goals. Western observers at the time were impressed. A long-time British resident concluded that " . . . by the end of the second season [1917], the enormous crowds of people of every age and rank, shouting themselves hoarse and sometimes breaking the ropes even in the presence of royalty, showed conclusively the entire success of this device for dispelling the erstwhile apathy."[98] An American writer was even more sweeping in his praise. In an article in the *New York Times* the writer gave full credit to the English-educated Vajiravudh for deliberately introducing football as an instrument of national policy. And the policy had worked, he said: football, together with the Boy Scout movement, had "made over" the Thai nation; it had changed the youth "from a life of enervation and luxury to one of vigorous athletic competition"; it had produced a "moral regeneration that reduced to a minimum the two greatest vices of Siam," opium and gambling; it had awakened the Siamese youth to a "patriotic impulse and a sense of national obligation."[99]

The American writer undoubtedly went too far and claimed too much. But some claim for sports is justified. Never before in Siam's history had masses of thousands of people gathered to cheer on "their side," to dare cheers even at the risk of incurring royal displeasure. Feelings were aroused, mostly in Bangkok but to some extent also in the provinces. Not all these feelings were nationalistic or patriotic in a broad sense. But some were. And almost all feelings of loyalty to a group larger than a family were new to Siam and could be built upon to fashion national patriotism.

Status of Women

In furthering the cause of nationalism, women in Siam came into the King's program in two principal respects. First, Vajiravudh felt strongly that women as well as men must be imbued with a sense of nation. Second, he believed that the status of women in Thai society should be elevated so that Thai women could be compared favorably with their sisters in the West. In both respects, Western ideas affected the King's attitude.

The West as Model

Insofar as nationalism was concerned, the main thrust of the King's arguments seemed to be directed toward men. When Vajiravudh used terms such as "warrior spirit," he obviously had men in mind. He, therefore, on occasion made special reference to women so that no one would assume that the need for nationalism was confined to men. Such references appear in several of his plays, essays, and speeches. Women, he made clear, should also love their nation. And this love could be expressed in a number of ways. In wartime, for example, women could serve as nurses. Women could also contribute to fund drives such as that for the cruiser fund. Says one heroine: "I am a woman. I cannot be a soldier or a Wild Tiger. Since I cannot pay homage to His Majesty with the strength of my body, I must do so with money."[100] Vajiravudh's heroine understands the reasons behind her devotion to her country: "Although I'm only a woman, I've sense enough to see that if our Thai nation is destroyed, that will be the end of us Thai."[101] The heroine is even willing to defy her husband, who is opposed to nationalistic fund drives; she thus exhibits, with the obvious approval of the royal author, that devotion to nation outranks devotion to one's spouse.[102] The principal way in which women could exhibit their nationalism, however, in the King's view, was by doing a good job at their main work in the home. They should provide their husbands with happy and comfortable surroundings so that the men could at work apply themselves to their fullest capacities.[103] They should teach their children proper values, including love of nation.[104] And in times of stress they should support their menfolk, never undermining their bravery or willingness to fight.[105]

On the status of women, Vajiravudh's policy had several circumstances in its favor. First, the traditional position of women in Thai society was high. It was a fact that the vast majority of Thai women, those of the countryside, had social rights and status equal to men in all important respects. Most Westerners were convinced that such women occupied "as high and honourable a position as the women of the people in any country."[106] In the words of one contemporary Britisher: "... the women of the lower orders have always enjoyed absolute freedom."[107] The King knew this and commented that the equal status of women in rural areas meant that, in this respect, "our Thai country people are much closer to 'civilization' than people in Bangkok or large towns."[108] Another favorable circumstance was that some steps toward the elevation of upper-class women had already been taken during Chulalongkorn's reign. Queen Saowapha had been

The West as Model

much honored by the King; she had emerged out of the harem to take part in various public functions, and she had established girls' schools and sponsored the training of Thai nurses.

Although Vajiravudh was able to build on programs of the past, he moved much more boldly than his father had. The King's interest was apparent as early as his coronation, and Thai women were called upon to play a role in court functions of the time "to an extent that took their own breath away and astonished the public."[109]

Vajiravudh made the purpose of his reforms in the status of women abundantly clear, and in doing so he also made clear his reliance on ideas of the West. The status of women in a society, he stated in an essay specifically on the subject, is a symbol of the degree of civilization in that society.[110] Where women are elevated, there is civilization; where they are not—where they are slaves, workhorses, or chattels of men—there is not. The "jungle people" of Malaya, Borneo, and Africa, he said, treat their women as slaves. In England, by way of contrast, men and women are more or less on equal terms. In ancient India, noted for its high civilization, men and women were equal in many respects; the decline of India coincided with the coming of the Muslims and the degradation of women, including the imposition of purdah. The history of mankind was spotted with the record of men's mistreatment of women. In some societies men took many wives. In some, men even ensured their hold on women by resorting to extraordinarily cruel tactics such as the footbinding in China that made it impossible for women to run away. Men even used religion as a weapon; men, the priests, instructed women to be acquiescent as part of their religious duty. While Buddhism, said the King, included no such religious instruction, in other ways Siamese women of the upper class were taken advantage of by men. And foreigners criticized the Thai for their treatment of women. The King concluded:

> This situation is most shameful! Are we Thai so callous—with the hide of an elephant or a rhinocerous—that we are not disturbed? Even if you yourself are not a bad person as are some of our nationality, and many of them are nobles, shouldn't you help by speaking up and complaining? Can you silently look on while the outside world speaks of our customs as those of a jungle people? Please understand that others are taking our measure! Please do think this over.[111]

In his essay on the status of women, Vajiravudh enumerated two major and two minor restrictions on Thai women. The major restrictions were the limited freedom women had to socialize with men on equal terms and the practice of polygamy. The minor restrictions were women's black teeth (a consequence of betel chewing) and their short hair styles. In other writings, the King added one other major restriction, limited access to education, and one other minor restriction, the wearing of the trouserlike *phanung*.

The King's desire that women be given freedom to meet and mix with men socially was evidenced in word and deed. He deplored the argument that men had put forth that, if women attended public affairs together with men, they might become exposed to suspicion and become objects of gossip. He sarcastically remarked that there was indeed some danger of giving women a chance to meet men: they might find out just what special creatures men really were![112] To promote social intercourse between men and women, the King regularly included women in theater parties and other social affairs he attended. His half-sister, Princess Walai, frequently accompanied him to such affairs.

In November 1920 Vajiravudh became formally betrothed to Princess Vallabha Devi, a daughter of Prince Naradhip. Although this betrothal ended in an annulment four months later, the alliance with the Princess, and with other women who followed, gave the King an opportunity to set an example for elite society. The Princess during the four-month engagement went everywhere with the King. The press reported some twenty-seven functions they attended together, including dinner parties, theater performances, horse races, school inspections, and football matches.[113] By this tactic His Majesty gave a royal nod in favor of the association of the sexes.

One innovation in Bangkok elite circles that created quite a stir in the 1920s was Western social dancing. The Teachers Club staged a debate on the subject early in 1920, and a less formal debate continued to be waged in the columns of the local press, both Thai and English.[114] The pros argued for dancing as a means of promoting social intercourse; the cons protested that dancing would lead only to the further degradation of Thai women. One Thai writer editorialized that Europeans "know how to behave when dancing; we don't."[115] While the argument continued, social dancing apparently became increasingly popular. Although the King took no part in the debate, nor, as far as is known, on the dance floor either, the government-sponsored annual fair did provide a dancing hall, which "helped on the movement,"[116] and the King and his fiancée did attend dance exhibitions (one on October 30, 1920, in which a Thai couple displayed the steps of the foxtrot and tango)[117] and formal balls. (The press had

The West as Model

noted at the time of the betrothal that Her Royal Highness was "fond of dancing.")[118] Again, the sign of royal approval was unmistakable. By early 1921, Bangkok society was in the grip of a "dancing craze," and the annual fair provided a dance hall "on a much larger scale than formerly."[119] Even after the displays of royal favor, arguments on dancing continued. But so did the dance.

Opponents of Thai social dancing relied heavily on the argument that in a polygamous society in which women were not given proper respect, dancing became but another means for men to extend their sway over women.[120] Discussions of dancing, indeed, seemed inevitably to lead to discussions of polygamy; one Thai correspondent suggested that the Teachers Club debate on dancing give way to a debate on the Siamese practice of keeping lesser wives.[121]

The King, however, kept the two subjects separate. He approved of dancing; he strongly disapproved of polygamy. Polygamy had been one Thai practice that had consistently aroused Western antipathy. And Siamese kings, starting with Vajiravudh's grandfather, had been on the defensive about the practice.[122] Vajiravudh, at once more familiar with Western notions of propriety and more anxious than any of his predecessors to excise customs that Westerners regarded as barbaric or uncivilized, spoke out frequently against Thai multiple marriages.

In an important essay of 1915 on the conceptual "cakes of mud" that were clogging the wheels of Siam's national progress, the King devoted many pages to problems in the area of marriage and the family.[123] He castigated "temporary marriage," that is, informal cohabitation, as a custom that encouraged promiscuity, gave no security to women, and was subversive to morality. He wrote: "Have pity on our women and girls! Help them to obtain some justice and equality. Help them to become honoured as the future mothers of our nation." He castigated the "parental irresponsibility" that resulted from temporary marriages in which the partners, having joined together for sexual enjoyment, gave little heed to "their duty to bring up their children so as to become useful members of the community, and good, loyal citizens of Siam." And lastly, he castigated "traffic in young women," which he described as a new fashion worse than polygamy. The old custom had been for a well-to-do man to have a principal wife and, in the same household, a number of female servants who also served as lesser wives. The new custom favored by the "modern young Siamese" who claimed to be opposed to polygamy was to acquire a number of secret wives, often by paying the parents for them. The old custom had the virtue of being a more or less permanent arrangement; the new custom was highly temporary. Wealthy men simply used young, ignorant girls, tossing them off when they tired of them.

At one time the King suggested that improvement in the status of women would require "a correction of both the customs and laws of the country."[124] With respect to change in customs, the King hoped that his writings urging men to behave, urging parents to care for their children and not sell their daughters, urging women not to "marry" a man who kept wives the way a farmer kept chickens would have some effect.[125] On the matter of legal change, there was much discussion and thought, but in the end no law emerged.

The legal discussions reveal the King's mind exceptionally well. The King first aired his views on the need for some marriage legislation in January 1912 in a private discussion with Prince Damrong and Prince Devawongse.[126] The Princes agreed on the need, and by June 1913 M. Padoux, the legal adviser, had drawn up a draft code to which the King reacted with extensive comments.[127] The most significant aspect of the code was that it did not outlaw polygamy, and Vajiravudh, despite his personal preference for monogamy, approved. A marriage code, he said, should not reflect the King's "personal convenience" alone. A marriage code, above all, had to reflect realities, and the reality in Siam was that polygamy existed, it had long existed, it would not cease to exist automatically on the passage of a law. Some councillors, Prince Svasti for one, disagreed with the King and advocated the institution of monogamy at least on paper. The King was vehemently opposed to a law for show:

> Finally, I beg to express an emphatic opinion, that if we are going to practice Polygamy, there is no need to hide it, but if it is thought best to hide it, then do not practice it at all. It would be better to act so than to act the Pious Old Tiger; in other words, let us not be hypocrites.

Vajiravudh marshalled other arguments. A law against polygamy, he said, would antagonize the Thai nationals in the southern provinces who were Muslim. He wrote: "I do not wish to do anything, which would force my Malay subjects of Patani and Satul to run away from the harshness of our laws, to seek refuge under the more equitable laws of the English, who (very wisely) do not interfere with the marriage customs of their subjects." As to the plea for monogamy on moral grounds, Vajiravudh wrote that the issue was by no means clear, that Buddhism did not consider plural marriage immoral, that European and Siamese moral values were too different to be compared, and that "it is most difficult to judge who is on the higher plane and who on the lower."

One modification of marital practice the King did support was the civil registration of marriages. It was true that lesser wives were disadvantaged and exploited, but through institution of marriage registration such wives would acquire status and protection by law. The law might, further, adopt the principle, which already had some social sanction, that "all children of a man, no matter by which kind of wife, should be recognized as his legitimate children...." In this way, the King wrote, "we Siamese would then actually be going in advance of Europe in the way of providing justice for children!" By September 4, 1913, a draft "Law on Family Registration" had been prepared, incorporating the King's ideas by making no mention of monogamy but including a system of registration.

No marriage code, however, was enacted during the reign. Indications are that the King was unwilling to assume full responsibility for a decision on such a delicate matter. And none of his councillors seemed anxious to share the burden. In a meeting of the Council of Ministers on June 4, 1917, for example, a tentative decision was made to send the draft to the Legislative Council (Ratthamontri Sapha). The problem was that the Legislative Council chairman (Prince Rabi) had resigned and no satisfactory replacement was willing to serve.[128] The matter seems to have been permanently deferred at this point.

There was one other approach open to His Majesty to bring about a change in Thai marriage custom: setting the example for others to follow. This approach, indeed, had been suggested to King Mongkut in 1853 by an American missionary. Mongkut had claimed the times were not right, and he had walked away. Vajiravudh did not walk away. He fully intended to set an example of monogamy for his people. On November 10, 1920, he announced his betrothal to the Princess Vallabha Devi, and ten days later, at a party given for the King and his fiancée by Thai students who had studied abroad, he publicly announced his decision to take but one wife.[129]

The King did not adhere to his decision. His desire to set a moral example was outweighed by his desire for an heir. In fact, there is considerable reason to suppose that the only reason he married at all was to provide the dynastic line with a suitable and indisputable successor, a son of his own. The text of the annulment of his betrothal to Princess Vallabha Devi on March 15, 1921, owing to their "incompatibility of temperament," said as much. It said that His Majesty, in proclaiming his betrothal, "had no other desire than firmly and definitely to ensure the succession to the Throne with a view to the

The West as Model

good of the country, the welfare of the Royal House as well as the happiness of His Majesty's Own Person."[130] The fact that the King, whatever his reasons may have been, had failed to contract any alliances with women until shortly before his fortieth year was in itself indication that policy rather than passion motivated him. His continued bachelorhood, "regarded by the people as a national calamity,"[131] must have seemed indeed tinged with possible calamity as, one by one, his full brothers began to die off. By August 1925 there remained only himself and Prajadhipok, and Prajadhipok's health had never been good. There were, of course, half-brothers, but the feeling that the line would best be preserved by remaining with the sons of Queen Saowapha was strong.

Four women succeeded Princess Vallabha Devi. Princess Lakshmi Lavan was elevated to the rank of Royal Highness in September 1921 and became consort in August 1922. Two sisters were ennobled as concubines, one with the title of Phra Sucharit Suda in October 1921 and the other with the title of Phra Indrasakti Sachi in June 1922. Phra Indrasakti, who reportedly had several pregnancies ending in miscarriages, was elevated to queen late in 1922, but was demoted from that rank in September 1925. The last wife, Suvadana, was named consort and raised to royal status in October 1925, during the eighth month of her pregnancy. Princess Suvadana bore the King a daughter, Princess Bejaratana, on November 24, 1925, thirty-six hours before Vajiravudh's death. Since tradition and the King's own testament on succession ruled out female succession to the throne, Prajadhipok, the King's last remaining full brother, who was named in the testament as his successor, came to the throne on November 25.

A third major restriction on Thai women was their limited access to education. Tradition had encouraged that boys receive the rudiments of learning in temple schools. These schools were not open to girls. School education for females, supported by Western missionaries and some Thai, most notably Queen Saowapha, had started some years before 1910, but the educational opportunities for females were still severely limited. Vajiravudh was determined to advance the status of women in this respect. One significant step taken early in the reign to promote education for females was the opening of Siam's first teachers' training college for women in December 1913.[132] A Ministry of Religious Affairs and Education report for 1917–18, pointing to the serious lag in female education, stated that 7,411 girls were in school as compared with 389,806 boys.[133] The King, in his birthday speech of 1918, had declared: "The question of female education is one of importance and necessity in view of the fact that to women belongs the care of children from infancy and the work of teaching and training them while in the home."[134] And in a didactic poem on the virtues of women, Vajiravudh devoted several stanzas to women's need for learning as an ornament more valuable than beauty or wealth: "For knowledge runs deep like a branch of the Indus / Which no amount of bailing can ever empty."[135] Perhaps as a consequence of the King's interest, the Ministry of Education in 1918 exhibited a "new interest" in education for girls and cited a new policy of allowing girls up to the age of twelve to attend government schools for boys.[136]

The most important step, however, in advancing the education of women was taken in 1921. The Elementary Education Act of that year, which set forth the principle of compulsory primary education, made no distinction between the sexes. The act stipulated that, in all areas in which the law came into force, every boy and every girl was required to attend school.[137] The effects of the law were dramatic: the percentage of girls in school skyrocketed from 7 percent in 1921 to 29 percent in 1922 and reached 38 percent in 1925.[138]

The minor hindrances to the progress of women in Siam—hair styles, dress fashions, and tooth color—were obviously all in the category of appearance. Vajiravudh looked on Thai women with Western eyes and found the old styles distinctly unattractive. He wrote: "Every book I have read by a Western writer has commented on the great oddity that, for whatever reason, women cut their hair short. And they state that many Thai women would be very pretty except for their short hair which makes them ugly." On the Thai women's preference for betel-stained black teeth, he wrote that it had "long been a subject of foreign criticism" and added: "I myself very much detest black teeth."[139] What Westerners thought was obviously of great importance to the King. What Westerners thought became fact to him, so that traditional Thai fashions were seen not as fashions but as facts that could be explained only as deliberate devices fostered by Thai men to keep their women in bondage. Thai men, he said, wanted to keep their women unattractive so that they could hold them back better.[140] And so, the King reasoned, whatever he could do to help Thai women improve their appearance would forward the emancipation of women.

The King's ideas on fashion were translated into action by the women with whom he associated. His favorite half-sister and sometime companion, Princess Walai, was one of the first Thai women to wear her hair long,[141] and long hair "under the personal influence of His Majesty" became the favored style.[142] The King's first fiancée,

The West as Model

Princess Vallabha Devi, established the skirtlike *phasin* as the style to be favored over the trouserlike *phanung*. The Princess first wore the *phasin* at a party on November 23, 1920. It was an immediate success. One newspaper rhapsodized that the day would "go down in history" as the day a new fashion was set for the ladies of Siam.[143] By the end of 1920 the *phasin* had become the "national dress" for women.[144] The *phasin* was a fine compromise from a nationalistic point of view. It looked like a skirt, it was pleasing to Western eyes, but it was a genuine Thai style that had long been favored by women in the northern provinces. It had an additional advantage over Western dress in that it did not have to be imported. Promoters of the *phasin* were aware that they were not putting Thai weavers and sewers at a disadvantage.

One female fashion developed late in the reign that had nothing whatsoever to do with Thai tradition: the wearing of hats. The hats of the day were large and floppy brimmed. At their first appearance in late 1920 a letter to the editor of the *Bangkok Times* pleaded that Siam be spared "the glorious, and notorious, hat of the European one million varieties on Siamese Ladies heads."[145] Siam was not to be spared: the appearance of the King's companions "gloriously" behatted put the new Western mode beyond censure.

The fashion reforms sponsored by the King were eminently successful from all points of view. An article in the army magazine summed up the effects: the hair and dress styles of the King's companions, as expected, were imitated widely, for "what the upper class do, the lower class will follow"; the new styles won general Thai approbation, for they tended to put "the Siamese lady more on a level with ladies of the West"; and, as for the Westerners' reaction, "the Europeans all smile approval."[146]

Education

Taken in its broadest possible sense, education was the main concern of King Vajiravudh. For his strongest aim was to educate his nation to its nationhood. His speeches, his writings, and many of his projects, including the Wild Tigers, the Boy Scouts, and the pro-sports activities, were all educational. They were meant to teach his people the values of hardiness, self-reliance, and industry for their own good and for the good of the nation. Given this didactic bent, it would be surprising if the King had not also been keenly interested in education in its more restricted usual sense. He was.

Royal concern for education did not start in the Sixth Reign. In a sense, support for education was part of Thai tradition in that

The West as Model

aid to the monastic order was a recognized obligation and the order provided young boys with the rudiments of learning. This traditional aid to education was expanded by King Rama IV, who instituted the beginnings of modern (i.e., Western) education by bringing Western tutors into the palace, and further expanded by Rama V, who adopted the principle of public education for the masses and began to construct a school system to put that principle into effect. In the main King Vajiravudh was a continuer of educational policies already started. But some features of his program for education bore unmistakable signs of his nationalistic purpose.

A measure of the King's strong espousal of education can be seen in his declaration that he regarded the building of a school as an act of Buddhist merit and that, in fact, he would not follow the practice of his predecessors and build a new royal temple as a meritorious act but would, instead, build schools. The first formal declaration in favor of schools by Vajiravudh grew out of a request from a noble who had built a school and asked His Majesty to dedicate it. The King wrote: "Well done. I am certain that this meritorious act will yield better results than the building of a temple for the shelter of sham monks who don yellow robes in order to escape their obligations." The King asked the Minister of Education to prepare a royal declaration that "If anyone wishes to make merit, achieve beneficial ends, and please His Majesty, let him build schools. To build new temples is not to my liking."[147] The declaration was prepared and issued by August 1911.[148]

The King's declaration was accompanied by action. By June 1911 he had established a new private school under royal patronage and supported by the privy purse. The school, which had its precedent in the school for pages at Saranrom Palace, was called Royal Pages College (Rongrian Mahatlek Luang). It was expected to be "a model school for the Kingdom,"[149] whose exemplary ideals and practices would spread, in the utopian fashion, throughout Siam. In fact two other schools followed the model of the Royal Pages College: King's College in Bangkok, which had been a special school under the Ministry of Justice and came under the King's patronage in 1916;[150] and a new school, the Royal Pages College of Chiangmai, set up on the same lines late in 1917.[151] The original Royal Pages College was given a large piece of land near the King's Chitralada Palace, and temporary structures built in the early years were later replaced by elaborate permanent buildings in a modified temple style. The complex came to be, in effect, the memorial "temple" of King Vajiravudh; after his death the school was renamed Vajiravudh College in his honor.[152]

Royal Support for Education. A cartoon by the King to advertise the 1919 Winter Fair, the proceeds of which were designated to support the Royal Pages College. The original drawing by the King was sold to help raise funds for the college. The advertisement appeared in *Dusit samit*; the original text was in Thai.

The West as Model

Many of the King's notions on education were put into effect at the Royal Pages College. The school was deliberately organized on the lines of an English public school: it was a boarding school with teachers living in; it had several houses; lower classmen were expected to serve upper classmen. The aim was to produce an educational environment that promoted not only book learning but total mental, physical, and moral training for boys and young men. Vajiravudh stated explicitly that he did not want "walking school books" but "*manly* young men, honest, truthful, clean in habits and thoughts." He wanted a school that would turn "a boy into a fine young man and a good citizen."[153] The King took a personal interest in the school; he appointed its masters and visited it several times a year. He gave talks at the school twice a year—in November near the anniversary of his coronation, and in May at the *wisakhabucha* ceremonies (ceremonies commemorating the anniversary of the birth, enlightenment, and death of the Buddha). The November speeches stressed the importance of education, the need to respect and obey the masters, the overriding necessity for adherence to high ethical standards.[154] The *wisakhabucha* speeches were usually in the style of sermons on the values of Buddhism and the ways to be a good Buddhist.[155] These and other speeches the King gave to school audiences also contained nationalistic messages urging the boys to fulfill their duties to the nation by improving their knowledge, exercising their bodies, and observing proper moral behavior. "A country's advancement," he said, "depends on its education," and Siam's advancement depended on a youth with education, morality, and national devotion superior to those of their fathers. Siam, he said, had to advance in order to survive, for, with the continued advancement of other nations in the world, to stand still was to fall behind.[156]

The main means of inculcating nationalism among students, however, was not to make speeches directly on the subject but rather to stimulate a school spirit that would become the building block for national spirit. The English concept that "no one can love his country who does not love his school"[157] seems to have been absorbed by Vajiravudh as his own. The theory of larger loyalties developing out of smaller loyalties was one of the King's abiding faiths; it was the theory behind the moves to strengthen the family and to create groups such as the Wild Tigers and Boy Scouts. Out of loyalty to a smaller group—family, club, team, or school—would grow group solidarity, regard for the interests of one's fellows, willingness to make concessions, discipline, and other virtues essential for the true expression of loyalty to the nation. So within the Royal Pages College small sodalities—houses, debating teams, athletic teams—were fostered. These groups competed with each other. In encountering the world outside the school, however, school fellows were expected to act as one. To promote such a school spirit, schoolboys wore special identifying dress and competed with other schools in athletic and other events. As boarders, the boys were expected to regard the school as home, with their teachers serving as father substitutes. The honor and good name of the school, the boys were repeatedly told, depended on the good behavior of each. By contributing to the good name of the school the boys were serving their own best interests and the interests of their school, their nation, and their king. As graduates of a "good school" the boys would have earned a passport to a favorable reception in the world outside.[158]

One other school associated with the Sixth Reign was Chulalongkorn University. It was formally inaugurated as Siam's first university in 1917. The basis for the university, however, had been laid many years earlier in the civil service training school in the Ministry of Interior. Early in his reign, King Vajiravudh decided to enlarge this school to serve all ministries, to support it with the surplus of money subscribed by the people for the equestrian statue of King Chulalongkorn, and to rename it King Chulalongkorn's Civil Service College.[159] By 1915 a campus had been donated by the King and buildings begun. Vajiravudh seems not to have been deeply involved personally in the details of the university, leaving its organization to an expert board of governors headed by Prince Damrong, but he did support the board and undoubtedly took pride in the prestige of presiding over the establishment of Siam's first Western-style university.

Probably the most noted educational achievement of the reign was the enactment of a compulsory Primary Education Act in September 1921. The act was a logical development from successive educational steps taken in the reign of King Chulalongkorn. By 1910 the fundamental decisions had been made for the organization of provincial schools under the Ministry of Interior, for reliance on local committees and local financing of schools, and for the eventual institution of compulsory education. The records show that in promoting public education King Vajiravudh did not assume personal leadership but relied heavily on an energetic, Western-educated official, Čhaophraya Thammasakmontri,[160] who had already emerged as a prominent consultant on educational matters to King Chulalongkorn during the last years of his reign. Čhaophraya Thammasak was appointed Minister of Religious Affairs and Education in 1915, and, on the reorganization of the ministry in 1920, became Minister of Education. He seems to have been primarily responsible for most of the changes in education, such as the institution of model schools in every *amphoe* ("district") in the country and the creation of district educational promoters (*thammakan amphoe*), that led to the adoption of the compulsory Primary Education Act.[161]

The act, which was to come into effect on October 1, 1921, called for compulsory attendance at school of all boys and girls from the age of seven to fourteen. Noncompliance with the act could result in heavy penalties. All schools, whether supported by the national government, local communities, or private bodies, were to adhere to standards set by the Ministry of Education for syllabus, length of term, textbooks, and the like. National and local schools were to be tuition free, supported in the capital and in impoverished areas by the government and in most provincial areas by a school poll tax and voluntary contributions. Although the act was to come into effect on October 1, it was never intended that on that date, or indeed on any specific date, the full force of the act would come into effect. Indeed it could not. There simply were not enough schools or teachers to make total compliance with compulsory education possible. The act was initially limited to certain village groups (*tambon*) where reasonably adequate facilities existed. These groups were specified; by the end of 1922 they totalled 45.76 percent of the village groups in the country.[162] Furthermore, even in these village groups enforcement of the act was not made automatic for all members of the age groups specified. Students who lived too far from a school were exempted. And in areas where facilities were limited, only children in the higher age brackets were required to go to school.[163]

The act did not revolutionize mass education in Siam. It was not intended to. Most of its provisions were in fact already in effect in the areas in which it was first applied.[164] The act more than anything else signified the coming of age of the idea of public education. Commitment to the ideal of free public education for all the people was confirmed.

Public education received one new impulse during the Sixth Reign that did closely reflect the King's concepts. This impulse was toward practical education, training in arts and crafts, rather than just book learning. Schemes for vocational training had been drawn up as early as 1899, but it was not until the Sixth Reign that the first vocational school was started. The School of Arts and Crafts was formally opened by the King early in 1914, and over the years he periodically visited

The West as Model

the school, admired students' workmanship, awarded prizes, and in other ways showed particular royal favor for this aspect of education.[165] The main object of the school was to help revive the traditional handicrafts of Siam. But emphasis on practical skills went beyond the establishment of special schools; the curriculum in all schools reflected this new concern. The basic curriculum of five years was divided into two parts, the first three years retaining "ordinary school studies," the last two years concentrating on useful studies such as carpentry, tailoring, and farming.[166]

The need to make education relevant to Siam's farm population was frequently enunciated by the King and the Minister of Education. In presenting his report on discussions of the draft act on compulsory education, the minister pointed out that, while a certain level of general education was needed by the population at large, after Siam's school children had learned the basics they would best serve their own interests and the interests of the nation by acquiring special skills in agriculture, handicrafts, and business. Siam was essentially an agricultural nation; its progress depended upon advances in agriculture. Therefore, "It is necessary that we begin to train people to acquire knowledge in the agricultural field and to increase respect for agricultural pursuits." And so with crafts and with business. If the Thai were ever going to be able to compete with foreigners, specifically Chinese immigrants, in such fields, they must gain the requisite knowledge in school. The Thai had aptitudes and capabilities enough; they merely lacked the opportunity to develop those capabilities.[167]

The earlier educational emphasis on training for government service was deplored by both Vajiravudh and Chaophraya Thammasak. Such education was producing "a nation of clerks." It stimulated farm boys to leave the farms. It led to the abandonment of business and the trades to foreigners. The Thai weakness for "clerkism" was criticized by the King in more than one essay. He went into the subject most fully in an essay of 1915[168] in which he stated:

> Any man with a grain of commonsense must surely understand that for a country like Siam, the agriculturist and cultivator is much more likely to contribute to her wealth than the clerk, who after all is as much an instrument as the pen or typewriter that he uses (or misuses). As a producer his value is very low in comparison to what he consumes. And yet the clerk thinks himself superior to the farmer, and the worst of it is that we others go on allowing him to think it too!
>
> When will our young men understand that it is quite as honourable to be a farmer, a cultivator, or an artisan, as it is to be a quill-driver?[169]

The West as Model

The King laid the blame for clerkism in part on the schools but principally on the society at large. He deplored the general attitude of according more prestige to the lowliest and least efficient paper shuffler, who would willingly "starve on a beggarly" salary in order to live in the "gaiety of the City," than to the "*active* producers of wealth for the country." The King's essay was an attempt to sway public opinion; the educational reforms were an attempt to expand the options—both in order to cure the national vice of clerkism.

While most of the changes in education introduced by Vajiravudh aimed at simultaneously enhancing national strength and national pride, some changes belong solely in the category of stimulating nationalism. The use of schools to recruit and train members of the Boy Scout movement, already discussed in chapter 3, is one such change. Schools were also used to disseminate the essential messages of love of nation.

Patriotic songs were written specifically for school children to sing. One, for example, went:

> All of us youths are proud to be of Thai descent.
> Our hearts are strong to protect the power who loves the land,
> King Vajiravudh, who has encouraged us all
> To offer our bodies and our lives to the royal need.
> We are heedless of sacrifice to save our freedom
> So that we Thai will endure till the end of time.[170]

Another method of spreading the idea of nation to all the country's youth was dissemination of the King's writings on the subject. This practice was instituted in 1911 with the distribution of copies of the King's essay *Plukchai sŭapa* (Instilling the Wild Tiger Spirit) to the schools. The Ministry of Religious Affairs and Education, uncertain as to how the essay should be used, wrote the palace for instructions. Instructions were duly sent. Teachers, it stated, should read this "great treasure for the nation" to all the boys and girls, making clear any parts that the students might have trouble understanding. The essay should be read in a room containing the King's portrait, so that the reading might be conducted in an atmosphere of respect. At the end of the reading, students should stand and bow respectfully. The readings were to be conducted periodically on suitable occasions.[171]

Economic Nationalism

Some of the most virulent expressions of nationalism in late nineteenth- and early twentieth-century Europe were in the economic sphere. The competition for empire in the Golden Age of Imperialism and the fierce commercial and financial rivalries of European states were to become important contributory elements in the bloody confrontation of World War I. Nor were the postwar years to see any abandonment of the belief that each nation must pursue its own economic interest without concern for long-range consequences. Presaging the catastrophe of the Great Depression of the 1930s was the agricultural depression of the 1920s, in which the leading nations pursued policies of autarky, protecting local producers by imposing political and fiscal obstacles on foreign competitors. And national self-sufficiency not only was regarded as the answer to economic problems but became an article of faith, a basis for pride.

King Vajiravudh and many of his officials were well aware of the main economic tenets of European nationalism. The Minister of Agriculture, in a prescient memorandum to the King written four years before World War I, pointed out that "... all civilised states are putting every power they have at their disposal to support their agriculture, trade and commerce, even to the verge of war." Siam, he said, must do likewise. And Siam must prevent foreign domination of its economy: "... we have to see to [it] that foreign wealth shall not come in to the purpose of grinding down our people as they have ground down their own. ..." Siam must develop an economic policy that would wean the people away from their "thriftless" habits, introduce improved farming methods, stimulate new enterprises, and, in short, bring about an "important national movement" to "increase production and promote the national wealth." Such a movement would make "our beloved Fatherland ... a recognized power among the civilised nations."[172]

The basic economic philosophy presented by the minister corresponded with the King's own views. The practical working out of a policy of economic nationalism, however, was beset with difficulties. In fact, the common view of the reign today is that economics and finance were its areas of greatest weakness. Cited as evidence by writers of the day and subsequent writers are the budgetary deficits inherited by King Prajadhipok in 1925, the lavish expenditures on ceremonies and courtiers, the large allotments to the military as opposed to the small outlays for internal improvements, the two foreign loans (totaling five million pounds) floated in the London market, and the periodic crises arising from rice shortages, silver shortages, bank failures, and inflation. However, a thorough study and evaluation of the reign's entire economic and fiscal history has just begun.[173]

The easy supposition that the King's profligacy was the root source of all the country's economic ills is highly vulnerable.[174] In

The West as Model

fact, the total income of the national government was small, and while different appropriations of money would have had different effects, the effects, given the limited resources, would, in any event, have been slight. Further, a basic cause of much of the reign's economic distress in the 1920s seems to have been the depression in prices of agricultural commodities, and this was a worldwide phenomenon that Siam could do little to contend with. For not only was Siam unable to affect the asking price for rice, it was unable to raise tariff walls against foreign imports because the country lacked tariff autonomy. The essential economic difficulties of the Sixth Reign may then have stemmed from external sources.

Nonetheless, there is no doubt that within limits some things might have been done to promote economic development and ameliorate economic hardships that were not done. In the field of agriculture, for example, the ministerial budget was kept at a low level and most projects proposed remained unfunded. At the start of the reign the *Bangkok Times* commented that the country was in need of "improved methods of agriculture" and that the ministry, "hitherto much neglected," was beset with problems and required the leadership of a "strong man."[175] The press kept up a continuous barrage of criticisms of agricultural policy, even to the point of saying that the agricultural policy of the Siamese government was "that it has not got any such policy."[176] In a letter to the editor in 1918, a writer bluntly stated what seems to have been the common view:

> The plain fact is that agriculture is not, and, so far as my experience carries me, never has been a serious interest of the state. For some time now that has been cynically emphasized by the notorious fact that the Minister does not attend office.... the Ministry has not on its staff an agricultural chemist, and has never shown the faintest recognition of the fact that there is a scientific side to successful rice growing.[177]

Clearly critics in the press and elsewhere believed that more should be done to help farmers organize their efforts so as to secure a more advantageous bargaining position in the market place, more should be done to secure credit facilities for farmers, more should be done to build irrigation and flood control systems.[178] And these "mores" should be done by the government. The plea for government attention, for government acceptance of its responsibility, was insistent. As one editorial put it, "Whatever is done, the initiative must come from the Government."[179]

King Vajiravudh was aware of the criticisms of his economic policies. His reaction was a curious mixture of denial of problems,

The West as Model

criticism of the critics, introduction of some remedial measures, and, most significant from the point of view of nationalism, exhortations to his people to take economic initiatives on their own for love of country.

The workings of economics and finance were something of a mystery to Vajiravudh, and on occasion he admitted as much. In 1912 he wrote, "When I come to the question of finance, I never feel quite happy about it, because I never had a head for finance."[180] In a long and scathing review of a book on political economy, the King stated that such books had only one use for him: they helped to put him to sleep. Economic theory, he held, was useless. What other conclusion could be drawn from the fact that rich men never studied political economy, and political economists were never rich men?[181]

The King took strong exception to the "loud laments" that the Thai peasantry was impoverished and exploited. The Thai were not poor: there was no starvation in Siam; the people even had money enough to indulge in gambling. The "so-called poor people in Bangkok," he said, "are quite rich" compared with the urban poor in Europe. As for people in the countryside, "Our provincial people do not lack necessities; they have got decent roofs over their heads, and ground to till and cultivate." The only "poor" people in Siam were the extravagant spenders in Bangkok whose luxurious tastes ran beyond their means.[182] The King even wrote letters to the press, under the pseudonym Asvabahu, questioning the wisdom of publishing articles on "The Poverty of the People." On the basis of his extensive travels, said Asvabahu, "I am able to attest that no other country has fewer poor or needy people than Siam."[183]

The King also argued that the government had limited resources and must maintain its essential priorities. Defense, he said, was more important to the nation than economic development. If Siam became much more prosperous than it was, how could its increased wealth be defended? Acquisition of wealth was a worthwhile endeavor only if one had the means to protect it. Siam's defenses must come first.[184]

The King admitted, however, that the Siamese economy needed improving in various ways. And, he argued, the government was doing what it could. Every birthday speech contained references to the new railway lines that had been laid, the financial measures that had been taken, the agricultural improvements that had been begun. In some areas the record was impressive: railway mileage at the end of the reign was more than treble the mileage that had existed in 1910. In other areas such as irrigation, little had been done by Chula-

The West as Model

longkorn and little was done by Vajiravudh until the last years of the reign.

Some innovative approaches in the economic field were tried by King Vajiravudh. They all bore a clear relationship to the King's philosophy that Siam should learn to be self-reliant. The message of Siam for the Siamese thus spilled over into the economic sphere.

One new approach, already mentioned under education, was the introduction of an arts and crafts curriculum into the schools. By training Thai artisans in these schools, it was hoped that a new class of craftsmen would be created so that Thai would be able to buy locally made products.

A second new approach was an effort to provide farmers with a source of credit so that they would become less dependent upon moneylenders, many of whom were Chinese immigrants. A law establishing National Savings Banks was proclaimed on April 1, 1913. The idea of such savings banks was the King's and apparently had come to him when he was in England and saw such banks in operation there. The purpose of the savings banks was to encourage people in the provinces to place their modest savings in an accessible institution where their money would be safe and would accrue interest. Loan policies were also designed to favor the small-farmer provincial clientele.[185] In 1916 another move in the same direction was taken with the establishment of the first cooperative societies. Some 60 societies had been established by October 1922. It appears, however, that neither the banks nor the societies were much of a success. Government support was maintained at a low level. After ten years of existence, the banks had not yet made a "very serious appeal to the people" and had had little general effect on the rural credit scene.[186] The cooperative societies still belonged in the category of an experiment.[187]

A third approach of the government in fostering economic nationalism was its direct sponsorship of new economic enterprises. The first manufacturing enterprise of any size in Siam, and the only one to achieve success during the reign, was the Siam Cement Company, which was founded in 1913. Siam possessed the basic raw materials for cement manufacture; the prospect of Siam's producing its own cement caught the King's imagination. He encouraged plans for the company and invested half of the needed capital from the privy purse. The goal was for the company to supply all of Siam's internal needs. By the end of the reign this goal had been reached. Further, the company had expanded its work force to 300 men, and annual dividends had averaged 12 percent.[188] A much smaller effort

The West as Model

at paper manufacture, sponsored by the Army Survey Department, met with only mixed success.[189]

The most ambitious effort of the government in promoting new enterprise, its inauguration of the Siamese Steamship Company in January 1918, was an unmixed catastrophe. The idea of a Siamese merchant marine started with the seizure of the German merchant vessels on the day Siam entered World War I. Within days of the seizure, the King and Prince Paribatra, Minister of Marine, were laying plans for a fleet of Thai merchant vessels that would be owned by Thai, be captained by Thai, fly the Thai flag, and enter the export carrying trade early enough to be able to withstand postwar competition from the major trading nations. The navy also argued the military benefits of a merchant fleet, which could serve as a naval arm in times of war.[190] The demands of international politics compelled the Thai to lease many of the most desirable vessels to the Allies during the war.[191] But before the charters came into effect the Siamese navy pressed several of the vessels into merchant service. The largest ship, the *Yiam Samut* (formerly the *Trautenfels*), returning fully laden from Japan, foundered on rocks off the China coast in February 1918.[192] The loss of the *Yiam Samut* was but the first of a series of profound shocks and disappointments experienced by the Siamese navy and, later, by the Siamese Steamship Company. In December 1920 another Thai vessel, the *Kaeo Samut*, was wrecked off the Siamese coast; both ship and cargo were a total loss.[193] In addition to the mishaps at sea, the company experienced managerial difficulties at home. Early in 1922 the Borneo Company, a British shipping concern, was appointed managing agent of the Thai company.[194] The Thai "experiment in national commercial enterprise," as the King called it,[195] had failed.

By far the most characteristic form of government sponsorship of Thai economic development, however, was exhortation. In numerous speeches and essays the King made the case for Thai economic self-reliance. Part of national self-awareness was awareness of the economic responsibilities of Thai to Thai.

In an essay of 1915 whose title translates into English as "Wake Up, Siam," the King dealt exhaustively with the theme of the economic dimensions of nationalism. The essay started with a definition of the problem. At one time, Vajiravudh wrote, the Thai people produced the articles they needed. With the advent of peace and prosperity, the expansion of foreign trade, and the immigration of Chinese laborers, the Thai came to rely excessively on foreigners. Foreign

The West as Model

imports drove Thai manufacturers out of the market. Cheap foreign labor replaced Thai workmen in many crafts and industries. The Thai accepted the new emergent economy because it was convenient. The Thai, who "by nature do not like to work hard," were content to leave manual labor to the Chinese. The Thai became lazy, giving up skills they once had, depending on foreigners for products they once made. Locally, the Chinese took over food marketing in Bangkok; they dominated the construction industry and carpentry trades. The international market supplied machinery, petroleum, benzine, coal, sugar, and cloth. Some of these imports were necessary, but not all. Petroleum for lamps could be replaced by locally produced coconut oil. Homegrown castor oil could easily supplant imported lubricating oil. Siam had once been self-sufficient in sugar and cloth and could again be. The disadvantages in economic dependence were apparent enough in peacetime; they would expand manyfold in wartime and make Siam extremely vulnerable.[196]

How were these economic problems to be solved? The repeated suggestions in the press that the government do something, that the government take corrective measures, said Vajiravudh, were unfair. The government's responsibility was to protect the people and to encourage their enterprise. But the government could not accomplish miracles. It could not act alone. The government, in the last analysis, could not be "Commercial Magnate and Captain of Industry."[197] It was up to the Thai people to help themselves:

> For commerce and industries to flourish and grow, the proper business men, men of integrity, to direct commercial and industrial concerns must be forthcoming as well as a sufficient number of labourers. If people in our own country would only realise this elementary truth, there would be a little more energy among our Siamese business men, and a little less fanciful talk. What is the use of always blaming the Government for not making industries flourish in Siam? What do you think business men are there for? Do you think all you need to do is to *look* like splendid millionaires, and loll about in your arm-chairs planning the latest additions to your gorgeous mansions? ... If you do not help yourselves, how could you expect the Government to help you?[198]

To those who looked on the government as the father of the Thai people and then faulted the father for not caring for his children, Vajiravudh responded by pointing out that fathers did indeed have responsibilities. But were these responsibilities endless? Once a father

The West as Model

had raised, trained, and educated his child, should not the child then assume his own adult responsibilities?[199]

It was the responsibility of all the people to improve Siam's economic lot. Businessmen should invest in Siamese industries. Farmers should plant crops to compete with imports. And consumers should buy Thai products whenever possible. To those who said local products were more expensive than imports, he answered that the flow of capital abroad was an expense that had to be considered. "If we want to retain monetary assets in our country, we must buy only those goods made in our country."[200] The consumer complaints that foreign products were better made should prompt Thai craftsmen to perfect their skills. The Thai in general must learn the virtues of thrift, of accumulating capital. The values the King hoped to instill were exemplified by a character in one of his plays, an inventor, who refused Western bids for his invention because he wanted to sell it to a Thai businessman: "I am Thai, so I want us Thai to reap the rewards of my invention."[201] All Thai should be like this inventor. All Thai should conduct their economic lives in ways beneficial to the Thai; a patriotic people would enable Siam to become productive, self-reliant, and strong.

The King advertised his views not only in speech and on paper but also in deeds. He made regular visits to exhibitions of Thai arts and crafts, to agricultural and trade fairs, to the openings of new industrial plants, all in an effort to stimulate Thai economic endeavors by displays of royal favor. Under the King's auspices Siam participated in foreign trade fairs and expositions, including those in Turin in 1911 and in San Francisco in 1915, in order to show to the world the best of Thai silver, pottery, lacquerware, and other products. Finally, in 1924 the King began preparations for a great Siamese Kingdom Exhibition, slated to open late in 1925. There were many foreign precedents for such an exhibition; the closest in time and place was the Malaya-Borneo Exhibition of 1922, which its promoters hoped would "be a help to the revival of trade."[202] Vajiravudh had the same hope. His fair, he believed, would bring exhibitors from around the world who would be able to show machinery that could modernize Thai farming. And it would permit Thai from all parts of the country to put their own goods on display for new international buyers.

The Siamese Kingdom Exhibition was Vajiravudh's last important project before his death. He donated to the government a large tract of land he owned personally, naming it Lumphini Park, and began to develop it with money from the privy purse. The land was

The West as Model

leveled, and a gateway, clock tower, permanent exhibition hall, and several temporary stalls were erected. Electric generators were ordered from Germany to light the fair grounds. A brochure was prepared as a guide to exhibitors and fairgoers. The work was well advanced by November 25, when the King died. Within days the new government came to a decision to abandon the project.[203]

7

The Concept of Nationality

King Vajiravudh advocated the adoption of many Western ways to promote Thai national progress and national pride. But, he pointed out, there were limits to what Siam could learn from the West. In the choice of Western cultural elements, discretion had to be rigorously and constantly exercised so that Thai culture would not be swamped and destroyed. On this point he once stated:

> I don't at all object to all Western knowledge, for I myself have obtained much knowledge from the West. So I don't take exception to the point that Westerners have much to offer in the way of techniques and abilities. But I do question that if something is good for Westerners it must necessarily be good for everyone else.[1]

Western civilization, he noted in his diary, was like a medicine. It had to be used with great care. Put to good use it had good effects, but used indiscriminately it became a virulent poison with rapid and fatal results.[2]

The Concept of Nationality

Vajiravudh was obviously aware that, because of his Western schooling and some Western preferences, he himself might be subject to a charge of being indiscriminately pro-Western. To counter such a charge he told a story of the gods who mask their inner divinity by taking on rude outer shapes. "As for me," he said, "I am a rude man within, and wear a golden exterior.... Although I may use language and diction in the foreign style, when you examine me closely you will surely see that my dip in European educational waters has given me but a European gloss; the flesh inside is still very much Thai."[3] This view was seconded by one longtime British resident in Siam who commented that the King was "passionately attached to the traditions of his country, that his intention in pursuing western methods is only to adopt such foreign customs as may contribute to the happiness and material welfare of his people, and that the very last thing he desires is to see the nation divest itself of its own ideals in favour of that veneer of so-called civilisation which has upset the national equilibrium and subverted the morals of more than one Eastern race."[4]

Whatever his personal predilections,[5] Vajiravudh realized that the Thai nation to be Thai must stress its unique values. The Thai people must understand what being Thai meant, what being a nation meant. Promotion of nationalism depended on comprehension of nationality.

To aid in that comprehension he coined a word, heretofore lacking in Thai, for nation. The word was *chat*, from the Sanskrit *jati*. In fact, *chat* was not a new word; it had long been used in its old Indic meanings of origin or birth or, by extension, caste. Even more common in Buddhist Siam was the definition of *chat* as a life span in the circle of rebirths. The word *chat* had desirable connotations of common ancestry, common origin. It was easy to extend the meaning to "nation," used in the sense of "race" in terms such as "Aryan race" or "French race." In the King's usage the word played an important role in fostering an idea by giving that idea a name. Siam was no longer just a country (*prathet thai* or *mūang thai*) with a Thai population (*chao thai* or *phonlamūang thai*), it was now also a nation (*chat thai*) with its own national identity.[6]

What was a nation? The King defined it often. He started with the ancient meaning of the term, family line or caste,[7] and said that the term later came to mean a group of people who had originally been relatives or friends and lived together in one place. But the meaning of nation in the modern world had grown much larger. Nationality was an indispensable part of every individual. Who a

The Concept of Nationality

man was depended on his nationality. And since nationality was so important to modern man, man must do his utmost to preserve his nation as his birthright. He wrote: "Any man who does not know how to preserve his nation cannot be a man."[8]

King Vajiravudh often compared the relationship between a man and his nation to the relationship between a man and his family. The nation was a unity, like a family. Only by feeling the oneness with fellow members could a nation exist. The members of a nation must live in agreement and harmony with each other. All the faults that weakened families, such as jealousy, self-aggrandizement, disrespect, and disobedience, inevitably also weakened nations.[9] If any individual behaved badly toward the nation, by failing to give it respect or by shirking his obligations toward it, he was helping in the destruction of the nation. His behavior was a reason for sorrow, as it would be in a family, in which "if even one member behaves badly, all relatives are saddened." A nation should be loved, as one loves one's father and mother, and that love must be continually demonstrated.[10] The true nationalist loved all fellow nationals as his brothers. He helped people of his nationality in times of distress; he refrained from harming his fellow nationals; he redirected fellow nationals who went astray; and he taught the young to love the nation.[11]

The Thai nation must know what constituted a nation; it must also know what constituted its "Thainess." In the King's words: "We must remember that we Thai have characteristics basically different from those of foreigners."[12] What set the Thai nation apart? A combination of things including Thai history, Thai art, Thai language, Thai literature, Thai Buddhism, Thai love of the royal leader, and an essential Thai spirit, a fierce devotion to *thai* in the sense of "free," a warrior spirit that the King frequently called the Wild Tiger spirit. It was vital that all of these characteristics of the Thai be preserved. That, indeed, they be built upon and strengthened. The King's views on the monarchy and militarism as essential foundations of the Thai nation have already been discussed; his views on history, art, language, literature, and religion will be examined in the next chapter.

One of the greatest dangers to the Thai nation was the failure of its own people to appreciate the strengths and the virtues of Thai culture. In a speech to a group of Thai students going to study in Europe the King advised:

> Finally, I beg to remind all of you students that we are Thai. Don't disparage your nation, for in doing so you are in effect disparaging

The Concept of Nationality

yourselves. All peoples have both good and bad intermingled in their characters. There is no nation that is absolutely good or bad. There is much that is good in the Thai nation. We must nurture the merits and the good characteristics of our race and not let it be said that we are inferior and not the equals of others.... A nation without its own traditional culture is not regarded by outsiders as a nation at all. It is looked down upon by the world and is a subject of derision.[13]

The King spoke often of the Thai inclination to self-disparagement, the "slavish habit of self-abasement."[14] In one address, in which he exhorted the Wild Tigers to love their nation and give it respect for its own true worth, he said: "If our nation does decline so that others look down upon us, if our nation does fall, it will be our own fault! For we ourselves do not know how to cherish it, how to save it. We ourselves do not appreciate its value. We ourselves continually look down upon it."[15]

Westerners

The tendency of the Thai to deprecate their own nation, said Vajiravudh, grew out of an excessive admiration of the West. Bangkok Thai of the educated classes were particularly subject to this error. They placed Europeans "on pedestals" and treated their own "kith and kin as less than dust beneath the feet" of Westerners. Nothing was praiseworthy to them unless it bore a Western stamp. A "habit of mind" had developed, an assumption that "to have anything done at all well, it must be done by a Farang [Westerner]." The *farang* had been exalted "to undreamt of heights" and the Thai abased "to almost the lowest depth."[16]

The extraordinary esteem given Westerners had brought into being in Siam the "cult of imitation," which the King identified as "the biggest and worst clog" on the wheels of Siam's progress.[17] The unreasoning imitation of Westerners had been carried by some to the ridiculous extremes of choosing Western woolen trousers over Thai silk *phanung*, passing time in shooting "inoffensive" birds, drinking brandies and sodas, and indulging in other Western vices, thereby ruining "both their physiques and their brains."[18] These imitators were also inclined to engage in "smart" talk that was critical of the government, comparing Siam unfavorably with one Western state or another. But, the King asserted, bad-mouthing one's own society did not earn foreign respect; in fact, just the opposite was true: "Those Thai who respect themselves and their nation the most are the most respected by foreigners."[19] Nothing could be further from the truth, said Vajiravudh, than the mistaken idea that the flattery

The Concept of Nationality

of imitation would provide the imitators with "a passport to the esteem of Europeans."[20] Imitators might be tolerated, might even be liked, but they could not win real esteem:[21] "It is human nature to *look up* to one's superiors, *look level* at one's equals, and *look down* upon one's inferiors. And what is imitation but a patent confession of inferiority?"[22] Imitators could hope for no more than a "patronizing pat on the back."[23] One image Vajiravudh was fond of and used more than once was a comparison of imitators to puppy dogs. Europeans, he said, reacted to the flattery of imitators by feeling

> ... rather kindly disposed toward the imitators, as one does towards a little puppy that knows how to sit up! The fact of his being able to sit up does not change the puppy into a human being, inspite of what the puppy itself may think about it. One likes the puppy better than the other dogs which do not know how to sit up and do not try to do so, not because one accepts the sitting puppy as a human being, but merely because it knows how to imitate one of our own postures, and one therefore pats it on the head and calls it an intelligent dog! Why will not Asiatics, who slavishly imitate European ways and customs, realize this truth?[24]

Thai imitators, further, were entirely too indiscriminate in their choice of Westerners to imitate. They usually associated with the worst *farang* elements in Bangkok, the managers of hotels, bars, and houses of prostitution, people who did not practice the virtues of their own culture. Unlike the better elements, the diplomats and merchants, who maintained their distance from the Thai, the vagabond elements were quite willing to associate with anyone who had money. From them the Thai imitators were picking up habits of indolence, boasting, criticizing, and carousing. Foreigners of the better classes did not behave this way. They did not, for example, criticize the monarchy or the Thai government officers. The King posed to the imitators the rhetorical question "Why do you wish to behave like the common *farang* drunken in the middle of the street?"[25] On occasion he supplied his own answer to this question: the aper of Western ways merely sought a rationalization for doing as he pleased, claiming the Western right of freedom to excuse his lack of discipline or respect, his entire devotion to self, and his basic immorality. The assumption that Westerners were superior in all things, an assumption made by themselves and by their admirers, was entirely unwarranted, said the King.[26] Not all Westerners were moral exemplars. If they were, there would be no need for jails in Western countries. But on the contrary, he pointed out, "there are plenty of jails everywhere

The Concept of Nationality

and they are not empty either."[27] The war in Europe should be a further lesson to those who steadfastly regarded Europeans as "our preceptors in the ways of Progress and Civilisation," for "all the good that Progress and Civilisation have been able to do for them has been utterly incapable of saving the great Powers from the most frightful war the world has ever seen!"[28]

The cult of imitation, wrote the King in an essay on this topic, was "a brake upon our National Progress," for it stifled originality and imagination, made one perpetually dependent upon the actions of others, and wasted time. "We should realize," he wrote, "that we may now venture to think and act for ourselves without waiting for the lead of our preceptors...."[29]

Vajiravudh, of course, was not unalterably opposed to all Western ideas "so long as one does not bind one's self hand and foot to always follow some one else's lead." What was necessary was that the Thai feel "free to adopt or reject or originate as it best suits our national purpose."[30]

A relatively new Western philosophy that had begun to make an impact on educated Thai during the Sixth Reign was socialism. The King reacted to this ideology and its spokesmen with the same degree of vehemence with which he reacted to revolutionary Western political concepts.[31] Both social and political revolutionaries were, he said, afflicted with "unrest fever" or "new mania," a "fairly contagious disease" spread by "arrant humbugs" among ignorant and gullible people who would "enthuse" over everything Western and everything new.[32]

The King wrote a witty essay entitled "Uttarakuru" exposing what seemed to him the foolishness of these imitators of Western fads. Uttarakuru was an Asian utopia first described in Thai in a fourteenth-century work which was based on a much older Brahmanic text.[33] In Uttarakuru the people all observed the moral precepts and never strayed from righteousness and so were blessed with beauty, longevity, and happiness. The best blessing of all, noted Vajiravudh, was contained in the sentence "Of all forms of wealth, no man knows which is his and which is of another, all being common (property) everywhere, and no man ever cultivates lands, or ploughs fields or engages in trade." Here, said the King, is "pure, idealistic Socialism" with "no individual property, and no manner of work."[34] The King pointed out other aspects of Uttarakuruan society that he regarded as anticipating socialist thought. One was a "providing tree" that gave men clothing and jewelry at their wish; this, the King said, was a literary device that really implied communization or nationalization of all forms of property. Another was a short-term marriage system, which, he pointed out, was very much like the free marriage ideas of such socialists as George Bernard Shaw. A third was a child-raising system in which "children grow up by themselves"; presumably, said the King, this meant that children would belong to and be reared by the state.

The irony and sarcasm of the essay made its point clear. What need had the Thai for the foreign utopian thought of Westerners such as Shaw or Keir Hardie, or their Chinese variants such as K'ang Yu-wei and Sun Yat-sen, when Siam had its own depictions of the ideal? The King wrote, "As long as human nature remains as it is, so long shall we have new apostles of Social Reform, who prate of 'New' theories, which are as old as the hills! Shall we get any nearer to such an idealistic state? Will such theories ever become really practicable outside Dreamland or the Lunatic Asylum?"[35]

A continuous thread running through the King's thought on the West was his awareness of Western racial prejudice. Although evidences of this prejudice had never been so obvious in Siam as in neighboring Western colonies in Burma, Indochina, or Malaya, they existed and occasionally surfaced. The most patent evidences were the unequal treaties that restricted Siamese fiscal and judicial autonomy, and, as has been pointed out earlier, considerable state energies were devoted to ridding Siam of these treaties. Other smaller evidences of Western feelings of superiority abounded. The English-language press, although usually very careful on this score, sometimes slipped into a note of condescension. Foreign travel accounts were more openly slighting or insulting, as, for example, this report:

> Careless and heedless, pliable and open to influence, anxious and easily intimidated, and when left alone gay and full of life, easy to get on with, amiable, busy at *fêtes*, a witty chatterer, this is the Siamese who with his small, well-built body and pretty face, forms a sympathetic nation, but in no way an imposing one.[36]

King Vajiravudh was well aware of Siam's foreign press image and in a charitable mood once commented: "To most people Siam is a country full of White Elephants and nothing much besides."[37]

Foreign residents in Siam by and large preserved their distance and their privileges. One British officer in the Siamese service, queried as to the "general attitude of Europeans to constables and Siamese officers," replied: "It varies very much, but as a general rule it is not very polite."[38] Francis Sayre, early in his career as foreign affairs adviser, discovered that Western diplomats were not in the habit of

The Concept of Nationality

acknowledging diplomatic *faux pas* to the Siamese and reported that, in one instance when he felt that an American apology to the Siamese was in order, it took "a long heart-to-heart talk" with the American minister before he "rose to the occasion."[39] Among the Westerners in Bangkok, the Germans had the best reputation for treating the Siamese as equals. While the Siamese appreciated the German attitude, the British did not. A British writer castigated the Germans for their willingness "to descend" to the Siamese level and praised his own people for not doing so; he added that, if they did, they would soon lose "that priceless possession their prestige, which the native, even if he is not regardful of his own, recognizes in the white man and respects."[40]

The main means of contending with Western racism, whenever it obtruded, was to refuse to concede to it insofar as possible. The King usually avoided out-and-out denunciations of Western assumptions of superiority; rather, he insisted that the Thai were equals and must act as equals. He even allowed that some Western expressions of superiority were natural, for "ordinarily people of different nationalities feel that their own nationality is first in the world and other people are less good." That in itself was not harmful. Indeed, the Thai were not above such feelings; in casual speech a Thai was apt to refer to Westerners with the vulgar pronoun *man* ("it") and to a foreign king with the undignified pronoun *kae* ("he," but not suitable for royalty).[41] It was to be expected that "every patriotic man would naturally have his own country's interests at heart above the interests of all others"; one could hardly look for "foreigners to have the interests of Siam at heart as much as we ourselves."[42]

Private feelings of Western superiority were one thing, but naked insults and demands for special privilege were quite another. Several incidents occurred during the reign that put to the test the King's determination to be equal. He came out well.

The most highly publicized incident occurred in March 1915. Two Thai soldiers, returning from maneuvers, took shelter in the shade under the house of Mr. P. A. Lewin, a British engineer in the Siamese Railway Department. Lewin, annoyed, drove the soldiers out by kicking them. The Ministry of War, enraged at the "moral insult," persuaded the Ministry of Communications to dismiss Lewin from government service and issued an official communique accusing certain foreigners of looking "down upon us as non-equals." The communique closed with a veiled threat to foreigners that ". . . you cannot expect our soldiers to remember every foreigner's face and distinguish those who treat us nicely from those who do not."[43] The

The Concept of Nationality

Ministry of War's blast, undoubtedly written by the mercurial Prince Chakrabongs, created a big stir. The *Bangkok Times* editorialized that Lewin should not have taken the law into his own hands, but questioned the severity of the punishment and particularly objected to the general accusation at the communique's end.[44] Prince Chakrabongs immediately countered with a letter denouncing the editorial in strong language:

> ... the Siamese do feel, as probably all Asiatics do, that the Europeans consider them (Siamese) as an inferior race. The ordinary Siamese feel it by instinct, while the educated ones can read about it in any foreign newspaper or book. You cannot deny the fact that men of the white race in general consider us to be inferior to themselves in every way. Well the ordinary Siamese do not like it and they, by their ignorance, return the compliment.[45]

The Lewin affair finally drew in the British minister, the Siamese Minister of Foreign Affairs, and the King. Lewin was allowed to submit a full apology, in return for which the King granted him clemency and reinstated him in his position.[46] Some months after the Lewin affair, Vajiravudh, in a statement to Thai students in Europe, again referred to it:

> Formerly it was not at all unusual for a Westerner to slap or kick a Thai and to do so with impunity. But if a Thai did anything to a Westerner, even the smallest thing, it became a big affair requiring us to beg their humble pardon. Nowadays this is all changed, and if a Westerner does bodily harm to a Thai, he must be punished no less than if a Thai injures a Westerner.[47]

A few minor episodes further illustrate the Thai disinclination to accept insults or discourtesies. In 1911, when three high-ranking Thai princes stopped off at Singapore on their way back to Siam, they paid a courtesy call on the British governor. The governor kept the princes waiting for some minutes. An objection to the governor's discourtesy was communicated to the British Legation in Bangkok, and this soon brought a "fullest apology" from the governor.[48] In 1915 Father Colombet, a French cleric, complained that Thai soldiers marching in column were deliberately insulting Westerners by failing to give way to them on the street. The King noted that in Europe soldiers in column had the right of way; he disallowed the Frenchman's charge and advised that it be ignored.[49] In 1916 the British consul in Siam, T. H. Lyle, objected to the use of the term *nai*, a Thai translation of "mister," before his name. The King, who had in-

The Concept of Nationality

augurated the policy of using *nai* for "mister," dismissed Lyle's objection by saying that it presumably arose because he was "of the older generation of consuls and cannot overcome the habit of looking down on the Thai."[50] The minor quarrel over *nai* and "mister" continued to surface occasionally in the press. The Thai held that *nai* was but a simple translation, in no way demeaning; the Westerners objected that the Thai practice of entitling all officials tended to make a *nai* "a nobody."[51]

One important affair involving racism and Westerners was the internment of German and Austrian prisoners of war by the Thai in 1917. The Thai obviously intended to keep the enemy prisoners in Siam; they immediately began to build a permanent camp for them at Nakhọn Pathom. The British minister strongly objected to this policy, citing as his principal reason the danger that the Germans might escape and cause trouble in India.[52] The matter was laid before the King. He decided to accept a British offer to house the prisoners at a British encampment in India,[53] and, after six months' internment in Siam, the prisoners were transported to India on two Thai ships.

There were problems from the start about the internment of the Germans and Austrians. The internment policy itself was adopted largely to please the British. The Thai were acutely aware that Germans in England and Japan were not imprisoned whereas those in British colonies were. And the decision to move the prisoners to India was also made in response to British insistence. The Germans wanted to stay in Siam, and many Siamese preferred to hold them. Most vociferous on this subject was Prince Chakrabongs, who as Army Chief of Staff had done much to see to the orderly arrest and the provision of respectable quarters for the enemy aliens. The Prince resented the presumed British belief that the Siamese might not be able to guard the prisoners adequately; he resented the "colonial" implications he saw in the British policy and the severity of the British demands on Siam as compared with those on Japan; he was deeply troubled by the seeming disregard of the British for Siamese *amour propre*.[54] Vajiravudh, however, was inclined to make the best of things; he seemed to accept the logic of British arguments and also the political reality that Siam was not Japan.[55] Siam, after all, had made a significant step forward in merely taking white men as prisoners:

> I know that it is regarded by many people as a great compliment, not to say glory for Siam that she should not only be able to intern Europeans, but that these same Europeans are even anxious and willing to be kept interned by us rather than their fellow Europeans. Indeed,

The Concept of Nationality

being a Siamese myself I cannot but help feeling elated that we have been able to intern Europeans which has undoubtedly increased our prestige a great deal, in the eyes not only of our own people but in those of the other Asiatic races residing in our country.[56]

There is no question that Vajiravudh believed significant progress had been made by Siam in achieving equality with the West. And equality was the goal, not racial enmity. He specifically warned his people not to hate foreigners, for "it is not necessary to show our love of nation by being insulting in word or manner or by hating other nations."[57]

The signs that equality was being achieved were summarized by the King in a letter to Thai students abroad in 1916. At one time, he said, the Thai had been as afraid of Westerners as they were of great demon *yakshas*, and Westerners, sensing this fear, had been correspondingly demanding. But the Thai had got over their fear, and Westerners no longer acted the bully. Westerners had learned that the Thai could not be intimidated and were now determined to "walk in equality" with the Thai. Westerners who came to Siam to make a living "feel a lively respect for us Thai and know better than to make us angry." At one time Westerners would not associate with the Thai; nowadays, "it is impossible to see one who doesn't."[58]

The example of new international respect that Vajiravudh was proudest of was his appointment as an honorary general in the British army, which he reciprocated by offering George V a generalship in the Siamese army. King Vajiravudh referred often to this "mutual bestowal of military ranks." He was exceedingly proud of it and saw in it "the meaning that the Siamese Nation has already shown to the world that they deserve equal treatment with other countries." He took particular pleasure in the special favor shown Siam, for no other Asiatic sovereign, not even the Japanese emperor, had been similarly honored. He wished his people to know that this honor was for all of them. And the language Vajiravudh used, referring to King George as a "Brother and Friend" who "stretches his hand over the ocean in order to grasp mine,"[59] is not merely the grand language of a formal speech, it represents a conviction that Siam had entered a new era of national and racial equality.

The Chinese Minority

King Vajiravudh's views on the relationship between the Thai and all other Asians were somewhat ambiguous. On the one hand, the King recognized a certain similarity between Thai and other East Asian

The Concept of Nationality

peoples; at least they shared a common lot with respect to their treatment by the West.[60] He occasionally used the phrase "we Asiatics." On the other hand, his main objective was to strike out for recognition—by the Thai and by outsiders—of the existence of the Thai as a separate people, not to be confused with any other people or to be judged by any other label but that of Thai. For example, in commenting on an article on Yuan Shih-k'ai by a British writer, who had accused the then President of China of being guilty of "opportunism of the Oriental type," Vajiravudh expressed no objection to Yuan's being called an opportunist but took exception to "of the Oriental type" as a purely gratuituous and unjustified smear of Eastern peoples. "Opportunists," he said, "are bad whatever their nation or language," and opportunism "has nothing to do with a person's country or skin."[61] The King took even more violent exception to the term "yellow peril" that had gained currency in Europe early in the twentieth century. There was no "yellow" peril, he said. There might be a Chinese peril, but the Thai were also a "yellow" people, and they were a peril to no one.[62]

One problem for Vajiravudh in defining the Thai nation or "race" was the Chinese community in Siam. Chinese had long resided in Siam; the Chinese had come to occupy an important role in Siamese trade; and the Chinese were accepted. Many had intermarried with the Thai. Many members of the Siamese nobility and royalty were part Chinese in ancestry.[63] Vajiravudh did not seek to deny any of these facts; however, he did wish to heighten awareness among the Thai of their identity by fostering the idea that the Chinese and the Thai were different peoples, that the ethnic Chinese were not Thai.

The insistence on Chinese separateness was part of the King's policy of nationalism, but the idea of separateness was growing in any event. It was a product of the times, of the developing nationalism within China itself—a nationalism associated with Sun Yat-sen, the fall of the Manchus, and the soliciting of moral and financial aid from overseas Chinese communities for political changes in China. Proselytizers for the new China came periodically to Siam. Dr. Sun himself had paid a brief visit in 1908. Signs of Chinese national fervor had begun to appear in the last years of King Chulalongkorn's reign: the first Chinese-language school was established in 1909; Chinese newspapers in Siam, which had been founded as early as 1905, became more and more politicized; and a major Chinese strike, lasting three days, posed a serious threat to Thai authority in June 1910.[64] The strike constituted a Chinese protest against a new government policy of increasing head taxes on Chinese residents to the level

The Concept of Nationality

paid by Thai. Although swift government action brought the strike quickly under control and showed Chinese residents the effectiveness of Thai power, the very fact that the Chinese had been able to organize, that Chinese secret societies had been able to marshal mass support, that the grievances aired had gone beyond the tax issue gave the Thai reason for apprehension.

The Chinese problem that had begun to emerge at the close of Chulalongkorn's reign grew rapidly during the fifteen years of Vajiravudh's. Chinese immigration swelled, and for the first time included significant numbers of women. New Chinese schools opened; there were at least six by 1916, forty-eight in 1925. The overthrow of the Manchus and establishment of the Chinese Republic late in 1911 focused the attention of overseas Chinese more sharply than ever on events in China and heightened Chinese nationalistic inclinations and activities. During the summer of 1915, for example, local Chinese organized a boycott of Japanese goods to protest against Japanese political demands on China. In 1924 the Chinese of Siam sent delegates to the first National Congress of the Kuomintang Party. And there were constant rumors during the reign that a new strong government in China would demand the opening of diplomatic relations with Siam so that it could better protect the interests of its overseas citizens. Local Chinese on occasion urged the government in China to take such a step.

In terms of administrative policy, the government of the Sixth Reign undertook little that was new with respect to the Chinese minority. It watched; it worried; it acted only when laws were transgressed.

The government kept particularly on the alert for signs of another strike. Fears of a new strike, perhaps even a revolt, were most lively in the summer of 1911. Several letters from Prince Chakrabongs and Čhaophraya Yommarat to the King reported rumors that Chinese were collecting funds and arms and drawing up detailed plans to challenge the government.[65] The Thai Ministry of War was ready; a seven-page secret plan detailed the steps that would be taken in the event that the Chinese acted.[66] No Chinese action came, and only minor outbreaks between rival Chinese groups marred the tranquillity of the reign.

The necessity of being on the ready absorbed considerable government attention. There were continual reports from the Ministry of Local Government and the Ministry of the Interior about the actions of individual Chinese suspected of being agitators, about activities of Chinese secret societies, about the Chinese press, about

The Concept of Nationality

Chinese subscription drives, about Chinese schools, about Chinese manipulations in trade and finance, about virtually every aspect of organized Chinese activity. On occasion individuals were arrested and deported;[67] on occasion newspapers were closed and circulars or handbills seized. Fund drives for political purposes were banned, although the effectiveness of the ban is doubtful.[68] But harshly repressive measures were rigorously avoided. When danger threatened, the government was inclined to call in leaders of the Chinese community, explain the government's point of view to them, and enlist their support. When the Chinese boycott of Japanese goods started in 1915, the Minister of Local Government held a meeting with leaders of various Chinese associations and editors of Chinese newspapers to point out the government's view that such a boycott endangered Siam's relations with Japan, a power friendly to Siam; the minister was pleased with the Chinese reception of his message.[69] The policy of friendly persuasion seems also to have been the first choice in the provinces.[70] Persuasion was reinforced from time to time by warnings, such as the King's reflection in 1913 on the 1910 strike: "Just another 'strike' and I should be very loth to answer for the consequences."[71]

Only two laws passed during the reign were aimed at "the Chinese problem." Neither could be called repressive. And neither was legally anti-Chinese.

The first was a law of 1914 calling for the registration of associations.[72] The already existing criminal code barred secret societies and criminal associations; the new law provided a positive screening for clubs and associations. On registration an association became a juristic person, liable to legal penalty. Associations that could not show a constructive program and provide a list of acceptable officers could be denied a license to operate.[73] The law was aimed particularly at preventing the formation of Chinese associations reflecting the new political enthusiasms generated by events in China.[74] Such associations, which were not secret societies nor strictly speaking criminal organizations, were much easier to control under the new law than under the criminal code. After the passage of the law, several arrests were made of Chinese attending meetings of unregistered societies.[75]

The second law aimed particularly at the Chinese was the law on private schools of June 1918. The law required that all students in private schools be "(1) taught to read, write and understand the Siamese language with reasonable facility; (2) instructed in the duties of a good citizen, in the love of Siam, and in a knowledge of the country including at least its history and geography."[76] Other provisions called for the registration and inspection of schools and specified that headmasters must be proficient in the Thai language. Mission schools and most other private schools were already being conducted along the lines of the new law; Chinese schools were not. The law was meant to bring about an end to the indoctrination of young Chinese "in a purely Chinese atmosphere" and to give Chinese youths an education "in sympathy with the people of the country."[77] In fact, however, the law was so weakly enforced that it achieved no more than "a measure of purely nominal control" and Chinese schools continued to "flourish and increase" as before.[78]

What the private school law of 1918 was supposed to do was facilitate the assimilation of Chinese. Assimilation had long been the Thai way, be it largely an unconscious way, of solving or avoiding a "Chinese problem." By the 1910s and 20s the swell of Chinese migration, the influx of Chinese women, and the heightened political awareness of the migrants had slowed the pace of assimilation. But the policy of assimilation continued. The first Thai nationality act, promulgated in 1911, indeed seemed designed to facilitate assimilation, since it defined as a Thai national everyone born on Thai soil regardless of racial background or parentage.[79]

Assimilation of the Chinese in the past had been successful. This success, it would seem, had had less to do with government policy than with the basic receptivity of the Thai to strangers and the lack of "racial feelings," as this term is generally understood in the West.[80] Chinese had intermarried freely with the Thai at all levels of society; Chinese had been ennobled and appointed to high positions in government; Chinese had been granted all privileges of Thai citizens and, indeed, had possessed some freedoms, such as freedom from corvée requirements, that the Thai themselves did not have. And the contributions of the Chinese, as traders, laborers, and craftsmen, had been appreciated. Although the Thai and Chinese had held some uncomplimentary stereotypes about each other, the relations between the two peoples had been remarkably amicable and smooth.

Vajiravudh sought to continue the good relations. The King understood the value of the Chinese in Thai society. He undoubtedly agreed with an analysis of Chinese contributions made by Chaophraya Yommarat in a report in 1916.[81] The report stated that the Chinese added people, industrious and productive people, to an underpopulated land. Siam, with a population of but eight million in 1910, was considered by both Thai and Westerners to be weak

The Concept of Nationality

partly because it lacked people. Where Chinese had come into Siam, such as in the tin-mining provinces in the South, production had soared. Further, the wealth the Chinese produced was a taxable wealth, providing needed government revenues. The capital that the Chinese had invested and the specialized labor they supplied would be hard to replace. The report ended with the comment that if Chinese were discouraged from coming to Siam, there was a danger that their economic role might be filled by Indians, Japanese, or Europeans, none of whom were as desirable or as culturally assimilable as the Chinese. These economic arguments were undoubtedly persuasive in convincing the government to live with the growing Chinese problem and not to impose any curbs on Chinese immigration. The fact that the Chinese did not involve themselves in Siamese politics, as the King himself noted, was also a point in their favor.[82]

The King showed his good feelings toward the Chinese in innumerable ways during the reign. Starting with the cremation rites for King Chulalongkorn in December 1910, Vajiravudh received Chinese delegations at many important public functions and often addressed them. At the December 1910 rites, for example, the King said:

> The Chinese people and our own people have long been of one heart; the Chinese have acted like people of the same race as our people from ancient times to the present day. I am resolved, therefore, always to assist and protect all the Chinese who come to live in this country.[83]

The attitude displayed in this comment is remarkably similar to that displayed by King Chulalongkorn, who in 1907 said: "I regard the Chinese not as if they were foreigners but as a part of our country and equally entitled to share in the fruits of the country's prosperity."[84]

At the coronation festivities in 1911 Vajiravudh made a special stop at the Chinese section of town to receive the congratulations of the Chinese community. On this occasion His Majesty promised that he would always treat the Chinese with justice and would make no impositions on them that he did not make on his own people.[85] On provincial tours the King often received Chinese delegations; in one town he bought a large pig in the market as a present to the Chinese. Other evidences of favor included a royal donation to a Chinese hospital in 1912, emphasis on the Chinese descent of King Taksin during the royal *kathin* in 1916, the dedication of a Chinese school and a Chinese theater in 1917, and sponsorship by the Ministry of Education of athletic events at Chinese schools in 1918.

The Concept of Nationality

One policy of showing favor that was probably new was the awarding of honorary noble titles to individual Chinese. The ennobling of Chinese in government service was not new, but Vajiravudh seems to have been the first to give noble titles without any duties or salary as a means of strengthening the bonds between wealthy Chinese and the government. Conclusive figures are lacking, but one source indicates that some ninety-two Chinese were given such noble titles during the reign. There is no doubt that the awarding of noble titles was also used as a means of repayment for donations to the King's projects.

The relations between one wealthy Chinese, Yi Ko-hong, and the government will illustrate the King's methods of dealing with the Chinese. Yi was so wealthy and powerful that Prince Chakrabongs suggested in 1910 that his power be curbed by taxing much of his wealth away.[86] This advice was not followed. Rather, Yi was ennobled as Phra Anuwat Ratchaniyom and in 1920 was awarded a special royal order. Yi in return gave bridges, various pieces of property, and a school to the government.[87] Typical of the reciprocity between well-to-do Chinese and the government were two acts associated with a theater opened by Yi Ko-hong in 1917: on December 13 the King honored Yi by visiting the new theater; on December 22 Yi lent the theater to one of the "King's Own" Wild Tiger units for a benefit performance.[88] The King's methods of winning over wealthy Chinese were effective; Chinese businessmen in general were particularly generous donors to the King's fund drives—the cruiser fund drive, the Siamese Expeditionary Force drive, the Wild Tiger rifles drive.[89]

The King often expressed his gratitude to the Chinese for their gifts, given, as he expressed it, in gratitude for the benefits extended them in Siam. In an article whose title would be translated into English as "Thanks to Our Chinese Friends," written by Vajiravudh under the pseudonym Asvabahu, he praised the Chinese who had subscribed to the cruiser fund. He complimented them for realizing that a stronger Siam, free from danger, would be a better place for them to live and work. Chinese and Thai, he said, were after all "both Asians and ought not be enemies." In the article the King also included some typical admonitions. The Thai and Chinese could remain friends to the mutual advantage of both peoples, but the Chinese must understand that in Siam the Thai were the masters and the Chinese the guests. The host planned no injury to the guests, but the guests must be good citizens and not listen to agitators or instigators of trouble who spoke against the Thai.[90] The generosity

The Concept of Nationality

of Chinese to fund drives was even used by the King to shame his own people. In the play *Mahatama* a Chinese peddler makes his small donation, saying "Even though I'm Chinese, I live in Thailand; I want the Thai to like me." And a Thai servant says, "Everyone I see makes contributions to the cruiser fund. Even the Chinaman gives. If I don't give I'll feel shamefaced before the Chinese."[91]

The "Chinese problem" in Siam during the Sixth Reign had two dimensions. The first dimension, how to deal with the Chinese community, brought forth, as we have seen, a government policy that was notably consistent with the easygoing policies of the past. The second dimension, how the Thai should view themselves with respect to the Chinese, brought forth something new. It was this second dimension that related directly to Thai policies of nationalism; it was this second dimension that aroused Vajiravudh's greatest interest.

The Thai habit of ready acceptance of strangers, in the King's view, bore the great danger that the Thai would lose their own identity. An important part of the King's nationalistic message thus became the sharp differentiation between Thai and Chinese. In this differentiation the Chinese came off poorly. Chinese faults were contrasted with Thai virtues. The message was distinctly anti-Chinese. But anti-Chinese statements were not made to arouse the Chinese, or even to arouse the Thai, to hatred or to any rupture of relations. They were made to help the Thai realize who they were and what values Thai culture had so that the Thai would bestir themselves to save themselves.

The best known of the King's anti-Chinese writings was an essay published simultaneously in Thai and English in July 1914. The English title was "The Jews of the Orient."[92] The essay began with an analysis of the Jewish problem in Europe. The Jews in Europe, said Vajiravudh, differed from other Europeans not only because of their religion but also because of their racial exclusiveness. They always remained aliens, never became real citizens of the country they lived in. The Jews also held to a feeling of racial superiority, regarding themselves as the chosen people and Gentiles as inferior. And, most important, the Jews were thoroughly possessed by the moneymaking instinct. They had raised moneymaking to a cult for which they were willing to endure any hardship or privation, including obloquy and persecution.

After having provided this background of anti-Jewish stereotypes, Vajiravudh proceeded to point out parallels between the Jews and the Chinese. The Chinese also preserved their allegiance to their

The Concept of Nationality

race, taking advantage of all the benefits of foreign citizenship but giving no loyalty in return. The Chinese also possessed the concept of racial superiority, regarding only Chinese as civilized and classifying all other peoples as barbarians. And, lastly, the Chinese shared the Jewish moneymaking instinct; they had indeed "discovered the Art of living on nothing." In their devotion to money the Chinese were without morals or conscience or pity. They would cheat, rob, or murder for money. The wealth that Chinese produced was sent back to China; in effect the Chinese were "like so many vampires who steadily suck dry an unfortunate victim's life-blood." In this respect they were worse than the Jews, said Vajiravudh, for at least the Jews, who had no country, spent their wealth in the country in which they resided. (The King did begrudgingly allow one point in favor of the Chinese: that at least the Chinese, who, unlike the Jews, had a country of their own, did not get involved in local politics.)

"The Jews of the Orient" represents the King's views at their most extreme. The essay was scathing in its denunciations. Needless to say, it borrowed heavily on anti-Semitic thoughts of the West, thoughts the King had certainly become familiar with during his long years in England. And it borrowed from a growing body of anti-Chinese Western literature. Indeed, the comparison of the Chinese to the Jews was not new with Vajiravudh; it had been used at least as early as 1898 by a Britisher in the employ of Siam who had written that the Chinese were "the Jews of Siam."[93] There is good reason to believe, in fact, that the essay was written with a European audience in mind: the Jewish comparison might be expected to appeal to Westerners, but it would be meaningless to the Thai, who were hardly aware of the existence of the Jewish people. After the essay appeared, the King noted with particular pleasure its good reception by Europeans.[94]

Far more typical of the King's anti-Chinese writings were those that compared the Chinese with the Thai with the aim of enhancing Thai feelings of national pride. Vajiravudh wrote often of the "true Thai," and by this he meant someone who spoke Thai and was loyal to king, religion, and country. Mere residence in Siam was not enough. Nor was citizenship enough. Citizenship by naturalization or even by virtue of birth in Siam did not necessarily produce "true Thai."[95]

The Chinese were not true Thai because their basic identity was Chinese. Their loyalty was to China; most of them lived and worked in Siam only in order to accumulate wealth enough to return to

The Concept of Nationality

China. If war with China should ever come, the Chinese in Siam who could afford to do so would certainly flee to China. Even in peacetime, whenever there was any trouble or even rumor of trouble in Siam, Chinese immediately readied themselves to take passage on boats leaving the country.[96] In the areas of heaviest concentration of Chinese, notably in Bangkok's Sampeng district, the Chinese lived in almost totally Chinese communities, spoke Chinese, were closely involved with Chinese secret societies, and were virtually divorced from Thai associations.

Many of the Chinese, the King wrote, were remarkably like chameleons. These Chinese called themselves Thai. On occasion they spoke Thai. They had Thai friends. They went to Thai temples. They were Thai when it was in their interest to be Thai. But on other occasions they spoke Chinese, associated with Chinese, took the Chinese side in disputes. Their apparent acceptance of Buddhism was a matter of convenience, and when it suited his purposes a Chinese could as readily become a Christian, a Muslim, or a Hindu.[97] Vajiravudh distrusted such people. They were not "true Thai," for "one is either Thai or Chinese; he cannot be both."[98]

The Thai tendency not to regard the Chinese as foreigners arose, said the King, out of Thai lack of understanding of Siam's long-range interests. The Chinese were a convenience: they worked hard for little pay. The Thai were too ready to accept the easy way. As a result the Thai had become dependent on the Chinese. This dependence made many Thai reluctant to look at the problem that had arisen, to balk at saying anything critical about the Chinese. Such dependence, which led some Thai to say "If the Chinese go on strike again, we will all die," was woeful.[99] Other Thai asserted that, if the Chinese were not counted as Thai, there would be few Thai left to count at all.[100] Not so, said Vajiravudh. The congestion of Chinese in Bangkok gave a false picture, for in the countryside the Chinese were not numerous and, further, were much less Chinese. The Thai must not feel so abjectly beholden to the Chinese. The Thai must have more self-reliance and self-pride. The King wrote:

> I do not ask you to hate the Chinese; I ask only that you think more of yourselves. You who are Thai must do more for your own nationality than you do for the Chinese. Whenever you must choose between what is of benefit to the Chinese or to the Thai, there should be no question, you should choose the Thai. That is my only wish.[101]

Many of the concepts about the Chinese that the King attempted to foster were summed up in Chinese characters in his plays. A minor

The Concept of Nationality

character in *Mahatama* represents the good Chinese who appreciates the life Siam offers him and is openly grateful. In *Huačhai nakrop* the most villainous character in the play, named Sunbeng, is often referred to by the derogatory Thai term for Chinese, *ai čhek*. Sunbeng is depicted as completely selfish, with no loyalties to anything other than his personal interests. Sunbeng obviously stands for the self-seeking, chameleonlike Chinese who cannot be relied upon. In the words of one character in the play, such people "readily switch nationalities. They join the Thai as Thai; they join the other side and become something else.... we can never be sure what they are."[102] In still another play, *Wiwaha phra samut*, a Chinese "boy" provides much of the comedy. He becomes the butt of jokes because of his pigtail and his mispronunciation of Thai. The humor is pointed, but it is not vicious. And a song, sung by the "boy" in broken Thai, provided Thai audiences with a clever encapsulation of royal views, a neat and memorable poetic stereotype, of the average career of Chinese immigrants to Siam:

> Chinaman very smart; no look down on him.
> He know how to make living in unfancy job.
> He can be humble cook or boy;
> He take hard work to make money.
> Master trust him to buy things;
> He diligent in getting good bargains.
> He buy at cheap price in his way
> And keep the change as he please;
> He get old clothes of master to wear.
> If the master scold, he can take it.
> Little by little he save up money;
> Before long he become rich
> And leave the master to set up shop.
> Soon the shop become full store;
> Then he become a very smart big businessman.
> The Secret Society choose him as third brother;
> He can go about and throw his weight around,
> He can do what he like and get away with it.
> He watch out for police so they not bother him,
> And then he be happy forever after.[103]

Other Asian Minorities

Second in size among the minority groups in Siam were the Malays. The Malays were a distant second; they comprised only about 2 percent of the total population. But the fact that the Malays were

The Concept of Nationality

concentrated in southern Siam, where, indeed, in the southernmost provinces they comprised a population majority, did make the Malays a special problem in terms of Thai nationalism. Unlike the Chinese, the Malays had not migrated to Siam; they had become Siamese nationals by virtue of Thai political expansion southward over territories populated by Malays. The Malays, therefore, had every right to consider the provinces they lived in as home. Their allegiance to the Siamese nation could not be assumed. The nationalistic symbols the King relied upon all heavily stressed the "Thainess" of the Thai. And the Malays of Siam were not ethnically Thai; they were Muslim and not Buddhist, and their language, customs, dress, and dietary habits were different from those of the Thai. Furthermore, their history was that of a conquered territory once in vassal status.

Vajiravudh was aware of the special Malay case insofar as nationalism was concerned. He was anxious not to antagonize the Malays, for he keenly felt the vulnerability of the area that he frequently described as a rich jewel that Siam might well lose if it were not treasured. And so he gave the Malays more attention, accorded them more favors, than any other minority group.

The King's favor was exhibited by official royal tours in the southern provinces. In 1915 the royal progress in the South lasted two months; in 1917 it lasted six weeks. In fact the South was the only region, outside of the Central Plain, to which the King paid extensive visits. He visited Khorat in the Northeast once, in 1921, but spent only a few days there, and, as King, he never visited the North. On the southern tours he extended courtesies to Malay Muslim groups on many occasions. At Nakhọn Sithammarat in 1917, for example, he granted an audience to the heads of the Muslim communities and to the imams and hajis of the various mosques in the area. At this audience he received a loyal address by the Governor of Saiburi on behalf of his coreligionists, thanking the King for his protection, and was presented with a "sacred sword." Vajiravudh, in his return speech, pointed out that he regarded the protection of Islam as his duty. He said:

> We intend always to give all the people under our government our protection and the opportunity to pursue their activities in the religious sphere to the full in freedom, without oppression or any pressure to change their faith or believe in a religion they do not favor. All of you who are adherents of the religion of Muhammad, we feel, are our subjects in no way different from those who hold other religions. And so we have declared our intention to protect all adherents of Islam who live in our country.[104]

The Concept of Nationality

He also expressed the hope that, if the need arose, he could count on his Malay subjects to rally round the sacred sword they had presented to him, to participate in the defense of the nation. Although the King's tours in 1915 and 1917 undoubtedly had several purposes, including the wish to end rumors that the South was a breeding ground for seditionists training to work against the British in India, the basic purpose seems clear: to strengthen the bonds between the government and its Muslim Malay subjects. The King apparently considered his person as a bonding instrument. Showing himself before large numbers of his people in the South would, he felt, convince them that Vajiravudh was their king and that he was a king who cared.

The King's reception of Muslim Malays was by no means restricted to his visits to the South. There were Malay communities, which owed their origin to groups of prisoners of war taken in the early nineteenth century, sprinkled around the Bangkok area, and on local tours the King passed through such communities and accepted their "enthusiastic welcome."[105] Vajiravudh also received Muslim and Malay representatives at court on his birthday and on other occasions.

At his birthday celebration in 1916 the King took the unusual step of accepting a petition from Muslim representatives who asked him to extend his protection over Muslim communities in the Bangkok area. A Muslim representative read a loyal address in which the Malays expressed their "deep gratification" and promised to give "unalterable loyalty to the Throne" even to the extent of laying down their lives in the defense of the king and the kingdom. The King was thenceforward termed "the Protector of the Faith of the Prophet Muhammad." The King's reply continued the theme of the original address. Vajiravudh said that he was certain the Muslims in Siam would indeed come forth to offer themselves in the defense of the realm, ". . . for in so doing, they do but follow the precepts of their Prophet, namely, that to die in defence of one's religion is a meritorious act, and indeed they would be serving the cause of Islam when they serve the country that gives it her protection."[106] In an audience with Muslim representatives on his birthday in 1917, Vajiravudh received pledges similar to those of 1916 and, in addition, the "Aden Staff of Islam," which was described as "a holy emblem of Faith entitling the holder to the loyalty of all the Faithful."[107]

With respect to law, the Malays in southern Siam seem to have continued to be given, through their religious leaders, the right to decide cases "of Islamic nature."[108] Under the Education Act of 1921, no bars were placed on instruction in Malay, although the teaching

The Concept of Nationality

of Thai became compulsory. And a small concession made to Malay Boy Scouts is highly indicative of His Majesty's attitude: the King himself gave Malay boys in the Boy Scout movement in Pattani permission to wear Malay-style caps in place of regulation caps, which the local boys considered "not suitable."[109] This concession was undoubtedly based on His Majesty's overall delight with his southern compatriots because of their enthusiastic acceptance of the Wild Tiger Corps and the Boy Scouts.

Aside from the Chinese and Malays, there were various other minority groups, but their numbers and their position in Thai society were so insignificant that they did not require special consideration. On occasion, however, one or another of these small groups was accorded special attention: for example, the Vietnamese in Bangkok participated in the funerary rites for the Queen Mother in 1919[110] and for Prince Chakrabongs in 1920;[111] the small Japanese community was honored by the presence of the King at the cremation of the Japanese minister in 1921.[112] One governmental action with respect to the Indians resident in Siam was of nationalistic significance: in 1917 an order was issued that the use of the designation *khaek* (literally "guest," but also a somewhat deprecating term for "Indian") in front of personal names of Indians in government records was to be abandoned. The use of the similar designation *čhin* in front of Chinese names had been abandoned some time earlier.[113]

It would have been possible to view the various Thai dialect groups in Siam as comprising ethnic elements different from the Thai of the country's center. The Lao of the Northeast and the Thaiyai of the North could have been regarded as separate from the Thai of the Čhaophraya Plain on historical and, to some extent, on cultural grounds. The basic linguistic and cultural affinities of all Thai groups, however, are very close, and these groups have commonly been seen as comprising one ethnic family. In any event and for obvious reasons the Siamese government, even before Vajiravudh's time, had decided on a policy of treating all these peoples as Thai and using the term "Thai" for all of them.

The practice of using the term Thai for the Thaiyai of the North and the Lao of the Northeast had apparently not extended below the top levels of government during Chulalongkorn's reign. Its spread to all levels of government was vigorously promoted during the Sixth Reign. Consistent with the policy of seeing all Thai dialect groups as Thai was the decision to use only "standard Thai," that is, the Bangkok dialect, in public schools; the Lao script was to be discouraged.[114] In a report on the Northeast in 1915, Prince Chakra-

The Concept of Nationality

bongs stressed the necessity for a policy of national identification for the Lao, who, he said, "must be regarded as Thai."[115] And in a report on the northern provinces written after his trip there in 1916, Prince Chakrabongs went into considerable detail about the problem. He commented that high officials were careful not to use the term Lao and were following the government policy so that "all the people will feel themselves to be part of the Thai nation and abandon the idea that they are in a subservient territory." Lower officials, however, he reported, were not consistent in calling the local people Thai and tended to look down on them "as do Westerners with regard to all Asians." Some officials used the terms *thai nŭa* ("northern Thai") and *thai tai* ("southern Thai") to differentiate the dialect groups. This practice, said Prince Chakrabongs, should also be discouraged. If distinctions were needed, terms such as "inhabitant of Chiangmai" or "inhabitant of Bangkok" would suffice. The Prince further said that instructions to officials were not enough and suggested that sanctions be imposed on erring officials, such as denial of promotion or pay increases—or even dismissal.[116]

A logical extension of the broad application of the term Thai to all Thai dialect groups in Siam would have been an attempt to apply the term to such groups outside of Siam as well. This idea, and the political concept of a pan-Thai state that would go with it, was apparently never put on paper by any government official or any other Thai during the Sixth Reign. The one expression of the idea on record during the reign was made by a Westerner who suggested that the Thai race be preserved by creating for it a solid, substantial government "from Yunnan and Kwang-Si, in China, down to the southern limit of Thai speaking people, and reaching from the Mekong Pacific watershed on the East to the Salween river and Indian Ocean on the West." In such a fashion there would come into being "a separate ethnological entity," a structure for "the whole Thai race." The idea was presented as a dream "that will alarm no one since it is not even dreamed by one of the Thai race.... And as in these days the young men of Siam are given to dreaming dreams this may give them food for thought that should be sobering in its possibilities."[117]

Whether Vajiravudh and his contemporaries ever dreamed the pan-Thai dream, it is impossible to know. It can be assumed, though, that if they did they certainly considered it an impossible dream. And highly impolitic to ever mention or even hint at. The rumor that reached Siam in 1912 that the French were thinking of breaking up Laos and attaching pieces of it to other portions of French Indochina evoked no Thai response. The press reported that Siam, both

The Concept of Nationality

officially and unofficially, was "entirely uninterested in what is after all purely an internal administrative measure beyond her frontier."[118] Interested or not, the Thai were determined to be diplomatically correct. And, with respect to neighboring states, this meant keeping scrupulously out of their affairs. As has been mentioned in chapter 4, all efforts were made to allay French suspicions of Thai intentions. In the 1910s and 1920s Siam was still too close to its period of territorial losses, still too much in awe of its neighbors' power, to dare dream of a larger sway at the expense of others. This dream would come when power relationships changed with the fall of France in World War II. But at the time of Vajiravudh's death in 1925, the pan-Thai dream still lay fifteen years in the future.

8

The Past as Model

A vital element in Siamese nationalism under King Vajiravudh was an emphasis on tradition, the cultural inheritances of history. Siam needed to be proud of its Western-style progress; it needed also to be proud of the values of its own culture and its own past.

The stress on the past seems an inescapable part of any nationalist movement. In many, however, the look backwards has created severe tensions, strains, and fundamental insecurities. Nationalist movements led by revolutionaries against their own traditional social elites and classes have tended to be iconoclastic, repudiating any and all symbols of tradition. The anti-Manchu, anti-Confucian, anti-Mandarin reformers of China, for example, had great difficulty coming to terms with their own tradition; at one time they sought to "convert the Temple of Heaven in Peking into a school of forestry."[1] Yet the tug of the cultural inheritance on such revolutionaries could not be denied. However it might be expressed—in arguments for reappreciation of the values of the Chinese family or Chinese mysticism or

The Past as Model

Chinese peasant life—it needed to be expressed for the very sake of nationalism itself. A total rejection of all the past could only mean a total rejection of everything distinctively Chinese, that is, a rejection of the Chinese nation, an impossible stance for a nationalist.[2]

Tradition makes a very different claim on nationalist leaders reacting against foreign rule. Here the philosophic way seems clearer. The history before the dark colonial present is seen as the golden age to which a people, once free of colonial mastery, may return. Early in the history of Indonesian nationalism Sukarno put the problem clearly: "... first we point out to the people that they have a glorious past, secondly we intensify the notion among our people that the present time is dark, and the third way is to show them the promising, pure and luminous future and how to get there."[3] The problem with tradition for the modern anti-colonialist is how to define it, how to reconnect the thread that, in fact, colonialism and Westernization have broken.

Compared with the problems faced by most modern nationalists in adjusting to the past, Vajiravudh's task was simple. There had been no foreign rule; the threads of Siamese tradition were still intact. Nor had there been any revolution against the country's own social elites. There was, therefore, no reason to repudiate the Siamese cultural inheritance. Traditional links need not be severed; on the contrary, they required reinforcing and reemphasizing. Whatever the problems a traditional leadership may face in stimulating nationalism, they do not include that of finding threads of continuity. Such threads abounded in Siam; it was the role of the King as the nationalist leader to identify the ones that would serve best in weaving the fabric of a proud nation.

The ancient elements that Vajiravudh chose as having greatest value for his nationalist program were four: history, Buddhism, the arts, and literature.

History

While there were few philosophical or psychological obstacles for King Vajiravudh in his use of history as a means of stimulating nationalism, some problems did exist. First, Siamese historical records were sketchy; second, the mass of the people had only the meagerest knowledge of their history. In a sense there were assets inherent in these problems: historical research and popular notions of history could both be expanded in ways favorable to nationalistic purposes. To a large extent this is what occurred.

The sketchiness of the Thai historical record had several causes.

The Past as Model

White ants and wars with Burma had both taken their toll. But perhaps even more important was the traditional lack of interest in compiling historical accounts. It is too much to say that the Thai were ahistorical; the lucid and lively description of Sukhothai in 1292, partly in the words of the reigning king, shows a feeling for man's place in time that is historical in a very real sense. And other inscriptions, portions of chronicles, and references to lost chronicles are evidence that records of past events were of some interest to the court. Yet that interest seems not to have been institutionalized or to have played a central role in the ideology of governance. In the Bangkok period, which saw some quickening of historical interest, at first because of the newness of the dynasty and later because of the intellectual challenge of the West, histories were compiled by members of the royal family and high nobles. The impact of these histories on the country at large was minimal, however, for they were written for an extremely small educated elite surrounding the court.

The concept of history presented in a style that would be meaningful for the masses was an innovation of King Vajiravudh's. The King possessed to a degree the antiquarian interest and eye of his father and of his uncle, Prince Damrong.[4] He was well read in the chronicles and epigraphs that had survived from Siam's past. As a prince he had in 1908 made an extensive trip into the heartland of the first Thai kingdom in Siam, traveling across difficult terrain by boats, horses, and elephants. He described the ruins at Kamphaengphet, Sukhothai, and Sawankhalok and came up with theories related to history that he hoped would be useful to the experts on antiquity.[5] He made other trips to historical sites during the reign, and in several literary works he set forth various ideas on Thai history. Essentially, however, his scholarly interests were far outweighed by his interest in the use of history as a means toward nationalism.

Some of the King's concepts on the uses of antiquity and history are revealed in his description of his trip to the North in 1908. He expressed the hope that, because of his account of the Thai past, "the Thai will become more aware that our race is not a new race, is not a race of jungle folk, or to use the English word, 'uncivilized.'"[6] To put it simply, the King believed, and sought to persuade others to believe, that the Thai had a proud past, a past worthy of emulation in the present:

> Our Thai race has achieved much progress, so we ought to feel shamefaced today not only before others but also before our own ancestors with whom we cannot compare.... The ancient Thai had the imagination

The Past as Model

and industry to build large and beautiful buildings that lasted. Thai today demolish and destroy old sites or let them decay because of their infatuation with new things from the West. They do not know how to select what is best for our country.[7]

There is little question that the King himself believed in past Thai achievements. In describing one temple in Sukhothai, for example, he marvelled at its construction and remembered how he had also marvelled, years before, at the monuments of Egypt: "I felt gratified that we also have something unusual and worth being proud of."[8]

The ways in which Vajiravudh sought to use history to stimulate nationalism included emphasizing the need to preserve old sites, encouraging the production of historical materials, popularizing the stories of the past, and utilizing particular episodes or aspects of the past for present purposes.

The King's policies of seeking to preserve old sites and ancient objects and of stimulating production of historical works were continuations of policies begun under Kings Mongkut and Chulalongkorn. King Mongkut, while he was still a prince-monk, had been responsible for bringing a number of important stone inscriptions, including that of Ramkhamhaeng, to Bangkok. And King Chulalongkorn, particularly after an order of 1887 directing officials to search for old inscriptions, received many stone steles into the royal museum. New appeals for inscriptions and rubbings of inscriptions were made in the Sixth Reign, and the collection was considerably expanded.[9] This work was given a firmer foundation with the creation of the Archaeological Service in January 1924.[10] The work of preservation, research, and restoration of archaeological sites was placed under the control of the National Library. Within weeks after the establishment of the service, important sites were being given new attention. Prince Damrong and Prince Naris visited the ruins at Lopburi and Ayutthaya; G. Coedès inspected old monuments at Phitsanulok, Sawankhalok, Sukhothai, and Kamphaengphet—all with the aim of preparing a list of protected areas and planning for future research.[11] The King was personally interested in this preservation work and was particularly vehement on the subject of the despoliation of ancient monuments by those who dug into them for buried treasure. He once wrote: "If these people would use the efforts and the strength they employ in destroying our antiquities in good and proper ways, our country would advance not a little."[12]

The King realized that in the process of modernization some monuments of past glory might have to be destroyed. But he noted with regret that bricks from sites at the ancient capital at Ayutthaya had been used to construct railroad embankments; he expressed the hope that such exchanges of antiquities for progress would not occur often.[13]

The strengthening of the National Library and the expansion of publication of historical texts followed a dynamic begun before the Sixth Reign. Vajiravudh gave support to the library by assigning it new quarters in 1916. On the death of the head of the library in 1915, the King appointed Prince Damrong to the post. The Prince, whose vigor and power as Minister of Interior had rankled the King, was able to redirect his considerable energies into the politically harmless pursuits of scholarship and scholarly publishing.[14] A similarly fortuitous, and similarly unexpected, change came to the library as a result of Siam's entry into World War I in 1917: the elderly German curator, Dr. Frankfurter, was replaced by a young French epigraphist, G. Coedès, who was to become the premier scholar of Southeast Asia's classical period. In 1924 Coedès as curator published a definitive edition of the inscriptions of Sukhothai, Siam's first Thai kingdom.

It was in his own writings on history, however, that King Vajiravudh could fully apply his nationalistic notions. Although Vajiravudh did not write historical texts,[15] his work was sprinkled with historical references and historical views. Historical justifications were freely supplied for old institutions he wished to preserve, such as the monarchy, and for new institutions he wished to establish, such as the Wild Tigers. And in history were found the values, the ideals, the goals the King hoped to instill in the Thai nation.

All the virtues the King hoped to reawaken in the Thai people—their loyalty to their king, their devotion to Buddhism and morality, their sense of unity and willingness to fight to preserve that unity—were discovered by him to be ancient virtues. History showed that Siam was strong when its kings were strong; history showed that Siam was weak when the royal authority was in dispute, as, for example, when King Thammaracha died, when King Songtham usurped the throne, and when King Chakkraphat died.[16] In the sweep of Thai history the King tended to see the earliest epochs, the Sukhothai period in the thirteenth and fourteenth centuries and the early Ayutthaya era through the fifteenth and sixteenth centuries, as the most glorious. He felt that a decline had begun in the seventeenth century and noted that the whole last hundred years of the Ayutthaya period were marked by irregular accessions, petty rivalries, and a lack of harmony or feeling of national purpose, which had given the

The Past as Model

Burmese the opportunity to invade and lay the country to waste.[17] The Bangkok period, however, under the dynasty of his forebears, had seen a return to glory: a succession of wise rulers, appreciating the force of the "stream of progress," had been wise enough to welcome civilization and progress with open doors, "without being *forced* to do so at the cannon's mouth."[18]

Vajiravudh's interest in history was not restricted to the episodical or illustrative or the brief literary allusion that provided background for a specific argument. Certain historical figures intrigued him. Not surprisingly these figures were all "heroes." They were all warriors. They were men, and a few women, who had met the challenges of their times. They were Thai of the past whose lives and values merited emulation by modern Thai.

Three men received more attention than most; they were Naresuan, Taksin, and Phra Ruang. As might be expected, all three were kings, all three were military leaders, all three were unifiers of the Thai people.

King Naresuan the Great, as Vajiravudh called him, had been the Thai monarch during the last years of the sixteenth century. He had successfully brought an end to a fifteen-year period of Burmese suzerainty in Siam. According to Thai chronicles, Naresuan had fought a decisive battle against a new invading Burmese army in January 1593 and, to commemorate this victory, had erected a stupa, or *čhedi*, at the scene of the victory. The stupa and the victory had subsequently been forgotten. The new interest in history and the rediscovery of old Thai historical accounts led Prince Damrong to direct provincial officials to search for Naresuan's stupa. A likely site, called Dǫn Čhedi, was found and reported to the King in 1913.[19]

King Vajiravudh, who had extolled King Naresuan for his bravery and for exemplifying the true ideals of a "Wild Tiger" as early as May 1911,[20] decided to make use of the discovery of Naresuan's stupa in a large public display. During the Wild Tiger maneuvers early in 1914, the King organized a march of almost a thousand men from the Tiger camp at Nakhǫn Pathom to the stupa site in Suphanburi Province. After a seven-day march, the stupa remains were reached. The site was verified through various artifacts that were identified as dating from Naresuan's time. On January 28, approximately on the day 321 years after Naresuan's "glorious victory," a great commemorative service was held, a service that concluded with the King's delivery of a ringing patriotic address.

In the address Naresuan was praised as the king whose victory

The Past as Model

"upon this very spot secured our national freedom and made our nation respected by the Burmese and Talaings [Mon]." Naresuan, however, did not act alone; he was able to rely upon a Thai people who were loyal to him and gave him their full confidence. The historical lesson to be learned from Naresuan's time was that a united and patriotic people who were loyal to a capable leader could overcome any adversity. Vajiravudh said:

> When every Siamese shall begin to think and speak as one man, then will the time have arrived when there will be no longer any anxiety for the well-being of our nation. Individually each one of us is comparable to a lump of earth which goes to form part of a mountain. It would be great folly to look after only the small lump and allow the mountain to crumble. We must exert ourselves to preserve the mountain in order to preserve the existence of its component parts.[21]

The way to become "the worthy successors of our ancestors who fought for King Naresuan the Great" was for all Thai to resolve "to think and act together" and so become the unified patriotic people they had once been.

King Vajiravudh's glorification of Taksin, the King of Siam from 1767 to 1781, would at first glance appear to be a paradox, since the Chakkri dynasty had taken over the throne that Taksin had been forced to vacate. Although the first Chakkri ruler, Vajiravudh's great-great-grandfather, had not deposed Taksin, he had accepted the accession and had ordered the execution of the king who had been imprisoned as a madman. Vajiravudh restored King Taksin to respectability by stressing the virtues of the early years of his reign. Whatever his later faults, Taksin had, Vajiravudh noted, been responsible for ridding Siam of the Burmese hosts and reuniting the kingdom. Taksin, he said, was a brave leader who exemplified the true ideals of a Wild Tiger. Unlike some kings who thought only of their personal pleasure, Taksin always put the needs of his country first and, heedless of his own safety and comfort, risked all in his desire to save Siam.[22] In addition to making favorable comments about Taksin, Vajiravudh in 1916 devoted the "people's" *kathin* (the ceremony of the giving of robes to monks) largely to celebrating that king's memory. A temple particularly associated with King Taksin was made the site of the King's pilgrimage. The temple had never been visited before by a reigning king of the Chakkri dynasty. The barge on which the King was transported to the temple was deliberately designed in the shape of a Chinese dragon, and the royal pavilion

The Past as Model

on its back was fashioned as a Chinese house.²³ These were stylistic references to King Taksin's part-Chinese ancestry.

The hero nonpareil in Vajiravudh's estimation, however, was Phra Ruang. The name Phra Ruang is a name that appears often in early Thai legend. In the Chronicle of the North (*Phongsawadan nüa*) Phra Ruang refers to the Thai leader who established the independence of the kingdom of Sukhothai, that is, the first king of Sukhothai, who is called Si Intharathit in inscriptions. King Vajiravudh used the term Phra Ruang in this sense, but he also understood the term as a name applying to the entire dynasty founded by Si Intharathit. When he used the term to refer to a particular individual, he meant either Si Intharathit, who reigned early in the thirteenth century, or his son, Ramkhamhaeng, who reigned late in the century.²⁴ The glory of the former was his establishment of Thai independence from Cambodia; that of the latter, the expansion of Thai power over much of present-day Thailand.

References to Phra Ruang abound in Vajiravudh's writings. His best-known travel account is that of his trip to "Phra Ruang country" (*Thiao müang phra ruang*), and his most highly regarded historical play is about Phra Ruang's success in winning Thai independence. A number of poems celebrate Phra Ruang's memory. And, as has been mentioned, the object of the great patriotic drive organized by the Navy League was to purchase a warship that the King named *Phra Ruang*.

The play *Phra ruang* was prepared in at least three versions: a traditional dance drama, written in December 1912; a modern drama, written before February 1914; and a musical, first presented in 1924.²⁵ The modern drama is the version that is best known and most frequently performed. The King, in fact, deliberately wrote it in a style that would make it relatively easy for Wild Tiger groups and other amateur players to perform. The play eventually became a standard text in secondary schools.²⁶

Phra ruang exemplifies Vajiravudh's historical technique, patriotic didacticism, and dramatic skill at their finest. The historical method he used, which probably borrowed not a little from Prince Damrong,²⁷ was to subject his legendary sources to a critical and logical examination, conjure up a rational explanation, and present that rationalized account as history. This method depended on the theory that careers of heroes in history undergo a continuous embellishment in time, that there is a natural inclination to endow heroes with extraordinary powers, to see their noble acts as arising from

The Past as Model

superhuman attributes; the historian merely has to peel away the fabulous to get back to the real personality.[28] The legend of Phra Ruang in the Chronicle of the North, for example, described him as possessing various magical powers. Phra Ruang's difficulties with his Cambodian overlords began when the vassal prince sent tribute water to the Cambodian king in loosely woven baskets. The baskets retained the water because of the power of Phra Ruang's words commanding that they do so. The Cambodians became alarmed at a vassal whose magic was so great and decided that they must take action against him. Vajiravudh rejected the magic of the legend, but retained the story by supplying the reasonable element that he was sure history had lost. The Thai of Phra Ruang's time, he said, had suffered keenly from the Cambodian exactions. To reduce the difficulty in sending the water tribute, Phra Ruang, who was extraordinary only in his intellect and compassion for his people, decided to replace the heavy and breakable water jars ordinarily used to contain the tribute water with much lighter containers, and so he devised baskets coated with waterproof lacquer. On receiving the water in such an unorthodox fashion, the Cambodians became aware of the potential danger this clever vassal posed. At another point in the traditional Phra Ruang story, a Cambodian was sent by his king to capture Phra Ruang. He started on his mission by miraculously plunging into the earth, and emerged hundreds of miles away in Thai territory. This Cambodian "earth diver" of legend, the King said, was simply a popular distortion of what originally was a commonplace spy mission; the figurative "going underground" had acquired a fantastic literal meaning.

The Phra Ruang story, as finally rationalized by Vajiravudh, became a straightforward history of a Thai hero leading a valiant people out of bondage into freedom. Phra Ruang outsmarts the Cambodians; his people resist the Cambodian armies; and, at the play's end, the populations of Sukhothai and Lopburi combine to offer fealty to Phra Ruang as the monarch of a new independent Thai state.

Phra Ruang is brought out of legend and into life by Vajiravudh, but he remains very much the hero. He is the epitome of all virtues. He is extolled by other characters in the play as loving his people as if they were his own children and as being courageous, compassionate, beneficent beyond the beneficence of parents, incomparable:

> A magnificent example for the Thai
> Whose name will surely last through all the ages.[29]

The Past as Model

In the earlier version of the Phra Ruang play, one noble says of him, "Not once in a thousand years does there appear a man with his merit."[30]

Phra Ruang is the brave leader, but a brave leader to be successful needs a loyal and courageous people. The hero—be he Phra Ruang or Naresuan or Taksin or, indeed, Vajiravudh—cannot work miracles all alone. The final speech of the play, delivered by Phra Ruang as he accepts the throne of Sukhothai, is a stirring patriotic call to all Thai to realize their great promise as a free people. The speech is, of course, Vajiravudh's own call to the Thai of his time rather than an attempt to recreate Phra Ruang's sentiments. In this speech—and occasionally in some other contexts as well—Vajiravudh identified himself with Phra Ruang.[31] Phra Ruang urges his people to maintain their armed might and their unity so as to leave no opportunity for an enemy to destroy the state. He says, in part:

> I ask the Thai to join in love,
> To join in fellowship,
> So that when the enemy comes
> We can fight him in full strength.
> The Thai combining their power
> Will be able to raise a staunch defense.
> Even if a powerful foe comes,
> He will be defeated.
>
> I ask only that we Thai not destroy our nation.
> Let us unite our state, unite our hearts, into a great whole.
> Thai—do not harm or destroy Thai,
> But combine your spirit and your strength to preserve the state
> So that all foreign peoples
> Will give us increasing respect.
>
> Help one another to further our progress
> So the name "Thai" will redound throughout the world.
> Help one another to sustain
> Both our nation and our faith
> So they will last to the end of time.
> Let us progress, Thai! Chaiyo![32]

The patriotic purpose of dramatizing the Phra Ruang story, which is abundantly clear in the text itself, was made explicit by the royal author. In a preface to the first version Vajiravudh wrote: "I hope it will serve for more than casual reading. I hope it will be a means for our Thai race to reflect on our history and make us feel that our race is not a new race but an old race with an admirable history."

The Past as Model

The King continued in the preface to point to the lessons of the past: the lesson of a king who loved his nation so much he was willing to suffer and die for it; the lesson of a loyal people who respected their leader and obeyed him. This relationship between the king and his people, Vajiravudh stated, was proper and good in Sukhothai times, and this relationship was "suitable for us Thai today to emulate."[33]

Vajiravudh extolled Phra Ruang in several poems in addition to his dramatic works. One long poem was a versification of a collection of old Thai proverbs known as The Maxims of Phra Ruang (*Suphasit phra ruang*).[34] The maxims, which include the well-known saying that Thai are free men and not slaves, were introduced by the King with lines praising Phra Ruang and his moral teachings—teachings which, the King said, despite their age, retained relevance and value. Another poem refers to Ramkhamhaeng, "the most daring of men in battle," as Phra Ruang and urges Thai to contribute to the fund to purchase a warship that will bear his name.[35]

Historical figures other than the three heroes already mentioned were honored by Vajiravudh. Among them were two women: Queen Suriyothai, a sixteenth-century heroine who sacrificed her life to save her husband; and Khunying Mo, the wife of a governor of Khorat who helped defeat an invading Lao army in the early nineteenth century. One important work, a verse-play entitled *Thao saen pom*, was devoted to the demythologized history of the father of the founder of Ayutthaya; here, however, Vajiravudh made little attempt to turn the principal character into a major patriotic hero.[36]

The evoking of the past for nationalistic purposes extended beyond the preservation of historical sites and objects, the encouragement of production of historical works, and the heralding of old heroes. A deliberate attempt was made, for example, to revitalize traditional ceremonies and customs in order to focus attention on the nation. King Vajiravudh's elaborations of the homage to dynastic ancestors, resulting in the creation of a "National Day," and his additions to the celebrations of the king's accession day and the king's birthday have already been discussed in chapter 6. Vajiravudh's revival of the first plowing ceremony is another example of his use of traditional ceremonies for new purposes. This ceremony, an old Hinduist rite meant to insure good crops, had almost disappeared by Vajiravudh's time. Vajiravudh brought it back into favor. While the ceremony had little direct bearing on nationalism, it had been popular among Siam's large farm population, and its resuscitation could not help but bring the people closer to their government. This fact was

The Past as Model

appreciated by the King, as an article on the plowing ceremony either written by or approved by him made clear. The article pointed out that, although the ceremony had no tangible use, it was popular among the people and had meaning for them. "And when most people think it useful, then it is!"[37]

A number of other ceremonies and social customs received the King's support. The old popular festival of *loi krathong*, the floating of candle-lit offerings on the rivers, had received no royal attention for more than twenty years; in Bangkok it had ceased to be celebrated. King Vajiravudh in 1915 revived the festival by fixing three evenings for its celebration, by encouraging members of the royal family and certain officials to take part in it, and by himself going to watch the procession of floating decorations.[38] The festival was a huge success. In the following year, however, royal support for it was not continued because of the augmentation of the ceremonies for the anniversary of the King's accession (at which the new dynastic name was introduced) and the augmentation of the ceremonies for the King's birthday (his thirty-sixth, the end of his third cycle). And the King made no further attempts to revive the festival.

King Vajiravudh supplied some reasons for his support of old Thai custom in a rejoinder he wrote to a newspaper criticism of the tonsure ceremony as a waste of money. The King grouped the topknot-cutting ceremony with ordination, marriage, and funeral rites as all belonging in the same category. All could be regarded as wasteful, as "grinding pepper sauce in the river." Yet, held the King, they were no more wasteful than Western social affairs—coming-out parties, balls, and concerts—which the Thai did not indulge in. Such social affairs were, said Vajiravudh, earmarks of civilized peoples. Peaceful and pleasant social intercourse, the gathering of friends, the mingling of peoples from various stations of life were all part of the necessary cement of society. If topknot ceremonies were to go, the King wryly queried, what would take their place? Western barroom bashes perhaps?[39]

It is impossible to measure with any accuracy the effect of the King's campaign for increasing Thai historical awareness. But there can be no doubt that it had some effect. Even as early as 1921 the *Bangkok Times* was able to conclude that "... practically up to the time when the present King came to the throne, the history of Siam for the average Siamese began with his own earliest recollections. Young Siam to-day is gaining a wider vision and some sense of the fact that the roots of the national life go deep into the past."[40]

The Past as Model

Buddhism

Buddhism occupied a very special and important place in the nationalistic program of King Vajiravudh. For adherence to Buddhism was seen by the King as one of the essential characteristics of the Thai as a people. A primary element in the definition of Siam was that it was a Buddhist nation.

Regard for Buddhism was, of course, nothing new for kings of Siam. The relationship between the monarchy and the Buddhist Order had been close since earliest history. It was a symbiotic relationship: the Buddhist Order supported the state, the state supported the order. The religious and civil administrations complemented each other; very rarely did either interfere in the vital concerns of the other. In addition to supporting Buddhism, Thai kings had also long maintained a body of court Brahmins whose role was limited to the performance of certain royal ceremonies, such as the coronation ceremonies. During the reign of King Mongkut, however, the Buddhist ceremonial role in state affairs had been expanded and the significance of the court Brahmins had declined.[41]

Vajiravudh, as a prince, had received traditional instruction in Buddhist principles. This instruction had been maintained even during the Prince's period of education in England. Indeed, the experience abroad may have sharpened Vajiravudh's conscious adherence to Buddhism, for in the European setting, young Thai students often encountered Christian arguments against and Christian challenges to their Buddhism. Vajiravudh may have been reflecting on his own experience when he pointed out that young Thai studying abroad were particularly vulnerable to Christian arguments: they did not know their own religion well enough to defend it; they were apt to remain silent before the voluble European and his criticisms of Buddhism.[42] Vajiravudh apparently met this Western threat successfully, and his faith in Buddhism emerged, if anything, stronger from the encounter. When he returned to Siam, he underwent the traditional ordination for Thai young men and spent four months in late 1904 in the monkhood, studying Buddhist discipline, Pali and Sanskrit texts, and the administration of the Buddhist Order.

Vajiravudh, as king, was Buddhism's prime patron. He maintained traditional support of the order and traditional Buddhist rites of merit-making such as the *kathin* (giving of robes to monks) and the *wisakhabucha* (celebration of the birth, enlightenment, and death of the Buddha). In an effort to popularize *wisakhabucha* Vajiravudh attempted to make it a special day for children. At the Royal Pages

The Past as Model

School a *wisakha* tree made of bo tree branches was decorated "like a Christmas tree" and presents were distributed by the King to the young boys.[43] Special Buddhist ceremonies in the palace were also continued. One such ceremony was the fashioning of a special Buddha image for the reign to insure prosperity and victory. This image, known as the Phra Chai Watthana, was cast on January 8, 1911, and consecrated in a two-day ceremony and celebration in October 1912.[44] There were countless other such ceremonies dotting the royal calendar.

The customary administrative tasks related to the Buddhist Order were also performed by the King. By and large, appointments, promotions, and awarding of names to monks in high administrative posts were given routine royal approval, but in some cases the King scrutinized them carefully and asked questions or made suggestions. On one submission on October 16, 1925, for example, Vajiravudh approved the promotion of forty-nine monks, suggested the promotion of one additional monk, and suggested name changes for four monks.[45] At ministerial meetings the King discussed revisions of examinations for monks and the amount of aid to be given royal monasteries for maintenance.[46] A crucial decision on the successor to the Supreme Patriarch, who died in 1921, was also made by the King, who chose the new patriarch's rank and even decided on the proper translation of his title into English ("Patriarch of the Kingdom," later changed to "Prince Patriarch of the Kingdom"). The King, in an interesting aside on this subject of patriarchal titles, wrote his secretary: "I rather like the style of the Archbishop of Canterbury, who is called 'PRIMATE OF ALL ENGLAND.' But it might sound too imitative."[47]

One policy of the reign toward religion that marked a change from previous policy was the King's encouragement of merit-making in practical and progressive ways. His favor for the building of schools over the building of temples has already been noted in chapter 6. This policy marked an extension of an idea expressed in a rescript of King Chulalongkorn that called for a more modest than usual cremation for himself so as to reduce the customary "display of pomp and circumstance" and "waste of labour and expense" that conferred "no lasting benefit on the public."[48] This rescript was often referred to during the Sixth Reign by the King, by Queen Saowapha, and by other individuals when they made donations for public works such as schools, hospitals, or book publishing. Vajiravudh carried the meaning of the rescript considerably farther, however, by deciding not to follow tradition by building a temple dedicated to his reign but to build schools and a memorial hospital instead. In the dedication of Vajira Hospital in 1913, the King stated that, although tradition "mentions that the King after his Accession ... erects and consecrates a monastery as a pious memorial of Thanksgiving," Siam already had a great number of monasteries and "to add more to the number ... would be of no immediate benefit to the people." However, since some sign of "Our gratitude for the Virtues which have raised Us to Our exalted position of power and wealth" was proper, he had chosen to build a hospital, which would be infinitely more beneficial to the people and "far more gratifying to Our heart than the sowing broadcast of money and presents to casual mendicants." The King prayed that the "Virtues of the Holy Trinity of the great Religion" which "We devoutly observe and defend" would shower blessings on his act of devotion "towards the People whom We regard as Our beloved children."[49]

The great change in the role of Buddhism in Siam initiated by Vajiravudh, however, was his use of Buddhism to buttress nationalism. One of the three essential attributes of a patriotic Thai, along with loyalty to king and love of nation, was devotion to Buddhism. A true Thai was a good Buddhist. Adherence to the Buddhist faith was necessary for the well-being of the state. Previous kings had supported Buddhism publicly for somewhat different reasons. They had favored Buddhism as a means of increasing royal virtue, as a means of public welfare, and as a means of adding miraculous power to the state. But Vajiravudh identified Buddhism with patriotism; a devoted Buddhist was a devoted citizen.

The Buddhist messages of the King consisted of four main elements. First, a good Buddhist was a moral citizen and a strength to the state. Second, a moral state would be strong in competition with other states. Third, for the Thai at least, Buddhism was a better route to morality than any other religion. And, fourth, the Thai had a mission to preserve and protect the Buddhist faith. These messages were conveyed in various ways—in plays, speeches, essays, and poems. Particularly noteworthy was a series of lay sermons to the Wild Tigers delivered on Saturdays during 1914 and 1915.[50] The sermons were preceded by Buddhist devotions performed before the King's own Buddha image that was brought along with him wherever he went. Also noteworthy were the lectures the King gave on Wisakhabucha Day to students at the Royal Pages School[51] and an essay on the knowledge gained by the Buddha on his enlightenment.[52]

Vajiravudh's first message, that a good Buddhist was a moral citizen and a strength to the state, was supported very simply.

The Past as Model

Buddhism, in the King's view, was primarily a system of morality. The moral codes and moral laws of Buddhism kept men from barbarism. These moral codes had been discovered by an extraordinary man, the Buddha, not through divine revelation, but by "researches and experiments in nature's own laboratory."[53] The Buddha then out of his infinite kindness and compassion had dedicated his life to teaching others what he had learned. The golden rule of Buddhism was "Do good, receive good; do evil, receive evil." Indeed, said the King, through a character in one of his plays, "If you plant weeds, how can you expect to reap rice?"[54] A man consumed by selfishness, lusts, passions, and desires inevitably had to suffer, for subjugation of desires was essential to one's own well-being. But it was also essential to the well-being of society. No society could tolerate individuals "without moral decency"; such individuals were "just as dangerous as a ferocious beast of the jungle." Vajiravudh wrote: "Therefore, if we wish to live in peace and happiness in any community of people it is really necessary that we conform ourselves to the principle of morality and Dharma so that our neighbors can be friendly with us without suspicion and distrust."[55] No man, after all, could stand alone, no matter how strong, wealthy, or wise he was. He needed at least a wife, parents, children, servants. He was dependent on others. And, being dependent, he was obliged to consider the welfare of others.[56]

Some Westernized Thai, the King said, thought it modern to deprecate Buddhism as old-fashioned and outdated. But morality, said the King, knew no time, and true righteousness was worldwide. Buddhism had always had and always would have its carpers, men who for their own private interests preferred not to be bound by any code of morality. But civilization in any country depended on peace and order, on a system of morality.[57]

King Vajiravudh could hardly expect that, even with his encouragement, all Thai would immediately become exemplary Buddhists. Indeed, he explicitly stated, in the traditional mode of Buddhist tolerance, that different men had different levels of achievement. All that was necessary was that one try to exercise control over himself. If a man were born with a low karmic balance sheet, he could not do much, but "No matter how little it is that you can do, that little is better than nothing at all."[58] More, much more, might be expected of government servants. A persistent effort of the King was to improve the ethical standards of government officials. And in part this effort had a religious purpose. Government officials, after all, could be seen as agents of His Majesty's own karmic capital.

The Past as Model

His Majesty's Buddhist virtue, accumulated in previous births, was the ultimate source of his servants' authority. It was particularly important, therefore, that government servants be honest and trustworthy so as to protect the good name of the king and the nation. "Better an honest official," said Vajiravudh, "than one who is cleverer but less honest."[59]

The adherence to Buddhist morality of each and every Thai could not help but strengthen Siam. Thai who loved the nation, the King said, should be attentive to their moral behavior. Since every Thai person was a part of the Thai nation, it was necessary for each person to tend his morals for the advantage of the nation. For, as the King once said, "a good nation is made up of moral people."[60] And a good nation endured. In the "sublime" and "truthful" words of an old Thai cosmological work, "the length of a nation's days are greater or less in accordance with the righteousness of the individuals thereof."[61]

Adherence to Buddhism contributed to the strength of the state not only in a general way but also in a very specific way: it contributed to the bravery of soldiers. Buddhism, no less than Christianity or Islam, steeled the hearts of warriors, converted the timorous into the brave. In former times, Vajiravudh pointed out, Thai soldiers had carried amulets into battle or had worn protective symbols on their bodies as reminders of the protective power of the triple gems of Buddhism.[62]

The King's second message, that a moral state would be strong in competition with other states, followed an argument that flowed logically from the arguments for individual morality. An immoral nation was one that used its strength to oppress other nations. Such a nation not only earned a bad name in the world, but also, eventually, earned the ruinous fate it deserved. An immoral state might succeed in getting away with its oppressions for a time, but sooner or later its immorality would lead to its downfall. It was like the immoral official who might rise in rank through cheating; eventually he would be discovered and would lose all. Vajiravudh buttressed his arguments with numerous examples. In an obvious reference to Germany, he pointed out that states which proclaimed the doctrine of "might is right" had fallen into disgrace. Other examples, he said, were closer to home. He wrote:

> The great nations that once were our enemies and fought the Thai nation, that once oppressed us, what is their fate today? The Chinese, who were our masters for 2,000 years, and the Cambodians, who once

The Past as Model

caused us hardships to the point of tears, and the Burmese and Mon, who once oppressed us so that our hearts and bodies ached beyond describing, what is their status today? Anyone with eyes and ears can answer.

The Thai, he said, had withstood the oppression and had been able to retain their freedom because, unlike their neighbors, they had remained steadfast in morality.[63]

The third message of the King, that Buddhism was, for the Thai at least, the best route to morality, led Vajiravudh into lengthy comparisons of Buddhism with other religions—comparisons that were inevitably to Buddhism's advantage. Vajiravudh said that, as a Buddhist, he was bound to think that Buddhism was the best religion in the world. But beyond this bias, he declared, there were good reasons for his preference of Buddhism.[64]

First of all, Buddhism was tolerant. The Buddha was a teacher who, having found what he felt to be the true path for men to follow, proclaimed it to others. The Buddha's proclamation, however, was a generous deed; it was not a command. Men could follow or not, as they chose. There was no dogma, no set of beliefs—not even a belief in a god-creator (such as Jehovah or Allah)—that it was necessary to accept in order to avoid being in eternal sin.[65] Buddhism set forth a philosophic way for men to become happier, to help themselves. There was no god who demanded obedience and threatened terrible punishments for those who did not obey.

Secondly, the Buddha, the predecessor of Jesus and Muhammad, was the most remarkable of the three teachers. The Buddha taught without setting forth commandments. He made no claims of being a god or speaking for a god. The truth he proclaimed commended itself to men simply on its own merits as truth. In his personal life the Buddha, born a wealthy prince, had renounced his easy life and voluntarily assumed a life of hardship. Neither Jesus nor Muhammad had made such a sacrifice, for both had been born poor and had been used to poverty. Muhammad, in fact, had become a well-to-do ruler during his lifetime.[66]

The Jewish and Christian concept of a single god, Vajiravudh felt, contained weaknesses. The Jewish god, for example, sided with his "chosen people," yet he was supposed to have created all mankind. How could a god, who should above all be just, love some of his creatures and hate others?[67] As for the Christian god, his multiple personalities gave Vajiravudh pause. How could Jesus be the son of God? How could a disembodied holy spirit be the husband of a

The Past as Model

woman? And if Jesus were the son of God, why did Matthew bother to provide Jesus with a royal genealogy by tracing Joseph's line back to King David? Vajiravudh suggested that Mary had indeed been the mother of Jesus but that some man other than Joseph had been his father and, after Jesus became a famous teacher, the Holy Ghost story had been invented to cover Jesus' unsavory past. The superiority to Jesus of the high-caste and pure-born prince who became the Buddha was manifest. The Thai could be proud of the Buddha, could be happy that his birth was no cause for shame. There was no need for the Thai to beat an implausible story into their heads.[68]

To Vajiravudh, the role of faith made the vital difference between Buddhism and Christianity. Christianity placed great stress on faith. A Christian had to begin, for example, by believing in the virginity of Mary. Not all Christians had the same beliefs, but there was an essential core of belief. Not so with Buddhists. The Buddha taught men how to be good, but he fashioned no articles of faith. Men followed the Buddha because they recognized the merit of his teachings, because they recognized the goodness of his person. This recognition led to love. And love led to faith. The basis of Buddhist faith, said Vajiravudh, was not superstition and fable, but intelligence.[69]

Buddhism, it was true, had miraculous and superstitious elements, as did Christianity, Hinduism, and Judaism. But rejection of the miracles in Buddhism need not lead, as some misguided people thought, to rejection of the entire faith. Miracles, said the King, were a religion's embellishments. A great religious teacher or a great king who aroused extraordinary respect during his lifetime was apt to have his wondrous life improved upon after his death. He became larger than life, superhuman. But these heroic embellishments were not intrinsically important. They were like the ornaments on a house —curtains, pictures, lights—that dressed it up but were in no way essential to its architecture. The story of Christ's resurrection, for example, was but the vehicle for the real message of the persistence of his teachings. And the miracle of the Buddha's single-handed victories in his contests with Mara, the evil tempter with a thousand arms and an army of a hundred thousand, was but the means for illustrating the power of the human spirit when committed to the way of truth.[70]

King Vajiravudh's religious comparisons were meant to make Buddhists proud of their Buddhism; they were not meant to make Thai Buddhists disrespectful of other religions. Time after time the King pointed out the basic similarities of all religions. All religions taught their adherents a similar moral code; they taught men to do good, not to harm others. The important messages of Christianity, said the King, had already been enunciated by Buddhism. Christian criticisms of Buddhism amounted in fact to an admission of similarities between Christianity and Buddhism, for only relative equals debated; Christians did not bother, for example, to argue the relative merits of Christian love and the cannibalism practiced by some primitive faiths. Christian criticisms of Buddhism also amounted to an appreciation of the challenge that Buddhism posed to Christianity as a rival claimant to universal belief.[71]

Only one specific criticism of Buddhism was attacked by the King. This criticism was that Buddhism was a negative faith, that it taught quiescence and was thus a religion for lazy people. Vajiravudh argued that messages of asceticism, surrender, and otherworldliness were common in religion. And he quoted the Sermon on the Mount to make his point: "Behold the fowls of the air: for they sow not, neither do they reap, nor gather into barns; yet your heavenly Father feedeth them." The intention of such words was not to make people lazy, but to get them to appreciate that the true values of life do not lie in material things. The heart of Buddhism was contained in the words "Do good, receive good; do evil, receive evil." If one did nothing, one would receive neither good nor evil. Those who criticized Buddhism for its passivity, said the King, were poorly informed on Buddhism and were wrong.[72]

The conclusion Vajiravudh drew from these religious comparisons—that Buddhism was at least the equal of other world religions—was not the end of his arguments in favor of Buddhism for the Thai. History and national identity provided Buddhism's final substantiation. For Buddhism had come early to Siam. It had preceded Christianity in Asia as Christianity had preceded Buddhism in Europe. For a European to become a Buddhist or for an Asian to become a Christian was unnatural. Such conversions amounted to a repudiation of one's ancestors and of one's nation. They were signs of weakness, vacillation, and opportunism. Europeans converted to Buddhism were looked down upon by other Europeans. And Thai who became Christians won the favor of no one except the missionaries. The Thai should realize, the King said, that one's religion was an essential element in one's nationality. Religion and nation were inseparable. The Thai were fortunate in having a religious faith of such outstanding value, a religious faith that was truly in accord with a high state of civilization.[73]

The fourth Buddhist message the King brought his people was

The Past as Model

that they had a duty in the world to preserve Buddhism. There was no place other than Siam where Buddhism could be properly studied and understood. Siam was Buddhism's last line of defense. The first and second lines had already fallen; only Siam, the third line, remained. (Although Vajiravudh did not specify what he meant by first and second lines, it is probable that he was regarding India as the first fallen line and Burma, Cambodia, and Ceylon together as the second.) Siam was Buddhism's great citadel, and the Thai must be soldiers proud to defend it against all internal and external enemies.[74] The main weapon of defense was practice of true Buddhist principles.

The image of Thai Buddhists as soldiers defending the last bastions of their faith was probably no accident. Although it was only natural that Vajiravudh's military enthusiasms would be reflected to some extent in his rhetoric, the King was undoubtedly also aware of an undercurrent of Thai thought that saw the pairing of Buddhism and militarism as inherently inappropriate. He disagreed with this view. The allegory of the Thai Buddhist bastion defended by its citizen soldiers corresponded with the King's view that real soldiers were necessary to protect the Buddhist state. Those who cited the Buddhist injunction against taking life as proof that military duties were immoral and that soldiers could not be good Buddhists had only a superficial knowledge of Buddhism, said the King. The Buddha himself understood that defense of a nation was a necessity and that those responsible for a nation's defense could indeed be moral individuals.[75] The Buddha, he said, "never expressly forbade war"; indeed, there was evidence that he approved of the waging of war to defend a state against an outside enemy.[76] The King told the story of a Buddhist king of Magadha named Bimbisara whose soldiers were deserting the ranks to enter the monkhood. The Magadha king appealed to the Buddha, who laid down the rule that thenceforward no soldier would be accepted for ordination as a monk. "This," said Vajiravudh, "could only mean that the Lord Buddha, who was himself a prince of the warrior caste, fully understood and appreciated the necessity of national defence."[77] Other clues to the Buddha's attitude toward soldiers existed. The *vinaya*, or rules for the behavior of monks, gave monks permission to preach to soldiers. Further, monks had long been in the habit of conducting prayers for military men and performing rites to protect men in battle. Neither of these actions were prohibited by the *vinaya*, as would certainly have been the case if the Buddha had disapproved.[78]

The real meaning of the prohibition of the taking of life, said

The Past as Model

Vajiravudh, was to end aggression. It was counsel for those who would use their strength to inflict injury on others. It was not meant to deter the innocent from protecting themselves. The soldier engaged in defending his countrymen from the depredations of an aggressive enemy was not behaving immorally. Quite the contrary, such a soldier was, or should be, a particularly moral man because the arms he bore gave him special means of harming others. The soldier must be outstandingly moral in order to be worthy of the trust he had been given. The Thai soldier, engaged purely in defense, was a man with such compassion for the group that he was willing to sacrifice his life for his neighbors and a man with such a commitment to his faith that he was willing to sacrifice his life to protect and preserve the Buddhist *dharma*, or moral law.[79]

The close association in the King's mind between Buddhist morality and the military was exhibited in the long sermons Vajiravudh gave to Wild Tiger troops and the various religious devotions in which he led them. In the latter the King embellished and "improved" standard prayers, or *mantras* (*mon* in Thai), by adding pertinent lines of his own. A prayer to be recited by navy men added lines calling for Siamese victories at sea,[80] and the daily prayer for Wild Tiger units was supplemented with the lines:

> Though there be a special enemy
> With the strength of Mara,
> May the Thai fight and destroy him
> As did the holy Buddha.[81]

When Siam entered World War I against the Central Powers, Vajiravudh carried his argument further. The Central Powers were viewed as evil incarnate. If evil were allowed to triumph, how could the *dharma* survive? Going to war to defend the *dharma* was no sin.

> And why is it "no sin"? Because we go to war in defense of right. If there were no right there would be no religion. If there were no right we could not exist as nations, as communities, or even as households. This principle is so important that we have to fight for it.[82]

The opposition to the pairing of Buddhism and militarism already mentioned as an undercurrent in Thai thought did not always remain an undercurrent. On at least one occasion an opposing voice was heard publicly. The voice was that of Phra Deb Mori, a prominent monk who was abbot of a Bangkok monastery. Early in 1916 this monk delivered a sermon, later printed, in which he labeled the military profession as evil and stated that those in the military

The Past as Model

establishment and those associated with it as manufacturers of arms were all guilty of sin. Public espousal of such views could not be tolerated. The monk was deprived of his rank by the King and removed to another monastery where he was placed "under close watch in order that he may not do such a thing again." The monk was castigated for his misinterpretations of the teachings of the Buddha, who, it was held, had never condemned the military life and had never interfered with politics. The strong action taken against Phra Deb Mori was meant as a warning "in order that no other monk should make such mischief again, and interfere with politics, which are not his profession." The Supreme Patriarch, it was announced, thoroughly sympathized with His Majesty in the action taken.[83]

The Supreme Patriarch, Prince Vajiranana, was a close and dependable ally of King Vajiravudh not only on the subject of the compatability of military defense and Buddhism but also on the King's nationalistic program in general. The correspondence of the ideas of the Prince and the King was not surprising. Prince Vajiranana had been Vajiravudh's preceptor during the latter's indoctrination as a monk, and the relationship between a novice monk and his preceptor was customarily very close in Siam and lasted throughout life.[84] The Prince Patriarch, further, was Vajiravudh's uncle. And Vajiranana's family and dynastic loyalties were strong. His decision to remain in the monkhood had been due, in large measure, to the urging of his brother, King Chulalongkorn, who wanted a trusted and capable relative in the monkhood who could one day assume a position of authority in the order and who could be relied upon to be sympathetic to the King's program of government reform. Vajiranana had not disappointed King Chulalongkorn; among other things, the important initial steps in bringing mass provincial education into being had been entrusted to Prince Vajiranana and the Buddhist Order.[85]

During the Sixth Reign, Prince Vajiranana on numerous occasions gave clear indications in word and action of his support of the administration. The Prince, for example, gave a benediction to the Wild Tiger Corps at its inauguration in May 1911. The benediction itself constituted an act of support for the paramilitary corps. And to the standard Pali verses asking that those he blessed be accorded respect, honor, and freedom from harm, the Prince added a verse that showed his specific approval of the idea of the corps.[86] On the same occasion the Prince gave an address that echoed the King's own comments on the need for Thai to be united and to support and love their nation. The nation, he said, must be cherished more

The Past as Model

than life itself. And loyalty to nation must precede loyalty to family, for the continuation of a family depended on the continuation of the nation; the nation, therefore, must be cherished "much more" than the family. The nation, he pointed out further, needed a leader who would give it direction; without a leader, a king, the nation was like a body with arms and legs but no mind. The Prince also spoke of the need for individual morality as a prerequisite for national survival. He pointed out that nations that lacked morality had lost their independence to colonial powers. As for the Wild Tiger Corps specifically, Vajiranana praised its members and said that their act of membership in itself was proof that they were already imbued with the highest national ideals. Vajiranana urged the corps members to maintain their integrity and always honor their sacred vows.[87]

Among the other addresses, or sermons, delivered by Prince Vajiranana, three stand out as particularly important for their support of national policy. These three were part of the series of addresses the Prince Patriarch gave each year on the occasion of the King's birthday on January 1. The three were delivered in 1916, 1918, and 1919 and were subsequently translated into English "by one of his disciples"—undoubtedly the King.

The sermon of 1916, termed "a special allocution," was entitled "The Buddhist Attitude towards National Defence and Administration." In it the Prince praised the King for his righteous rule. On the subject of national defense he made his position clear: "The defence against external foes is one of the policies of governance, and is one that cannot be neglected." He added, in much the same terms as Vajiravudh had used, that "war must be prepared for, even in time of peace, otherwise one would not be in time and one would be in a disadvantageous position towards one's foe."[88] The historical picture of Siam as a country that had once been a nation of warriors but had lost its military skills through long years of peace—a picture also drawn by Vajiravudh—was now being changed, said the Prince, by a vigilant and wise King who was promoting the welfare of the army, improving the navy, and creating units to teach civilians the arts of war and to give schoolboys the warrior spirit.[89]

The sermon of 1918, another "special allocution," was entitled "Right Is Right." The sermon was delivered after Siam's entry into World War I and clearly defended the King's action. Vajiranana said:

> Your Majesty has broken off friendly relations with and declared war on the Empires of Germany and Austria-Hungary in the name of the

The Past as Model

Kingdom of Siam, and has put an end to peace, because of Your desire to uphold International Rights.

When Right is in question, Wealth, Limbs, and even Life itself, all must be sacrificed should the occasion so demand it, any other policy is thereby practically forbidden.[90]

In other passages the Prince Patriarch strongly upheld "the duty of those who are in the right to chastise those in the wrong," and he ended the sermon with the invocation: "... may the success of glorious victory attend Your Majesty at all times henceforth."[91]

This sermon of 1918 particularly delighted the King, who, in the translator's foreword, pointed out to those who "affected to find in Buddhism grounds for conscientious objection to war" that they need no longer take the King's word that his policy was correct but could now rely on the "pronouncement of the head of the Buddhist Church of Siam," who said that "to fight for Right is not only a patriotic duty but also eminently a *moral* one." The King used Vajiranana's words of support, quoting liberally, in an important speech of his own given before the Wild Tigers on February 3, 1918.

The third sermon, that of 1919, also termed a "special allocution," was entitled "The Triumph of Right." It was essentially a victory address by the Supreme Patriarch. Siam had allied itself with nations opposed to the Central Powers, who had been "making war in an unrighteous manner" and threatening the freedom and equality of all nations. In so doing Siam had come to the defense of the right, and "in the end the Allies have achieved victory and Right has been upheld." The policy the King had followed thus constituted a special blessing that had resulted in "enhancing Your dignity throughout the world."[92] The Prince enlarged his remarks into a general principle on "The Policy of Governance":

... the Defence of Right forms part of the Policy of Governance which the King must consider one of his chief duties, chastising the wicked within his dominions who trespass against right and liberty of others, causing everyone to enjoy the blessings of his government in equal measure with one another, and likewise defending the realm from invasion by an enemy from without.[93]

To illustrate the propriety of righteous men's going to war to defeat the unrighteous, Prince Vajiranana in his 1919 sermon told a story from the *Dharma Jataka*. It was an allegory concerning two minor gods, Dharma ("Morality") and Adharma ("Immorality"), each of whom rode chariots in the air around the world. Dharma exhorted his fellowers to seek the ten paths of virtuous action; Adharma

The Past as Model

gave his followers opposite advice, exhortations to perform unvirtuous acts. Dharma's circumambulatory route was by the right, or auspicious, side; Adharma proceeded by the left, a sign of disrespect. The two chariots eventually met face to face. Each god demanded the right of way. Each presented his case for precedence, Dharma arguing that he deserved it because he caused men to do meritorious deeds, Adharma insisting that he would go forward because he had the power to do so. Adharma challenged Dharma to fight. A battle ensued, and just as Dharma was about to be overcome, Adharma fell from his chariot, the earth held him firm, and he was slain. Prince Vajiranana saw "a striking similarity" between this story and the course of the Great War in Europe.[94] Vajiravudh certainly agreed; in fact, he used the tale, inserting contemporary allusions, in a verse dance drama he wrote in 1919.[95]

Another example of Prince Vajiranana's support of the King's policies was his participation in the ceremonies that greeted the returning members of the Siamese Expeditionary Force on September 21, 1919. The Prince praised the troops who had volunteered for service in the war in Europe "to help the Allies defend the right and to prevent the victory of immorality." He commended the men for having brought pride to the Thai nation. And he blessed the troops "in the name of the Buddha," wishing them health, happiness, and future success. After the speech, the Prince Patriarch sprinkled consecrated water on the flag of victory and successively on each soldier as he passed in line before him.[96]

One other matter concerning the Prince and state policy deserves mention, although it only indirectly concerned nationalism. This was the Prince's handling of Phra Siwichai, a village monk from Lamphun who had won great reverence in northern Siam for his piety. The popularity of the monk, the adulation accorded him by thousands of people, the stories that circulated regarding his miraculous powers all aroused considerable suspicion among local civil and religious officials that the monk might become the center of a northern separatist movement. Harassment of Phra Siwichai ended in his being sent by the Viceroy of the North down to Bangkok. There his case was examined by a committee of monks and finally by Prince Vajiranana himself, who concluded that Phra Siwichai had committed only minor errors, for which he had already been punished "more than he deserved," and that most of the charges against him were without merit. The Prince recognized the danger of making a martyr of the monk and, in order to repair the damage that had been done, sent Phra Siwichai back to Lamphun under the official protection of the Supreme Patriarch.⁹⁷ The Phra Siwichai case exemplified to the full the political astuteness of Vajiranana, his appreciation of the best course to follow in order to discourage the growth of regionalism and prevent disruption of national unity.

King Vajiravudh's enlistment of Buddhism in the course of Thai nationalism was by and large a safe policy, for the vast majority of the people of the country were Thai and virtually all Thai were Buddhists. Nonetheless, there were minority elements in the population who were not Buddhists, and the King had no wish to antagonize these minorities. The special treatment accorded the Muslim minority has already been discussed in chapter 7. With respect to the very small number of Christians, the almost century-old royal policy of toleration was retained. Early in 1911, for example, Vajiravudh made donations in memory of King Chulalongkorn to several Christian groups—Christ Church, the Catholic mission, the Presbyterian mission, the Bangkok Nursing Home, and the St. Louis Hospital.⁹⁸ Periodically during the reign other similar gifts were made. In 1921 the King and his consort paid a long visit to the charity sale at St. Joseph's Convent.⁹⁹ There is no evidence of local Christian or missionary antipathy toward the reign. On the contrary, there is evidence that at least some Christian groups eagerly took up the King's nationalistic cause. The American Presbyterian Church mission in northern Siam, for example, composed and distributed patriotic hymns, published prayers for the King and officials, and wrote a flag song for the schools. In 1915 a mission conference adopted the following resolution: "We agree together that whenever Christians meet for worship or prayer, they should always pray for our King first, and for all those in authority and for our fellow Tai citizens. This should never be forgotten. Let us truly love those of our blood and nation."¹⁰⁰

In addition to their belief in the world religion Buddhism, the Thai also had a great body of informal religious notions. There was a vast ideational world peopled by spirits, angels, and demons that formed part of Thai religious concepts. This world was not part of formal Buddhism, but neither was it in conflict with Buddhism. The Buddha's attitude toward notions of heavens and hells and gods and demons had been tolerant; in general, he had neither confirmed nor denied such popular ideas. Vajiravudh's attitude was also tolerant. For the most part he said little on these subjects. To an extent, however, he attempted to utilize these popular beliefs for state and nationalistic purposes.

Vajiravudh himself seems to have been freer from superstition than most of his subjects. A Western observer called him "sober-minded" and "far from superstitious or fanciful" on supernatural subjects.[101] One of the few mystical phenomena he seems to have given credence to was the appearance of a miraculous light ringing the top of the Phra Pathom stupa on October 24, 1909. The then Prince Vajiravudh reported to his father that he and sixty-nine of his courtiers had seen the light, which lasted for seventeen minutes. He tried to explain the phenomenon scientifically, decided he could not, and so concluded it was a miracle. He ordered various religious ceremonies performed, presumably as a safeguard.[102] Much later he explained the meaning of the phenomenon as a portent of a change in reign.[103] And, indeed, the reign change did occur one year almost to the day later. Other portents in which the King apparently believed, such as the miraculous finds of "the Bow and Arrows of Rama's Strength,"[104] were intimately associated with the monarchy and betokened an auspicious reign. Belief, or professed belief, in such matters could hardly have been avoided.

One supernatural idea that the King encouraged was belief in a tutelary personal deity of his named Hiranhu or Hiranphanasun. Hiranhu was large and powerful, and his divine function was to keep King Vajiravudh and his retinue free from harm. As long as Hiranhu was propitiated with incense, candles, and food the King would remain safe and well. A portion of the King's food was allotted daily to this royal genie.

The story of Hiranhu's first appearance is revealing. In 1906, during his northern tour, Crown Prince Vajiravudh and his party were about to enter a jungle trail. Several members of the royal party expressed anxiety over the perils they would face in the jungle. The Prince assured the group that royal persons in their travels were always protected by supernatural beings who continually watched over them and kept them from harm. A short time after these comments, one member of the party had a dream in which a tall, powerful man appeared, telling the dreamer that he was Hiranhu, a forest spirit whose appointed duty was to protect the royal party. Vajiravudh heard of the dream and ordered that propitiatory gifts be laid out for Hiranhu. Several people subsequently reported seeing the spirit, the custom of propitiatory gifts became set, and the idea of Hiranhu was established. After he became King, Vajiravudh had a statue of Hiranhu prepared and set up on the grounds of Phya Thai Palace; it was dedicated in April 1911 in a ceremony in which the spirit was invited to occupy his bronze image.

In the royal announcement telling the Hiranhu story, there is no indication that the King ever saw Hiranhu or even that he believed

The Past as Model

in his existence. Rather the royal opinion is given that "Such beliefs, whether there is reason for them or not, serve their purposes for the common people." Belief in a supernatural force for good, for protection from danger, made people less afraid, and, being less afraid, they were less likely to encounter danger; unnatural fear, after all, was a danger in and of itself.[105]

The establishment of Hiranhu as Vajiravudh's personal deity did not contribute directly to the enhancement of nationalism, but to the degree that it enhanced the power and prestige of the King, it lent some strength to all of his programs.

The Arts

The arts of Siam, by almost universal account, were in a sorry state by the beginning of the reign of King Vajiravudh. This was true of painting, sculpture, architecture, the handicrafts in metal, leather, and lacquer, and the performing arts of dancing and music. The reasons for the decline were not hard to see. As a contemporary newspaper put it, the eclipse of native genius in the arts was due to the "all invading" impact of the West.[106] A longtime British resident in Siam noted that with the opening of Siam to the West "her own arts and crafts suffered. Many of them disappeared." He added that Kings Mongkut and Chulalongkorn "did nothing to stop the decline; it is doubtful indeed if they desired it. To Europeanize his country became with Chulalongkorn one of the dominating passions of his life...."[107] King Vajiravudh came to the same conclusion about the status of the arts—but without, of course, attributing any blame to his royal predecessors. It was "Young Siam," he said, that was to blame. The young people were obsessed with the idea of "Civilisation-at-any-price," turned their backs on everything traditional in Siam, wanted Siam to "start with a clean slate." It was their "shallowness of thought" that was responsible for equating civilization with an outward show of European tastes. It was enthusiastic "Young Siam" that had committed "all sorts of vandalism" against Thai arts "in the name of Civilisation." He wrote:

> Instead of treasuring objects of Art which have been in the family for generations, such objects are sold or exchanged for more "civilised" articles; priceless *"thom"* bowls have been exchanged for Thermos flasks, beautiful mother-of-pearl boxes for cheap cigarette cases, lovely pieces of cloth for the latest product of Lancashire looms, and so on *ad nauseam*.

And he added:

The Past as Model

> The best example of Siamese decorative painting with beauty and grace in every line is despised and has to make way for a piece of lithographic horror, whose colours knock you down at the distance of ten yards; for we prefer to defile our walls with the horror in order to show people that we are civilised.[108]

These analyses by the King and Western writers were essentially correct. For the productions of the fine arts and the expert crafts had always been destined for elite consumers, and the elite class of Siam was the most Westernized element. The elite were most influenced by Western tastes and most anxious to make a good impression on Westerners. When the demand for Thai arts began to decline among the elite, the decline of the arts had to follow.

The King saw Siamese art as a very sick creature that needed "general appreciation and public support" in order to survive. And its survival was to be desired not solely for the sake of the real merits of the art itself but also for the sake of the nation: art was "part and parcel of our national life." Art, Vajiravudh wrote, expressed "the individual ideas of our nation" and if such individual ideas were lost "then we shall cease to be Thai."[109] The nation was not merely a political unit, it was a totality of culture that most certainly included the arts; if the political unit survived but the culture it was designed to house died, then the nation would truly be lost. The King thus took on the role of a strong defender and patron of Thai arts for both aesthetic and nationalistic reasons.

Part of the King's work was in the area of propaganda. He wrote newspaper pieces on Thai art; he gave speeches urging the Thai to support their arts and crafts;[110] he wrote poems extolling the work of Thai artisans. The poetic lines on art appear most profusely in a work called *Samakkhi sewok* (Harmonious Officialdom), written as an accompaniment for dance performances. Part 2 of this work praises Ganesha as god of the arts, and part 3 praises Visvakarma as god of architecture and the crafts. The poems are meant to instill pride in the Thai arts and to urge their continued support. For example:

> Thailand is as civilized as other lands,
> For we have craftsmen who are expert
> In carving and in drawing
> And in the composing of music
> And in all sorts of work in gold
> And in fashioning superbly in silver.
> We also have many excellent painters
> And talented jewelers.
> . . . .

The Past as Model

> We Thai should nourish our crafts,
> The beautiful products in Thai style.
> We should support our artisans
> And not let them shamefully decline.
> . . . .
> Helping our artisans is helping our country,
> Because then our art will enhance our reputation
> So we can take our place without shame
> Among the great nations of the world.
> . . . .
> The civilized arts are a nation's glory.
> . . . .
> A nation without artists
> Is like a man without a woman.
> It is not a pleasant sight;
> He is derided and shamed.[111]

Vajiravudh's sponsorship of the arts was not confined to words, however. The Thai arts were supported in administration, in education, and in government projects.

Administratively, the most significant move was the establishment of a Department of Fine Arts in April 1912. The department was created in connection with changes that transformed the Ministry of Public Works into a Ministry of Communications. The technicians and artisans not needed in communications, and craftsmen from other ministries as well, were placed in the new department. The Department of Fine Arts was put under the immediate supervision of the King, "whose object is to preserve and develop the art and craftmanship of the country under one control." Prince Nares, who had been Minister of Public Works, was placed in charge of the new administrative unit.[112]

In education, one important step taken was the creation of a School of Arts and Crafts at Wat Ratchaburana. The school, which was officially opened by the King in January 1914, accepted from other schools students who had shown particular promise in manual skills. One objective was to revive the old handicrafts by training a new generation of artisans. For example, the school taught the art of niellowork, which by 1914 "had become almost a lost art in the country."[113] Other schools with more conventional curriculums were also encouraged to include training in art. As early as 1914 the press noted that the "arts and crafts now occupy an important place in the general scheme of education."[114] Even the Boy Scouts were introduced to "practical training" in the form of classes in woodworking, metalworking, and the like; proficiency medals were instituted for boys who showed exceptional skill.[115]

Allied to education were the various arts and crafts exhibitions sponsored by the King. The exhibitions served several purposes: they encouraged art students to improve their work so that they could compete; they helped the students financially through the sale of their works; and they helped advertise the Thai arts to a wide public. For Vajiravudh realized that to encourage production without stimulating demand was to build a road that led nowhere. The first Arts and Crafts Fair was held at Suan Kulap School in January 1913. The fair became an annual event and was held at various sites thereafter until the King's death in 1925. Vajiravudh always opened the fair; he frequently gave a short address on the utility of the arts; he admired the various productions; and he bought articles for his own use.[116] The fair seems to have been popular. By 1920 the exhibits included furniture, drawings, paintings, photographs, woodblocks, baskets, and works in silver and ivory, and, according to a news account, "a large part of the exhibits" was sold the first day.[117] Art exhibits were also included in other fairs sponsored by the King at various temples and palaces.[118]

As a means of promoting Thai arts and winning worldwide recognition for them, and for Siam, King Vajiravudh underwrote Siam's participation in international exhibitions—those at Turin in 1911, at Leipzig in 1914, and at San Francisco in 1915.[119] At Turin and at San Francisco a building of the traditional Siamese style was erected to house examples of Thai art and industry. His Majesty took a personal interest in these exhibits; for the Leipzig show he even contributed some of his own photographs and books.[120] The Siamese exhibits were well received abroad; at Turin the Siamese displays won a total of ninety-three prizes, medals, and awards.[121]

Among the foreign residents in Siam, a few took active interest in Thai arts. These few were given hearty support by the King, who once presciently commented: "The Art of my Country will only find its salvation through the interest that Europeans take in it."[122] Foremost among these foreigners was Karl Doehring, a German architect who had served in the Siamese Ministry of the Interior for several years. Doehring, "under the protection of the scientifically and highly educated King Vajiravudh of Siam and of Prince Damrong," made extensive studies of Thai art, producing "architectural surveys, drawings, and photographs."[123] Doehring, again with Siamese government support, published the first careful examinations of Thai architecture and Thai lacquer designs.[124] Doehring's role in Siam was similar to that of Ernest Fenollosa in Japan: the role of the respected Westerner whose appreciation of the Asian aesthetic reopened the eyes of the Asian to the value of his own art heritage.

Direct sponsorship of art production was, of course, another route of artistic revival. Vajiravudh's main contributions here were in the fields of architecture and the performing arts. He did give some attention to other fields such as book production and illustration, however; many of the King's works were issued in special editions with designs and drawings by leading artists such as Prince Naris.[125]

In architecture there is evidence that the King disapproved of the heavy intrusion of Western styles and sought a return to Thai motifs. He apparently rued the very expensive Italianate throne hall, Anantasamakhom, that his father had started and that he felt obliged to complete. He is said to have stated that, although the hall was large and grand and unique in Siam, there was nothing Siamese about it and Westerners were not apt to be impressed by it since grander and larger structures of this style were to be seen all over Europe.[126]

Among the public buildings erected during the reign, many marked a return to traditional forms: for example, the buildings at the Royal Pages School, at Chulalongkorn University, and at Sanam Chan. These buildings adopted a modified Khmer-Thai style that had begun to emerge at the end of Chulalongkorn's reign (for example, in the building that formerly housed the National Library). These buildings, however, continued to rely on Western engineering to supply the multistories and the large enclosed spaces that old Siamese society had not needed but that new Siam did.

By and large it seems that the attempts at resuscitation of traditional architecture were not successful. Buildings of European design continued to be built, some undoubtedly with the King's approval. Notable among such buildings is Samakkhichai House, an imposing pile in Venetian Gothic built by the King for his favorite courtier, Chaophraya Ram. Unequivocally high marks can be given to only one type of building, the wooden towers called *phra men* (*meru* in Sanskrit) that were built for royal cremations. These buildings were constructed for but a single purpose and a single occasion; they were destroyed after the cremation rites were over. Consequently they survive only in verbal and graphic depictions. The funeral structure for King Chulalongkorn won lavish praise as the most "perfectly constructed" building of its type ever fashioned in Siam.[127] Later *phra men* designed by Prince Naris for the Queen Mother and for Prince Chakrabongs, and other *phra men* executed for high members of the royal family, received similar words of adulation.

The Past as Model

A final field of artistic promotion that received extraordinary royal attention and achieved considerable success was that of the traditional performing arts. Certainly a good deal of the royal attention was due to the King's personal interest in the theater, but there is no doubt that Vajiravudh also saw revival of Siamese drama, dance, and music as a part of the essential task of preserving Thai national culture. He suspected, in fact, that the Thai had not grown so far from these old theatrical tastes as some supposed: "We may, in our innermost hearts, really prefer to sit through the performance of a *'Khon'* or *'Lagor'* of the old Siamese style, but instead we go and sit through a fearful entertainment called an 'operetta' at the Pramothai or some one of the other houses, because we think that style of entertainment is more like what they give in European theatres."[128]

Vajiravudh's support of the traditional theater began while he was still a prince at Saranrom Palace. There he sought out old teachers and performers of the classical music and dance and, as was mentioned in chapter 1, organized an amateur dance company. After his coronation, Vajiravudh expanded on his early work, establishing a special Department of Entertainments (Mahorasop) and a school of the performing arts. He recruited a number of teachers who were specialists in ballet and in music.[129] These men were given noble titles according to merit and in the same fashion as other government officials. Apparently the awarding of high noble titles to performers was an unprecedented step; it aroused considerable criticism among "his orthodox and conservative ministers."[130]

The theater in all its forms received a powerful stimulus during the Sixth Reign, and among these forms the classical styles were given full attention. The old styles, which had been seriously in decline at the end of Chulalongkorn's reign,[131] were revived under Vajiravudh's patronage. Once again carefully rehearsed troupes of *khon* and *lakhon* players, musicians, reciters, and singers brought to life on stage, in the proper costumes and with the necessary sets, the old dramas of *Inao*, *Anirut*, and *Rammakian* (the Thai *Ramayana*) as well as newer dramas that borrowed much from the old forms. The revivification of the classical theater, however, depended too much on the King personally to be permanent; with his passing the revival came to an end.

Literature

On September 13, 1913, King Vajiravudh started a poetic story that was to become his longest work. A little less than eight months later, on May 9, 1914, the first draft was completed. There followed two

The Past as Model

years of editing and of revising, after consultations with other scholars, before the work was ready for printing.[132]

The poem, *Phra non kham luang*[133] (The Story of King Nala in Classical Verse Forms),[134] began with traditional stanzas that offered homage to the author's teachers, and proceeded with the following preamble:

To begin, this story of King Nala
Is translated from a Sanskrit epic
Into *khlong, chan, kap,* and *klọn* verse forms combined
As a work called *kham luang,* or classical model of prosody.

May all Thai scholars
Appreciate the value
Of Siamese poetry present and future
And not let it disappear.

The aim of the author of this Nala story
Is to show our young men examples
Of interesting poetry in various forms
So they can use them as models to compose their own.

Listen, young men of the Thai nation:
Our nation is brilliant and shining.
If we had no poetry we would be shamed
And laughed at for having no scholars.

Great poetry is like a jewel;
Beautiful words are a begemmed sash.
We should add to the works of Vedic poetry
And treasure them unselfconsciously.

Don't be afraid of being criticized.
If you are teased, don't be discomfited.
Whoever ridicules us Thai
And our literature is a boor.

Peoples abroad all respect
Scholars and writers.
Those who reject literature are savages;
Whoever downgrades poetry is a barbarian.

Don't be misled by the words
Of sophomoric men who are brash boasters
And would sinfully lead you nowhere;
Our scholars will bring back joy to your hearts.

Don't try to emulate any other race.
Think only of Thailand right now.

The Past as Model

> Our country is civilized and should so remain.
> Don't listen to glib talkers who would lead you to madness.
> Be careful to choose the good;
> Choose poetry as your guide.
> Be a good citizen, work hard,
> And Thailand will be honored as a bright jewel.[135]

"Choose poetry." Choose the glorious classics of Siam's past. Value Thai literature, a mark of civilization. And continue the literary traditions uncorrupted and undefiled. These were some of Vajiravudh's messages to his countrymen to help them find national pride in their literature.

The threat to traditional literature was real. The nineteenth century had seen the introduction of printing, the spread of reading beyond the royal elite, and the development of a popular prose literature—all with deleterious effects on many classical forms. Old dance dramas were rarely staged except in truncated versions. "The present day Siamese are forgetting the old songs," one writer complained.[136] And the King commented that, although Siam had "a great deal of genuine literary genius," many people preferred "to read execrable translations of European 'penny-dreadfuls' and 'shilling-shockers.'"[137] On top of all this, the King reported that "foreigners say the Thai nation has no books or records."[138] This foreign view was particularly irritating to His Nationalistic Majesty.

The solutions Vajiravudh turned to—in addition to making known the value of Thai letters and the danger to Thai letters—were to preserve the classics, to write himself, to encourage others to write, to inveigh against pernicious influences on the language, and to work for language purity.

Preservation of the classics was advanced by sponsoring the publication of old poetry and the performance of old dramas. As mentioned above, the Royal Company of Players put on a succession of classic dramas, including *Anirut*, *Inao*, and episodes of the *Rammakian*. The publication of Thai classical poetry had already made much progress in the reign of King Chulalongkorn through the issuance of a monthly literary journal, *Wachirayan*, and the growth of the habit of making merit, particularly at cremation rites, by the distribution of texts chosen by the National Library.[139] Vajiravudh continued to encourage such publications. In 1913, for example, to commemorate the opening of Chitralada Palace, he printed at his own expense the first complete edition of the *Rammakian* of Rama II, together with

The Past as Model

his own study of the sources of the Thai *Rammakian*. In the introduction to the *Rammakian* the King specifically pointed out that he had chosen to publish a volume that would do honor to the Thai nation and would repudiate the Western argument that the Thai had no books that could be called literature.[140]

In the area of his own writing, Vajiravudh was by no means a classical purist, but he did compose a large number of works on classical themes, in classical meters, and in classical styles. There is hardly a genre—*nirat* ("travel poem"), *lilit* ("narrative poem"), *suphasit* ("proverb"), *nithan* ("story" or "fable"), *lakhon* ("drama"), *he rüa* ("boat song")—that he did not try his hand at. As a crown prince he wrote a long narrative poem, *Lilit phayap*, about his journey through northern Siam. In 1923 he wrote another long *lilit*, *Lilit narai sip pang*, which was a poetic narrative of the ten incarnations of Narayana, or Vishnu, including his incarnations as Rama, Krishna, and the Buddha. He wrote several *nirat*. He also wrote a succession of *he rüa*, a literary form that had practically ceased to exist with the death of its great exponent, Prince Thammathibet, in the early nineteenth century. And he wrote the long poetic romance *Phra non kham luang* quoted from above, which was based on the popular Indian story called *Nala and Damayanti*. The largest number of his works in classical style, however, were written for the theater. These works include several episodes of the *Rammakian*; three plays from the Sanskrit: *Savitri, Priyadarshika,* and *Shakuntala*; and several original works, including *Phra ruang, Thao saen pom,* and *Matthanapatha*. The Sanskrit plays and several other works by the King were based on English versions of the Sanskrit classics; the King stated more than once that he did not read Sanskrit.[141] Whatever the literary value of these works by Vajiravudh, the King fully demonstrated, simply by using the old literary forms, that he intended to keep them alive.

Closely allied in spirit to the King's rendering of Sanskrit classics into Thai was his translation of outstanding classics of the West into Thai. Although this enterprise can be seen as an aspect of the Westernization process, the King justified his work on the grounds that Shakespeare and other such writers transcended national boundaries and their works were a universal heritage for all mankind. In his preface to his translation of *The Merchant of Venice* the King wrote that the plays of Shakespeare were read in all the languages of Europe and some were even available in Japanese; that his works had not also been rendered into Thai poetry was a reproach the King could not bear.[142] Vajiravudh rendered into Thai verse four Shakespeare

The Past as Model

plays: *The Merchant of Venice, As You Like It, Romeo and Juliet,* and *Othello.* He also translated *School for Scandal* by Sheridan, *Le Médecin malgré lui* by Molière, and several lesser works by other European dramatists.

Another measure taken to accord official recognition to literature of value—old works and new—was the establishment in 1914 of a Literary Society (Wannakhadi Samosǫn).[143] The society was patterned after the Historical Research Society (Borankhadi Samosǫn) that had been organized by King Chulalongkorn in 1907. The Literary Society, like the Historical Society, was headed by the King and composed of a select group of Thai intellectuals. Works that the society deemed meritorious were to be allowed to use the society's seal, a design featuring the god Ganesha, patron of the arts. The society considered literary works in all fields except history, which was already under the purview of the Historical Society and certified by its dragon seal.[144] Shortly after its formation the society issued a special list of outstanding works in Thai literature. One work was singled out in each of seven fields. Winner of the award in the field of Western-style drama was Rama VI's own *Huačhai nakrop* (The Soul of a Warrior).[145] In later years the king also won certificates of merit and the privilege of using the seal for at least two additional works—*Phra non kham luang* in 1917[146] and *Matthanaphatha* in 1924.[147]

The Literary Society was also given the charge to become "the guardian of correct style," by which it was meant that the society should help prevent the corruption of the language with foreign words and foreign locutions. King Chulalongkorn had taken a step in the direction of maintaining language standards in 1907 by appointing an Etymological Commission (Nirukkati Samakhom) composed of Prince Vajiranana, Prince Devawongse, Prince Damrong, and Prince Naris. However, the commission, composed as it was of extremely capable but extremely busy men, had long been inactive. Three new members seem to have been added to the commission in 1916 or 1917, but there is no indication that this move brought the commission into action. By 1921 there apparently were serious discussions about the formation of a new Institute of Etymology and Orthography (Sapha Photčhanabanyat lae Akkharawithi) to handle the problems of finding the right words for foreign scientific and technical terms and for transliterating Thai into Roman letters, but the institute was not established.[148]

Whatever may have been the King's reasons for failing to bring into being a working commission to guard the Thai language, he was exceedingly active himself in the matter. His role as a drumbeater

The Past as Model

for language purity grew out of his annoyance with what he regarded as the corruptions in diction and style that had come largely from Western influence. One poem dealt exclusively with this theme:

> Feeling lonely and alone,
> I chose a book for solace.
> The more I read, the more I missed
> You beside me, inducing laughter.
>
> Feeling lonely and forlorn, I thought of you with sad heart,
> So I chose a book to while away my boredom and read on.
>
> The more I read, the more I grew annoyed at modern writings
> In ununderstandable style. They don't write in Thai.
>
> The language of today that students like
> Makes me dizzy. They excel at destruction.
>
> The modish language, presumably Western,
> Is unbearably dull to read, nauseating to hear.
>
> It is incomprehensible to read, irritatingly boring,
> Composed in excessive disorder like the language of drooling idiots.
>
> Oh, the Thai language is going to wrack and ruin;
> The Thai people are becoming shamefully "smart."
>
> The more I read of the book that I hoped would give momentary respite
> The madder I got, so I finally had to throw it into the sea.
>
> I looked for another work and chanced on verse,
> A play that I understand has gained quick fame.
>
> Oh, I lose heart. Why are we so unfortunate?
> Thai poetry is finished; no people are more unlucky.
>
> All is worthless; all forms are of fleeting value.
> The stories ramble on in disorder; their vocabulary is vulgar.
>
> I go back to find a good story that I brought with me
> And read to gain contentment and to ease my sad loneliness.[149]

The Westernisms and the vulgarisms that Vajiravudh deplored were constant objects of his attention and criticism. By 1910 a host of words from European languages, mostly English, had found their way into Thai. Vajiravudh warred against these "unThai" words and tried to reverse the trend. He suggested alternates, for example, for such borrowings as "editor," "steam," "motor," "lecture," "policy," "empire," "economics," "goal" (in football), and "toxicology."[150] The new words coined by the King depended on Thai roots or on Sanskrit, the traditional Thai source for new vocabulary. The King's national-

The Past as Model

istic purpose here was obvious. It was even clearer in the King's suggested name change for the loose black pajamalike trousers commonly called *kangkeng chin* ("Chinese trousers"); the King preferred they be called *kangkeng thai* ("Thai trousers"), justifying the change with the comment that although the trousers may have been Chinese in origin, they had become thoroughly domesticated in Siam.

Apparent contradictions of Vajiravudh's announced policy of maintaining language purity may be seen in some of his own writings. Many of these are in early writings that date from the time before he became king and began to be more rigorous in his use of "pure Thai." Others, for example the many Westernisms, misspellings, and uses of "improper" language that abound in the play *Tang chit khit khlang*, are found in works that belong in the category of humorous writings, in which, said the King, ordinary rules of propriety need not apply.[151]

Spelling was always of particular concern to the King. He wrote a number of newspaper articles proposing spelling changes that would return words to what he regarded as their correct etymologies.[152] He also made his preferences known as to the best way to render Thai in the Roman alphabet. His system was a transliteration of Thai writing into Roman letters, without dependence on phonetics. He used the system in awarding surnames, giving his transliteration in each case.[153] He believed that a letter-by-letter transcription of the writing was most important since it preserved a word's etymology, that is, the linkage of a word to its past.[154]

Vajiravudh's most remarkable effort in the direction of linguistic nationalism was a scheme he developed for the radical reform of the Thai system of writing.[155] The scheme was put forth as a trial balloon, not a royal order. It never achieved popularity, and it was quietly set aside.

The reformed spelling scheme of the King, from the point of view of nationalistic analysis, was derived almost equally from Western and from traditional inspiration. It showed an almost perfect placement of a logical and efficient change in the context of old Thai culture. The scheme, thus, was not solely a Westernizing reform, nor was it solely a return to the past; it was both simultaneously.

The spelling scheme, in brief, prescribed that all Thai letters be written on a single line and in the sequence in which they were pronounced. The existing Thai system in which vowels that were pronounced after consonants were sometimes written in front of, sometimes after, sometimes above, sometimes below, and sometimes in a combination of positions with regard to the consonants would

The Past as Model

be abandoned. The scheme would, he noted, mark a return to the system of the earliest Thai writing, that used on the stele of King Ramkhamhaeng in the thirteenth century, in putting all letters on a line, but it would modify that system by adopting the Western practice of placing vowels and consonants in the order in which they were pronounced. In addition, the Western practice of leaving spaces between words would be adopted.

In urging use of the new system, Vajiravudh argued his case strongly in terms of making it easier for Westerners to read Thai. Thai native speakers had the advantage of knowing the spoken language so well that spelling peculiarities gave them little trouble; foreigners learning Thai did not have that advantage. And the Thai habit of leaving no space between words caused much trouble to Westerners. The King, however, also urged the new system as a means of removing ambiguities that even Thai speakers often had to face. The existing writing system, he wrote, served as a block to progress; it posed problems even for the Thai. The older generations, he admitted, would have trouble adjusting to the new system, but the new generation of Thai, learning their language at school, would be able to progress much faster at their studies if the new system were available. And this new generation deserved the fullest consideration.

Although Vajiravudh invited comments on the system, there seems to have been little open discussion of it. Some of the English-language newspapers praised the idea.[156] And at least one official wrote several letters to the King's secretary in August and September of 1917 using the new system.[157] But the system died a quiet death.

The idea behind the system, however, showed the subtle forms that nationalism under Vajiravudh could take; in concept the system represented a delicate balance between the new and the old, between the practical and the traditional, that nationalistic formulas at their best seek. The difficulty with the idea was that it called for changes in an area that is heavily weighted with habit and emotion in every culture. It failed for much the same reasons that an attempt by King Mongkut to reform the spelling of religious texts failed. And that efforts by Premier Pibulsonggram in the 1940s to simplify all spelling failed. And that, indeed, despite Shavian persistence and wit, reform of the spelling of the English language remains a subject of dreams.

9

The Media

Long before Marshall McLuhan made his well-known declaration that "The medium is the message," King Vajiravudh was aware of the importance of the media. The "messages" of Vajiravudh's nationalistic campaign were transmitted to the Thai people in a prodigious variety of ways. The "media" were exploited by a king who was often acutely aware of what he was doing. What Vajiravudh was trying to do, above all, was affect the hearts of his people. Although legislation and decrees could have a role in reaching this objective, such measures were obviously more effective in bringing about changes in people's acts than in their minds. Decrees smacked too much of the concept behind paid weepers at royal funerals; they had too little of the spontaneous show of love of nation, king, and religion that Vajiravudh hoped for among his people.

Legislation, however, cannot be ignored. Although nationalism cannot be legislated, certain acts of legislation undoubtedly aid in the development of nationalism. Laws, in this regard, can also be considered media. The legislative acts that provided for the formation of the Wild Tiger Corps and the Boy Scouts, the adoption of surnames, the change in flag design, the inauguration of special medals, the entrance into World War I, the institution of compulsory education, the attempt to develop a Thai merchant marine, can all be seen as instrumentalities that in whole or part were meant to make the Thai people strong, united, and proud. These acts were designed to produce habits that would eventually affect attitudes.

In the stricter meaning of the word, however, the media Vajiravudh used to make direct emotional appeals included speeches, plays, essays, letters to the press, poems, songs, films, pageants, fetes and fairs, various celebrations, fund-raising campaigns, and royal appearances and visits. Usually, each of the nationalistic messages the King attempted to convey to his people was conveyed by a variety of media. And each medium was used for a variety of messages. The message that Siam was a nation of warriors, for example, was brought home by all the media mentioned—from speeches to royal appearances. And fund-raising campaigns were used to elicit interest in and support for the Wild Tigers, the Siamese Expeditionary Force, the Navy League, the Siamese air units, and the Red Cross.

A mere list of the media gives but scant clue to the diversity of uses to which each medium was put. The fund-raising technique alone involved such means as showing films; staging plays, shows, and pageants; sponsoring sports events; holding auctions and lotteries; issuing special postage stamps; putting on art shows and fairs; staging air displays and military tournaments; organizing motor races; and making out-and-out appeals for contributions. The conclusion of one newspaper writer that "the frequent appeals to help patriotic movements by gifts is surely a distinctive feature of today" is abundantly borne out.[1] Much ingenuity went into the planning of such events. In July 1920, for example, there was at Bang Pa-in a special art exhibition of amateur drawings by the King and various government officials. The drawings went on sale—the King's satirical cartoons of some of his officials drew the largest bids—and the proceeds were used to purchase rifles for the Ayutthaya contingent of Wild Tigers.[2] In January 1924, another Tiger benefit fund was aided by the extraordinary fund-raising method of having His Majesty man the photographic booth at the annual Winter Fair. As might be expected, this method was a great success, with long lines of people waiting each evening "for the attention of the Photographer Royal."[3] Fund-raising as a means of promoting nationalism, however, was put to its most telling use during the reign in the sustained campaign to

Cartoon of Prince Purachatra by King Vajiravudh. Prince Purachatra, running the Siamese Railway Department, bumps former German aides off the line. One of a series of cartoons by the King published in *Dusit samit*. Originals were sold in various fund-raising drives.

purchase the warship *Phra Ruang* as a gift from the Thai people to their King and navy.

There is no doubt that Vajiravudh was media-conscious. He was very much aware, for example, that his royal appearance in and of itself made any occasion a special event for his people. Therefore, to encourage the arts he attended arts and crafts shows; to encourage sports, he attended sports events; to promote enthusiasm for the war effort, he attended special celebrations connected with Siam's participation in World War I. The King explicitly pointed out that his trips to the provinces had the clear goal of letting his people see him so as to increase their devotion and loyalty.[4] And he often planned his appearances for maximum effect. On one of his southern tours he travelled from Chumphọn to Ranọng by elephant and made his entrance into Ranọng riding a "big handsome tusker" in a "fine roomy howdah" followed by a retinue of more than 300 elephants.[5]

The King's Speeches and Essays

The King also approached his speechmaking with great deliberation. Vajiravudh delivered hundreds of speeches. The largest number were given before Wild Tiger assemblies. Other audiences included students at the Royal Pages School, the Boy Scouts, the army, the navy, and the princes and officials who attended his birthday celebrations. Some of the speeches were the formal and routine kind that any monarch or head of state is obliged to give. The annual "Birthday Speech," a sort of state of the nation address, was competent but rarely inspired.[6] But many were ringing nationalist appeals. The *Bangkok Times*, commenting on several of the King's speeches during the coronation events, said they were "marked by earnestness and imagination, and by a power of compelling thought and of getting into direct touch with those he is addressing." The *Times* added that His Majesty's speech to the children "was certainly a happy effort."[7] The Wild Tiger speeches were outstanding examples of Vajiravudh's speech-making abilities. The *Bangkok Times* singled these out for a special accolade: "There the object was to be stirring and effective, and His Majesty was able to make the most of a freedom that is denied to more formal occasions."[8] According to the King's own comment, the Wild Tiger speeches were given without notes. He aimed at spontaneity and simplicity. He aimed at easy comprehension. He told one Tiger audience directly: "I intend to speak in Thai that is most easily understood."[9] He pointed out, for example, that the "sermons" he gave to the Wild Tigers, that is, his expositions of the value of Buddhism and Buddhist morality, were not like the sermons

The Media

of monks; they were just his own views of the truth that he wished to share with friends.

As a speaker it appears that Vajiravudh was effective among the special audiences he preferred—the Wild Tigers and student groups. His voice is said to have been low, his manner quiet. He was not, by accounts of his listeners, a spellbinder. He was not an orator for the multitudes.

The King's nationalistic writings bear a close relationship to his speeches. In fact, some speeches were later published as essays, and, on occasion, some essays were later read as speeches. Several series of addresses were issued in printed form during the reign—after the King had made minor emendations in the scribe's transcriptions. His first series of Wild Tiger lectures, which ended in July 1911, was in print "for all to read" by December.[10] The King hoped that the speeches, in their simple spoken style and with their everyday images, would, in print, convey his ideas to a large audience.

The King even made suggestions as to how his printed speeches should be used to attain maximum effect. His instructions on how *Plukchai sùapa* (Instilling the Wild Tiger Spirit) should be used in the schools have already been noted.[11] The long speech *Sadaeng khunnanukhun* (A Definition of Virtue), which Vajiravudh edited and printed for distribution within a few months of its delivery in May 1918, was also meant to be read aloud. The King said it should be read to soldiers, to Wild Tigers, and to schoolchildren. But, he elaborated, it should not be read at one sitting; it should be broken up into smaller sections. And whenever the reader felt the audience did not fully understand the text he should stop and explain its meaning in his own words.[12]

In an effort to have his ideas reach a large public audience, Vajiravudh also wrote and published a great number of essays, many of which were republished in various forms. Some of his more important essays were "Wake Up, Siam," "Clogs on Our Wheels," "The Cult of Imitation," "On Becoming a Real Nation," "Might Is Right," "Victory," "The Jews of the Orient," "Principles of Government," "Grinding Pepper Sauce in the River," "A Comparison of Surnames with Clan Names," "The Affairs of China," "Education and Unrest in the East," "The Failure of the Young Turks," "The Fruits of Turkish Constitutionalism," "Japan for Example," "Uttarakuru," "Isn't a Four-Wheeled Vehicle More Stable Than a Two-Wheeled Vehicle?" "A Definition of Virtue," "A Symbol of Civilization: The Status of Women," "Freedom of the Seas," "A Visit to the Land of Phra Ruang," and "What Is the Knowledge Attained by the Buddha on His Enlightenment." The majority of these essays were nationalistic in content. Although the King did publish prose writings on other subjects—for example, some short pieces on the spelling of specific words and some literary commentaries (usually written as introductions to poetic works)—the prose works designed for a mass audience were, by and large, attempts to stimulate public devotion, loyalty, and morality as a means of strengthening the nation.

Vajiravudh used several tactics to make his prose essays more effective. One was the use of pseudonyms. The name Asvabahu ("horseman")[13] was most frequently attached to nationalistic essays. As Asvabahu the King could write as if he were an ordinary citizen who approved of government policies and wished to urge others to approve of them. A similar motive probably applied to the King's use, in other essays, of the pen names Ramachitti ("the wisdom of Rama"), Phan Laem ("thousand-pointed"), and Sukhrip (the name of a monkey king in the *Rammakian* who assisted Rama). To broaden his audience, the King ordered the widespread distribution of free copies of some of his works. The printed speeches on "Instilling the Wild Tiger Spirit" were issued to schools and were made prescribed reading there.[14] The King's essay "A Definition of Virtue" was apparently also made available to schools.[15] His patriotic address to the members of the departing Siamese Expeditionary Force was issued in print as an army order.[16] The King also sought to develop a sympathetic audience among Westerners in Siam by making many of his works available in English—"the King's English," in fact, since he usually undertook the translations himself.

The King's Plays

In the realm of the theater, a world he particularly loved, the King made extensive use of plays for nationalistic purposes. During his reign Vajiravudh wrote some sixty Western-style plays—thirty-four original dramas and about twenty-six translations or adaptations. The introduction of the Western-style play, or "spoken" play (*lakhǫn phut*), in Siam has been attributed to Vajiravudh, who is also credited with introducing sets and, by 1919, the practice of allowing actresses to play female roles.[17] In addition to plays, the King composed many *khon* and other forms of the traditional poetic drama.

A large number of the King's Western-style plays had a distinctly didactic quality; they were intended to instruct, to enlighten, to rally the Thai people behind some cause or other. Not all the plays had such motives; many were light entertainments, pleasant farces, melodramas, or drawing-room comedies. But even some of these were made to serve useful purposes.

The "moral" plays all contributed in a broad way to the King's program of stirring up Thai nationalism. Some were direct and open patriotic appeals; others approached nationalism more indirectly by recommending a course of social or cultural improvement to strengthen the nation. All were performed on many occasions, even in the provinces.

The nationalistic message is loud and clear in many of Vajiravudh's most famous plays. Again and again, in play after play, the main theme is the necessity for the Thai to be united, to put their nation first, to love their land, their religion, and their king above all, to be willing to give up even life itself for these three. The nationalist call is particularly strong in the plays *Phra ruang*, *Huachai nakrop* (The Soul of a Warrior), and *Mahatama*. It appears to a lesser degree in other plays such as *Sia sala* (Sacrifice), *Phuan tai* (Friends to the End), and *Wiwaha phra samut* (Neptune's Bride). Other plays with political and social themes include *Chuai amnat!* (Coup d'état), *Khanom som kap namya* (The Right Amount of Noodles for the Sauce), *Noi inthasen* (Noi Inthasen), *Topta* (Deception), *Phurai phlaeng* (The Evil Doer), *Phongphang* (Fishtrap), *Chatkan rap sadet* (Preparing for a Royal Visit), and *Khwamdi mi chai* (The Triumph of Virtue). The best known and most frequently performed of all of Vajiravudh's nationalistic plays was *Huachai nakrop*. It was produced very often in Bangkok, and it was also performed in the provinces: in Songkhla, in Nakhon Sithammarat, and in Phuket. The play has been described by one appreciative viewer as a "hit" that never palled. And that Vajiravudh succeeded in getting his nationalistic message across is clearly demonstrated by this viewer's further comment: "You got excited seeing it and wanted to help the good people who loved their nation. It made you hate traitors and want to slap them on both sides of their faces."[18]

Many of Vajiravudh's plays with a didactic or propagandist purpose are, from a purely aesthetic point of view, overburdened with message. Some of the patriotic speeches are perhaps longer than the dramatic structure can comfortably carry. But in this whole area the King was breaking new ground. Dramatic literature of this sort had not been known before in Siam. The whole technique of using the theater to instruct, to propagandize, to influence an audience in favor of an idea, was a contribution of the King's. Although all literature to an extent teaches (even the *Ramayana* sets forth ideals of proper behavior), this kind of instruction is much attenuated and is unconscious. The conscious, deliberate fashioning of literature for the stage in order to sell an idea was King Vajiravudh's gift to Thai drama.

The majority of King Vajiravudh's plays were not message plays; they were written to entertain. They were farces, comedies, light romances. He enjoyed writing them; he enjoyed producing them; he enjoyed acting in them. Yet even here a nationalistic purpose was not completely absent. The plays were not arguments for any causes, but they were used as fund-raisers for causes. The play *Buang man* (Noose of Evil), for example, which tells the story of a man whose wife runs off with a lover, was first produced on October 12, 13, and 14, 1916, and all three times the proceeds went to help fill the coffers of the Red Cross of Siam. And so with play after play after play. The idea of benefit performances of royal plays started in 1915 with a performance of *Mahatama*, the proceeds in this case going to the cruiser fund of the Royal Navy League. And other benefits were held in later years for other pet projects of the King such as the Siamese Expeditionary Force sent to Europe in World War I, the Wild Tiger rifle fund, and various hospital funds. The fund-raising aspect of the theater was very important in Vajiravudh's eyes. One advertisement for a benefit performance for a royal charity starts out: "Are You a Friend of Siam?"[19] It became, then, one's patriotic duty to go to plays. It is possible even that the rather large number of plays the King wrote in English (ten of them) were written, at least partly, to tap some of the *farang* money in the community for one or another of the King's favored benefits.

Vajiravudh used traditional theatrical pieces—"sung dramas" and masked dance-dramas—as well as Western-style plays to convey his patriotic messages. The poetic rendering of the Phra Ruang story, *Khom damdin* (The Cambodian Earth Diver), is outstanding in this regard. And two dance-dramas, *Mit mi chai* (The Triumph of Friendship) and *Thammathamma songkhram* (The War between Good and Evil), were propaganda pieces for the Allied cause in World War I. These dance-dramas presented their messages in the transmutation of classical-style ballets. *Mit mi chai*, first performed in October 1917, shows Phra Mit, the god of friendship, leading the gods and goddesses in dance. The envious demon Phalasun appears to interrupt the proceedings, claiming that the gods and goddesses are trying to deprive him of his "place in the sun." A great fight between gods and demons takes place. The gods win and celebrate their victory with a joyful dance in which the dancers, in a charming touch to guarantee that the audience will not miss the true meaning of the

The Media

allegory, wave on stage the flags of the Allied nations.[20] *Thammathamma songkhram* has a very similar theme. Although written shortly after the end of the war, the drama reflected the King's thoughts on the war's meaning. It was inspired by a sermon by Prince Patriarch Vajiranana on the victory of the forces of good over the forces of evil. In Vajiravudh's version the leader of the forces of evil argues that might makes right and, making the intended identification with the Germans inevitable, echoes the infamous phrases chosen by the German chancellor to justify the violation of Belgian neutrality:

A solemn treaty is but a scrap of paper;
Laws are disposable when necessity requires.[21]

For his dramatic works, as for his essays, the King frequently resorted to pseudonyms. Classical pieces and serious plays such as *Phra ruang*, *Mahatama*, and *Huachai nakrop* bore his own name, but informal plays were written under the pen name Si Ayutthaya or Phra Khanphet. Perhaps by this means the King hoped to dispel some of the criticism that he was excessively devoted to the stage.

The Press

The one medium that caused Vajiravudh some trouble was the press. The King appreciated the press. He used newspapers often as an outlet for his views. But the press was a problem. It had its own voice. Newspapermen presented their own views. And these views the King often regarded as antithetical to his own and pernicious to the kinds of development he desired for Siam.

Some of the King's most prominent essays appeared first in the press. *Nangsuphim thai* carried his articles, frequently in series, in Thai, and the *Siam Observer* followed later with English translations. Other papers, of course, gave considerable prominence to all the King's words and actions as newsworthy items. In 1917, as a sign of particular favor, Vajiravudh invited members of the press to the official audience at which he delivered his speech from the throne about entering the war; this was the first time the press in Siam had been honored by an invitation to attend such an audience.[22] And to ensure that there would be accurate reporting of affairs at court, the King instituted the "Court Circular" on May 21, 1912. By this move he made the main events of life at the court, which had been "a sealed book to the bulk of the Siamese people," known to all newspaper readers; as the *Bangkok Times* put it, he "substituted facts for gossip."[23]

The King was an avid newspaper reader. He read all of the Bangkok papers and some of the leading British news journals, and he subscribed to a press clipping service for "cuttings related to Siam."[24] Vajiravudh also wrote, under a variety of pen names, rejoinders to press comments of which he disapproved. On July 17, 1915, for example, he sent a long criticism to the editor of the *Nangsuphim thai* concerning an earlier two-part article on the poverty of the people. The article had said that the poor people of Siam were being driven to robbery and had blamed the government for the people's distress. Vajiravudh's rejoinder vehemently denounced the writer, likened him to a senseless yapping dog, refuted the logic of his arguments, and criticized the newspaper for wasting paper on such nonsense.[25]

Similar criticisms of critics abound in Vajiravudh's writings. In general what the King objected to were writings that exposed government weaknesses—inefficiency, inattention to rural problems, financial difficulties, and the like. Although he claimed that "I do not and cannot possibly object to ... fair comment or criticism,"[26] in fact he objected to all criticism. Even a mildly unfavorable review of the diction in his translation of *Romeo and Juliet* evoked a scathing attack on the English critic. The King wrote that he had not written the play for a European "with some knowledge of Siamese" but for well-educated Thai.[27]

Vajiravudh had a theory as to the reason why so many writers for the press were so critical. He saw them as men who were "of very indifferent education, or dismissed officials with mountains of grievances against the Government." Journalists in Siam thus were men without responsibilities and so were "practically always critical and destructive." The people of Siam bore their share of blame for the "trashy news and irresponsible vapourings of disappointed, dismissed Government servants" because they read these writings and bought the papers.[28] The King (as Asvabahu) spoke as a "well-wisher" who felt the need to warn the people that Siamese journalists were concocting their sweet offerings from "water from the nearest street gutter."[29]

Although his own sarcasm may have provided the King with a momentary catharsis, the press problem remained. And the problem was real, not merely the product of the King's sensitivity. The Siamese-language papers in particular were noted for their carelessness in handling facts and for their defamations of character. Their attitude was made clear by an editorial in one paper which stated that the paper's only duty was to print what it received; if someone were defamed in the process, he always had the option of refuting the defamation.[30]

Control of the press was one way to solve the press problem.

The Media

But Vajiravudh was loath to resort to control or censorship. He admired the free press of England; he was proud of his own tolerance, of Siam's record of liberality. As Phraya Arthakar Prasiddhi, Siam's Attorney General, put it, "No restrictions have been placed on the press in Siam of any nature whatsoever, and the press in Siam since its birth became free, whereas it took hundreds of years in England to attain that end."[31]

Many high officials in Vajiravudh's government, however, did not share the King's compunctions with regard to the press. In June 1912 Prince Paribatra recommended the passage of a press law.[32] In July of the same year Prince Chakrabongs came forth with the same recommendation.[33] By August 1912 an accord had been reached to draft a law. But, the King noted in his diary, a severe law such as existed in Russia and Germany was to be avoided. Such a law would not end adverse criticism, it would only direct it into other channels.[34] His philosophy here was clearly stated in another diary entry: "It is important that we not cut off people's means to air their grievances."[35] At a special meeting of the Council of Ministers in 1915 agreement was reached that a mild law to ensure press responsibility should be enacted.[36] Nothing was done. In 1916 Chaophraya Yommarat urged the King to ban immoral books; Vajiravudh promised to consider the matter.[37] In 1917 a fairly harsh newspaper act patterned after the Japanese law was drafted, probably on the initiative of Prince Chakrabongs.[38] In a note on this law Vajiravudh characterized Japanese methods as "glorified caricatures" of Western laws, as containing the appearance of justice but in fact enabling the government to discriminate "between its favourites and those it has a down upon...."[39] The King again suggested deferment. The subject of a press law came up again in 1922, and a new draft was prepared.[40] After several revisions, the draft in 1923 became the Law on Books, Documents, and Newspapers. This law required that all newspapers be licensed. Licenses could be denied or could be revoked in the interest of "public order," but a newspaper had the right to court appeal. The *Bangkok Times* editor made it clear that, although he was not delighted with the law, it could be lived with.[41] It would appear that, insofar as application of the law was concerned, the government during the Sixth Reign continued to act circumspectly.

The mild control of the law of 1923 added little to the controls already present in the civil and criminal codes. And these codes were on occasion used. A Thai paper, the *Sam samai*, was closed in May 1911 on a charge of *lèse majesté* for an indiscreet reference to the running aground of the royal yacht.[42] The editor of the *Chino-Siam*

The Media

Daily News was imprisoned on losing a court case in which he was charged with defaming a prince.[43] Another case of libel, this time by a writer of the *Bangkok Daily Mail* against the Minister of Justice, was settled by a formal apology.[44] The *Chino-Siam Daily News* was in trouble again briefly in 1918, but the matter was settled with a light fine.[45] In 1925 two Chinese papers were closed for printing articles regarded as inflammatory.[46] Although very few papers were closed, many were warned. Generally a newspaper accused of printing errors rushed to make retractions. But not always. The *Bangkok Daily Mail* not only refused to retract a statement it had made about an action taken by the Ministry of War, but also refused to print the ministry's own explanation. The ministry consoled itself by denouncing the *Daily Mail* in other papers for its discourtesy.[47] On other occasions the government, although very much irritated by sly innuendos in the press, decided not to press charges for fear of making a "big clamor ... for the public's benefit."[48]

Probably the most effective means the government found for exercising influence over the press was buying it. At least two newspapers, the *Nangsuphim thai* and the *Nangsuphim chino*, received government subsidies.[49] The *Siam Observer*, it seems clear, had government connections.[50] And in 1917 the *Bangkok Daily Mail* and its Thai-language edition, the *Krung Thep Daily Mail*, were purchased by a government official, Phraya Boribun Kosakon, from the American proprietor, P. A. Huffman; the purchaser, it was noted by another paper, was not acting on his own account.[51] The *Daily Mail* had been an annoyance to the government from the start, and as early as 1912 Chaophraya Yommarat had suggested to the King that a controlling interest in the company should be bought secretly by government officials.[52] The *Nangsuphim thai* was widely known as the voice of the government.[53] It had been receiving aid secretly before the Sixth Reign started, and in December 1910 the paper was reorganized and given increased financial support on a regular subsidy basis.[54] Government officials up to the King seem also to have become increasingly concerned with the paper's circulation, rates, and effectiveness. In a memorandum of March 1912, for example, an official suggested that in order to make the circulation of the *Nangsuphim thai*, then about 500, match the 1,000 figure of the *Daily Mail* the rates should be reduced, the subsidy should be increased, and government offices should break news to the paper first so as to give it an advantage over the competition.[55]

A certain number of journals were openly owned and published by the government or government-supported agencies. Most of these,

The Media

however, were specialized or professional journals with little popular appeal. Several journals were initiated by the King, who had played the role of editor himself since his issuance of *Thawipanya* as a prince. In the days of Dusit Thani, two newspapers, *Dusit samai* and *Dusit sakkhi*, and one monthly, *Dusit samit*, were published there. These publications, however, were virtually limited in circulation to the courtiers of Dusit Thani. The King also sponsored several journals: *Chotmaihet suapa*, the Wild Tiger monthly; *Samutthasan*, the Navy League monthly; and a literary magazine entitled *Sap thai*. *Chotmaihet suapa* and *Samutthasan* served as outlets for some of the King's more important speeches, essays, and poems, but, again, their circulation was not wide.

The outstanding newspaper of the reign in terms of fairness, reliability, and absence of sensationalism was the English-language *Bangkok Times*. The *Times* was English owned. Its editor, W. H. Mundie, knew the Thai language and people well. He was sympathetic to Siam, but not to the point of sycophancy. The editor's ideal, as he once expressed it, was to produce the kind of paper admired by Robert Louis Stevenson, a journal that appeared "to have been written by a dull, sane Christian gentleman, solely desirous of imparting information."[56] Despite its caution, the paper sometimes got into trouble. In March 1914, for example, the King's private secretary objected to an editorial concerning alleged government involvement in or mishandling of the failure of a bank. The secretary asked the editor, who had a "well deserved reputation for fairness," to correct the "false impressions" he had produced. The editor did so, although in so doing he wrote that more meaning had been "read into" his words than was intended.[57] The *Times* was aware that it had won the reputation of "constantly 'grousing' against the administration." The paper saw itself not as a grouser but as a constructive critic "keenly and honestly interested in the advancement of the land we live in."[58] The editor by and large realized how far he could go without getting into trouble. He once wrote: "If one has to write in this country, one has to learn to convey a meaning and at the same time to use great restraint in doing so."[59]

Although restraint was the watchword of the *Bangkok Times*, articles of great frankness were published. One series of such articles, written by a Westerner under the pseudonym Junius, began appearing in September 1919.[60] The articles were not sensational; they did not indulge in personalities; they were calmly reasoned analyses of "The Future of Siam"—the future Siam might have if, Junius said, the prevailing inefficiencies, corruption, short-range policies, lack of leadership, and policy of drift were to give way to a firm program of economic development led by honest and practical men. The Junius articles were exceedingly strong. And they were exceedingly critical, calling into question fundamental principles of government in Siam.

In 1923 a new series of articles of much the same nature began appearing under the name Hermit.[61] Hermit, a Thai, argued for an increase in funds for national development, a reduction in military spending, and a more rapid movement toward democracy. Hermit expressed his ideas clearly and pointedly, and his ideas were far from congenial to the King.

Yet no actions were taken against Junius or Hermit or any other such writers. The King was disturbed. But he did nothing but pen the following, in English, to one of his officials:

> You know I have been ill and my nerves are in anything but good condition. I am being continually annoyed by having to read such foolish (or knavish) correspondences as those of "Hermit" and such like in the "Bangkok Times." As I feel that nothing could be done to stop such annoyance, the only thing that I can ask you to do is to stop sending up the "Bangkok Times" for the present, otherwise I shall become quite a nervous wreck, for I feel it more and more difficult to control my temper![62]

It appears that the King shielded himself from the barbs of the *Bangkok Times* for a total of eight days![63]

Long-time newspapermen such as Sathitya Semanil,[64] Ome Palangtirasin,[65] and Chalerm Vudhikosit[66] have given complimentary assessments of the freedom permitted to the press in Vajiravudh's days. And their assessments seem thoroughly justified. One of the earliest acts of Vajiravudh's successor was to issue a rescript warning the press in effect that the new government was not going to be so tolerant of journalistic excesses as its predecessor had been. But it was not until the absolute monarchy came to an end in 1932 that full censorship of the press was instituted.

10

An Assessment

King Vajiravudh died on November 26, 1925, at the age of 44. He had had periodic bouts of illness during the reign and was sick through most of 1918; his final illness, which began in August 1925, centered on an infection of the intestinal system.

The last months, indeed the last years, of the King were filled with much sorrow and bitterness. Deaths of high-ranking members of the royal family occurred with alarming frequency in those last years. From 1919 to the end of the reign six half-brothers, three full brothers, the Queen Mother, Prince Vajiranana, and Prince Devawongse all died. The most frightening losses, from the political point of view, were those of the heirs to the throne. In 1910 Vajiravudh had declared that succession to the throne would pass presumptively through the line of Queen Saowapha's sons: Princes Chakrabongs, Asadang, Chudadhuj, and Prajadhipok. Prince Chakrabongs died in 1920 at the age of 37; Prince Chudadhuj died in 1923 at the age of

An Assessment

31; and Prince Asadang died in 1925 at the age of 33. Only one son of Queen Saowapha remained to carry on the line, Prince Prajadhipok, the youngest of King Chulalongkorn's sons. Vajiravudh had, of course, hoped for a son of his own to carry on the succession. But his only child, born two days before the King's own death, turned out to be a girl and therefore, by the King's law on succession of 1924, not eligible to succeed.[1] The King's question when the baby brought to him and placed by his side was, "Is it a girl or a boy?" The answer was, "A girl." The King paused for a moment, then said, "It's just as well."[2]

Contributing to the mood of depression that grew during the last years of the reign was the downturn taken by the economy. Poor rice harvests, budget deficits, and growing criticism of administrative policies could not help but affect Vajiravudh adversely.

Characteristic of the King were the plans he made to boost the economy and the national morale. In a new burst of enthusiasm early in 1925 he decided to hold special festivities commemorating the end of the fifteenth year of his reign—a reign that would then be equal in length to that of Rama II, Vajiravudh's great literary predecessor. He planned to join these festivities with those for his birthday and the annual Winter Fair to create one great celebration. The celebration's chief feature would be a Siamese Kingdom Exhibition, patterned after England's annual Wembley Exhibition, that would combine all the attractions of the Winter Fair—the booths, the lotteries, the games, the dancing—with an elaborate display of Siamese arts, agriculture, and industry. The principal aim of the exhibition would be to promote the economic development of the nation; its by-product would be a new permanent park for the people and an exhibition ground for future fairs. The exhibition had proceeded to within two months of its opening when Vajiravudh died. One of King Prajadhipok's first acts was to cancel it.

Vajiravudh's exhibition and Prajadhipok's cancellation symbolize in microcosm the vast differences between the two kings and their reigns. The ethos of the Sixth Reign, and many of its accomplishments, were to stand embodied in the exhibition. It was to have, in addition to exhibit halls for agriculture and industries, a palace of art, sports stadia, theater halls, and displays illustrating the progress of the army, the navy, and the Wild Tigers. The Boy Scouts were to be featured in yet another display. Various sports events were planned, and football teams were invited from Rangoon, Colombo, Penang, Singapore, Saigon, Hong Kong, Manila, and Batavia to compete in "the first great Asiatic Football Competition." But what Vajiravudh undoubtedly

An Assessment

hoped would happen at the Siamese Kingdom Exhibition was what a writer for the *Bangkok Times* described as happening at Britain's Wembley during the final torchlight tattoo. The tattoo was staged in a great arena with flags, lights, bands, marching men, horses. It was "just a parade on a big scale," and yet it was much more. For the performance had a magic, a thrill. And that thrill came from the audience "in the strung up excitement and admiration and emotion of thousands of people, all stirred by a common feeling." That feeling was pride in nation, pride in unity, pride in fellowship. It was the proof, despite "all the terrible things happening or about to happen to our country," that "England isn't done."[3]

Prajadhipok and his advisers saw the exhibition in a different light: it was expensive, and much of it was wasted show; at a time when the economy was in difficulty, retrenchment rather than lavish spending on fairs was the practical course to follow. The exhibition was cancelled in good conscience. Only a small pagoda clock-tower and a few small buildings remained as evidence of what had been planned. The Wild Tigers died quietly soon after. Arts shows ceased. The Boy Scouts failed to get financial support. Even the army and navy felt the financial pinch as the new government cut all expenses it could to keep a balanced budget in a time of worldwide depression.

The overriding question about the nationalistic program in Siam during the Sixth Reign remains: Did it work? Did it survive, if not in the form of the Wild Tiger Corps, in the impression it made on men's minds?

"On the day that King Vajiravudh died," said one former Boy Scout, "I put on my Scout insignia and stood for a long time in honor of the leader of our nation with a heart deep in sorrow ... the whole Thai nation had lost its guiding national star."[4] Another writer, commenting many years after the King's death on the King's patriotic songs, said that the songs remained moving and unforgettable.[5] Such stories, such vivid memories of men of the times, demonstrate beyond doubt that the King's messages affected some people. And in addition, the latter-day assessments of the reign by most Thai writers, even those not generally sympathetic, do credit the reign with success in its nationalist program. One severe critic of Vajiravudh, for example, allows that the "one political success of his was sowing the seeds of nationalism in the Thai people."[6] Favorable Thai surveys of the reign usually count the drive to stimulate nationalism as the foremost achievement of the reign.

The question of the effectiveness of the nationalist movement then does not deal with absolutes. It becomes a question of the degree

An Assessment

of effectiveness. How many people were affected? How many people remained aloof or uninvolved? Such questions cannot be answered absolutely. No Gallup or Roper polls are available to give quantified answers. Answers, at best tentative, must remain impressionistic.

It seems unlikely that the population at large, the vast mass of Siam's farmers, was deeply influenced by the King's nationalistic messages. In those areas in which farmers were affected—in the drive for adoption of surnames, for example—the nationalistic meaning was probably not even understood. Yet the farmers were not completely isolated from the new emphasis on patriotism. School boys and school girls even in the provinces learned the patriotic songs penned by Vajiravudh. The King's birthday and other national holidays were celebrated in provincial capitals with parades, Wild Tiger and Boy Scout marches, and displays of the King's photograph. The provincial holidays were on a smaller scale than those in Bangkok, but they were stirring nonetheless.

To a degree, also, the Wild Tiger movement and, even more so, the Boy Scout movement brought the patriotic ideas of the King to rural Siam. The number of men directly involved in the Wild Tigers was not large, and most members seem to have come from the ranks of government officials. The Boy Scouts were less elitist, although the expense of buying a uniform undoubtedly kept many boys from joining. In any one year, it seems, there were never more than 22,000 Scouts. Perhaps a total of 40,000 to 50,000 Scouts received training during the reign. But each Scout was given considerable exposure to nationalistic slogans and ideals, and it is hard to believe that a Scout would remain unaffected by appeals to his patriotic sentiments. Further, his parents, who had to be willing to buy his uniform, and another member or two of the family would be likely also to be aroused. Putting all these probables together, for Boy Scouts alone, would give a total of perhaps 200,000 people who to some degree saw the nation in a new and favorable light.

Although it is impossible to approach an estimate of nationalism through figures, another figure, that of the number of people who subscribed to the Navy League in the great patriotic drive to purchase the warship *Phra Ruang*, may reveal something. In the five-year campaign some 130,000 people made contributions. Certainly not all contributed for purely nationalistic reasons, yet some undoubtedly did.

Still a third audience for nationalistic messages that can be numbered is the armed forces. Obviously, not all army, navy, and gendarmerie conscripts were equally susceptible. But all were sub-

An Assessment

jected more than most citizens to patriotic slogans, songs, and words. On the basis of an approximate military establishment of 10,000 men made up mostly of two-year enlisted men, there must have been, during the fifteen-year reign, roughly 75,000 men who received military training, a military training that included a strong element of nationalist indoctrination.

It is tempting to play with numbers further and add up the figures for the various audiences—the Wild Tigers, the Boy Scouts, the contributors to the many campaigns, the viewers of the nationalistic pageants and plays—to obtain a final audience figure. But such an exercise would be meaningless, for the audience overlap would be very large; how large there is no telling.

In general, however, the nature of the appeals the King made shows that his primary audience was the educated element in the population—the elite, the leaders. Most of the Wild Tigers were, after all, civil servants. The heavy stress on writings is also evidence of reliance on the educated, for, as simple as Vajiravudh's writings were, they could be read only by the minority of the population that was literate. And, even if no reading barrier had existed, many of the King's finest nationalist expressions—for example, the play *Phra ruang* or the essay "Clogs on Our Wheels"—were not likely to be comprehended by farmers. Not even the King's plays reached a mass audience, for they required actors experienced in "spoken plays" and they required theaters, neither of which were available except in Bangkok and some of the largest towns.

King Vajiravudh realized, of course, that he could reach only a small percentage of his people with his vital messages. He saw this as no insuperable problem if his select audience helped him spread his ideas. If the Wild Tigers informed others, if government servants, including teachers, passed on the word, then the idea of nation would spread. He enunciated this idea clearly to one Wild Tiger audience. "If all of us here, though we are only few in number, were to be of one mind and speak with one voice, that voice would strike the ears of others, one person after another, and soon would be heard throughout Siam."[7]

There was a certain logic in the King's view of how ideas could spread in Siam. But there were also problems. The King's ideas of patriotism were given to groups that were undoubtedly already more nation-conscious than most Thai. These groups needed nationalistic reminders less than most Thai. And as disseminators these groups had both natural advantages and natural shortcomings.

The advantages lay in their influence. Men such as Čhaophraya

An Assessment

Yommarat and Prince Chakrabongs had large circles of influence in their ministries. Such men could and did help spread the King's word. They gave speeches echoing the ringing nationalistic phrases of the King. Prince Abhakara composed songs for the Siamese navy fully as patriotic as those of the King. Other men also picked up the messages. The Commander of the Fifth Army Division in Khorat, for example, in 1918 wrote and staged an operetta (*lakhǫn rǫng*) involving a hero who served in the Siamese Expeditionary Force. In one scene the hero tells the weeping mother and wife of a friend about the friend's death in battle and "suddenly amid thunder, flames of fire and smoke, the spirit of the departed shows itself and exhorts his dear ones not to grieve for his glorious death, but to bring up his little son to become a courageous and daring 'Nak bin' [aviator]." The boy rises to the occasion and "swears to his father's spirit that he will worthily follow his father's footsteps and combat the fatherland's enemies." The play's reviewer commended it for its "ardent patriotism."[8] Certainly in this regard the play was a worthy successor to His Majesty's own products.

A disadvantage in using the elite classes as purveyors of the King's ideas was that the links between the elite and the masses were usually not intimate. The social gulf between even lowly government officials and rice farmers was considerable. Officials were respected. They were obeyed. But they were not always understood. And a sentiment such as nationalism is not easily communicated under such circumstances.

Another possible disadvantage in relying on the Siamese elite to transmit nationalism was that many of its members were not sympathetic to Vajiravudh on personal and political grounds.

That a gulf existed between the King and many members of the royal family and other educated Siamese cannot be gainsaid. A detailed examination of the dimensions of the gulf and its causes would be relevant, of course, to an overall evaluation of the reign, but such an evaluation is beyond the scope of a study of nationalism; the gulf is relevant here only to the extent that it may have interfered with the King's nationalistic program. A catalog of some elements of the gulf, however, will substantiate its existence.

The lack of rapport, of intimate contact, between King Vajiravudh and the other members of the royal family is well documented. King Chulalongkorn had been in the habit of meeting regularly with his Council of Ministers, most of whom were members of the royal family. In addition, ministers and other royal councillors would dine with the King and meet him informally. They would even attend the King

An Assessment

when he was residing outside of the capital. Vajiravudh did not follow this pattern. Although he continued to assign important positions in government to his relatives, he met these relatives much less often than his father had done. Meetings of the Council of Ministers were held irregularly and with less and less frequency during the reign. The King and Prince Chakrabongs, for example, "hardly ever had a quiet chat together, let alone a quiet meal" during the entire period of the reign.[9] To cite but one example of the differences between Chulalongkorn and Vajiravudh in their contacts with relatives: Prince Paribatra, who had been in the habit of seeing Chulalongkorn every evening no matter where the King was residing, went to attend Vajiravudh during the King's first visit to Bang Pa-in in 1911. Paribatra waited for an audience. He waited several days. He was not called. The Prince drew the obvious conclusion and thereafter ceased to expect the call that would not come.[10]

It is much more difficult to establish the reasons for the rift than to demonstrate its existence. On the King's side, many reasons are cited by one source or another. Vajiravudh, according to some, wished to do things his own way, without interference from his relatives. The King was anxious not to fall under the sway—or have the government remain under the sway—of strong elder princes such as his uncle, Prince Damrong. Old Thai custom did not allow a King to remove officials, not even cabinet ministers, from office without extremely good cause. King Chulalongkorn had had his problems because of this custom. And so did his son, who had to proceed circuitously to achieve his objectives. Prince Damrong, who as Minister of the Interior had been the most powerful minister during the Fifth Reign, found his ministry reduced by Vajiravudh. In 1915 Damrong resigned for "reasons of health." Shortly thereafter, the Ministry of the Interior, under the stewardship of one of the King's most trusted counsellors, Chaophraya Yommarat, found its powers enhanced again.

Another frequently cited reason for the rift between the King and his relatives was Vajiravudh's shyness. Foreigners as well as Thai remark on this personality characteristic. The rarity of the King's visits to his mother, for example, has been attributed in part to his uncomfortableness in her female-dominated household; he reportedly "never seemed at home" in surroundings in which he was "in the midst of women."[11] His disinclination to call meetings of the Council of Ministers early in the reign has been attributed to his shyness in presiding over a group of men whose years and experience elicited the King's deep respect.[12] This reputed shyness of the King, however,

An Assessment

may have been primarily a reflection of his unwillingness to expose himself to criticism.

There are several indications that Vajiravudh was less tolerant of hearing opinions that did not agree with his own than his father had been. The King was aware that on occasion his policies were not popular; he was also aware that many people did not approve of his lifestyle. Just as Vajiravudh wished to rule according to his own lights, he wished to live according to his own lights. On social occasions he preferred the company of his courtiers in the royal household to the company of members of the royal family. He enjoyed having dinner with Čhaophraya Ram or Phraya Anirut or Phraya Sucharit or other long-time friends from his years as prince at Saranrom Palace, and so he dined with them. If important business in a ministry arose, the King would meet the minister informally in settings of his own choosing.

One astute commentator on the probable source of the King's distance from his relatives observed that it was a natural result of the King's long separation from his family during his years of schooling in England. The young sons of Chulalongkorn "were scattered over the Continent" and could meet one another "only on rare occasions." Thus "those impressionable and formative years for family contact were lost ... and never regained."[13]

On the side of the King's relatives, the reasons given for the rift are also many. They include criticisms of the King's displays of favoritism, his reluctance to marry, his suspicions of his relatives, his excessive generosity to his courtiers. Aspects of Vajiravudh's administrative policies were also called into question, particularly his stress on militarism and his nationalistic drives that seemed to crowd out attention to practical problems. Whatever the merits of these criticisms, they do not account for the rift. For the rift did not exist because the princes refused to see the King or resented the King. The princes simply were not called upon. Whether the specific criticisms of and uncomplimentary gossip about the King were true or not, it was the King who called the tune, not the princes. Vajiravudh did not work as closely with his brothers and uncles as they would have liked. That was the principal reason for the resentment they felt.

In the end, however, the distance between the King and his relatives bears on the history of nationalism only if this group, out of resentment, refused to cooperate, or cooperated half-heartedly, with the King in forwarding the nationalist cause. It would be very difficult to prove that royal bickering had this effect. It may be

An Assessment

assumed that some princes, resentful of their low status in the Wild Tiger movement, were less than enthusiastic about the Wild Tiger cause. Yet none dared refuse roles assigned them in the movement by the King: Prince Damrong did research for Wild Tiger pageants, and Prince Paribatra wrote music for them. Prince Abhakara, according to rumor, was one of the princes the King suspected of plotting his downfall. But that rumor seems not to have interfered with the Prince's continuing an outstanding career in the navy and, not incidentally, contributing his bit toward nationalism by writing a number of patriotic navy songs. By and large it seems clear that all the princes of Vajiravudh's generation shared his nationalistic inclinations. They may have resented the King's approach, his aloofness from them personally, but their ideas of Siam's needs were not dissimilar from the King's own. And, in any case, they would not have dared to oppose him directly.

There may have been some individuals who held back, who did not throw themselves enthusiastically behind the nationalistic program because of their general feeling of estrangement and resentment of the King. It is difficult, however, to see this kind of a reaction as a serious obstacle to nationalistic growth in Siam during the Sixth Reign. It has been speculated that Prince Damrong's opposition to the Navy League drive to purchase the *Phra Ruang* was the direct cause of his subsequent resignation. Yet the drive continued to a successful conclusion without the Prince's support. The resentment of some princes may have been more of a factor in the reign of King Prajadhipok when the princes came back to favor and proceeded, in a mood of pique and practicality, to dismantle sections of Vajiravudh's nationalistic edifice.

The evaluation of King Vajiravudh's nationalism cannot stop with consideration of possible personal dissatisfaction from princely quarters. There was dissatisfaction from other quarters for other reasons. The abortive coup of 1912 was the clearest demonstration of dissatisfaction. The young military men who were the members of the coup group had personal grievances against the King; they also took exception to his policies, particularly those they felt to be injurious to the best interests of the army. Insofar as they conceptualized their ideals in their plans, they reflected the growing spirit of democratic thought that had shown its strength in Turkey and China. But in the area of ideology, there is little question that their main emotion was nationalism. They were ardent patriots who shared the King's desire for the advancement of Siam. And the very words

An Assessment

they used showed royal inspiration. Thus the coup group of 1912 provided in a sense an indirect tribute to the effectiveness of the King's nationalistic propaganda.

Dissatisfaction with the reign was also reflected in the press of the time, and press criticism showed the growth of an intellectual rift between the King and some of the educated elements in the society. Criticism of specific policies was aired in the press from time to time throughout the reign, but a general critical mood became apparent in the last years of the reign. Several series of very frank, although carefully worded, articles began appearing in the *Bangkok Times* in late 1919 and continued through 1925. The articles were written by various contributors under the pen names Junius, Hermit, Fiat Lux, Perspectiva, and Simplicitas.

In these articles, which were written in a period of growing economic difficulties and postwar pessimism and fear, Siam's policies were examined from a broad perspective—and generally found wanting. The first article by Junius, for example, stressed the theme that, now that "Siam has taken her place in the family circle of the nations," Siam must live up to the responsibilities of that position. Siam must develop its resources to prevent the growth of a "spirit of unrest" internally and to answer the threat of the irresistible force outside that demanded "higher development." To develop its potential Siam needed honest and able administrators and not "her common run" of men better known for "paltry cleverness" than "straightforward work." Siam needed also to throw open its gates to foreign business and to Chinese labor. Siam must invest in its own development, and to do this must "cease to dissipate her resources on armaments." Waste of all sorts must end, particularly "private profit arising out of government acts, nepotism and the power of personal influence." The article concluded: "Siam needs a strong leader. She has him, if he will trust himself and the right helpers."[14]

Subsequent criticisms by Junius and others attacked government policies in four main areas: economy, administration, defense, and the political system. The principal governmental shortcoming in the economic sphere, according to the critics, was its lack of attention to the development of Siam's main resources. Above all, the government was faulted for doing little to improve the Thai rice industry; the Thai rice farmer, said Perspectiva, is "getting poorer and poorer every year ... if we cannot tackle this question of the rice industry and put it on an efficient basis then there is no hope for us." Government efforts at economic development were regarded as misdirected;

An Assessment

for example, said Perspectiva: "The cities of Siam are all trying to subscribe to aeroplanes and making flying grounds, while fundamentals like drains, water supplies, hospitals and streets are forgotten."[15]

In the administrative sphere innumerable shortcomings were identified. The bureaucracy was termed too big, unwieldy, inefficient, graft-ridden, self-serving. It needed drastic pruning; it needed "a cold, common-sense, business-like programme, and the will to carry it through."[16] And the government "broadcasting of honours" in the awarding of titles and decorations, said Hermit, defeated the object of encouraging talent, merit, and character.[17]

The principal waste of government funds pointed out by the critics was that in the area of national defense. One critic suggested that the armed forces be cut by half. The mood in general was that Siam no longer was in peril from abroad and, in any case, its armed forces, despite the large proportion of the budget spent on them, could not really face a serious threat if one should pose itself. The Wild Tigers were too close to the King to be directly opposed, but Hermit, who praised the organization, did dare to air doubts about its funding and the soundness of its organization.[18]

In the sphere of Siam's political system several writers alluded to the stifling of public opinion and to popular unrest. Hermit wrote openly in favor of democratic reform.[19] He did admit that Siam was not ready for full democracy, but he suggested that the institution of advisory councils of citizens who would consult with government administrators would be a large step in the right direction. He recommended that such councils be formed at all levels, from the provinces up to the cabinet level. A cabinet council would be advisory to the cabinet ministers, who, in Hermit's view, should be presided over by a prime minister.

All of these suggestions for reform in a country that remained an absolute monarchy had to be understood as implying a criticism of the King. Some indeed came very close to *lèse majesté*: a sly reference to the waste of money on "fine uniforms," which was a veiled criticism of the Wild Tiger organization; a delicate mentioning of excessive expenditure "in a certain quarter," which probably meant the privy purse; and an even more veiled reference to "evil influences" on the King. Probably even more repugnant to the King than such daring remarks were overall conclusions that Siam was in peril and Siam's leaders were not doing enough about it. Assessments such as Junius' "Siam has no national ideal, no cohesion of soul, no inheritance of common interests" and Perspectiva's "we really do not

An Assessment

have the slightest idea of where we are going" could not help but disturb Vajiravudh deeply.[20]

The purpose of the articles in the *Bangkok Times*, however, was not sensationalism, not a desire to inflame either the King or country. The articles, it is clear, were written by honest men, by well-informed men, by representatives of Siam's intellectual elite who seriously disagreed with some things the government was doing and were seriously disturbed about many things the government was not doing. These men comprised a kind of "loyal opposition" of monarchical times.

What was the effect of these men on Thai nationalism? Did they tend to undermine the King's program? It is doubtful if they did. For one thing, they were but a small group, and their influence could not have been large. Their articles were scholarly and not popular, and they wrote in English, a safer language for criticism[21] and, quite possibly, a language that would reach a larger number of like-minded people than the Thai language could. Far from trying to undermine Thai nationalism, these critics were themselves nationalists. It was because the critics loved Siam that they dared to express views that were dangerous but that they believed needed to be expressed if Siam was to progress.

The objectives, and even many of the specifics, of the national program outlined by the critics were very close to those of the King's program. Both the critics and the King wanted a strong, prosperous, and united Siam. Both criticized the inefficiencies in government, the self-centeredness of many government officials, the Thai preference for "clerkism." Both believed Thai should be more active in commerce and trade. Both believed in furthering education, particularly practical education. The critics, of course, could point to failures, such as the disastrous government effort to build a Siamese merchant marine. But that effort, misguided though it may have been, was a sincere attempt to launch Siam into the postwar commercial world, which was one of the aims of the critics.

The intellectual opposition to King Vajiravudh may even constitute evidence of the effectiveness of his reign-long drive to stimulate nationalism. Although the critics undoubtedly received their nationalistic transfusion from many sources, it is at least possible to wonder if the King's blood had not indeed added to the richness of their national ardor. Some of the critics' phrases on occasion are very reminiscent of the King's. All write as patriots and argue policy changes in the interest of increasing national strength and enhancing nationalism. Inculcation of love of nation in the schools and in the

An Assessment

military is urged. The Boy Scout movement is praised for instilling "in the youth of our country patriotism, honesty, and humanism."[22] It cannot be proved that Vajiravudh's loyal opposition learned any of their nationalism from him, but, wherever they got it, it was there. Love of nation was one point on which the King, the princes, and the critics were in complete harmony.

One important touchstone of the degree of success of Vajiravudh's nationalistic efforts is the question "What elements survived his time?" The obvious survivals—his flag design, the institution of surnames—are dubious evidences of nationalism. Other survivals, such as compulsory education, Chulalongkorn University, and Vajiravudh College, were logical developments of policies begun before the Sixth Reign and have meanings broader than nationalism. Some institutions, such as the Boy Scout movement and the arts and crafts shows, went into a decline or ceased altogether at the end of the reign, but were later revived. More important than any of these, however, are the literary survivals. The patriotic plays *Huachai nakrop* and *Phra ruang* have been performed often in Thailand since Vajiravudh's time. And, on occasion, they are still performed. Some of the King's plays, including *Phongphang* and *Chuai amnat!*, have been featured on Thai television in recent years. Vajiravudh's essays, his proverbs, his poems have gone through countless editions. His song *Sayam manutsati* is one of Siam's best-known patriotic songs today. His first volume of lectures to the Wild Tigers was used as a school text for many years; by 1958 it was in its seventh printing. And *Phra ruang*, also used as a school text, had reached its eighteenth printing of 40,000 copies by 1959. Countless other writings of the King have been reissued as commemorative volumes at cremations and in commercial editions.

Indeed, the nationalistic message of King Vajiravudh has undoubtedly reached many more people since his death than it ever did in his lifetime. The King's writings and his patriotic spirit inspired Thai of later generations. His contributions in the area of nationalism were drawn upon by many later nationalists.

The clearest illustration of the use of Vajiravudh's ideas as a nationalist model is provided by the regime of Premier P. Pibulsonggram. Pibulsonggram, one of the military promoters of the coup d'état of 1932 that ended the absolute monarchy in Siam, rose to the premiership at the end of 1938. Pibulsonggram's power base was the army, and his program was militaristic and nationalistic. It would be a distortion of truth to attribute all of Pibulsonggram's nationalistic notions to his royal predecessor, for the nationalism of the premiership

An Assessment

of World War II years could and did draw heavily on other sources, particularly the ultranationalism of the rising dictatorial regimes in Italy, Germany, and Japan. But some of Pibulsonggram's notions seem clearly to go back to Vajiravudh.

The main elements of Pibulsonggram's nationalist program were militarism, economic nationalism, chauvinism (particularly directed against the Chinese minority in Siam), and cultural nationalism. The militarism of the regime undoubtedly derived in part from the military background of the premier himself. It seems also to have borrowed heavily from Japanese warrior codes. But some of the phraseology—"The Thai love nation above life"; the Thai are "eminent warriors"[23] —is strongly reminiscent of Vajiravudh's. The economic nationalism of the Pibulsonggram years also seems to hearken back to the exhortations of the Sixth Reign to the Thai people to work hard, to buy Thai products, to take increased interest in occupations in industry and trade. In the expressions of anti-Chinese sentiments, parallels are again easily noted, even to the point that a close associate of Pibulsonggram in a public lecture compared the Chinese in Siam to the Jews in Germany. The cultural nationalism of the Pibulsonggram regime seems in many ways but an extension of the cultural nationalism of the Sixth Reign, with heavy attention paid to language purity, historical glory, and Buddhist piety. And, in addition to this emphasis on traditional Thai values, Pibulsonggram, like Vajiravudh before him, felt the need to modernize the culture, obviate possible outside criticism, by introducing Westernizing reforms such as Western dress and Western social manners. Some cultural reforms in both regimes defy the East-West label: Vajiravudh's new system of writing that found precedent in Siam's past as well as in Western styles is akin in this regard to Pibulsonggram's promotion of social dancing through the medium of an old Thai peasant dance, the *ramwong*. There are aspects of Pibulsonggram's nationalistic program that could have been inspired by either Vajiravudh or the fascist states. The militaristic youth movement, the *yuwachon*, that Pibulsonggram created in 1935, for example, certainly partook of the flavor of the Italian *ballilla* and the German *Hitlerjugend*; it undoubtedly owed something as well to Vajiravudh's Boy Scout movement.

But although there are similarities in their methods and motives, Pibulsonggram far outstripped Vajiravudh in the intensity of his program. Vajiravudh by and large relied on voluntarism, exhortation, and propaganda; Pibulsonggram frequently resorted to force, underlining his convictions by fines, threats, and, on occasion, assassinations. Vajiravudh made some anti-Chinese remarks; Pibulsonggram enacted

King Vajiravudh Memorial (Statue at entrance to Lumphini Park).

An Assessment

severe anti-Chinese legislation. Vajiravudh initiated promilitary measures; Pibulsonggram embarked on a program of military opportunism and aggression against Siam's French Indochinese neighbor. The nationalism of King Vajiravudh can be seen in the nationalism of Premier Pibulsonggram as through a lens that magnified and distorted.

Despite their differences, Pibulsonggram felt the tie between himself and his royal predecessor. He expressed it in word and deed. In January 1940 the government made a decision to honor the Sixth Chakkri monarch by building him a tribute in the form of a statue to stand at the entrance to Lumphini Park. At the opening of the campaign to solicit funds for the statue, Premier Pibulsonggram gave high praise to Vajiravudh; he asserted "there does not to-day exist an individual comparable with such a Monarch." The premier recited the various accomplishments of the King and concluded with the statement:

> The most important and highly beneficial kindness handed down to the Thai country and nation, however, lies in the fact that King Vajiravudh was responsible in rousing the Thai nation as a whole from its lethargy to realize the importance of carrying out patriotic and other good acts for the betterment and glory of the nation.[24]

The days of wartime supernationalism have long been gone in Siam. The process of nation-building goes on in quieter ways, in ways that seem more congenial to the spirit of Siam's "great literary monarch."[25]

Although all the connecting lines between Vajiravudh's nationalism and modern Thai nationalism cannot be precisely charted, the lines are there; they are perceivable, and they are perceived. In a reflective, and perhaps harried, mood, Vajiravudh once made a prediction that was also a wish, a wish that now is in large part fulfilled: "When I die, it will be many years before those who come after me will realize what good I have done for the country."[26]

Notes

Abbreviations Used in the Notes

BT   *Bangkok Times*
CMHSP *Čhotmaihet sǔapa* (Wild Tiger Records)
NA   National Archives, Documents of the Sixth Reign
         (NA 37/1 = National Archives, Documents of the Sixth Reign, File 37, Folder 1)
RKB   *Ratchakitčhanubeksa* (Royal Government Gazette)

Introduction

1. Malcolm Smith, *A Physician at the Court of Siam* (London: Country Life, 1947), p. 92.

Chapter 1

1. M. C. Poon Pismai Diskul, *Sarakhadi* (Bangkok: Mahamakut Ratchawitthayalai, 1964), p. 303.

2. Ibid., p. 304. See also Prachoom Chomchai, *Chulalongkorn the Great* (Tokyo: Centre for East Asian Cultural Studies, 1965), p. 165.

3. Vajirunhis died on January 3, 1895; Vajiravudh was installed as Crown Prince on March 8. One source (*BT*, December 4, 1911) states that Chulalongkorn named Vajiravudh heir thirteen days after the death of his older son.

4. Chula Chakrabongse, *Lords of Life* (New York: Taplinger, 1960), p. 268.

5. For example, see Chulalongkorn to Vajiravudh, February 11, 1895, in Thawi Muktharakosa, *Phramaha thiraratčhao* (Bangkok: Phrae Phittaya, 1963), pp. 36–42.

6. Chulalongkorn, *Phrabǫromrachowat nai phrabatsomdet phra čhulačhǫmklao čhaoyuhua phraratchathan phračhao lukyathoe song phraratchaniphon mǔa p.s. 2428* (Bangkok: Sophon, 1931), pp. 10–11 (English translation).

7. For the King's instructions on the conduct of the government during his absence, see Chulalongkorn's decree of March 16, 1908, in Thawi, pp. 100–103. It appears that Vajiravudh's performance of duties in substitution for his father continued after Chulalongkorn's return: Chulalongkorn had not been cured of his illness abroad and immediately on his return to Siam went for an extended rest in Phetburi. See Chamun Amorn Darunrak, *Phraratchakaraniyakit samkhan nai phrabatsomdet phra mongkutklao čhaoyuhua rǔang phraratchaniphon nai ratchakan thi 6, kharomrak, mahasinlapin ek khǫng thai* (Bangkok: Khurusapha, 1968), p. 8.

8. Dhanit Yupho, *Khon* (Bangkok: Department of Fine Arts, 1957), p. 50.

9. Khon Samak Len, *Rainam tua khon kap bot rǫng lae phak čheračha* (Bangkok: n.p., 1909), pp. 1–2.

10. *Ha lo, Wang ti, Nǫi inthasen*, and *Khwamdi mi chai*.

11. The student publications were *The Screech Owl* and *The Looker-on*; the thesis was *The War of the Polish Succession*, published in English in 1902.

12. A diary in three volumes for 1902, in English, is preserved in the National Library. There are references to other diaries; these may be in the possession of the Royal Secretariat. Portions of a diary have been published as *Čhotmaihetraiwan nai phrabatsomdet phra mongkutklao čhaoyuhua* (Bangkok: Mahamakut Ratchawitthayalai, 1974).

13. *Lilit phayap* (Bangkok: Prasoet, 1968).

14. *Čhotmaihet praphat huamǔang paktai r.s. 128* (Bangkok: Khurusapha, 1963).

15. *Thiao mǔang phra ruang* (Bangkok: Ministry of the Interior, 1954).

16. Ibid., preface.

17. Phraya Sunthǫnphiphit, "Suan anusǫn," in *Wachirawutthanusǫn* (1967). Apparently the telling of tales to children was common at court. Vajirunhis, the first Crown Prince, noted in his diary that he and his younger brother Vajiravudh (nicknamed To, meaning "large") enjoyed stories told them by Princess Somawadi and Krommaluang Samǫnratsirichet; see Thawi, p. 14.

18. For a collection of the Prince's riddles, see Rama VI, *Phraratchaniphon pritsana* (Bangkok: Mahamakut, 1960).

19. Phraya Sunthǫnphiphit, "Sǔapa–luksǔa," in *Wachirawutthanusǫn* (1953), pp. 25–45.

20. Sunthǫnphiphit, "Suan anusǫn," p. 236.

21. Thawipanya Samosǫn is written "Dvi Panya Club" in the contemporary English-language press.

22. The principal officer was called secretary in 1904 and chairman in 1905; see *Thawipanya*, no. 1 (April 1904) and no. 12 (March 1905).

23. On the Thawipanya Club activities, see Sunthǫnphiphit, "Suan anuson," pp. 231–233; remarks of Prince Phitthayalongkǫn, quoted in King Vajiravudh, *Chumnum nithan* (Thonburi: Bannakhan, 1966), pp. iii–iv; *Thawipanya*, no. 1 (April 1904) and no. 2 (May 1904).

24. *BT*, October 9, 1916. The small theater, in the northern part of the garden, was later supplemented by a 100-seat theater in the southwest corner; see Sunthǫnphiphit, "Suan anusǫn," p. 232.

25. Sunthǫnphiphit, "Suan anusǫn," pp. 232–233.

26. Malcolm Smith, *A Physician at the Court of Siam* (London: Country Life, 1947), pp. 113–114, 106.

27. The Prince mentions Claridge's and the Russian ballet in his diary for 1902, part 1, under January 12.

28. Esmé Wingfield-Stratford, *The Victorian Cycle* (New York: Morrow, 1935), p. 260.

29. Ibid., p. 340.

30. H. G. Quaritch Wales, *Siamese State Ceremonies* (London: Quaritch, 1931), p. 136.

31. Phraya Wisut Suriyasak to Chulalongkorn, September 20, 1895, in Thawi, pp. 59–66.

32. Smith, pp. 115–116. Smith states that Chakrabongs "was always the first favorite, both with his father and mother.... he was regarded as the ablest as well as the handsomest of all the sons."

33. Chamun Amorn Darunrak, *Dusit thani* (Bangkok: National Library, 1970), p. 28.

34. Thawi, p. 27.

Notes to pp. 13-16

Chapter 2

1. King's reply to speech of Prince Svasti, January 5, 1915, in *Phraratchadamrat nai phrabatsomdet phra mongkutklao čhaoyuhua* (Bangkok: Bamrung, 1929), p. 134.

2. W. A. Graham, *Siam* (London: Moring, 1924), vol. 1:226.

3. King to Prince Chakrabongs, December 2, 1911, in Chula Chakrabongse, *Lords of Life*, p. 272.

4. Second coronations were unusual but not unprecedented. Rama I had a second coronation when he moved to his new palace in Bangkok in 1785; Chulalongkorn had a second coronation at the end of the regency period in 1873. See Hophrasamut Samrap Phranakhǫn, *Čhotmaihet phraratchaphithi bǫromrachaphisek* (Bangkok: Sophon, 1924), pp. 3-4.

5. For general remarks on Thai coronation rites, see Wales, pp. 67-120; for a general description of Vajiravudh's coronations, see Hǫphrasamut, *Čhotmaihet ... bǫromrachaphisek*.

6. Hǫphrasamut, *Čhotmaihet ... bǫromrachaphisek*, p. 3.

7. *BT*, December 9, 1911.

8. Introduction to *Phra sunhasep* (Bangkok: Khurusapha, 1961), pp. viii-xii.

9. On auguries in general, see Wales, p. 62 and passim. There were also omens portending the end of a reign. One "miracle," the appearance of mysterious lights circling the peak of Phra Pathom Čhedi, Siam's tallest and oldest Buddhist stupa, was reported by Prince Vajiravudh to his father as having occurred on October 24, 1909; see Vajiravudh to the King, October 26, 1909, and the King's reply, October 27, 1909, in Chamun Amorn Darunrak, *Kamnoet phraratchawang sanamčhan* (Bangkok: Khurusapha, 1968), pp. 22-26. This miracle, occurring within a day of the date of the death of Chulalongkorn a year later, was subsequently interpreted as portending his death; see Prince William of Sweden, *In the Lands of the Sun* (London: Nash, 1915), pp. 122-123.

10. Thawi, pp. 167-176, who quotes Prince Damrong to the King, March 26, 1911, and the King to Damrong, March 26, 1911. The manuscript letters are in NA 37/1. See also *RKB* 28, April 9, 1911, p. 37.

11. *BT*, December 5, 1911; Hǫphrasamut, *Čhotmaihet ... bǫromrachaphisek*, p. 145.

12. Rama VI manuscript quoted in Amorn, *Kamnoet phraratchawang*, p. 21.

13. King's address to the people on December 3, 1911, in *BT*, December 5, 1911, and Hǫphrasamut, *Čhotmaihet ... bǫromrachaphisek*, p. 149.

14. Thawi, p. 175.

15. Chula Chakrabongse, *Lords of Life*, p. 272.

16. Somphop Phirom, *Kutakhan* (Bangkok: Krung Sayam, 1970), p. 59. Also the throne called Pradamuk, built during the first reign of the Bangkok

dynasty, was replaced by the Manangkhasila throne, which was built around the stone used as a throne by King Ramkhamhaeng in thirteenth-century Sukhothai. See Chamun Amorn Darunrak, *Phraratchakaraniyakit ... rùang phraratchaprapheni* (Bangkok: Khurusapha, 1971), vol. 2:9–10.

17. *BT*, December 4, 1911. The details given in the English-language newspaper are in substantial agreement with those given in Họphrasamut, *Čhotmaihet ... bọromrachaphisek*, pp. 124–125. The Thai account does not stress the crowning itself. It seems likely, however, that for the benefit of the foreign guests Vajiravudh placed more emphasis on the actual "coronation" than was customary.

18. Họphrasamut, *Čhotmaihet ... bọromrachaphisek*, pp. 131–133; *BT*, December 4, 1911. The strong impression this moment made on the King himself is indicated by his choice of it as the subject of the mural of his reign on a wall of the throne hall, Anantasamakhom, which was opened in 1917.

19. On the foreign visitors to Mongkut's coronation, the royal chronicle states: "Being very well disposed towards foreign visitors, the King granted them audience, to enable them to view his royal person on the occasion of the coronation." See Čhaophraya Thiphakọnwong, *Phraratchaphongsawadan krung ratanakosin ratchakan thi 4* (Bangkok: Khurusapha, 1961), vol. 1:17–18.

20. *BT*, November 29, 1911.

21. Ibid., July 15, 1911.

22. Ibid., October 13, October 26, October 28, October 31, November 9, and November 30, 1911. Also Amorn, *Phraratchakaraniyakit ... rùang phraratchaprapheni*, vol. 2:14.

23. *BT*, December 7, 1911. Two previous balls are mentioned: one in 1897, celebrating Chulalongkorn's return from Europe; one in 1903, given in honor of Vajiravudh's return to Siam.

24. William, p. 28.

25. *BT*, December 4, 1911.

26. April 1912.

27. Early January 1912.

28. *BT*, January 2, 1912.

29. William, p. 59.

30. Ibid., p. 141.

31. Address of Čhaophraya Yommarat to the King, January 1, 1912, in *BT*, January 5, 1912.

32. King's reply to address of Čhaophraya Yommarat, January 1, 1912, in *Phraratchadamrat nai phrabatsomdet*, pp. 24–27, and *BT*, January 5, 1912.

33. The King's address to the people, December 3, 1911, in *BT*, December 5, 1911, and Họphrasamut, *Čhotmaihet ... bọromrachaphisek*, pp. 148, 150.

34. *BT*, December 9, 1911.

35. The Queen Victoria incident, dramatized by Laurence Housman in *Victoria Regina*, is reported as he saw it in *The Unexpected Years* (New York: Bobbs-Merrill, 1936), p. 184.

36. *BT*, December 6, 1911.

37. Ibid., December 5, 1911.

38. Ibid., January 5, 1912; *Phraratchadamrat nai phrabatsomdet*, p. 25.

39. *The Poetic and Dramatic Works of Alfred Lord Tennyson* (Boston: Houghton Mifflin, 1898), p. 527.

40. Smith, p. 84. See also *BT*, December 24, 1915, from a report by the Chiangrai correspondent on the visit of Prince Chakrabongs to Chiangrai in December 1915: "Europeans and Americans in Siam all notice the lack of popular *enthusiasm* over Royalty. The people think it is 'becoming,' 'proper,' to shrink and be discreetly silent in the presence of one of their rulers even at a public reception in the open. I asked a man this morning 'Were you really glad to see the Prince?' He said 'I was truly glad!' I remarked 'Well you *looked* like a stone image! *Why did you not shout and cheer?*' He said 'It would not be proper!'"

41. *Chotmaihetraiwan*, pp. 41–42.

42. The King's address to the people, January 1, 1912, in *BT*, January 5, 1912, and *Phraratchadamrat nai phrabatsomdet*, p. 26.

Chapter 3

1. *CMHSP* 1, no. 1 (May 1911); Sunthǫnphiphit, "Sǔapa–luksǔa," p. 46.

2. *CMHSP* 1, no. 1 (May 1911): 19.

3. *BT*, May 8, 1911; *CMHSP* 1, no. 1 (May 1911): 20–28, gives a list of the initial members.

4. *CMHSP* 1, no. 1 (May 1911): 10. For the genesis of the corps idea, see also the King's diary for April 1911 (*Chotmaihetraiwan*, pp. 32–33).

5. William, p. 67: "The inspection ... resembled in every respect a rally of Boy Scouts ... rich in comic interludes...."

6. See the Royal Remarks on Establishing the Wild Tiger Corps, *CMHSP* 1, no. 1 (May 1911): 3–4.

7. Collected in *Plukchai sǔapa*. The edition used here is *Plukchai sǔapa lae khlon tit lǫ* (Bangkok: Mahachai, 1951).

8. Speech to Wild Tigers, May 26, 1911, in *Plukchai sǔapa*, pp. 1–9.

9. Speech to Wild Tigers, June 6, 1911, in *Plukchai sǔapa*, pp. 10–22.

10. Ibid., p. 17.

11. Ibid., p. 18.

12. Ibid., p. 22.

13. Ibid., p. 19.

14. See David K. Wyatt, *The Politics of Reform in Thailand* (New Haven: Yale, 1969).

15. Brochure on the Wild Tigers (in English) reprinted in *BT*, December 4, 1911.

16. Speech to Wild Tigers, July 4, 1911, in *Plukčhai sǔapa*, pp. 58–71.

17. Ibid., p. 59.

18. *BT*, December 5, 1911; Hǫphrasamut, *Čhotmaihet . . . bǫromrachaphisek*, p. 148.

19. *CMHSP* 1, no. 2 (June 1911):73–82.

20. Ibid., p. 83.

21. Speech of June 6, 1911, in *Plukčhai sǔapa*, p. 21.

22. *CMHSP* 1, no. 2 (June 1911):79.

23. Sathǔan Supphasophon, *Phraratchaprawat phrabatsomdet phra mongkutklao čhaoyuhua lae prawattikan luksǔa thai* (Bangkok: Khurusapha, 1961), p. 24.

24. Prince Damrong Rajanubhab, *Khawamsongčham* (Bangkok: Social Science Association Press, 1963), pp. 160–161.

25. Brochure on the Wild Tigers, *BT*, December 4, 1911.

26. See, for example, *CMHSP* 1, no. 3 (July 1911):151; a royal order on the corps stated that what the Wild Tiger gained from sacrifices of free time to practice and drill was the benefit of "the honor of belonging to the same organization with His Majesty, the princes, and high government officials."

27. William, p. 67. See also *BT*, September 21, 1911, which said that membership "has been practically compulsory for the higher civil service officials."

28. Čhamroen Sawat-chutho, "Dusit thani," *Triam udom sǔksa*, no. 3 (1951):233; also, "Report of the Committee To Investigate Views on the Wild Tigers, March 26, 1912," in *CMHSP* 2, no. 12 (April 1912):733.

29. NA 169, His Majesty's Royal Secretariat, February 19, 1912.

30. NA 169, Department of the Palace to Phraya Sisunthǫnwohan, March 17, 1915.

31. *CMHSP* 1, no. 4 (August 1911):232.

32. William, p. 66.

33. *CMHSP* 1, no. 1 (May 1911):21–27.

34. NA 169, "Kanphraratchathan thong pračham . . ." (no date given).

35. *CMHSP* 1, no. 4 (August 1911):325, 332.

36. It is surprising that no definite figure appears in the sources. A guess can be made from some figures in the *BT*, October 13 and 16, 1911, and February 6, 1912.

Notes to pp. 38–41

37. Sunthǫnphiphit, "Sǔapa–luksǔa," p. 60. Clubhouses were later built in the provinces: mention is made of one in Nakhǫn Pathom in September 1911 (*BT*, September 18) and in Ayutthaya in October 1911 (*BT*, October 16).

38. See, for example, the twenty-one articles on saluting when wearing a cap, when not wearing a cap, when carrying a swagger stick, etc., in the Order on Wild Tiger salutes in *CMHSP* 1, no. 3 (July 1911): 143–151.

39. An Order To Prevent Infractions of Discipline, in *CMHSP* 1, no. 3 (July 1911):151–172. See page 154 for the punishments for tardiness.

40. Regular Sunday drills were abandoned on July 14, 1911; see *BT*, July 15, 1911.

41. *BT*, July 5, 1911.

42. Ibid., February 21, 1912.

43. Phraya Satčhaphirom Udomratchaphakdi, *Lao hai luk fang* (Bangkok: Aksǫnsat, 1955), pp. 68–70.

44. *BT*, June 19, 1911.

45. Ibid., June 29, 1911.

46. Sunthǫnphiphit, "Sǔapa–luksǔa," p. 65.

47. Ibid., pp. 62–66; *BT*, December 11, 1911.

48. *BT*, December 11, 1911.

49. *Nangsǔphim thai*, December 15, 1911.

50. *BT*, December 11, 1911.

51. Ibid., December 23, 1911. Prince William, pp. 139–140, states: "As usual when the Wild Tiger Corps was concerned, the King himself was the leading spirit of the undertaking ... [he] performed the difficult duties of stage manager with praiseworthy success." The inspiration for the pageant may go back to 1898, when the King, then a student in England, saw and very much enjoyed a "military tournament" complete with pantomime put on by British troops; see Vajiravudh to Chulalongkorn, in Thawi, pp. 72–73.

52. *BT*, December 23, 1911.

53. William, p. 139.

54. "Grand Pageant" announcement in NA 169.

55. *BT*, February 22, 1912.

56. *CMHSP* 2, no. 9 (January 1912):511.

57. See *CMHSP* 2, special number (February 1912):i–iv.

58. For details see *CMHSP* 2, no. 9 (January 1912):541–554.

59. NA 169, King to Prince Nares, Prince Devawongse, Prince Damrong, Prince Kitiyakara, Prince Charoon, Čhaophraya Yommarat, Čhaophraya Wongsa, Phraya Wisut, and Phraya Anurak, undated, but presumably January 26, 1912.

60. NA 169, reply of Devawongse, January 29, 1912.

61. For a full report see *CMHSP* 2, special number (February 1912): 559–601.

62. *BT*, February 13, 1912.

63. Ibid., February 14, 1912.

64. Amorn, *Kamnoet phraratchawang*, pp. 145–149.

65. *CMHSP* 1, no. 3 (July 1911): 101–142.

66. *BT*, December 9, 1911.

67. Ibid., December 5, 1911.

68. Ibid., February 6, 1912.

69. Interview with a former courtier.

70. *BT*, June 11, 1912, quoting from the *Daily Mirror* of May 13.

71. *CMHSP* 2, no. 10 (February 1912): 666.

72. Henri Cucherousset, *Quelques informations sur le Siam* (Hanoi: l'Éveil Économique, 1925), p. 48.

73. See sample examinations in *CMHSP* 5, no. 4 (August 1913): 147–148; 7, no. 6 (October 1914): 195–197, 197–199. A typical question asked the scoutmaster to explain how he would teach Scouts the meaning of the saying "Our nation was established because our fathers were Wild Tigers." By 1915 a special scoutmasters' school had been established; see *CMHSP* 9, no. 1 (May 1915): 233–246.

74. NA 127/8, Minister for Religious Affairs and Education to the Royal Secretary, "Letter Reporting on Developments in the Ministry for 1912."

75. NA 169, address to Boy Scout Reserves by Phraya Wisut Suriyasak, September 18, 1913.

76. *BT*, February 10, 1914.

77. NA 169, Phraya Phaisan Sinlapasat, "Kham tůan hai luksůa tham kanchuailůa phu ůn."

78. *BT*, September 1, 1917.

79. Cucherousset, *Quelques informations*, p. 49.

80. Personal interviews. All interviewees remembered the Boy Scouts favorably. Even one who regarded the Tigers as "a sort of farce" called the scouts "good."

81. Amorn, *Kamnoet phraratchawang*, pp. 124–125. The lyrics were composed by Čhaophraya Thammasakmontri; the music, by Prince Paribatra.

82. To give some idea of relative value: a provincial school teacher made from two to twenty-five baht a month; a courtier in the original list of Tiger members made sixty baht a month.

83. *CMHSP* 1, no. 3 (July 1911): 172–176.

84. The coup group was composed principally of young army officers, but not entirely; indeed, four were members of the Wild Tigers. See *CMHSP* 3, no. 1 (May 1912): 15–16.

85. Rian Srichandr and Netra Poonwiwat, *Prawat pattiwat khrang raek khọng thai r.s. 130* (Bangkok: Kim Li Nguan, 1960), pp. 20–21.

86. Interview with Netra Poonwiwat, October 22, 1969.

87. William, pp. 66–67.

88. *Nangsuphim thai*, March 19, 23, and 27, 1912.

89. *CMHSP* 2, no. 12 (April 1912): 713.

90. Ibid., 713–743.

91. Ibid., 743–758.

92. NA 169, Chakrabongs to King, April 16, 1912.

93. *CMHSP* 2, no. 12 (April 1912): 765–770; *Nangsuphim thai*, March 26, 1912.

94. *CMHSP* 2, no. 12 (April 1912): 758, 759–764.

95. *CMHSP* 6, no. 11 (March 1914): 405–412.

96. *BT*, January 6, 7, and 8, 1913.

97. Ibid., June 26, 1917.

98. See, for example, the nineteen speeches given from April 25, 1914, to August 28, 1915, in *Ruang thetsana suapa* (Bangkok: Khurusapha, 1958), and the thirty-one speeches given from February 17, 1912, to January 4, 1920, in *Phrabọromrachowat suapa* (Bangkok: n.p., 1920).

99. For 1913 see *CMHSP* 4, no. 12 (April 1913): 515–529; for 1915 see *CMHSP* 10, no. 8 (December 1915): 733–796; for 1917, *BT*, December 29, 1917; for 1918, *BT*, January 8, 1919; for 1919, *BT*, January 9, 1920.

100. Letter of January 28, 1916, quoted in Chamun Amorn Darunrak, *Suapa lae luksua nai prawattisat* (Bangkok: Khurusapha, 1971), vol. 1: 59–60. A participant in the maneuvers of 1917 commented on the King's total absorption in the maneuvers every day; see Satchaphirom, p. 98.

101. *CMHSP* 9, no. 6 (October 1915): 595–608; 10, no. 1 (November 1915): 679–711; 10, no. 8 (December 1915): 807–811; 10, no. 9 (January 1916): 897–916, show the addition of 1,000 members in Bangkok and 736 members in the southern provinces. The total membership to date was 4,956. This latter figure represents only full members who had taken the oath of loyalty.

102. Graham, vol. 1: 242.

103. NA 169, King to Prince Bhanubhandu, June 18, 1915.

104. *CMHSP* 11, no. 12 (April 1917), 1366–1370; *BT*, May 10, 1917.

105. Phraya Phahonphonphayuhasena. See *CMHSP* 4, no. 10 (February 1913): 317–411; *BT*, February 19, 1913.

106. *BT*, March 1, 1915.

107. See chapter 5.

108. NA 169, Vajiravudh, "Kham atthibai nathi sǔapa kǫngphon tang tang," February 11, 1915. This document was issued only to commanders and contains scathing criticisms of those who entered the corps for personal advantage, of those who criticized His Majesty's Own Guard units, and of those who treated the corps as if it were but another part of the bureaucracy and not a defense organization that could determine national survival.

109. *CMHSP* 7, no. 6 (October 1914): 200–222. See also the lecture to the Wild Tigers of January 31, 1915, in *CMHSP* 8, no. 9 (January 1915): 471–473.

110. See NA 169, speech of January 4, 1915; *CMHSP* 10, no. 9 (January 1916): 892–894; *CMHSP* 11, no. 9 (January 1917): 1005–1006.

111. *RKB* 34, July 18, 1917: 361–370. Also in Amorn, *Sǔapa lae luksǔa nai prawattisat*, vol. 4: 2–13. See also *BT*, July 24, 1917.

112. *CMHSP* 11, no. 12 (April 1917): 1361–1363.

113. Speech to Wild Tigers, March 5, 1919, in *Phrabǫromrachowat sǔapa*, p. 146.

114. NA 169, letters of Luang Phiphat, March 1, 1912, and March 4, 1912.

115. *BT*, January 23, 1912; December 16, 1914.

116. Ibid., November 21, 1919; December 2, 1920; March 19 and 28, 1921.

117. Ibid., December 18, 1919; September 5, September 21, and October 13, 1921.

118. Ibid., May 1 and November 1, 1920.

119. Ibid., February 4, February 5, February 23, and July 5, 1920.

120. Ibid., November 8, 1918; July 10 and December 16, 1920; January 11 and March 11, 1921.

121. Ibid., October 28 and November 15, 1919; February 2, February 3, and October 14, 1920.

122. Ibid., February 14, 1920.

123. NA 169, G. Kluzer & Co. to Phraya Nondisena, Chief of General Staff, Wild Tiger Corps, January 20, 1921; statement of G. Kluzer & Co., February 28, 1921. See also *BT*, November 20, 1919, and the appeal for contributions to the Wild Tiger Rifle Fund in *Dusit samit* 5, no. 48 (1919).

124. *CMHSP* 4, no. 12 (April 1913): 515–529.

125. NA 169, Vajiravudh, "Kham atthibai . . . ," February 11, 1915.

126. *Čhotmaihetraiwan*, pp. 34–35.

127. King's lecture to the Wild Tigers, March 11, 1918, in *Phraratchadamrat nai phrabatsomdet*, pp. 218–221.

128. NA 169, N series 209, report of meeting of October 4, 1921; NA

169/2521, Deputy Commander of the Bangkok Legion to the Commander of the Bangkok Legion, December 1, 1920; NA 169/1292, orders of the Bangkok Legion, October 4, 1921; NA 169/1292, Deputy Commander of the Bangkok Legion to the Commander of the Bangkok Legion, January 14, 1922.

129. *BT*, January 31, 1912. The article was based largely on an article by Lunet de Lajonquière in the *Bulletin de l'Asie française*.

130. *BT*, January 31, February 13, February 28, and August 27, 1912.

131. Chamun Amorn, Phraya Sunthǫnphiphit, Mǔn Sawatphakdi, Phraya Satčhaphirom. See works previously cited.

132. See, for example, Mǔn Sawatphakdi, quoted by Thai Nǫi (pseud.), in *6 phaendin* (Bangkok: Khlang Witthaya, 1960), p. 147.

133. Amorn, *Sǔapa lae luksǔa nai prawattisat*, vol. 4: 162.

Chapter 4

1. The fullest account of the 1912 abortive coup is by Rian Srichandr and Netra Poonwiwat: *Prawat pattiwat khrang raek khǫng thai r.s. 130* (Bangkok: Kim Li Nguan, 1960). This is an invaluable story by two of the principal participants (both of whom were interviewed by the author in 1969). Although the story was not written until almost fifty years after the beginning of the events described, it is in main outline remarkably consistent with contemporary records. The best of these records are the written testimonies (*kham chičhaeng*) and oral testimonies (*kham hai kan*) of 100 men suspected of complicity. These testimonies and other documents of the time are in NA 252/1. Unless otherwise noted, material on the coup party in the following pages is based on these archival sources.

2. *BT*, March 2, 1912.

3. The retirement of Prince Rabi in 1910 was probably a result of King Chulalongkorn's decision to support the heir. The Prince's retirement was officially attributed to poor health; one senior official stated that the real reason was that the Prince had had a dispute with his father and that feelings ran high in the Ministry of Justice in the Prince's support. See Sathaphǫn Malila, *Phračhaobǫromwongthoe kromluang ratburi direkrit* (Bangkok: Thai Khasem, 1953), pp. 45–46.

4. One rumor, for example, told of the King's demotion and beating of an official who refused to let his wife perform in one of the King's plays. This story, which made "a very unpleasant impression" on Europeans and upper-class Thai, was printed in *Lloyd's Weekly News* for December 17, 1911. The clipping and a Thai translation of it were found among the effects of one of the members of the coup party. The story was well known among coup members and strengthened their view that the "bad press" their King was receiving abroad was pulling their nation down.

5. In Thai: *Sia chip ya sia sat* (Wild Tigers); *Sia chip di kwa sia chat* (coup).

6. This view of various members of the coup party was undoubtedly

based on rumors that circulated in Siam of Chinese intervention during the Chinese strike of 1910 even before the fall of the Manchus. See *BT*, June 1 and June 3, 1910; May 12, 1911.

7. The rumor circulated that the Minister of Defense, Prince Chira, was out of favor with the King and had left for Europe because he was granted so little say in government. Although Prince Chira was certainly not one of the King's confidants, his reason for going to Europe early in 1912 was indeed his health. He was operated on in May 1912 and died in February 1914. See personal letter of Prince Chira to the King, May 8, 1912, in NA 252/1. The Prince spoke of the conspiracy as a "madman's dream" and prayed that the King "be preserved in good health, in order to lead, as *only you* can lead, the Destiny of our beloved country."

8. The formula of 10 percent of salary for the first month, 8 percent for the second month, and 5 percent for the third month was adopted, but it was never rigorously applied.

9. The median age of those sentenced to jail was twenty-three.

10. Rian and Netra, p. 70.

11. NA 252/1; Rian and Netra, pp. 137–138; interview with Čharun Sattamet.

12. Rian and Netra, p. 11.

13. See *BT*, May 6, 1912.

14. Rian and Netra, pp. 118, 148–151. The authors speak of the initial intention of the court martial to keep the sentences light, to between three and five years. After the threat, the King reportedly became very angry, demanded that the court reexamine some of the prisoners, and indicated his feeling that harsher sentences were in order.

15. Prince Rabi had resigned from the government in 1910. See Luang Čhakpani Sisinlawisut, *Ruang khǫng čhaophraya mahithǫn* (Bangkok, Tiranasan, 1956), pp. 76–78. The Prince resumed his government career immediately after the coup as Minister of Agriculture. It is possible that the new appointment was meant to insure the Prince's loyalty.

16. *BT*, May 6, 1912. See also Rian and Netra, pp. 157–161.

17. *BT*, May 6, 1912.

18. Ibid., March 5, March 14, April 3, and May 6, 1912.

19. Ibid., April 23, 1912.

20. Ibid., May 6, 1912.

21. *Siam Observer*, May 7, 1912.

22. *BT*, April 18, 1912.

23. Ibid. The personal property of the King was considerable, thanks in large measure to private investments in lands, buildings, and even provincial markets by King Chulalongkorn.

24. See chapter 3 on the Wild Tigers and chapter 5 on the military.

25. NA 146, "Khwamhen rŭang nai thahan khuan phrǫmkan khit tang samakhom phŭa utnun ratchakan thahan nai kǫngthapbok prathet sayam"; London *Times*, June 14, 1912; *BT*, June 12, 1912.

26. "Khwam pen chat doi thae čhing," *Phraratchaniphon thi naru* (Bangkok: Fŭang Aksǫn, 1963), p. 141.

27. *Plukčhai sŭapa*, pp. 36–45.

28. Ibid., p. 45.

29. November 13, 1915, in *Phraratchadamrat nai phrabatsomdet*, p. 145.

30. Speech to His Majesty's Own Wild Tiger Guards of Phuket, April 23, 1917, in *Phrabǫromrachowat sŭapa*, p. 101.

31. The moral rules for officials are the subject of a long essay by the King, "Lak ratchakan," in *Lak ratchakan lae khlong suphasit* (Bangkok: Krom Phaenthi Thahan, 1966) and in NA 210, dated February 20, 1915. See also speech to officials, April 1, 1914, in *Phraratchadamrat nai phrabatsomdet*, pp. 177–180.

32. "Khwam khaočhai phit," letter of May 7, 1915, in *Phraratchaniphon thi naru*, pp. 114–115.

33. See discussion of the "auspicious signs" in chapter 2.

34. For example, speech to the Wild Tigers on November 21, 1914, in *CMHSP* 8, no. 7 (November 1914): 277; speech to Boy Scout leaders, November 13, 1915, in *Phraratchadamrat lae phrabǫromrachowat* (Bangkok: Phračhan, 1958), p. 58.

35. See, for example, speech to Royal Pages School, November 13, 1914, in *Phraratchadamrat nai phrabatsomdet*, p. 100. This statement about the accessibility of Thai royalty is not quite true; traditionally, Thai kings were rarely exposed to public gaze. See discussion in chapter 2. See also Jeremy Kemp, *Aspects of Siamese Kingship in the Seventeenth Century* (Bangkok: Social Science Review, 1969), pp. 22–23.

36. *A Siam Miscellany* (Bangkok: Siam Observer, 1912), pp. 65–66. This *Miscellany* is a reprint of articles written by "Asvabahu" that appeared in the *Siam Observer* from August 5 to December 31, 1912.

37. Ibid., p. 54.

38. Speech of November 14, 1916, in *Phrabǫromrachowat sŭapa*, p. 88.

39. Poem on leadership quoted in S[awai] Watthanaset, *Kiattikhun phra mongkutklao*, (Bangkok: Watthanaphanit, 1957), pp. 724–725.

40. Ibid.

41. See Wyatt, pp. 89–90; Chula Chakrabongse, *Lords of Life*, pp. 261–263.

42. "Rŭang raingan kanprachum palimen sayam," in *Thawipanya*, no. 18 (September 1905), pp. 643–655. The author used the pen name Nǫila, a verbal switch for Nai Lǫ, i.e., Mr. Tease. The sketch contains many plays on words.

43. Thukthawin, "Palimen," in *Thawipanya*, no. 7 (October 1904), pp. 1–6.

Notes to pp. 66–70

44. "Sirat," in *Nangsŭphim thai*, May 18, 1917.

45. Speech to Royal Pages School, November 12, 1912, in *Phraratchadamrat nai phrabatsomdet*, p. 35. Along these lines is a pertinent remark in a play: "A king must regularly listen to the voices of the people; if he does not, he will be got rid of" (*Wiwaha phrasamut* [n.p., n.d.], p. 106).

46. "Sirat," in *Nangsŭphim thai*, May 18, 1917.

47. Speech to Royal Pages School, November 12, 1913, in *Phraratchadamrat nai phrabatsomdet*, p. 56.

48. "The Cult of Imitation," in *Clogs on Our Wheels* (Bangkok: Siam Observer, 1915), p. 161.

49. Speech of June 30, 1925, in *Phraratchadamrat lae phraboromrachowat*, p. 56.

50. "Sirat," in *Nangsŭphim thai*, May 18, 1917; "Mŭang thai chong tŭn thoet," *Pramuan bot phraratchaniphon (phak pakinnaka suan thi 2)* (Bangkok: Sirisan, 1961), p. 29; "Khwam pen chat doi thae ching," pp. 131–135.

51. See, for example, *A Siam Miscellany*, which includes "The Affairs of China," "The Failure of the Young Turks," "The Fruits of Turkish Constitutionalism," "Japan for Example." The articles in Thai appeared in *Nangsŭphim thai*; the articles in English, in the *Siam Observer*.

52. "Khwam krachat krachai haeng mŭang chin," in *Phraratchaniphon thi naru*, p. 306; this article served as the introduction to a translation into Thai of a long article on China by E. J. Dillon that had appeared in the October 1912 issue of *Nineteenth Century and After*.

53. "The Cult of Imitation," pp. 163–164.

54. *A Siam Miscellany*, pp. 1–18.

55. Ibid., pp. 17–18.

56. Ibid., pp. 27–48.

57. Ibid., p. 27.

58. Ibid., p. 30.

59. Ibid., p. 31.

60. Ibid., p. 76 (in the conclusion to the whole series of articles on foreign developments).

61. Ibid., pp. 31–32.

62. Ibid., p. 33.

63. Ibid., p. 47.

64. Ibid., p. 45.

65. Ibid., p. 26.

66. Ibid., pp. 49–76.

67. Ibid., p. 49.

68. Ibid., p. 71.

69. Ibid., p. 75.

70. See "Education and Unrest in the East," in *A Siam Miscellany*, pp. 19–26; the quotation is from p. 26.

71. *A Siam Miscellany*, p. 74.

72. Ibid., p. 76.

73. Ibid., p. 40.

74. Ibid., pp. 75–76.

75. Ibid., p. 37.

76. Ibid., p. 75. See also "Mửang thai čhong tửn thoet," p. 28.

77. *Čhotmaihetraiwan*, pp. 48–62.

78. NA 223/18, King to Prince Charoon, January 28, 1917, written in English.

79. NA 217/3, February 10, 1919.

80. NA 217/2, letter received June 8, 1912.

81. Chula Chakrabongse, *Lords of Life*, p. 290, based on unpublished documents found among the papers of Prince Chakrabongs (his father). The Prince's memorandum is dated April 21, 1917; the King's reply, April 30.

82. *Coup d'état* (Bangkok: Daily Mail, n.d.). In Thai, *Chuai amnat!* (Bangkok: Thanit, 1974).

83. *Coup d'état*, p. 70.

84. Ibid., p. 83.

85. Ibid., p. 19.

86. Ibid., p. 48.

87. Ibid., pp. 63–65.

88. Ibid., pp. 65–66.

89. Ibid., pp. 43–44.

90. Chamun Amorn Darunrak, *Phraratchakaraniyakit samkhan ... rửang hetphon* (Bangkok: Khurusapha, 1969), p. 217; Čhamroen Sawat-chutho, "Dusit thani"; Phraya Sunthǫnphiphit to Chamun Amorn, in Amorn, *Dusit thani*, p. 322.

91. Amorn, *Dusit thani*, p. 108.

92. Ibid., p. 40. Construction at Dusit Gardens started on July 21, 1918. When the Queen Mother died in October 1919, the King moved to her palace at Phya Thai, and Dusit Thani's new "city pillar" was erected at this site on December 19, 1919. Precursors of Dusit Thani were a small model city built at Amphawa Palace in 1903 and a model government, without the miniature city, established at Parusakawan Palace in 1907. The immediate stimulus for Dusit Thani would appear to have been a sand city the King built while on holiday for his health at his beach palace at Hat Čhao Samran in May, June, and July of 1918. See ibid., pp. 22–24.

Notes to pp. 75-80

93. The newspapers were *Dusit samai* and *Dusit sakkhi* (earlier called *Dusit Recorder*). The journal was named *Dusit samit*.

94. This "association" printed a rule book, *Khọ bangkhap pokkhrọng dusit nawik samosọn* (Bangkok, November 11, 1919). In all likelihood it was written by the King.

95. For the constitution and its amendment, see *Pramuan bot phraratchaniphon*, pp. 75-91. Also in Amorn, *Dusit thani*, pp. 57-73.

96. Amorn, *Dusit thani*, pp. 98-103; Čhamroen Sawat-chutho, "Dusit thani," p. 242.

97. Only a few very brief references have been found in the *BT*, for example. One newsman of the times suggested that public notices of Dusit Thani were forbidden.

98. Amorn, *Dusit thani*, p. iii.

99. Ibid., pp. 322-325, quoting from Phraya Sunthọnphiphit; Čhamroen Sawat-chutho, "Dusit thani," p. 246. One writer suggests that the King planned to consider adoption of a constitution for the whole country along Dusit Thani lines in 1926; see Amorn, *Dusit thani*, p. 325, quoting from Phraya Anuchitchanchai, *Saranukrom*, 3 (1934).

100. Quoted in Amorn, *Dusit thani*, p. 78.

101. Chula Chakrabongse, *Lords of Life*, p. 268.

102. Thai Nọi (pseud.), *6 phaendin*, pp. 149, 349; *Bangkok Daily Mail*, November 26, 1925; Rian and Netra, p. 225; various interviews in 1969-70.

103. *BT*, March 17 and December 6, 1911.

104. Ibid., October 27, 1913.

105. Ibid., November 1, 1913.

106. *Čhotmaihetraiwan*, p. 109. Entry for November 3, 1913.

107. A typical example: shortly after Vajiravudh became king, Prince Paribatra, the Minister of Marine, went to attend him, waiting for the call to come in audience as he had done earlier during the reign of Chulalongkorn; the call never came. See Mọmčhaoying Prasongsom Bọriphat, *Banthửk khwamsongčham bang rửang* (Bangkok: Phračhan, 1956), pp. 15-18.

108. Amorn, *Dusit thani*, pp. 311-312; King Chulalongkorn, *Samnao phraratchahatlekha ... kap prawat čhaophraya yommarat* (Bangkok: Bamrungtham, 1939), p. (115); Francis Bowes Sayre, *The Passing of Extraterritoriality in Siam* (New York: Institute of Pacific Relations), p. 17; Chula Chakrabongse, *Lords of Life*, p. 273.

Chapter 5

1. E. Alexander Powell, *Where the Strange Trails Go Down* (New York: Scribner's, 1921), p. 209.

2. Ibid., p. 241.

3. William, p. 37.

4. Lyman Bryson, "Imperialism at Home," *Atlantic Monthly* 134 (December 1924), 852.

5. As quoted in NA 223/18, draft of a letter by the King to Prince Charoon, June 17, 1918.

6. *Singapore Free Press*, as quoted in *BT*, January 18, 1921.

7. NA 223, Charoon to King, November 20, 1919.

8. John Nelson Mills, "Siam, the Last Stand of Buddhism," *Missionary Review of the World* 46 (May 1923): 357.

9. *Siamese Abuses in Patani* (London: Wightman, 1923), 17 pp.

10. "Kansadet čhak phranakhǫn," in *Phraratchaniphon thi naru*, pp. 170–178.

11. See treaty in Pensri Duke, *Les Relations entre la France et la Thailande* (Bangkok: Chalermnit, 1962), pp. 294–295.

12. NA 29, Phraya Kalyan to Phraya Sri, April 21, 1911.

13. *Opinion* (Saigon), August 12, 1912, as quoted in *BT*, August 27, 1912.

14. Articles from *Courrier d'Haiphong* quoted in *BT*, January 28 and February 25, 1914.

15. NA 232, report on the Northeast, Chakrabongs to King, October 15, 1915; NA 29/21, Phraya Kalyan, memorandum of February 15, 1915; NA 91/17, Prince Bovaradej to King, December 7, 1919, and King's reply, December 17, 1919.

16. NA 29/21, royal order of January 8, 1915. Vietnamese revolutionaries were also extradited; see *BT*, September 19, 1913.

17. *BT*, February 13, 1912, reporting on an article in the Saigon *Opinion*.

18. See Wyatt, p. 256.

19. NA 117, memoranda and letters, April 7, April 12, April 24, May 17, and May 19, 1911.

20. NA 29/50, memorandum of Lefèvre-Pontalis, July 25, 1917.

21. NA 29/50, King to Lefèvre-Pontalis, August 8, 1917.

22. Ibid.

23. NA 41/6, King to Phraya Phiphat, June 13, 1911.

24. NA 223/18, King to Prince Charoon, June 17, 1918. See also *BT*, March 30, 1916.

25. Graham, vol. 1: 383.

26. NA 223/18, Prince Charoon to King, September 26, 1918.

27. NA 223/18, King to Charoon, June 17, 1918. The King believed that the indiscreet comments the Frenchman had made to his Russian colleague, subsequently published by the communist government in Russia, prompted his recall. Said the King, the French would have to have seen "the advisability of withdrawing him, since they must surely have felt that their representative

was scarcely adding to the dignity of France in the eyes of the Siamese in behaving so much like a ridiculous buffoon!"

28. NA 133, Chakrabongs to King, June 3, 1910.

29. NA 29, Prince Devawongse to Phraya Kalyan, May 12, 1912. See also Prince Devawongse to French chargé, June 4, 1912.

30. Although there seems to have been little immediate fear of the Japanese, there certainly was distrust of long-range Japanese intentions. Japanese advisers had been hired for only a brief period; the reason they ceased being employed, said the King obliquely, was that "we ourselves began to grow apprehensive" (NA 223/18, King to Prince Charoon, June 17, 1918). Rumors of Japan's expanding interest in southern Asia, occasionally relayed by the British, continually reached Siam. One article by a Japanese journalist (*Pekin Daily News*, January 14, 1916) suggesting that Japan should take over Java and Sumatra and assume the burden of leading the Malayan races to civilization, earned the King's comment that this was no news; such stories of Japanese ambitions had been circulating in Siam for a long time. The King classified the Japanese, despite their paper alliance with Britain, as "the Germans of the East" (NA 10/28, King to Prince Devawongse, February 11, 1916). The most serious Japanese effort to play politics in Siam came in 1919, when a Japanese adviser to the steamship line Yamashita and Company secretly approached the Siamese government with a plan to help Siam form a shipping company in order to break the British trade monopoly. The adviser said that Siamese refusal would entail loss of sympathy of Japan's most influential class, whereas acceptance would bring Japanese surrender of extraterritorial rights in Siam (see NA 10/28, Prince Kitiyakara to King, September 2, 1919).

31. Of the nineteen sons sent to Europe, at least ten received military training: Chira, Abhakara, Vajiravudh, Paribatra, Purachatra, Chakrabongs, Vudhijai, Mahidol, Chudadhuj, and Prajadhipok.

32. See *BT*, December 13, 1910; Natthawutti Sutthisongkhram, *Phrakiat prawat khọng čhọmphonrưa čhọmphon somdet čhaofa kromphra nakhọn sawan wọraphinit* (Bangkok: Krom Phaenthi Sathan, 1965), pp. 560–563. A political motive of these actions may have been to bring to the fore the young Princes Chira and Paribatra, both brothers of the King, and to remove Prince Bhanurangsi, the King's uncle, from active leadership of the armed forces.

33. *BT*, December 8, 1911.

34. Ibid., July 28, 1914.

35. Ibid., January 25 and June 13, 1912; May 3, August 23, December 29, and December 30, 1913; January 14 and February 23, 1914; *Bangkok Daily Mail*, April 20 and 22, 1914; *BT*, June 24 and November 16, 17, 24, and 25, 1921.

36. *Čhotmaihetraiwan*, p. 112.

37. *BT*, July 24, 1920, quoting from H. Cucherousset's article in *l'Éveil Économique de l'Indochine*.

38. *BT*, April 5, 1920, quoting from the Saigon *Opinion*; *BT*, April 14, 1920.

39. Ibid., April 9, July 2, July 15, November 26, and December 2, 1920; January 19, October 1, October 18, and November 8, 1921.

40. Ibid., August 12, 1920.

41. *Kansongkhram pọm khai prachit* (Bangkok: Sophon, 1916). See *BT*, October 27, 1916.

42. From *Wiwaha phra samut*, p. 86.

43. NA 223/18, King to Prince Charoon, June 17, 1918.

44. "Mu̇ang thai čhong tu̇n thoet," p. 4.

45. Speech of June 13, 1911, *Plukčhai su̇apa*, p. 32.

46. Ibid., pp. 33–34.

47. NA 210/1, speech of January 1, 1915.

48. *Mit thae* (n.p., n.d.), p. 2.

49. *Nangsu̇ an lakhọnphut ru̇ang "Sia sala"* (Bangkok: Khurusapha, 1955), p. 82.

50. *Coup d'état*, p. 32.

51. A poem based on Shakespeare's "Cowards die many times before their deaths," in *Dusit samit* 2, no. 16 (1919): 39–40.

52. *BT*, February 14, 1914; *Phrabọromrachowat su̇apa*, p. 12.

53. Article written under the pseudonym Lekhanukan in *Thawipanya*, no. 3 (June 1904), 1–14.

54. *A Siam Miscellany*, p. 63.

55. Speech of August 14, 1915, in *Ru̇ang thetsana su̇apa*, pp. 205–206.

56. *BT*, August 13, 1913. The Prince also wrote a long, detailed, and exceedingly well-reasoned article on the principles and practices of conscripted armies, going back to the *levée en masse* of revolutionary France. The purpose of the article was to justify popular conscription and to point to the defects in the Siamese law of 1905. See "Phičharana phraratchabanyat laksana ken thahan p.s. 2448," in *Samutthasan* 2 (February 1915): 35–72.

57. NA 109, Notice of Changes in Conscription Law, December 27, 1910; NA 128/8, Minister of War to Prince Pravitra, December 14, 1911; *BT*, March 6 and 8, 1911; February 6, 1912.

58. *BT*, August 16, 1913.

59. Ibid., June 29, 1917. *RKB* 34, June 18, 1917, pp. 259–303.

60. Prince Chakrabongs, quoted in *BT*, August 16, 1913.

61. Prince Chakrabongs, quoted in *BT*, November 3, 1913.

62. *BT*, August 20, 1913.

63. *Plukčhai su̇apa*, p. 7. The device was not new with the King; it

Notes to pp. 91–95

presumably traces back to a proverb in the collection of the "Proverbs of Phra Ruang," popularly attributed to thirteenth-century King Ramkhamhaeng of Sukhothai. The ancient proverb read: "Being a freeman [Thai], do not associate with slaves." See G. E. Gerini, "On Siamese Proverbs and Idiomatic Expressions," *Journal of the Siam Society* 1 (1904): 53.

64. *Plukčhai sŭapa*, May 26, 1911, pp. 7–8.

65. The original version was slightly longer; see Maha Dhep Kasatarasamuha, *Sŭapa* (Bangkok: Mahamakut, 1968), pp. 38–39 for the longer version and p. 41 for the shorter version. The "official" English translation appeared in "The Pageant of Wild Tiger Traditions" program, reprinted in *Wachirawutthanusǫn* (1953), p. 48. The translation given here appeared in Prince William's book, p. 140; where Prince William obtained it is not known.

66. Speech to Wild Tigers, June 6, 1911, in *Plukčhai sŭapa*, pp. 19–20.

67. "Sadaeng khunnanukhun," in *Phraratchaniphon bang rŭang*, p. 28; originally given as a speech to civil and military officials on May 25, 1918.

68. *Bot lakhǫnphut rŭang huačhai nakrop* (Bangkok: Khurusapha, 1950), p. 72.

69. Speech to Wild Tigers, December 5, 1914, in *Phrabǫromrachowat sŭapa*, pp. 31–32.

70. *RKB* 31, August 6, 1914, pp. 316–317; *BT*, August 10, 1914.

71. In a diary entry for early 1915 the King noted: "I intend to make the greatest possible effort to preserve neutrality." See *Čhotmaihetraiwan*, p. 165.

72. NA 1414, August 26, September 9, and November 21, 1914. Speech of November 21 also in *Samutthasan* 1 (January 1915): 62–69.

73. *BT*, August 15, 1914; Thai original in *Phrabǫromrachowat sŭapa*, pp. 15–20.

74. *BT*, January 2, 1917; *Phraratchadamrat nai phrabatsomdet*, p. 198.

75. NA 2/2, Devawongse to Traidos, August 2, 1914. Prince Mahidol regarded his withdrawal from the German navy as "contrary to my military honor" (NA 2/2, telegram from Mahidol to Paribatra, July 31, 1914); the King's rejoinder was that he must withdraw, for "I have also my honour as Sovereign to think of" (NA 2/2, King to Traidos, around August 2, 1914).

76. NA 223, letter from a German mariner's wife, March 30, 1916, printed in *Tägliche Rundschau*, March 11, 1917, and sent to Siam by Prince Traidos.

77. *BT*, June 7, 1915; April 16, 1917.

78. Ibid., August 15, 1914; *Phrabǫromrachowat sŭapa*, pp. 18, 19.

79. *BT*, August 21, 1915.

80. It is not clear where the inspiration for this idea came from. Certainly public subscriptions for the war effort were in the air. See *BT*, October 27, 1914: "If we mistake not the people of Sweden not long since presented

their king with a warship, and at the present moment a great many countries are providing striking examples of what can be accomplished in the way of raising money by voluntary effort under the same stimulus of patriotism." In a speech of November 21, 1914, Čhaophraya Yommarat also speaks of such subscription efforts in foreign countries; see *Samutthasan* 1 (January 1915): 66.

81. An indication of the King's literary energy on these subjects is the fact that thirty-seven titles by the King appeared in *Samutthasan*, the Navy League's monthly journal, in the first year alone.

82. See King's letter of November 5, 1914, to the President of the Navy League (*BT*, November 6, 1914) and the president's reply of November 7, 1914 (*BT*, November 9, 1914); Thai texts in *Samutthasan* 1 (January 1915): 15–20.

83. Aside from the circumstantial evidence of the King's authorship, one of the original sponsors of the cruiser fund drive confirmed in an interview that the King indeed was the author of the drive and chose the members of the "sponsoring" committee.

84. "Khǫ chuan than pen malaeng wi," *Samutthasan* 13 (January 1916): 14–27.

85. "He rŭa yuk mai," *Samutthasan* 2 (February 1915): 32–33.

86. *Wiwaha phra samut*, p. 158; see also references to navies and the Royal Navy League on pp. 1–2, 160, 161.

87. "Prayot khǫng rŭarop tang tang," *Samutthasan* 1 (January 1915): 96–104.

88. "Chaiyo," *Samutthasan* 1 (January 1915): 87–88.

89. *BT*, January 4, 1915; *Phraratchadamrat nai phrabatsomdet*, pp. 117–118.

90. *BT*, December 31, 1914.

91. Ibid., March 31, 1916.

92. *Samutthasan* 12 (December 1915): 62–64.

93. Ibid., pp. 28, 31–37.

94. Ibid., 1 (January 1915): 80.

95. "Chaiyo," pp. 83–92. "Chaiyo!" is the Thai "Hurrah!"; see discussion in chapter 6.

96. *Mahatama* (Bangkok: Aksǫnnit, n.d.), p. 132.

97. Ibid., pp. 134–135.

98. "Khǫ chuan than pen malaeng wi," p. 15.

99. *BT*, December 31, 1914; January 6, 1915. See photograph in *Samutthasan* 2 (February 1915), facing p. 32.

100. *Samutthasan* 3 (March 1915): 5. Other advertisements appeared in *BT*, *Dusit samit*, and *Nangsŭphim thai*.

Notes to pp. 101–109

101. "Khǫ chuan than pen malaeng wi," pp. 25–26.

102. *BT*, January 6, 1916.

103. "Kan čhamlǫng yut thang rǔa," *Samutthasan* 15 (March 1916): 1–26.

104. See Amorn, *Phraratchakaraniyakit samkhan ... rǔang hetphon*, pp. 9–14; O-phat Sewikun, *Thai kap songkhram lok khrang thi 1* (Bangkok: Kasembannakit, 1968), pp. 7–10.

105. In his diary for March 1915, Vajiravudh made clear the necessity of not provoking his imperial neighbors. See *Čhotmaihetraiwan*, p. 165.

106. NA 139. See also *BT*, December 28, 1914, and NA 223/1, "Phrarachathibai," May 28, 1917, in which the King mentions that at various times the British in Singapore, the French in Saigon, and the Germans in Bangkok all protested at signs of Siam's departure from neutrality.

107. NA 117/43, Prince Devawongse to Dering, August 29, 1916.

108. *BT*, March 25 and 27, April 13, 15, 19, 20, and 25, and August 1 and 14, 1916.

109. NA 209/2, Phraya Maha-amat to Governor of Bandǫn, March 3, 1915; NA 209, Dering to Prince Devawongse, August 22, 1916, and Devawongse to Dering, September 6, 1916.

110. *New York Times*, November 30, 1915; *BT*, January 26, 1916; *BT*, April 24 and July 19, 1917; London *Times*, July 24, 1917; *BT*, July 31, 1917.

111. *BT*, August 14, 1916, citing the *Rangoon Times*.

112. NA 223/1, "Phrarachathibai," May 28, 1917.

113. Ibid.

114. *Samutthasan* 8 (August 1915): 69–111.

115. Ibid., 9 (September 1915): 81–112.

116. Amorn, *Phraratchakaraniyakit samkhan ... rǔang hetphon*, pp. 34–35.

117. NA 223/1.

118. The telegrams dealing with these communications are translated in *BT*, April 30, 1917.

119. *RKB* 34, April 12, 1917, p. 19; *BT*, April 16, 1917; *Nangsǔphim thai*, April 16, 1917.

120. NA 223/1, Prince Devawongse, secret memorandum on views concerning Siam's entry into the war, May 25, 1917.

121. At the end of May, Prince Chakrabongs was vacationing at his seashore home at Hua Hin. He spoke to the King there when Vajiravudh passed through on May 21. See *BT*, May 23, 1917.

122. NA 223/18, King to Prince Charoon, June 17, 1918.

123. NA 223/1, "Phrarachathibai," May 28, 1917.

124. NA 223, report of the Council of Ministers meeting of May 28, 1917. Present at the meeting were Prince Bhanurangsi (Inspector-General of All

His Majesty's Forces), Prince Devawongse (Minister of Foreign Affairs), Prince Kitiyakara (Minister of Finance), Čhaophraya Thamma (Minister of the Royal Household), Čhaophraya Wongsa (Minister of Communications), Čhaophraya Bǫdin (Minister of War), Čhaophraya Aphairacha (Minister of Justice), Čhaophraya Surasi (Minister of the Interior), and Phraya Thammasak (Minister of Religious Affairs and Education). Not in Bangkok for the meeting were Prince Chakrabongs (Chief of General Staff), Prince Paribatra (Minister of Marine), and Prince Nares (Keeper of the Privy Seal). Absent for illness were Prince Rabi (Minister of Agriculture) and Čhaophraya Yommarat (Minister of Local Government). In the further meetings of the council on June 1, 4, 11, and 18 only two members, Princes Rabi and Paribatra, were consistently absent. In the case of Paribatra, German-educated and reputed to be pro-German, the absence may have been a deliberate expression of disapproval of the decisions being taken.

125. NA 223, Chakrabongs to King, May 29, 1917.

126. See NA 223, telegram from King to Prince Chakrabongs, May 31, 1917.

127. NA 223, report of the Council of Ministers meeting of June 1, 1917.

128. Ibid.; NA 223, royal statement at the Council of Ministers meeting concerning the policy of dismissing Germans from the government, June 1, 1917.

129. The King said to his ministers on May 28, "I have my opinions" and "I have not tried to suppress them." In context, these remarks must refer to his pro-war views. See NA 223/1, "Phrarachathibai."

130. NA 223, report of the Council of Ministers meeting of June 18, 1917.

131. It is difficult to prove how well known the pen name Ramachitti was at the time. But, aside from stylistic "give-aways," an alert reader could probably have deduced the royal identity from the word Ramachitti itself, since the name means "the mind of Rama" and "Rama" was closely identified with the royal person in Siam.

132. Reprinted in *Samutthasan* 32 (August 1917): 96–140, and 33 (September 1917): 30–75. Translated into English under the title *"Might Is Right"* (n.p., n.d. [probably 1917]), 97 pp. At the start Ramachitti claimed he had taken up "an uncompromisingly anti-German attitude" since the Great War began, a statement that has some rhetorical power but is not borne out by the record.

133. *"Might Is Right,"* p. 95.

134. Ibid., p. 97.

135. *RKB* 34, July 22, 1917, pp. 333–340; *BT*, July 22, 1917.

136. Amorn, *Phraratchakaraniyakit samkhan ... rụ̄ang hetphon*, pp. 82–96; O-phat, pp. 55–65; Phraya Bamrung Ratchabǫriphan, "Phraratchaphithi pathomkam," *Wachirawutthanusǫn* (1969), pp. 231–235. Belief that the ceremony was more than symbolic is indicated by Phraya Bamrung, who

comments that, although men of science might scoff, in fact the fortunes of the Allied forces on the Western front began to improve after the ceremony was performed.

137. Quoted in *BT*, September 19, 1917. See also Amorn, *Phraratchakaraniyakit samkhan ... ruang hetphon*, pp. 115–118.

138. *BT*, January 4, 1918.

139. NA 223, report of the meeting of the Council of Ministers, August 18, 1917; Dering to Devawongse, August 17, 1917. Several documents in NA 35/49 deal with the discussions and negotiations pertaining to the disposition of the German ships.

140. NA 223, "Alien Enemies and Their Internment," no date, no addressee. Two ships left Bangkok with the prisoners on February 12, 1918.

141. *Clogs on Our Wheels* (Bangkok: Siam Observer, 1915), pp. 73–74.

142. *BT*, July 23, 1917.

143. *New York Times*, July 24, 1917.

144. *BT*, January 3, 1918.

145. NA 223, verbal note to London and Paris, July 26, 1917.

146. NA 223, Prince Charoon to King (in English), July 24, 1917.

147. NA 223/18, Charoon to King, December 7, 1917.

148. NA 223/13, Charoon to Devawongse, September 1, 1917; Chakrabongs to Phraya Buri, September 13, 1917; note of King around September 13, 1917.

149. *BT*, December 20, 21, and 22, 1917; *Phraya yun chingcha p.s. 2460* (Bangkok: Hang Hunsuan Chamkat Siwaphon, 1962).

150. *BT*, January 12, 1918.

151. *RKB* 35, July 22, 1918, pp. 169–182; *BT*, July 23, 1918.

152. NA 223. See also O-phat, pp. 83–84.

153. NA 223, King to Phraya Phichai, May 31, 1918.

154. See *BT*, October 19 and 26, 1917; July 6 and September 23, 1918; September 15, 1919.

155. O-phat, p. 88, contains a speech by Prince Chakrabongs to the troops reminding them that "the honor of the Thai nation rests in your hands."

156. *BT*, August 6, 1918.

157. Ibid., July 23, 1918.

158. Ibid., August 26, 1918.

159. NA 223/18, Charoon to King, August 14, 1918. To ensure that Thai troops would warrant good treatment, special orders were issued to the troops at the front. They were advised to be friendly and helpful to French peasants; the Thai proverb "When staying at someone's house, don't just watch him cut the grass" was cited as a guide to behavior. See O-phat, pp. 168–173.

160. *BT*, December 17, 1918; O-phat, pp. 215–216.

161. Royal Proclamation on the Occasion of the Great Victory of the Allies, November 19, 1918, in *BT*, November 19, 1918.

162. *BT*, December 3, 1918; Amorn, *Phraratchakaraniyakit samkhan... ruang hetphon*, p. 132.

163. *BT*, December 3, 1918.

164. Ibid.

165. O-phat, pp. 148–149; *BT*, November 19, 1918.

166. NA 223, Governor of Lopburi to Čhaophraya Surasi, December 5, 1918.

167. *BT*, December 6, 1918.

168. *BT*, January 22, January 24, January 28, and April 12, 1919.

169. Ibid., May 1 and 5, 1919.

170. Ibid., July 15, 18, 21, 28, 30, and 31, 1919.

171. Ibid., August 28, 1919.

172. Ibid., September 24, 1919; O-phat, pp. 282–283.

173. O-phat, p. 278.

174. *BT*, September 24, 1919.

175. Ibid., June 24, 1920.

176. Ibid., October 8, 1920.

177. Ibid., October 11, 1920.

178. *Samutthasan* 73 (January 1921): 124.

179. *BT*, October 11, 1920.

180. O-phat, pp. 302–305; *BT*, July 21, 1921.

181. *BT*, November 14, 1921.

182. Ibid., December 27, 28, 29, and 30, 1921.

183. NA 54/16, Charoon to King, May 8, 1919.

184. King's instructions to the special ministers plenipotentiary, in Amorn, *Phraratchakaraniyakit samkhan... ruang hetphon*, p. 135.

185. Wilson to Polk, February 27, 1920, quoted in Victor Purcell, "The Relinquishment by the United States of Extraterritoriality in Siam," *Journal of the Royal Asiatic Society, Malayan Branch* 37 (1964): 118.

186. NA 54/16, King to Dering, November 26, 1918.

187. Ibid.

188. NA 54/16, Charoon to King, March 22, 1919.

189. See *BT*, August 16, 19, 28, and 30, September 1 and 3, and December 31, 1918; January 3, 1919.

190. NA 54/16, Charoon to King, May 8, 1919.

191. NA 54/16, memorandum by Phraya Bibadh Kosha, London, March 26,

1919. For Japan's espousal of the role of champion of "Asia for the Asiatics," see *BT*, April 28, 1920. There are some indications that the Siamese may have been considering Japan as a counterweight to Britain; King Vajiravudh, for example, at one time planned to make a state visit to Japan in November 1920 (see *BT*, February 7 and April 28, 1920). In general, however, Siamese foreign policy continued to reflect the view, as expressed by Prince Charoon, that "the English will be masters of the World" and that "We, a small country on her borders are bound to be drawn closer into her orb." Charoon argued that there was no power "sufficiently strong to counteract the centrifugal force" of Britain. France, he wrote, was too weak, and the only other alternatives were the United States, whose interest was doubtful, and Japan. Charoon concluded, interestingly: "Of the two I need hardly say which would be preferable." See NA 54/16, Charoon to King, October 7, 1919.

192. *BT*, January 19, 1920; London *Times*, January 23, 1920.

193. "Mai tọngkan hia," *Dusit samit* 2, no. 16 (1919): 65–67.

194. Sayre, *Passing of Extraterritoriality*.

195. Francis Bowes Sayre, *Glad Adventure* (New York: Macmillan, 1957), p. 122.

196. Birthday speech of 1921 in *BT*, January 4, 1921, and *Phraratchadamrat nai phrabatsomdet*, pp. 247–255.

197. As quoted in *BT*, January 4, 1921.

Chapter 6

1. Although no exact number of given names has been tabulated, the impression that there is a great variety of personal names is borne out by the most casual observation. A random comparison made of the given names of 100 Thai and 100 American officials yielded 44 repeats of American names and 12 repeats of Thai names. The most frequently repeated American given name (John) appeared 9 times; the Thai favorite (Thawi) came up only 3 times.

2. For example, the names for the infinite kinds of lotus in Thailand were a source for many given names.

3. Vietnam, the one state in Southeast Asia in which Chinese culture was dominant, did adopt Chinese cognominal usage. The use of family names, however, was apparently restricted in early times to the elite classes. Even today Vietnamese usage of family names retains a Southeast Asian flavor in that the prime identifying name is the given personal name and not the family name.

4. "Chaya rŭ chŭsae," *Thawipanya*, no. 26 (May 1906), 121–128.

5. *BT*, August 12, 1910.

6. Ibid., October 3, 1911.

7. The decree is reproduced in Thawi, pp. 358–363. In January 1912 the King broached the subject of surnames in private discussions with Prince Damrong and Prince Devawongse; see *Čhotmaihetraiwan*, pp. 47–48.

8. S[awai], pp. 53–54; Thawi, pp. 347–349.

9. S[awai], p. 53.

10. Chamun Amorn Darunrak, *Phraratchakaraniyakit samkhan ... ruang kamnoet nam sakun* (Bangkok: Khurusapha, 1968), vol. 1:7–9.

11. *BT*, January 3, 1914; *Phraratchadamrat nai phrabatsomdet*, pp. 66–67.

12. "Priap nam sakun kap chusae," in *Pramuan bot phraratchaniphon*, p. 53.

13. "Priap nam sakun," pp. 45–53.

14. Mandarin: *hsing*. This word, and other Chinese words the King used, are from the Teochiu, the largest Chinese dialect group in Thailand.

15. "Priap nam sakun," p. 50.

16. Ibid., p. 51.

17. Ibid., p. 48.

18. Ibid., pp. 45, 53.

19. Ibid., p. 53.

20. The "of Bangkok" was replaced by "of Ayutthaya" in a decree of March 24, 1925.

21. S[awai], pp. 58–60.

22. The document is reproduced in Thawi, p. 353.

23. A table of Thai-Sanskrit-Roman equivalents favored by the King is reproduced in Thawi, pp. 354–358.

24. March 31, 1913.

25. In a decree of March 1915 enforcement of the decree was postponed three years. See *RKB* 32, March 30, 1915, pp. 33–34.

26. *BT*, June 2, 1924. NA 128/8, Report of the Ministry of the Interior for 1915, shows that a total of 100,979 individuals in the provinces had been awarded surnames by the end of 1915.

27. S[awai], pp. 61–115, lists the names.

28. *BT*, June 2, 1924.

29. Ibid.

30. Ibid., March 14, 1916.

31. *RKB* 32, March 2, 1916, pp. 490–491.

32. *BT*, October 9, 1925.

33. Unless a change in name was requested; then there was a fee. The fee was twenty baht in 1922 (*BT*, December 19, 1922).

34. *BT*, October 9, 1925.

35. Lauriston Sharp et al., *Siamese Rice Village* (Bangkok: Cornell Research Center, 1953), p. 80.

36. It may be worth noting that the old royal and noble names, although not divisible into first name and second name, had a perceptible first and second element, and the first element could be used alone: for example, (Prince) Damrong instead of the complete Damrongrajanubhab; Čhaophraya Thewet instead of Thewetwongwiwat.

37. For an explanation of the main principles of the system, see H. G. Quaritch Wales, *Ancient Siamese Government and Administration* (New York: Paragon, 1965), pp. 22–43; Akin Rabibhadana, *The Organization of Thai Society in the Early Bangkok Period, 1782–1873* (Data Paper 74, Southeast Asia Program, Cornell, 1969), p. 23 and passim.

38. *BT*, November 16, 1914. An earlier translation scheme for noble ranks, instituted in the Fifth Reign, was soon abandoned. See *BT*, October 5, 1911.

39. NA 6/17, Damrong's letter, May 25, 1911.

40. See Amorn, *Sŭapa lae luksŭa nai prawattisat*, vol. 4:61, 65–67, and *BT*, November 6, 1916. The formal procedure was for a group of high princes and nobles to petition the King to accept the name; see NA 221, letter of Čhaophraya Thamma of November 4, 1916.

41. NA 221, Prince Pravitra to members of the Council of Ministers, February 6, 1919. The signature Sayamin (Siam-Indra, "Indra of Siam," meaning "King of Siam"), used from Chulalongkorn's time, was abandoned.

42. *RKB* 34, July 12, 1917, pp. 326–330; *BT*, July 16, 1917.

43. NA 6/235, Čhaophraya Thamma to King, September 29, 1921; *BT*, October 11 and December 4 and 7, 1921.

44. Speech to Scout Masters' Training School, November 14, 1916, in *CMHSP* 11, no. 7 (November 1916): 745.

45. Chamun Amorn Darunrak, "Het thi phrabatsomdet phra mongkutklao song plian thong chat thai," *Wachirawutthanusǫn* (1953), pp. 81–102.

46. NA 184, report on Post and Telegraph Department flag, October 30, 1917.

47. *Rŭang thetsana sŭapa*, September 13, 1914, p. 122.

48. Speech to Scout Masters' Training School, November 14, 1916, p. 746.

49. Powell, p. 230.

50. *BT*, September 22, 1917.

51. NA 184, report of Devawongse and Paribatra, May 27, 1916.

52. Prince Paribatra held out only to request that the flags of the world be first carefully scrutinized to insure that Siam's new design would not be a duplicate of any of them. See NA 184, meeting of Council of Ministers, August 18, 1917.

53. *RKB* 34, September 30, 1917, pp. 436–440. The King was influenced

by an article in the *Bangkok Daily Mail*, August 15, 1917, that expressed disappointment with the red and white flag and suggested the addition of a blue stripe standing for the King. See Vajiravudh's diary entry for August 18, 1917, in *Čhotmaihetraiwan*, pp. 194–196.

54. According to an old Thai belief, each day of the week had its auspicious color: Sunday, red; Monday, yellow; Tuesday, pink; Wednesday, green; Thursday, brown or orange; Friday, blue; Saturday, purple. Although Vajiravudh was in fact born on Saturday, he chose to regard Friday as his birthday; therefore, "his" color was blue.

55. Thawi, p. 435.

56. *BT*, October 23, 1913.

57. Somphop, *Kutakhan*, pp. 80–84, 117–122; *BT*, April 4, 1918.

58. *BT*, April 8, 1918.

59. *Čhotmaihetraiwan*, p. 200; *BT*, March 26 and April 8, 1919. See poem on the sixth of April in *Dusit samit* 2, no. 17 (1919): 84.

60. NA 250, Charoon to Devawongse, June 30, 1920.

61. NA 250, Dhani to Devawongse, July 7, 1920.

62. NA 250, announcement of the Ministry of the Palace on Chakkri memorial day, March 1921; Čhaophraya Thamma to King, March 22, 1921.

63. *BT*, April 15, 1913, which mentions the "tiger" cheer, probably refers to "Chaiyo!"

64. Amorn, *Sŭapa lae luksŭa nai prawattisat*, vol. 3:48–50.

65. *BT*, December 6, 1911.

66. Ibid., August 23, 1911.

67. NA 216, typescript of an article on the popularity of football in Siam by Nisit Ǫkfǫt (Oxford alumnus) dated July 22, 1915. The attribution of this document to the King is circumstantial: it was written in Nakhǫn Sithammarat during the King's visit there; the style is that of the King; the "Oxford alumnus" points to the King.

68. Ibid.

69. *BT*, January 4, 1913.

70. Ibid., January 15, 1917.

71. Ibid., December 29, 1913.

72. Ibid., October 29, 1913.

73. Ibid., April 7, 1914.

74. NA 216, typescript by Nisit Ǫkfǫt (Oxford alumnus). See note 67 above.

75. *CMHSP* 9, no. 4 (August 1915): 427–429.

76. *BT*, August 31, 1915.

77. Ibid., September 6, 1915.

78. Ibid., September 28, 1915. Similar aims are reflected in an article by one of Vajiravudh's closest courtiers. See Phraya Anirut, "Khwam čharoen haeng futbǫn," *Dusit samit*, special issue (1919), pp. 43–44.

79. *BT*, November 24, 1915.

80. *CMHSP* 9, no. 5 (September 1915): 471–475; *BT*, September 13 through October 30, 1915.

81. *BT*, September 17, 1915.

82. Ibid., September 13, 1918.

83. Ibid., October 18, 1917.

84. NA 216, F. W. Margrett to Prince Pravitra, September 5, 1919.

85. NA 216, memorandum of the Football Association of Siam, undated.

86. NA 216, Prince Dhani to Margrett, September 20, 1919.

87. *BT*, October and November 1916.

88. *BT*, November 24, 1915, King's speech on opening of Royal Bangkok Sports Club's new building.

89. *BT*, December 20, 1915.

90. Ibid.

91. *BT*, December 27, 1915.

92. Ibid., December 24, 1915.

93. Ibid., December 31, 1915.

94. Ibid., August 18, 1919.

95. NA 216, draft of letter by Luang Sakdi, Secretary, Royal Pages Football Club, to the press; this draft is almost certainly in the King's handwriting. NA 216, Phraya Buri to editors of the *Bangkok Times, Siam Observer*, and the *Bangkok Daily Mail*, September 12, 1916. See also *BT*, September 12, 1916.

96. *BT*, August 19, 1919. The editor wrote: " . . . certain teams are specially favoured in obtaining players, and . . . against these teams certain other teams are not allowed to play their best." These statements have been corroborated in personal interviews.

97. *BT*, September 1, 1919.

98. Graham, vol. 1:243.

99. *New York Times*, February 17, 1924.

100. *Mahatama*, p. 12.

101. Ibid., p. 27.

102. Ibid., p. 18.

103. King's speech to princesses, January 3, 1914, in *Phraratchadamrat nai phrabatsomdet*, p. 76.

104. *Bot lakhǫnphut rūang huačhai nakrop*, p. 72.

105. Ibid., p. 92.

106. *BT*, December 18, 1911.

107. Graham, vol. 1:245.

108. "Khrüangmai haeng khwamrungrüang khü saphap haeng sattri," in *Phraratchaniphon thi naru*, p. 153.

109. Graham, vol. 1:245.

110. "Khrüangmai haeng khwamrungrüang khü saphap haeng sattri," pp. 146–166.

111. Ibid., p. 166.

112. Ibid., p. 163.

113. *BT*, March 15, 1921.

114. Ibid., February 6 and 10, 1920.

115. *Nangsüphim thai*, as quoted in *BT*, January 27, 1921.

116. *BT*, August 5, 1920.

117. Ibid., November 1, 1920.

118. Ibid., November 10, 1920.

119. Ibid., January 6, 1921.

120. *Sena süksa* (March 1921), as quoted in *BT*, March 23, 1921.

121. *Nangsüphim thai*, as quoted in *BT*, February 12, 1920.

122. See, for example, the exchange between King Mongkut and Dr. Bradley in which, according to Bradley, the King "confessed to me that polygamy was a sin but excused himself in it because of the power of custom," in the Journal of Rev. Dan B. Bradley (microfilm of original in Oberlin College Library), entry of January 4, 1855.

123. *Clogs on Our Wheels*, pp. 83–124.

124. "Khrüangmai haeng khwamrungrüang khü saphap haeng sattri," p. 165.

125. *Huačhai chainum* (Bangkok: Kaona, 1961), p. 59.

126. *Čhotmaihetraiwan*, pp. 46–47.

127. The King's views, presented here, are from NA 204, notes on the marriage laws, June 3, 1913, and additional notes, June 5, 1913.

128. NA 204, report of the Council of Ministers meeting, June 4, 1917.

129. Chula Chakrabongse, *Lords of Life*, p. 297.

130. *BT*, March 15, 1921.

131. Graham, vol. 1:231.

132. *BT*, December 15, 1913.

133. Ibid., January 8, 1920.

134. Ibid., January 3, 1918.

135. "Suphasit samrap sattri," *Wachirawutthanusǫn* (1966), pp. 133–136.

136. *BT*, January 8, 1920.

137. Ibid., September 26 and 27, 1921.

138. M. L. Manich Jumsai, *Compulsory Education in Thailand*, UNESCO Studies on Compulsory Education (Paris: UNESCO, 1951), p. 42.

139. "Khrŭangmai haeng khwamrungrŭang khŭ saphap haeng sattri," pp. 160-162.

140. Ibid., p. 162.

141. Chula Chakrabongse, *Lords of Life*, p. 278.

142. *BT*, February 23, 1921.

143. *Nangsŭphim thai*, as quoted in *BT*, November 27, 1920.

144. *BT*, December 11, 1920.

145. December 23, 1920.

146. *Sena sŭksa lae phae witthayasat*, as quoted in *BT*, February 23, 1921.

147. NA 84/16, King to Phraya Wisut, July 7, 1911.

148. *BT*, August 4, 1911.

149. Ibid., December 21, 1915.

150. Ibid., June 22, 1916.

151. Ibid., December 17, 1916; December 18, 1917.

152. The Chiangmai school was closed for lack of funds late in 1925 (NA 84, Čhaophraya Ram to King, September 9, 1925), and King's College was combined with the Royal Pages College in 1927 at the time the Pages College received the name Vajiravudh College. See decree of King Prajadhipok, April 16, 1927, in *Wachirawutthanusǫn* (1960), p. 35.

153. King to Čhaophraya Phrasadet, undated, in English in Chamun Amorn Darunrak, "Rongrian mahatlek luang," in *Wachirawutthanusǫn* (1969), pp. 257-258.

154. *Phraratchadamrat nai phrabatsomdet*, pp. 32-37 (1912), 54-60 (1913), 96-102 (1914), 143-147 (1915), 181-185 (1916).

155. Speeches of May 18, 1914, May 30, 1915, and May 18, 1916, in *Wachirawutthanusǫn* (1960), pp. 45-90.

156. King's speech to schools under His Majesty's patronage, December 27, 1913, in *Phraratchadamrat nai phrabatsomdet*, pp. 61-63.

157. Cited as a belief of the English middle class by E. M. Forster in "Notes on the English Character," *Abinger Harvest* (New York: Meridian, 1955), p. 4.

158. Speech to Royal Pages College, November 12, 1913, in *Phraratchadamrat nai phrabatsomdet*, pp. 58-59. M. L. Pin Malakul, "Wachirawut witthayalai," *Wachirawutthanusǫn* (1960), p. 129.

159. NA 84/5, announcement of the establishment of King Chulalongkorn's Civil Service College, January 1, 1911. Also *BT*, January 13, 1911.

160. See Wyatt, p. 363, fn. 117, for biographical details.

161. See NA 127/24, Čhaophraya Thammasak to King, November 21, 1917,

and May 23, 1919; NA 96/4, report of the meeting of viceroys and governors at the Ministry of Education, December 24, 1919.

162. NA 127/8, Report of the Ministry of Education for 1922.

163. *BT*, September 26, 1921; Manich, pp. 39–41.

164. For example, a report from Lampang in 1919 noted that there were then enough schools and teachers in the province to make compulsory education enforceable (*BT*, July 17, 1919).

165. *BT*, January 8, 1914.

166. Ibid., May 15, 1913; NA 127/8, Report of the Ministry of Religious Affairs and Education, 1913.

167. NA 96/4, report of the meeting of the viceroys and governors at the Ministry of Education, December 24, 1919.

168. "Clerkism," in *Clogs on Our Wheels*, pp. 38–48

169. Ibid., pp. 42–43.

170. Amorn, *Sùapa lae luksùa nai prawattisat*, vol. 2:14. The words were by Luang Phithakthepnakhọn and the music by Prince Paribatra.

171. NA 127, Minister of Religious Affairs and Education to the King, July 1, 1911, and typed, undated document of instructions.

172. NA 119/8, Phraya Wongsa, "Memorandum on Our Domestic Economy" (in English), December 7, 1910.

173. For the first study in depth, see Pornpen Hantrakool, "Kanchai čhaingoen phaendin nai ratchasamai phrabatsomdet phra mongkutklao čhaoyuhua," M. A. thesis, Chulalongkorn University, 1974.

174. Thai royalty traditionally had a record of "generosity." A fair comparison, for example, would have to balance the expenses of King Chulalongkorn on his trips to Europe, the palaces and temples he built, and his large harem with the personal expenses of his son. Queen Saowapha was noted for her lavish gifts (see Smith, p. 109, and Chula Chakrabongse, *Lords of Life*, p. 283). Figures available seem to show no marked change in the approximately 10 percent earmarked for the privy purse during the Fifth and Sixth Reigns. For a defense of the King from the charge of fiscal extravagance, see Amorn, *Dusit thani*, pp. 326–333.

175. *BT*, March 5 and April 16, 1912.

176. Ibid., June 28, 1912.

177. Ibid., February 7, 1918.

178. For important articles on these subjects see *BT*, August 11, 1911; February 15 and 24, 1912; March 12, 1914; February 8, May 17, November 18, and November 26, 1918; February 9, March 6, May 12, and July 8, 1920; September 7 and November 5, 1921.

179. *BT*, February 15, 1912.

180. *A Siam Miscellany*, p. 14.

181. "Sapsat," *Samutthasan* 9 (September 1915): 113–133.

Notes to pp. 170–176

182. *Clogs on Our Wheels*, pp. 74–80. See also speech to Wild Tigers, December 5, 1914, in *Phraboromrachowat sǔapa*, p. 31.

183. Letter to the editor, *Nangsǔphim thai*, July 17, 1915, in S[awai], p. 537, and *Phraratchaniphon thi naru*, p. 119.

184. "Sapsat," pp. 131–132.

185. Thawi, pp. 345–346; Praphat Trinarong, *Chiwit lae ngan khong atsawaphahu* (Bangkok: Watthanaphanit, 1963), pp. 425–444; *BT*, April 2, 1913.

186. *BT*, December 29, 1921.

187. Ibid., June 12 and October 31, 1922.

188. James C. Ingram, *Economic Change in Thailand since 1850* (Stanford: Stanford, 1955), p. 135.

189. Ibid., p. 139.

190. Paribatra to King, July 27, 1917, and Chakrabongs to Paribatra, August 1, 1917, in *Phraprawat lae čhariyawat khong čhomphonrǔa somdet čhaofa boriphat sukhumphan* (Bangkok: Krom Uthakasat, 1950), pp. 53–60.

191. NA 35/49, list of chartered vessels.

192. Among the more poignant of the documents on the loss of the *Yiam Samut* is Prince Paribatra's letter to the King, February 10, 1918, in NA 35/32.

193. *BT*, December 31, 1920.

194. Ibid., January 6, 1922.

195. King's birthday speech of 1923 in ibid., January 3, 1923, and *Phraratchadamrat nai phrabatsomdet*, p. 285.

196. "Mǔang thai čhong tǔn thoet," pp. 1–32.

197. *A Siam Miscellany*, pp. 59–60.

198. Ibid., p. 60.

199. Letter to the editor, *Nangsǔphim thai*, July 17, 1915, in *Phraratchaniphon thi naru*, p. 120.

200. "Mǔang thai čhong tǔn thoet," p. 31. See also King's speech of January 3, 1915, in *Phraratchadamrat nai phrabatsomdet*, pp. 124–125. The King developed his views on Thai economic independence very early. See the essay "Kho tham," almost certainly by the King under the pen name Thai Hua Het, in *Thawipanya*, no. 10 (January 1905), pp. 277–289.

201. *Mahatama*, p. 35.

202. *BT*, March 9, 1922.

203. Chamun Amorn Darunrak, "Kan ngoen khong lon klao r. 6," *Warasan luksǔa*, special issue (July 1, 1970), pp. 94–96; Thawi, pp. 708–715.

Chapter 7

1. "Sapsat," *Samutthasan* 9 (September 1915): 122.

2. *Čhotmaihetraiwan*, p. 39.

Notes to pp. 177–181

3. "Sapsat," p. 115.

4. Graham, vol. 1:240.

5. In his personal taste the King ranged widely—from a Western fondness for a cocktail before dinner to a Thai royal predilection for constant massage.

6. A search for the earliest uses of the word *chat* to mean "nation" has uncovered only one possible reference in a poem of 1893; see Sangop Suriyin, *Thianwan* (Bangkok: Suriyin, 1967), p. 7/2. King Chulalongkorn seems never to have used the term *chat thai*.

7. Speech to the Wild Tigers, June 27, 1911, in *Plukčhai sǔapa*, p. 46.

8. Speech to the Wild Tigers, November 13, 1915, in *Phraboromrachowat sǔapa*, p. 73.

9. Speech to the Wild Tigers, July 4, 1911, in *Plukčhai sǔapa*, pp. 58–71.

10. Speech to the Wild Tigers, November 13, 1915, in *Phraboromrachowat sǔapa*, pp. 72–75.

11. "Sadaeng khunnanukhun," pp. 25–27.

12. "Mǔang thai čhong tǔn thoet," p. 23.

13. Speech of June 30, 1925, in *Phraratchadamrat lae phraboromrachowat*, p. 56.

14. *Clogs on Our Wheels*, p. 14.

15. Speech of November 13, 1915, in *Phraboromrachowat sǔapa*, p. 74.

16. *Clogs on Our Wheels*, pp. 14–18.

17. Ibid., p. 6.

18. Ibid., pp. 18–19.

19. "Khǫ tham," pp. 277–282.

20. *Clogs on Our Wheels*, p. 8.

21. Ibid., p. 10; speech to the Wild Tigers, June 13, 1911, in *Plukčhai sǔapa*, p. 30.

22. *Clogs on Our Wheels*, p. 10.

23. Ibid., p. 11.

24. "The Cult of Imitation," pp. 151–152.

25. Speech to the Wild Tigers, November 13, 1915, in *Phraboromrachowat sǔapa*, p. 78. See also "Prayot haeng kan yu nai tham," *CMHSP* 8, no. 11 (March 1915): 33.

26. Speech to court officials, April 1, 1915, in *Phraratchadamrat nai phrabatsomdet*, pp. 137–138; lecture on Wisakhabucha Day, May 30, 1915, in *Phraboromrachowat nai ngan wisakhabucha* (Bangkok: Mahamakut, 1957), pp. 23–24.

27. *Lak ratchakan*, p. 21.

28. "The Cult of Imitation," p. 161.

29. Ibid., pp. 154–161.

30. Ibid., pp. 160–161.

Notes to pp. 181–187

31. See chapter 4.

32. *Uttarakuru* (Bangkok: Mahamakut, 1965), pp. 2–3.

33. For other references to Uttarakuru, see E. Sarkisyanz, *Buddhist Backgrounds of the Burmese Revolution* (The Hague: Nijhoff, 1965), pp. 58, 83–89.

34. *Uttarakuru*, pp. 7–8.

35. Ibid., p. 20. A long discussion of socialism also appears in the King's diary for April 1912 (*Čhotmaihetraiwan*, pp. 68–98).

36. H. Hackmann, *A German Scholar in the East* (London: Kegan Paul, 1914), p. 185.

37. *Clogs on Our Wheels*, p. 9.

38. *BT*, February 8, 1913.

39. *Glad Adventure*, p. 87.

40. NA 223, Peregrine, *Siam and the Germans* (London: Alabaster, Passmore & Sons, November 12, 1917), 31 pp.; the quotation is from p. 26.

41. NA 20, advice to students in Europe, August 18, 1916.

42. *Clogs on Our Wheels*, p. 22.

43. *BT*, May 13, 1916.

44. Ibid., May 16, 1916.

45. Ibid., May 17, 1916.

46. Ibid., May 25, 1916; NA 117, Dering to Devawongse, May 15, 1916, and Devawongse to Dering, May 18, 1916.

47. NA 20, advice to students in Europe, August 18, 1916.

48. NA 117, Peel to Devawongse, March 20, 1911, and memorandum, HBM Legation, Bangkok, April 6, 1911.

49. NA 204, report of a special meeting of the Council of Ministers, May 31, 1915.

50. NA 204/15, abstract of Department of Foreign Affairs No. 238/59, undated, but presumably before December 1916.

51. *BT*, October 12, 15, and 20, 1920.

52. NA 223, Dering to Devawongse, July 28, 1917.

53. NA 223, Devawongse to Dering, July 29, 1917.

54. NA 223, Chakrabongs to Phraya Buri, July 29, 1917.

55. NA 223, King to Chakrabongs, no date.

56. NA 223, "Alien Enemies and Their Internment," no date, no addressee.

57. NA 20, advice to students in Europe, August 18, 1916. See also *Clogs on Our Wheels*, p. 23.

58. NA 20, advice to students in Europe, August 18, 1916.

59. *BT*, November 13, 1915; *Phraratchadamrat nai phrabatsomdet*, pp. 140–142.

60. As a prince, Vajiravudh once commented on a controversy between

the Russians and the British: "It is fortunate that this affair is between two white peoples, or else...." ("Bettalet," in *Thawipanya*, no. 12 [March 1905], p. 509).

61. Footnote in his translation of "The Chinese Republic" in *Phraratchaniphon thi naru*, pp. 435–436.

62. *The Jews of the Orient* (Bangkok: Siam Observer, 1914), pp. 31–32.

63. Vajiravudh himself had Chinese ancestors; indeed, he may have been over one-half Chinese in ancestry. See G. W. Skinner, *Chinese Society in Thailand* (Ithaca: Cornell, 1957), p. 26.

64. For further details, see Skinner, *Chinese Society in Thailand*, pp. 155–159.

65. A letter from Prince Chakrabongs of June 9 (NA 133), for example, cited one Chinese plan "to attack the electric company so that power lines could be cut to deprive Bangkok of electricity."

66. NA 133, dated June 1911.

67. There were no massive deportations, however. In 1917–1918, for example, 219 Chinese were deported. See *BT*, September 3, 1920.

68. A fund-raising campaign to aid Chinese earthquake victims, for example, was allowed (see NA 133, Čhaophraya Yommarat to Prince Pravitra, October 14, 1918) whereas a drive to support Sun Yat-sen's Kwangtung government was banned (see NA 133, Čhaophraya Yommarat to Prince Pravitra, November 16, 1917). The flow of funds to China, undoubtedly consisting mostly of individual gifts to relatives, was large. The total was estimated at 16.5 million baht in 1910 (NA 133/1, Phraya Intharathibodi to Čhaophraya Yommarat, December 14, 1910) and 30 million baht in 1916 (NA 163, Čhaophraya Yommarat, report of March 1, 1916).

69. NA 133, Prince Bhanurangsi to King, July 2, 1915.

70. Satčhaphirom, *Lao hai luk fang*, pp. 154–155. When secret society activity became troublesome, the policy was to arrest only the leaders. See, for example, the report on secret societies in Chumphon Province (NA 163/4, Čhaophraya Aphairacha to Phraya Čhakrapani, March 3, 1920).

71. *The Jews of the Orient*, p. 60.

72. NA 146, Phraratchabanyat samakhom, p.s. 2457. Also in *RKB* 31, May 29, 1914, pp. 182–194.

73. *BT*, June 15, 23, and 25, 1914.

74. NA 133, report of the meeting of the Council of Ministers, June 24, 1912.

75. *BT*, November 21, 1914; September 9, 1915.

76. Ibid., June 10 and 11, 1918.

77. Ibid., June 11, 1918.

78. Graham, vol. 1:256–257. One Chinese girls' school seems to have

adopted the expedient of appointing a Thai headmistress (*BT*, December 11, 1918).

79. *RKB* 28, May 18, 1911, pp. 96–100; Richard J. Coughlin, *Double Identity: The Chinese in Modern Thailand* (Hong Kong: Hong Kong University Press, 1960), pp. 173–174.

80. See the provocative, if tentative, examination of the receptivity of the Thai as compared with the Javanese in G. W. Skinner, "Change and Persistence in Chinese Culture Overseas: A Comparison of Thailand and Java," *Journal of the South Seas Society* 16 (1960): 86–100.

81. NA 163, March 1, 1916.

82. *The Jews of the Orient*, p. 62.

83. *BT*, December 21, 1910.

84. King Chulalongkorn's reply to the Chinese merchants, November 17, 1907, in *Phraratchadamrat* (Bangkok: Thai National Bank, 1967), p. 211.

85. Họphrasamut, Čhotmaihet phraratchaphithi bọromrachaphisek, pp. 189–190.

86. NA 163, letter of July 24, 1910.

87. *BT*, January 9, 1919.

88. Ibid., December 12 and 24, 1917.

89. See, for example, *Nangsụphim thai*, November 14, 1914; *BT*, December 30, 1919; *BT*, February 4, 1920.

90. "Khọpčhai phụan čhin," *Samutthasan* 1 (January 1915): 93–95.

91. *Mahatama*, pp. 47, 74.

92. Originally published in four parts in the *Siam Observer* in July 1914.

93. H. Warington Smyth, *Five Years in Siam* (London: Murray, 1898), vol. 1:285. See Skinner, *Chinese Society in Thailand*, pp. 160–161, for other references to anti-Chinese remarks by Westerners.

94. "Mụang thai čhong tụn thoet," p. 5.

95. "Khwam pen chat doi thae čhing," p. 139.

96. "Mụang thai čhong tụn thoet," p. 14.

97. *The Jews of the Orient*, pp. 52–53.

98. "Mụang thai čhong tụn thoet," p. 10.

99. Ibid., p. 16.

100. "Khwam pen chat doi thae čhing," pp. 139–140.

101. "Mụang thai čhong tụn thoet," p. 13.

102. P. 91.

103. Pp. 100–101.

104. *Nangsụphim thai*, May 24, 1917. See also *BT*, May 22, 1917.

105. *BT*, December 2, 1912.

106. Ibid., January 4, 1916, and *Phraratchadamrat nai phrabatsomdet*, pp. 175–176.

107. *BT*, January 2, 1917. See also King's speech to the Muslims, December 31, 1916, in *Phraratchadamrat nai phrabatsomdet*, p. 187.

108. *BT*, May 22, 1917.

109. *CMHSP* 10, no. 12 (April 1916): 1181–1182.

110. *BT*, December 9, 1919.

111. Ibid., August 2, 1920.

112. Ibid., August 25, 1921. The minister was T. Masao, who had served as legal adviser to the Siamese government earlier in his career and was probably accorded special attention partly for this reason.

113. NA 204/15, February 15, 1917.

114. *BT*, July 9, 1913.

115. NA 232, Chakrabongs to King, October 15, 1915.

116. NA 232, Chakrabongs to King, January 3, 1916. For editorial comment on Thai attitudes toward the Lao, see *BT*, November 18, 1913.

117. *BT*, June 25, 1912. The quotations are from an editorial that discussed the suggestion, which had been received at the press shortly before.

118. Ibid.

Chapter 8

1. *BT*, January 8, 1913.

2. For a stimulating exploration of the problems of modern Chinese nationalists, see Joseph Levenson, *Modern China and Its Confucian Past* (Garden City: Anchor Books, 1964).

3. Sukarno's defense of 1930 as quoted by Bambang Oetomo in "Some Remarks on Modern Indonesian Historiography" in *Historians of South East Asia*, ed. D. G. E. Hall (London: Oxford, 1961), p. 75.

4. G. Coedès cites only four Thai as really interested in epigraphy after King Mongkut: King Chulalongkorn, King Vajiravudh, Prince Damrong, and the Prince Monk Pawaret. See *Recueil des inscriptions du Siam. Première partie: Inscriptions de Sukhodaya* (Bangkok: Bangkok Times, 1924), p. 4.

5. *Thiao mǔang phra ruang*, preface.

6. Ibid.

7. Ibid.

8. Ibid., p. 51.

9. Coedès, *Recueil*, pp. 4–6.

10. NA 37, decree of January 17, 1924. In 1922 the French minister had deplored Siam's failure to establish an archaeological department, which, he said, betokened a "lack of progress, moral as well as material, in this

fine country" (NA 37, Pila to Devawongse, June 17, 1922). The French minister's comments seem to have stimulated Vajiravudh to take action.

11. *BT*, January 22, February 11, and February 21, 1924.

12. *Thiao muang phra ruang*, p. 42.

13. Ibid., p. 140.

14. The rivalry between Prince Damrong and King Vajiravudh cannot be detailed here. The basic problem was that of a young inexperienced king, seeking to develop his power base, facing an older experienced uncle who was widely respected for his experience and for his close association with King Chulalongkorn.

15. An exception is the essay "The War of the Polish Succession" presented by Prince Vajiravudh as a student at Oxford in 1901.

16. *Plukchai suapa*, June 23, 1911, pp. 42-43.

17. Ibid., July 4, 1911, pp. 60-61.

18. *A Siam Miscellany*, pp. 54-55.

19. "Ruang sadet phraratchadamnoen pai namatsakan phrachedi somdet phra naresuan maharat mi chai chana yutthahatthi," *CMHSP* 6, no. 10 (February 1916): 333-358. See report on the march in *BT*, February 7, 1914.

20. *Plukchai suapa*, May 26, 1911, p. 4.

21. *BT*, February 14, 1914. *CMHSP* 6, no. 10 (February 1916), 347-352. For details on the January 28 ceremonies, the march to Don Chedi, and Vajiravudh's historical theories, see the King's diary entries for January 1914 (*Chotmaihetraiwan*, pp. 113-146).

22. *Plukchai suapa*, May 26, 1911, pp. 4-5.

23. *BT*, November 4 and 6, 1916.

24. Prefatory essay to *Phra ruang*, p. (9).

25. The dance drama, entitled *Khom damdin* (The Cambodian Earth Diver), has been republished in *Thi raluk nai ngan phraratchathan phloengsop phon ek phonrua ek mahasewok ek chaophraya ramrakhop* (Bangkok: Thannakhan Krungthep, 1967), pp. 1-52. The first edition of the modern drama, entitled *Phra ruang*, bears no date or publisher. The musical, entitled *Phra ruang, bot lakhon rong*, was first published in 1961 with an introduction by Prince Dhani. An earlier musical version of the story, first performed in 1894, was written by Prince Naris.

26. The seventeenth edition for school use was published in 1958.

27. The King notes his debt to the method of Prince Damrong, whom he calls "the person responsible for helping me in historical research," in "Ruang khom damdin," the introduction to *Khom damdin*.

28. Prefatory essay to *Phra ruang*, p. (6). The King's rationalizations of the Phra Ruang legend, which are summarized in the rest of this paragraph, are detailed in the prefatory essay, pp. (6)-(9).

29. *Phra ruang*, pp. 106–108. Quotation is on p. 108.

30. *Khom damdin*, p. 49.

31. One of the three places in which Vajiravudh directed that his ashes be deposited after his death was the base of a large standing Buddha attributed by experts to the reign of Phra Ruang. This image was found in Sukhothai, "invited" to move down to Bangkok (Buddha images are not transported; they are invited to change residence), restored by the King, and set up in front of the great stupa at Nakhon Pathom. See *BT*, June 18, 1914.

32. *Phra ruang*, pp. 116–117.

33. "Ruang khom damdin," pp. b, c.

34. *Samutthasan* 8 (August 1915): 1–29.

35. Ibid., 25 (January 1917). Another poem that has essentially the same message appeared in *Samutthasan* 2 (February 1915): 29–31.

36. The preface to the play contains, however, excellent examples of Vajiravudh's demythologizing technique.

37. Anonymous, "Kan raek na," *Dusit samit* 2, no. 23 (1919): 177–178. See also Graham, Vol. 2: 272.

38. *BT*, November 22, 1915.

39. "Tam namphrik lalai maenam," in *Phraratchaniphon bang ruang*, pp. 34–37.

40. *BT*, November 23, 1921.

41. See chapter 6.

42. *Plukchai suapa*, June 27, 1911, pp. 52–53; *Ruang thetsana suapa*, August 2, 1913, p. 78.

43. Maitri Buranasiri, "Kan pluk fang yaowachon khong chat nai ratchakan thi 6," in *Riangkhwam ruang phraratchaniphon nai ratchakan thi 6* (Bangkok: Khurusapha, 1961), pp. 282–283.

44. *BT*, October 14 and 15, 1912. In addition to the reign image, one image was cast for each year of the reign; see *BT*, April 8, 1913.

45. NA 106/1. The King's comment (*phraratcha krasae*) is dated October 18.

46. NA 74/7, report of meetings of the Council of Ministers, March 25 and April 22, 1912.

47. NA 106/1, King to Prince Dhani, August 30, 1921.

48. *BT*, December 10, 1910.

49. NA 128/8, proclamation of January 2, 1913.

50. *Ruang thetsana suapa*.

51. *Wachirawutthanuson* (1960) contains the lectures for 1914, 1915, and 1916.

52. *Phraphutthachao trat ru arai* (Bangkok: Khurusapha, 1964). This

edition contains a version in English by M. C. Upalisan Jumbala. Quotations are from the English version.

53. Ibid., p. 13.
54. *Mahatama*, p. 115.
55. *Phraphutthachao trat ru arai*, p. 34.
56. *Rŭang thetsana sŭapa*, March 24, 1915, p. 134.
57. Ibid., pp. 130–133.
58. *Phraphutthachao trat ru arai*, p. 32.
59. *Rŭang thetsana sŭapa*, March 24, 1915, p. 138.
60. Ibid., p. 146.
61. *Uttarakuru*, p. 6.
62. *Plukchai sŭapa*, June 27, 1911, pp. 55–56.
63. *Rŭang thetsana sŭapa*, March 24, 1915, pp. 144–146.
64. Ibid., April 25, 1914, p. 5.
65. Ibid., May 2, 1914, pp. 15–16.
66. Ibid., May 16, 1914, pp. 29–32.
67. Ibid., June 6, 1914, pp. 40–41.
68. Ibid., June 12, 1914, pp. 47–51.
69. Ibid., pp. 52–55.
70. Ibid., July 26, 1914, pp. 58–66.
71. Ibid., August 2, 1914, pp. 73–74.
72. Ibid., pp. 73–78.
73. Ibid., pp. 79–82.
74. Ibid., August 16, 1914, pp. 93–95.
75. Ibid., March 24, 1915, pp. 141–142; May 8, 1914, pp. 168–169; August 14, 1915, pp. 206–207.
76. Speech of August 9, 1914, in *BT*, August 15, 1914, and in *Rŭang thetsana sŭapa*, pp. 220–226.
77. *Rŭang thetsana sŭapa*, August 9, 1914, pp. 220–226; see also May 22, 1915, p. 194.
78. Ibid., March 24, 1915, p. 142.
79. Ibid., p. 143.
80. *Phraboromrachowat sŭapa*, November 21, 1914, pp. 27–28.
81. Ibid., August 9, 1914, p. 20.
82. Ibid., February 3, 1918, p. 111; see also January 4, 1916, pp. 81–82.
83. *BT*, January 5, 1916.
84. See Jane Bunnag, "Monk-Layman Interaction in Central Thai Society," in *In Memoriam: Phya Anuman Rajadhon* (Bangkok: Siam Society, 1970), pp. 87–106.

85. Niramol Kangsadara, "The Buddhist Order under Prince Wachirayan (1898–1921)" (M. A. thesis, University of Hawaii, 1972); Wyatt, pp. 233–255.

86. See translation of stanza in chapter 3.

87. *Prachum phraboromrachowat lae phra-owat* (Bangkok: Sutthisan, 1966), pp. 61–66.

88. *The Buddhist Attitude towards National Defence and Administration* [Bangkok, 1916], p. 19.

89. Ibid., pp. 20–21.

90. *Right Is Right* (Bangkok, [1918]), p. 24. In a memorial service for two Thai students who lost their lives on a vessel torpedoed by a German submarine, the Supreme Patriarch spoke pointedly about German evil deeds and about the sad loss to Siam of foreign-educated youths who might have helped Siam in its program of catching up with the West (*BT*, November 8, 1918).

91. *Right Is Right*, p. 29.

92. *The Triumph of Right* (Bangkok: Bangkok Daily Mail, [1919]), p. 11.

93. Ibid., p. 18.

94. Ibid., pp. 18–21.

95. *Thammathamma songkhram* (Bangkok: Sam Mit, 1971). The parallels in the literary allusions and figures of speech used by the King and the Prince are remarkable. It is hard to say who influenced whom, although in this case the Prince preceded, at least in print.

96. O-phat, pp. 280–281.

97. *BT*, June 7, July 3, July 13, July 28, August 5, and August 18, 1920. Vajiranana, *Pramuan phraniphon* ... : *Phrasommana winitchai* (Bangkok: Mahamakut Ratchawitthayalai, 1971), pp. 305–307.

98. *BT*, March 11 and 14, 1911.

99. Ibid., December 8, 1911.

100. Ibid., November 26, 1915.

101. William, p. 123.

102. Letter of Vajiravudh to King Chulalongkorn, October 26, 1909, in Amorn, *Kamnoet phraratchawang sanamčhan lae phra pathom čhedi*, pp. 22–25.

103. William, p. 122.

104. See chapter 2.

105. The royal announcement is in NA 37/3 and is published in *Khwamru kiao kap phraratchakaraniyakit nai ratchakan thi 6* (Bangkok: Phračhan, 1960), pp. 37–38. See also the pamphlet *Thao hiranphanasun* (Bangkok: Udom, 1969).

106. *BT*, October 8, 1910.

107. Smith, p. 92.

108. NA 30/27, "Siamese Art" by "Asvabahu," undated typescript in English presumably written for the *Siam Observer*. Internal evidence suggests January 1914 as the probable date.

109. Ibid.

110. See, for example, the speech to the Royal Pages College, November 12, 1913, in *Phraratchadamrat nai phrabatsomdet*, pp. 61-62.

111. *Samakkhi sewok (Witsawa kamma)*, as quoted in S[awai], pp. 673-674, 680-682. See also Saksi Yaemnatda, "Riangkhwam rüang phraratchaniphon praphet rọi krọng," in *Riangkhwam rüang phraratchaniphon nai ratchakan thi 6*, pp. 190-192.

112. *BT*, March 29, 1912.

113. Ibid., January 8, 1914.

114. Ibid., January 9, 1914.

115. Ibid., September 1, 1917.

116. S[awai], pp. 181-185. The fair was not supported by King Prajadhipok, probably in the interest of economy. It was resumed in 1948.

117. *BT*, January 6, 1920.

118. For example, the Dusit Park Fair, initiated by King Chulalongkorn as a means of raising funds for the upkeep of Wat Benčhamabọphit.

119. *BT*, July 5, 1911; December 17, 1913; June 28, 1915. See also G. E. Gerini, *Siam and Its Productions, Arts, and Manufactures: A Descriptive Catalogue of the Siamese Section at the International Exhibition of Industry and Labour Held in Turin April 29-November 19, 1911* (London: Stephen Austin, 1912).

120. The Leipzig show was previewed in Siam, and at the preview His Majesty's photographs won two gold medals, one silver medal, and a bronze (*BT*, January 12, 1914). The policy of participating in international expositions was started by King Mongkut with a Siamese contribution to the Universal Exhibition in Paris in 1867. Exhibits followed in 1868 (Havre), 1878 (Paris), 1885 (Antwerp), 1889 (Paris), 1893 (Chicago), and 1904 (St. Louis). See Gerini, pp. xliv-xlvi.

121. Gerini, p. 282.

122. NA 30/27, "Siamese Art."

123. *BT*, February 1, 1913, based on an article in the *Dresden Nachrichten*. Doehring organized an exhibit of Thai arts in Berlin in 1912 and inspired another at Dresden.

124. *Buddhistische Tempelanlagen in Siam* (Bangkok: Asia Publishing House, 1920), 3 volumes; *Kunst and Kunstgewerbe in Siam* (Berlin: Bard, 1925), 3 volumes. The latter, which illustrates Thai designs originally executed in lacquer and gold leaf, was issued in a regular and a special edition; the special edition, in which the illustrations were executed in gold on

black paper, is one of the most beautiful books ever published anywhere. There is a copy of this edition at Harvard University.

125. The King mentions, in the preface to *Thammathamma songkhram*, that he commissioned Prince Naris to do the illustrations for the work.

126. Amorn, "Kamnoet suan lumphini," as quoted in S[awai], pp. 169–171.

127. On architecture during the reign, see *BT*, March 17, 1911, and Amorn, "Mahasinlapin ek khọng thai," in *Phraratchakaraniyakit samkhan ... rửang phraratchaniphon*, pp. 171–207.

128. NA 30/27, "Siamese Art."

129. S[awai], pp. 175–179; Amorn, "Mahasinlapin," pp. 191–194; Dhanit Yupho, *Khon* (Bangkok: Department of Fine Arts, 1957), pp. 49–50, 60.

130. Powell, p. 236.

131. Prince Damrong Rajanubhab, *Tamnan lakhọn inao* (Bangkok: Khlang Witthaya, 1964), p. 206.

132. Prince Sommot is credited with inspiring the work, and Prince Kawiphot Supricha, Phraya Photchanasunthọn, and Phra Pọriyatthamthada are named as critical readers.

133. *Phra non kham luang* (Bangkok: Sinlapabannakhan, 1953), 574 pp.

134. *Kham luang* literally means "royal words." As applied to literary works, however, starting with the *Mahachat kham luang* of the fifteenth century, *kham luang* designates a poetic work composed in a variety of verse forms that has been either written by a king or commissioned by him. *Kham luang* literature, then, consists of royally approved, that is, classical, examples of prosody.

135. *Phra non kham luang*, pp. d–f.

136. *BT*, December 9, 1911.

137. NA 30/27, "Siamese Art."

138. King's speech on the opening of the National Library, January 6, 1917, in *Phraratchadamrat nai phrabatsomdet*, p. 205.

139. Encouragement of the printing of books to make merit by distributing them at funerals apparently was started in 1901 by Prince Sommot; see *Union Catalogue of Thai Materials* (Tokyo: Institute of Developing Economics, 1972), p. xxiv.

140. *Bot lakhọn rửang rammakian lae bọkoet rammakian* (Bangkok: Sinlapabannakhan, 1966), p. (17).

141. See preface to *Shakuntala* in *Sakuntala, matthanaphatha, thao saen pom, pramuan suphasit* (Bangkok: Sinlapabannakhan, 1966), p. 4, and preface to *Phra non kham luang*, p. 1.

142. *Baep rian kawiniphon rửang wenitwanit* (Bangkok: Khurusapha, 1961), 19th ed., p. b.

Notes to pp. 239–244

143. *RKB* 31, July 23, 1914, pp. 309–314.

144. NA 271, royal decree establishing the Literary Society, July 23, 1914; *BT*, August 8, 1914.

145. Bamrung Ratchabǫriphan, "Huačhai nakrop," in *Wachirawutthanusǫn* (1967), p. 251.

146. King's acceptance speech to the Literary Society, January 6, 1917, in *Phraratchadamrat nai phrabatsomdet*, p. 207; *BT*, January 8, 1917.

147. *Matthanaphatha rư̄ tamnan haeng dǫk kulap* (Bangkok: Aksǫnnit, 1951). This edition reproduces the letter of award which praises the play for its unique use of the difficult *chan* meters in a work for the theater.

148. NA 271/1, note of an opinion on establishing an Institute of Etymology and Orthography; no date, but probably before December 1921.

149. "He khruan thưng nangsư̄," *Sumutthasan* 2 (February 1915): 25–26.

150. In 1909 King Chulalongkorn's Royal Secretariat proposed the use of four Thai words to replace English words in common usage. This step Vajiravudh heartily endorsed. (See *Čhotmaihetraiwan*, p. 17.) Among the many writings of Vajiravudh as king on this subject, see "Kham chai thaen kham 'editor'," in *Nangsư̄phim thai*, reprinted in *Phraratchaniphon thi naru*, pp. 198–200; NA 2/28, King's note on Royal Naval Institute letter of February 11, 1916; NA 2/38, King's comments on maritime strategy, 1913; *BT*, September 16, 1915; Amorn, *Phraratchakaraniyakit samkhan ... rư̄ang phraratchaniphon*, pp. 9–11; NA 84/5, King's notes on Chulalongkorn University, undated. The new words suggested by the King for those listed above were *bannathikan*, *ainam*, *khrư̄angyon*, *banyai*, *ubai*, *annačhak*, *setthawitthaya*, *pratu*, and *phitsayasat*.

151. Vajiravudh as quoted by Amorn, *Phraratchakaraniyakit samkhan ... rư̄ang phraratchaniphon*, p. 111.

152. See "Phuket rư̄ phuket" and other such articles in *Phraratchaniphon thi naru*.

153. See Amorn, *Phraratchakaraniyakit samkhan ... rư̄ang kamnoet nam sakun*, vol. 1:36–38.

154. NA 30/25, undated, unsigned article in English on romanization.

155. *Withi mai samrap chai sara lae khian nangsư̄ thai* (Bangkok: Thai Khasem, 1950); the original document is dated April 6, 1917.

156. See, for example, *BT*, June 9, 1917.

157. NA 184, Phraya Siphuri Pricha to Phraya Buri, August 30 and September 2, 4, 10, and 22, 1917.

Chapter 9

1. *BT*, December 11, 1920.

2. Thawi, pp. 591–605; *BT*, July 10, 12, and 13, 1920.

3. *BT*, January 14, 1924.

4. "Kansadet chak phranakhǫn," in *Phraratchaniphon thi naru*, pp. 170–178.

5. *BT*, April 17, 1917.

6. The custom of giving such an address was started by King Chulalongkorn. Some of Vajiravudh's early speeches in this category were written by himself, but by 1916 the speech was drafted by officials, corrected by the King, and translated into English by Prince Devawongse. See NA 128/8.

7. *BT*, December 9, 1911.

8. Ibid.

9. *Ruang thetsana suapa*, p. 174.

10. *BT*, December 8, 1911.

11. See chapter 6, section on "Education."

12. "Sadaeng khunnanukhun," in *Phraratchaniphon bang ruang*, p. ii.

13. This strange pen name is explained in a letter of Chamun Amorn's as a term that derives from one of the epithets of the Buddha, who is called a vehicle for men as the horse is a vehicle. Since horses were highly valued in ancient India, particularly among the Kshatriya caste to which the Buddha belonged, the epithet had favorable connotations. (Probably in the way that "shepherd," applied to Christ, had special significance to the pastoral Near Eastern peoples.) Vajiravudh used a different word from that applied to the Buddha, but the meaning was the same. The implication was that the king as horseman or horse vehicle was playing the role of teacher to his people. See Chamun Amorn Darunrak, *Mahatlek nai thamniap* (Bangkok: Khurusapha, 1974), pp. 100–102.

14. NA 84, Ministry of Religious Affairs to King, July 1, 1911.

15. See preface to "Sadaeng khunnanukhun."

16. *BT*, January 17, 1918.

17. Sathitya Semanil, *Wisasa* (Bangkok: Phrae Phittaya, 1970), pp. 14, 21.

18. Phraya Bamrung, "Huachai nakrop," *Wachirawutthanusǫn* (1967), p. 249.

19. *BT*, December 23, 1914.

20. Ibid., October 8, 1917.

21. *Thammathamma songkhram*, p. 30.

22. *BT*, July 24, 1917.

23. Ibid., November 26, 1925.

24. NA 139, General Press Cutting Association, Ltd., bills and clippings. The service was apparently started by King Chulalongkorn.

25. *Phraratchaniphon thi naru*, pp. 117–122.

26. *A Siam Miscellany*, p. 50.

27. *BT*, November 25, 1922; *Bangkok Daily Mail*, November 27, 1922.

28. *Clogs on Our Wheels*, pp. 28, 33–35.
29. *A Siam Miscellany*, p. 50.
30. *Nangsŭphim thai*, as referred to in *BT*, November 3, 1920.
31. *BT*, January 14, 1913. The Attorney General was W. A. G. Tilleke, a Singhalese lawyer who was a life-long civil servant in Siam.
32. NA 217/2, Paribatra to King, June 1911.
33. NA 139/1, "Lek" to King, August 29, 1912.
34. *Čhotmaihetraiwan*, pp. 100–103.
35. Ibid., p. 97.
36. NA 263, report of meeting of Council of Ministers, May 31, 1915.
37. NA 263, Čhaophraya Yommarat to King, June 5, 1916; King's note on same letter.
38. NA 139/3, "The Newspaper Act of 2460."
39. NA 139/3, undated note by King.
40. NA 252/6, Čhaophraya Aphairacha to King, December 15, 1922.
41. *BT*, December 5 and 6, 1923.
42. NA 139, Čhaophraya Yommarat to King, May 3, 1911, and clippings from *Sam samai*, May 1 and 2, 1911.
43. *BT*, January 14 to July 22, 1913.
44. Ibid., February 26, February 27, and April 2, 1918.
45. Ibid., April 20 and May 10, 1918.
46. NA 133, Čhaophraya Yommarat to Čhaophraya Mahithǫn, July 2, 1925.
47. *BT*, June 18, 1912.
48. NA 139, Čhaophraya Yommarat to King, July 17, 1923.
49. NA 139, Čhaophraya Yommarat to King, January 24, 1911. The subsidy for the *Nangsŭphim thai* was 8,000 baht annually; for the *Nangsŭphim čhino*, 4,000 baht annually.
50. See NA 117/43, Acting General Adviser Pitkin to Phraya Arthakar, October 9, 1915. Pitkin denied that the government "as such" had connections with the *Observer*; his statement seems equivocal. *BT*, May 8, 1914, refers to the *Observer*'s "usual policy of 'buttering up' Government officials irrespective of what they do or contemplate doing."
51. *BT*, December 27, 1917.
52. NA 139, June 4, 1912.
53. *BT*, July 23, 1912.
54. NA 139, Čhaophraya Yommarat to King, December 21, 1910; *Nangsŭphim thai mai*, December 23, 1910.
55. NA 139, Phra Ratchasewok to King, March 24, 1912.
56. *BT*, October 24, 1913.

57. Ibid., March 9 and 10, 1914.
58. Ibid., September 20, 1919.
59. Ibid., October 13, 1921.
60. Ibid., September 24, 1919.
61. The first article appeared in *BT*, May 31, 1923. Further articles continued into the reign of King Prajadhipok.
62. NA 137, King to Čhaokhun Ratcha-aksǫn, undated but shortly before April 24, 1925.
63. The archives contain the unforwarded copies of the *Bangkok Times* from April 23 to May 1.
64. Interview with Sathitya, June 24, 1970.
65. *Bangkok Post*, September 6, 1970.
66. Ibid.

Chapter 10

1. NA 6/260, "Draft Law on Succession," November 10, 1924.
2. Čhaophraya Ram's account, given in *Sena sùksa*, October 1930, as quoted by Prayut Sitthiphan, *Phramaha thiraratčhao* (Bangkok: Sayam, 1972), p. 5.
3. *BT*, November 7, 1925.
4. S[awai], foreword.
5. Amorn, *Sùapa lae luksùa nai prawattisat*, vol. 2: 16.
6. Phra Sarasas, *My Country Thailand* (Bangkok: Golden Service, 1960), p. 143.
7. *Phrabǫromrachowat sùapa*, p. 13.
8. *BT*, September 10, 1918.
9. Chula Chakrabongse, *Lords of Life*, p. 273.
10. Prasongsom Bǫriphat, pp. 15–18.
11. Smith, pp. 112–113. Smith's views are at once revealing and untrustworthy. Smith was physician to Queen Saowapha. His reports, then, reflect views of the King prevalent in the Queen Mother's entourage. They are not objective and are not necessarily true or reflective of views in other quarters.
12. *Samnao phraratchahatlekha*, p. (115).
13. Smith, p. 114.
14. *BT*, September 24, 1919.
15. Ibid., April 4, 1925.
16. Ibid.
17. Ibid., February 23, 1924.
18. Ibid., May 24, 1924.
19. Ibid., May 31, 1923; February 23, 1924; February 6 and 28, 1925.

20. *BT*, December 31, 1919; March 8 and October 22, 1924; April 4, 1925.

21. See Hermit's hint on why writers "are compelled to write in English," in *BT*, September 4, 1925.

22. Hermit in *BT*, May 24, 1924.

23. Wan Waithayakon, "Thai Culture," *Journal of the Thailand Research Society* 35 (September 1944): 142–143.

24. *BT*, January 11, 1940; S[awai], pp. 827–828.

25. A translation of *Mahathiraratčhao*, an epithet for the King that is often used today.

26. A remark to Phraya Anirut, as quoted in the preface to Sangwan Phatthanothai, *Pathakatha rǔang phraratchaniphon khǫng ratchakan thi 6* (Bangkok: Phanit Suphaphon, 1941), p. i.

Bibliography

1. Archival Materials

The Thai National Archives are by far the most important and accessible depository of unpublished documentary materials on the reign. The materials for the Sixth Reign are grouped into subject categories comprising 293 files (*faem*), which are subdivided, as the volume of material requires, into folders (*puk*). The documents of the Sixth Reign are indexed in a volume of 424 legal-size pages. The index is dated September 24, 1964.

Other archival materials for the Sixth Reign are held by the National Library, the Damrong Library, various government ministries, the Royal Secretariat, and some individuals. Many of these materials are not accessible. Those that were accessible to me were few in number and, by and large, not of great importance in compiling this study.

2. Works by King Vajiravudh

"Amnat khu' tham" (Might Is Right). *Samutthasan* 32 (August 1917): 96–140; 33 (September 1917): 30–75.
"Appramat" (Diligence). *Samutthasan* 1 (January 1915): 47–53.

Bibliography

Bot lakhǫnphut rư̄ang huačhai nakrop (Text of the Play, The Soul of a Warrior). Bangkok: Khurusapha, 1950. 93 pp.

Bot lakhǫn rư̄ang minpramat san, topta, chuai amnat, lae nam yǫk ao nam bong (Text of the Plays: Contempt of Court, Deception, Coup d'état, and Use a Thorn to Pull a Thorn). Bangkok: Khurusapha, 1963. 348 pp.

Bot lakhǫn rư̄ang rammakian lae bǫkoet rammakian (Text of the Rammakian *and* the Origins of the Rammakian). Bangkok: Sinlapabannakhan, 1966. 1023 pp.

"Chaiyo" (Hurrah). *Samutthasan* 1 (January 1915): 83–92.

Čhatkan rap sadet. See *Lakhǫnphut rư̄ang* . . . .

Čhotmaihet praphat huamư̄ang paktai r.s. 128 khǫng phrabatsomdet phra mongkutklao čhaoyuhua (Documents on King Vajiravudh's Visit to the Southern Provinces in 1909). Bangkok: Khurusapha, 1963. 65 pp.

Čhotmaihetraiwan nai phrabatsomdet phra mongkutklao čhaoyuhua (The Diary of King Vajiravudh). Bangkok: Mahamakut Ratchawitthayalai, 1974. 200 pp.

Čhotmaihet ratchakan thi 6 sadet phraratchadamnoen prathet malayu p.s. 2467 (Documents on the Visit of Rama VI to Malaya in 1924). Bangkok: Mahamakut Ratchawitthayalai, 1968. 169 pp.

Chuai amnat! (Coup d'état!). Bangkok: Thanit, 1974. 50 pp.

Chumnum nithan phraratchaniphon nai phrabatsomdet phra mongkutklao čhaoyuhua (Collected Stories of King Vajiravudh). Thonburi: Bannakhan, 1966. 552 pp.

Clogs on Our Wheels. Bangkok: Siam Observer, 1915. 164 pp.

Coup d'état, a Play in One Act. Bangkok: Bangkok Daily Mail, [1924]. 96 pp.

"The Cult of Imitation." In *Clogs on Our Wheels.*

Ekasan rư̄ang sư̄apa lae pramuan rư̄ang kiao kap sư̄apa (Documents on the Wild Tigers *and* Collection of Accounts on the Wild Tigers). Bangkok: Khurusapha, 1960. 239 pp.

"He rư̄a yuk mai" (Boat Songs of a New Era). *Samutthasan* 2 (February 1915): 11–33.

Huačhai chainum (The Heart of a Young Man). Bangkok: Kaona, 1961. 71 pp.

Huačhai nakrop. See *Bot lakhǫnphut rư̄ang* . . . .

The Jews of the Orient. Bangkok: Siam Observer, [1914]. 63 pp.

Kansongkhram pǫm khai prachit (Trench Warfare). Bangkok: Sophonphiphatthanakǫn, 1916. 108 pp.

Khanom som kap namya (The Right Amount of Noodles for the Sauce). N.p., n.d. 16 pp.

"Khlon tit lǫ" (Clogs on Our Wheels). In *Phraratchaniphon thi naru* . . . .

Khǫ bangkhap pokkhrǫng dusit nawik samosǫn (Rules of Governance for the Dusit Naval Club). Bangkok, 1919. 17 pp.

"Khǫ chuan than pen malaeng wi" (Come Be a Fruit Fly). *Samutthasan* 13 (January 1916): 14–28.

Khǫm damdin. See "Rư̄ang khǫm damdin."

Bibliography

"Khruangmai haeng khwamrungruang khu saphap haeng sattri" (A Symbol of Civilization: The Status of Women). In *Phraratchaniphon thi naru* . . . .

Khwamdi mi chai (The Triumph of Virtue). Bangkok: Sophonphiphatthanakọn, n.d.

"Khwam khaochai phit" (A Mistake). In *Phraratchaniphon thi naru* . . . .

"Khwam krachat krachai haeng muang chin" (The Disintegration of China). In *Phraratchaniphon thi naru* . . . .

"Khwam pen chat doi thae ching" (On Becoming a Real Nation). In *Phraratchaniphon thi naru* . . . .

Khwamru kiao kap phraratchakaraniyakit nai ratchakan thi 6 lae bot lakhọn boek rong ruang dukdamban (Information on the Royal Duties of King Vajiravudh *and* Texts of Curtain-Raisers in Classical Style). Bangkok: Phrachan, 1960. 96 pp.

Kotmonthianban wa duai kharatchakan nai phraratchasamnak (Palatine Law concerning Officials in the Royal Household). Bangkok: Ministry of the Interior, 1960. 25 pp.

Lakhọnphut ruang chatkan rap sadet (The Play, Preparing for the Prince's Visit). N.p., n.d. 51 pp.

Lakhọnphut ruang khanom som kap namya, luang chamnian doen thang, phongphang, plọi kae (The Plays: The Right Amount of Noodles for the Sauce, Luang Chamnian Goes on a Trip, Fishtrap, Release). Bangkok: Khurusapha, 1969. 245 pp.

Lak ratchakan lae khlong suphasit (Foundations of Government *and* Proverbs). Bangkok: Krom Phaenthi Thahan, 1966. 159 pp.

"Latthi ao yang" (The Cult of Imitation). In *Phraratchaniphon thi naru* . . . .

Lilit phayap (A Poem of the Northwest). Bangkok: Prasoet, 1968. 131 pp.

Mahatama (The Mahatma). Bangkok: Aksọnnit, n.d. 155 pp.

"Mai tọngkan hia" (We Don't Need Lizards). *Dusit samit* 2, no. 16 (1919): 65–67.

Matthanaphatha ru tamnan haeng dọk kulap (Madanabadha, or Romance of the Rose). Bangkok: Aksọnnit, 1951. 146 pp.

"Might Is Right": A Siamese Opinion of the German Gospel. N.p., [1917]. 97 pp.

"Muang thai chong tun thoet" (Wake Up, Siam). In *Pramuan bot phraratchaniphon*. . . .

Nam yọk ao nam bong (Use a Thorn to Pull a Thorn). N.p., n.d. 83 pp.

Nangsu an lakhọnphut ruang "sia sala" khọng si ayutthaya (Reader's Edition of the Play "Sacrifice" by Sri Ayudhya). Bangkok: Khurusapha, 1955. 130 pp.

Narai sip pang (The Ten Incarnations of Vishnu). Bangkok: Sinlapabannakhan, 1960. 538 pp.

Phrabọromrachowat lae prakat tang chaophraya ramrakhop (The Royal Address and Proclamation of the Appointment of Chaophraya Ramrakhop). Bangkok: Mahamakut Ratchawitthayalai, 1962. 11 pp.

Phrabọromrachowat nai ngan wisakhabucha lae sadaeng khunnanukhun phra-

Bibliography

bǫromrachanusatsani khǫng phrabatsomdet phra ramathibǫdi sisinthǫn maha wachirawut phra mongkutklao čhaoyuhua (His Majesty's Speeches on Wisakhabucha Day *and* A Definition of Virtue). Bangkok: Mahamakut Ratchawitthayalai, 1957. 81 pp.

Phrabǫromrachowat sŭapa (Wild Tiger Speeches). Bangkok, [1920]. 152 pp.

Phra non kham luang (The Story of King Nala in Classical Verse Forms). Bangkok: Sinlapabannakhan, 1953. 574 pp.

Phrapenčhao khǫng phram (Brahmanic Gods). Bangkok: Rungrŭangtham, 1963. 82 pp.

Phraphutthačhao tratsaru arai, including an English version by M. C. Upalisan Jumbala entitled *What Is the Knowledge Attained by the Buddha on His Enlightenment*. Bangkok: Khurusapha, 1964. 37 pp. + 35 pp.

Phraratchadamrat lae phrabǫromrachowat (Royal Addresses and Speeches). Bangkok: Phrachan, 1958. 65 pp.

Phraratchadamrat nai phrabatsomdet phra mongkutklao čhaoyuhua (Speeches of King Vajiravudh). Bangkok: Bamrungnukunlakit, 1929. 330 pp.

Phraratchaniphon bang rŭang nai phrabatsomdet phra mongkutklao čhaoyuhua (Some Compositions of King Vajiravudh). Bangkok: Rungrŭangtham, 1958. 88 pp.

Phraratchaniphon phra ruang (The Royal Composition, Phra Ruang). N.p., n.d. (12 pp.) + 117 pp.

Phraratchaniphon pritsana: kham khlong lae khwamriang (Riddles in Verse and Prose). Bangkok: Mahamakut Ratchawitthayalai, 1960. 48 pp.

Phraratchaniphon thi naru khǫng lonklao ratchakan thi 6 (Significant Writings of King Vajiravudh). Bangkok: Fŭang Aksǫn, 1963. 440 pp.

Phra ruang. See *Phraratchaniphon phra ruang*.

Phra sunhasep (Lord Sunahsepha). Bangkok: Khurusapha, 1961. 363 pp.

Plukčhai sŭapa lae khlon tit lǫ (Instilling the Wild Tiger Spirit *and* Clogs on Our Wheels). Bangkok: Mahachai, 1951. 132 pp.

Pramuan bot phraratchaniphon (phak pakinnaka suan thi 2) nai phrabatsomdet phra mongkutklao čhaoyuhua (Compilation of the Writings of King Vajiravudh [Miscellaneous Pieces, Part 2]). Bangkok: Sirisan, 1961. 119 pp.

Pramuan phrabǫromrachathibai kiao kap prawattisat sayam (Collection of Royal Discourses on Siamese History). Bangkok: Songtham, 1935. 68 pp.

Pramuan suphasit phraratchaniphon khǫng somdet phra ramathibǫdi sisinthǫn maha wachirawut phra mongkutklao čhaoyuhua (A Collection of the Proverbs of King Vajiravudh). Bangkok: Phrachan, 1964. 193 pp.

"Prayot haeng kan yu nai tham" (The Benefits of Morality). *Čhotmaihet sŭapa* 8, no. 11 (March 1915): 609–625.

"Prayot khǫng rŭarop tang tang" (The Usefulness of Various Kinds of Warships). *Samutthasan* 1 (January 1915): 96–104.

"Priap nam sakun kap chŭ sae" (A Comparison of Surnames with Clan Names). In *Pramuan bot phraratchaniphon* ....

"Ramphŭng thŭng phra ruang" (Reflections on Phra Ruang). *Samutthasan* 25 (January 1917): i–iv.

Bibliography

"Rŭang khǫm damdin" (On the Cambodian Earth Diver). In *Thi raluk nai ngan phraratchathan phloengsop phon ek phonrŭa ek mahasewok ek čhaophraya ramrakhop* (Souvenir of the Cremation Ceremony for General Admiral Čhaophraya Ramrakhop). Bangkok: Thannakhan Krungthep, 1967. Pp. 1–52.

Rŭang phuak yiw haeng buraphathit (The Jews of the Orient). Bangkok: Charoenrat, n.d. 33 pp.

Rŭang thetsana sŭapa (Lectures on Religion to the Wild Tigers). Bangkok: Khurusapha, 1958. 226 pp.

"Sadaeng khunnanukhun" (A Definition of Virtue). In *Phraratchaniphon bang rŭang* . . . .

Sakuntala, matthanaphatha, thao saen pom, pramuan suphasit (Shakuntala, Madanabadha, Thao Saen Pom, Collection of Proverbs). Bangkok: Sinlapabannakhan, 1966. 771 pp.

"Sapsat" (Political Economy). *Samutthasan* 9 (September 1915): 113–133.

"Seriphap haeng thale" (Freedom of the Seas). *Samutthasan* 42 (June 1918): 1–33.

A Siam Miscellany. Bangkok: Siam Observer, 1912. 76 pp.

Sia sala. See *Nangsŭ an lakhǫnphut rŭang* . . . .

"Suphasit phra ruang" (The Maxims of Phra Ruang). *Samutthasan* 8 (August 1915): 1–29.

"Tam namphrik lalai maenam" (Grinding Pepper Sauce in the River). In *Phraratchaniphon bang rŭang* . . . .

Thamma mi chai (The Triumph of Morality). Unpublished typescript, n.p., n.d. 5 pp. In the Damrong Library.

Thammathamma songkhram (The War between Good and Evil). Bangkok: Sam Mit, 1971. 33 pp.

Thao saen pom: bot lakhǫn baep dŭkdamban (Thao Saen Pom: Text of the Musical Version). N.p., 1924. 41 pp.

Thetsana sŭapa (Lectures to the Wild Tigers). Bangkok, [1914]. 115 pp. + 6 pp.

Thiao mŭang phra ruang (Travels in Phra Ruang Country). Bangkok: Ministry of the Interior, 1954. 151 pp.

Uttarakuru (Uttarakuru). Bangkok: Mahamakut Witthayalai, 1965. 36 pp.

Withi mai samrap chai sara lae khian nangsŭ thai (New Method of Using Vowels and Writing in Thai). Bangkok: Thai Khasem, 1950. [25 pp.]

Wiwaha phra samut (Neptune's Bride). N.p., n.d. 173 pp.

3. Other Works in Thai

Amorn Darunrak, Chamun. *Dusit thani: mŭang prachathipatai khǫng phrabatsomdet phra mongkutklao čhaoyuhua* (Dusit Thani: The Democratic State of King Vajiravudh). Bangkok: National Library, 1970. 334 pp.

———. "Het thi phrabatsomdet phra mongkutklao song plian thong chat thai" (The Reason King Vajiravudh Changed the Thai Flag). *Wachirawutthanusǫn* (1953), pp. 81–102.

Bibliography

———. *Kamnoet phraratchawang sanamčhan lae phra pathom čhedi; mahathiraratčhao kap dǫn čhedi; anusǫn khǫng sǔapa lae luksǔa* (The Origins of Sanamčhan Palace and Phra Pathom Čhedi; The Philosopher King and Dǫn Čhedi; Remembrances of the Wild Tigers and Boy Scouts). Bangkok: Khurusapha, 1968. 184 pp.

———. "Kan ngoen khǫng lon klao r. 6" (The Finances of King Vajiravudh). *Warasan luksǔa*, special issue (July 1, 1970), pp. 85–96.

———. *Khon mai thuk nintha mai mi nai lok lae adit wira kasat thi song pen sot* (No One in the World Is Free from Gossip *and* Our Great Bachelor Kings). Bangkok: Khurusapha, 1974. 105 pp.

———. *Mahatlek nai thamniap; sunak pritsana; nam faeng khǫng mahaburut* (Court Pages; The Mystery of the Dog; Pennames of a Great Man). Bangkok: Khurusapha, 1974. 145 pp.

———. *Phraratchakaraniyakit nai phrabatsomdet phra mongkutklao čhaoyuhua lem 9 rǔang phraratchaprapheni (tǫn 1)* (The Duties of King Vajiravudh, Volume 9, Concerning Royal Ceremonies [Part 1]). Bangkok: Khurusapha, 1971. 2 vols.

———. *Phraratchakaraniyakit samkhan nai phrabatsomdet phra mongkutklao čhaoyuhua rǔang hetphon thi ratchakan thi 6 song prakat songkhram, dusit thani* (Important Achievements of King Vajiravudh: On the Reasons for His Declaration of War; Dusit Thani). Bangkok: Khurusapha, 1969. 225 pp.

———. *Phraratchakaraniyakit samkhan nai phrabatsomdet phra mongkutklao čhaoyuhua rǔang kamnoet nam sakun* (Important Achievements of King Vajiravudh: On the Origin of Surnames). Bangkok: Khurusapha, 1968. 2 vols.

———. *Phraratchakaraniyakit samkhan nai phrabatsomdet phra mongkutklao čhaoyuhua rǔang phrabǫrommarachobai thang kanmǔang* (Important Achievements of King Vajiravudh: Political Policies). Bangkok: Khurusapha, 1976. 170 pp.

———. *Phraratchakaraniyakit samkhan nai phrabatsomdet phra mongkutklao čhaoyuhua rǔang phraratchaniphon nai ratchakan thi 6, kharomrak, mahasinlapin ek khǫng thai* (Important Achievements of King Vajiravudh: On His Writings; His Love Poetry; His Position as a Leading Thai Artist). Bangkok: Khurusapha, 1968. 207 pp.

———. *Sǔapa lae luksǔa nai prawattisat* (The Wild Tigers and the Boy Scouts in History). Bangkok: Khurusapha, 1971. 4 vols.

Bamrung Ratchabǫriphan, Phraya. "Huačhai nakrop" (The Soul of A Warrior). *Wachirawutthanusǫn* (1967), pp. 245–251.

———. "Phraratchačhariyawat baep phudi angkrit" (His Majesty's Manners as an English Gentleman). *Wachirawutthanusǫn* (1968), pp. 217–225.

———. "Phraratchaphithi pathomkam" (The Royal First Action Rite). *Wachirawutthanusǫn* (1969), pp. 225–236.

Chaimongkhon Udomsap. *Phraprawat phonrǔa ek phračhao bǫromwongthoe*

Bibliography

kromluang chumphǫnkhet udomsak (A Biography of Admiral the Prince of Chumphǫn). Bangkok: Rung Witthaya, 1969. 600 pp.

Čhakpani Sisinlawisut, Luang. *Rưang khǫng čhaophraya mahithǫn* (An Account of Čhaophraya Mahithǫn). Bangkok: Tiranasan, 1956. 357 pp.

Chakrabongs, Prince. "Phičharana phraratchabanyat laksana ken thahan" (An Examination of the Law on Conscription). *Samutthasan* 2 (February 1915): 35–72.

Čhamroen Sawat-chutho. "Dusit thani" (Dusit Thani). *Triam udom sưksa*, no. 3 (1951), 231–248.

Čhotmaihet phraratchaphithi bǫromrachaphisek.... See Hǫphrasamut Samrap Phranakhǫn.

Chula Chakrabongse, Prince. *Čhao chiwit* (Lords of Life). Bangkok: Khlang Witthaya, 1962. 753 pp.

Chulalongkorn, King. *Phrabǫromrachowat nai phrabatsomdet phra čhula-čhǫmklao čhaoyuhua phraratchathan phračhao lukyathoe song phrarat-chaniphon mưa p.s. 2428* (Instructions of King Chulalongkorn to His Sons, Composed in 1885). Bangkok: Sophonphiphatthanakǫn, 1931. 16 pp. + 12 pp. translation.

———. *Phraratchadamrat* (Royal Speeches). Bangkok: Thai National Bank, 1967. 251 pp.

———. *Samnao phraratchahatlekha suan phra-ong phrabatsomdet phra čhulačhǫmklao čhaoyuhua thưng čhaophraya yommarat (pan sukhum) kap prawat čhaophraya yommarat* (Texts of the Personal Letters of King Chulalongkorn to Čhaophraya Yommarat *and* A Biography of Čhaophraya Yommarat). The biography during the Sixth Reign is by Prince Dhani. Bangkok: Bamrungtham, 1939. (154 pp.) + 274 pp.

Coedès, G. *Prachum čharưk sayam phak thi 1, čharưk krung sukhothai*. Bangkok: Bangkok Times, 1924. 168 pp. See French title in section 4.

Damrong Rajanubhab, Prince. *Tamra lakhǫn inao* (A Treatise on the Inao Drama). Bangkok: Khlang Witthaya, 1964. 216 pp.

Dhanit Yupho. *Khon* (Masked Drama). Bangkok: Department of Fine Arts, 1957. 166 pp.

Hǫphrasamut Samrap Phranakhǫn, compiler. *Čhotmaihet phraratchaphithi bǫromrachaphisek somdet phraramathibǫdi sisinthǫn maha wachirawut phra mongkutklao čhaoyuhua* (Record of the Coronation Ceremonies of King Vajiravudh). Bangkok: Sophonphiphatthanakǫn, 1924. 204 pp.

Khon Samak Len. *Rainam tua khon kap bot rǫng lae phak čheračha* (List of Masked Drama Players and Texts of Songs and Dialogue). Bangkok: n.p., 1909. 20 pp.

Laksaminusǫn (In Memory of Princess Laksmi). Bangkok: Maeban Kanrưan, 1961. 72 pp.

Maha Dhep Kasatarasamuha, Phra, compiler. *Sưapa* (The Wild Tigers). Bangkok: Mahamakut Ratchawitthayalai, 1968. 60 pp.

Natthawutti Sutthisongkhram. *Phrakiat prawat khǫng čhǫmphonrưa čhǫm-*

Bibliography

phon somdet čhaofa kromphra nakhǫn sawan wǫraphinit senabǫdi krasuang thahanrŭa phra-ong raek (Biography of Admiral and General Prince of Nakhǫn Sawan, First Minister of the Marine). Bangkok: Krom Phaenthi Sathan, 1965. 905 pp.

Noradhebprida, Phraya. "Khwamsongčham nai samai ratchakan thi 6" (Recollections of the Sixth Reign). *Khurusan* (March 1954), pp. 89–105.

O-phat Sewikun. *Thai kap songkhram lok khrang thi 1* (The Thai and World War I). Bangkok: Kasembannakit, 1968. 328 pp.

Phraprawat lae čhariyawat khǫng čhǫmphonrŭa somdet čhaofa bǫriphat sukhumphan kromphraya nakhǫn sawan wǫraphinit lae ekasan thi dai song pattibat ratchakan (The Life and Character of Admiral Prince Paribatra, the Prince of Nakhǫn Sawan, and His Government Papers). Bangkok: Krom Uthakasat, 1950. 113 pp.

"Phraprawat phonrŭa ek phračhaobǫromwongthoe kromluang chumphǫnkhet udomsak" (A Biography of Admiral the Prince of Chumphǫn). Typescript. 19 pp.

Phraprawat phraniphon lae phapfiphrahat khǫng somdet čhaofa kromphraya naritsaranuwattiwong (A Biography of Prince Naris and His Writings and Designs). Bangkok: Kaona, 1963. 96 pp.

Phraratchaniphon nai phrabatsomdet phra mongkutklao čhaoyuhua bannanukrom (A Bibliography of the Writings of King Vajiravudh). Bangkok: National Library, 1970. 84 pp.

Phraya yŭn chingcha p.s. 2460 (The Noble Presiding at the Swing Ceremony in 1917). Bangkok: Hang Hunsuan Čhamkat Siwaphǫn, 1962. 50 pp.

Pin Malakul, M. L. "Kam sǫmrop sŭapa p.s. 2462 lae phraratchawang sanamčhan" (Wild Tiger Maneuvers of 1919 *and* Sanamčhan Palace). *Wachirawutthanusǫn* (1968), pp. 161–172.

———. *Ngan lakhǫn khǫng phrabatsomdet phraramathibǫdi sisinthǫn maha wachirawut phra mongkutklao čhao phaendin sayam* (The Plays of King Rama VI). Bangkok: Khurusapha, 1973. 63 pp.

———. *Phramahakarunathikhun an lon klao* (The Accomplishments of Rama VI). Bangkok: Khurusapha, 1973. 53 pp.

———. "Rŭang khai luang hat čhao samran" (On the Royal Camp at Hat Čhao Samran). In *Phrabǫromrachanusatsani sadaeng khunnanukhun*. Bangkok: Khurusapha, 1973. 158 pp.

Poon Pismai Diskul, M. C. *Sarakhadi* (Essays). Bangkok: Mahamakut Ratchawitthayalai, 1964. 400 pp.

Pornpen Hantrakool. "Kanchai čhaingoen phaendin nai ratchasamai phrabatsomdet phra mongkutklao čhaoyuhua" (Government Spending during the Reign of King Vajiravudh). Mimeographed Master's thesis, Department of History, Graduate School, Chulalongkorn University, 1974. 277 pp.

Prachum bot lakhǫn dŭkdamban (Collection of Musical Plays). Bangkok: Department of Fine Arts, 1966. 248 pp.

Bibliography

Prachum kap he rŭa (A Collection of Boat Songs). Bangkok: Khurusapha, 1962. 121 pp.

Prachum phrabǫromrachowat lae phra-owat (Collection of Speeches by Kings and Princes). Bangkok: Sutthisan, 1966. 71 pp.

Praphat Trinarong. *Chiwit lae ngan khǫng atsawaphahu* (The Life and Works of Asvabahu). Bangkok: Watthanaphanit, 1963. 730 pp.

Prasit Suphakan, Phraya. "Kančhap rŭa chaloei nai nannam sayam wan thi 22 karakadakhom p.s. 2460" (Capture of Enemy Vessels in Siamese Territorial Waters on July 22, 1917). *Samutthasan* 32 (August 1917): 9–44.

Prasongsom Bǫriphat, Mǫmčhaoying. *Banthŭk khwamsongčham bang rŭang ... nai somdet čhaofa kromphra nakhǫn sawan wǫraphinit* (Some Reminiscences of the Prince of Nakhǫn Sawan). Bangkok: Phračhan, 1956. 48 pp.

Prayun Phitsanakha. *9 kasat thai haeng ratchawong čhakkri* (Nine Thai Kings of the Chakkri Dynasty). Bangkok: P. Phitsanakha, 1965. 864 pp.

Prayut Sitthiphan. *Phramaha thiraratčhao* (The Great Learned Monarch). Bangkok: Sayam, 1972. 509 pp.

———. *Ratchasamnak phra mongkutklao* (King Vajiravudh's Royal Household). Bangkok: Thammasewi, 1955. 583 pp.

———. *Ratchasamnak thai* (The Thai Royal Household). Bangkok: Khlang Witthaya, 1962. 660 pp.

Ratchasakunwong (Royal Genealogy). Bangkok: Phračhan, 1969. 209 pp.

Riangkhwam rŭang phraratchaniphon nai ratchakan thi 6 lae riangkhwam chabap dai rap rangwan thun phumiphon (Essays on the Writings of King Vajiravudh *and* Essays That Received the Bhumibol Prize). Bangkok: Khurusapha, 1961. 345 pp.

Rian Srichandr and Netra Poonwiwat. *Prawat pattiwat khrang raek khǫng thai r.s. 130* (A History of the First Thai Revolution, 1912). Bangkok: Kim Li Nguan, 1960. 263 pp.

Samutthara Surakkhaka. *26 kanpattiwat thai lae ratthaprahan samai 2089–2507* (Twenty-six Thai Revolutions and Coups d'état from 1546 to 1964). Bangkok: Sŭ Kanphim, 1964. 704 pp.

Sangop Suriyin. *Thianwan* (Thianwan). Bangkok: Suriyin, 1967. 663 pp.

Sanguan Ankhong. *Sangkhep phraratchaprawat lae phraratchaniphon nai phra mongkutklao čhaoyuhua* (A Brief Biography and Writings of King Vajiravudh). Bangkok, 1969. 104 pp.

Sangwan Phattanothai. *Pathakatha rŭang phraratchaniphon khǫng ratchakan thi 6 thang witthayu kračhaisiang* (Radio Talks on the Compositions of King Vajiravudh). Bangkok: Phanit Suphaphon, 1951. 108 pp.

Satčhaphirom Udomratchaphakdi, Phraya. *Lao hai luk fang* (Told for My Children). Bangkok: Aksǫnsat, 1955. 230 pp.

Sathaphǫn Malila. *Phračhaobǫromwongthoe kromluang ratburi direkrit* (The Prince of Ratburi). Bangkok: Thai Khasem, 1953. 66 pp.

Sathian Phantharangsi. *Phra mongkutklao; čhaofa phetcharat* (King Vajiravudh; Princess Bejaratana). Bangkok: Phrae Phitthaya, 1953. 395 pp.

Bibliography

Sathitya Semanil. *Wisasa* (Chats). Bangkok: Phrae Phittaya, 1970. 351 pp.

Sathŭan Supphasophon. *Phraratchaprawat phrabatsomdet phra mongkutklao čhaoyuhua lae prawattikan luksŭa thai* (A Biography of King Vajiravudh *and* A History of the Boy Scouts). Bangkok: Khurusapha, 1961. (42 pp.) + 492 pp.

S[awai] Watthanaset. *Kiattikhun phra mongkutklao, kasat nakprat khǫng chat thai* (In Honor of King Vajiravudh, the Thai Nation's Great Literary Monarch). Bangkok: Watthanaphanit, 1957. 833 pp.

Somphop Phirom. *Kutakhan* (Peaked-Roof Buildings). Bangkok: Krung Sayam, 1970. 154 pp.

Sunthǫnphiphit, Phraya. *Phramahakarunathikhun haeng phrabatsomdet phra mongkutklao čhaoyuhua* (The Virtues of King Vajiravudh). Bangkok: Kammakanpokkhrǫng, 1971. 337 pp.

———. "Suan anusǫn" (Remembrances of a Garden). *Wachirawutthanusǫn* (1967), pp. 229–238.

———. "Sŭapa–luksŭa" (Wild Tigers–Boy Scouts). *Wachirawutthanusǫn* (1953), pp. 23–80.

Thai Nǫi [pseud.]. *6 phaendin* (Six Reigns). Bangkok: Khlang Witthaya, 1960. 544 pp.

Thamrong Ratchabǫriphan, Phraya. "Song prot tang samosǫn" (Royal Favor toward the Establishment of Clubs). *Wachirawutthanusǫn* (1960), pp. 93–122.

Thao hiranphanasun (Lord Hiranphanasun). Bangkok: Udom, 1969. 22 pp.

Thawi Muktharakosa. *Phramaha thiraratčhao* (The Philosopher King). Bangkok: Phrae Phitthaya, 1963. 844 pp.

Thepchu Thapthǫng. *Winyan—phi* (Spirits—Ghosts). Bangkok: Phim Thai, 1968. 120 pp.

Thiphakǫnwong, Čhaophraya. *Phraratchaphongsawadan krung ratanakosin ratchakan thi 4* (Royal Chronicle of the Fourth Reign of the Bangkok Dynasty). Bangkok: Khurusapha, 1961. 2 vols.

Thi raluk sayam rat phiphitthaphan suan lumphini phraphutthasakarat 2468; The Souvenir of the Siamese Kingdom Exhibition at Lumbini Park B.E. 2468. First published 1928. Thai text 255 pp. English text 256 pp.

Thuan Wiriyaphǫn. *Prachum owat* (A Collection of Speeches). Bangkok: Niyomwitthaya, 1966. 377 pp.

Uthumporn Sundaravej. *Phraratchaprawat chiwit suan phra-ong somdet phra siphatcharinthara bǫrom rachininat phra bǫrom ratchonani phanpi luang* (Biography of Queen Saowapha). Bangkok: Phadung Sŭksa, 1972. 402 pp.

Vajiranana, Prince. "Phra mongkhon wiset katha" (A Special Discourse). *Samutthasan* 14 (February 1915): 1–20.

4. Other Works in Western Languages

Chula Chakrabongse, Prince. *Lords of Life: The Paternal Monarchy of Bangkok, 1782–1932*. New York: Taplinger, 1960. 352 pp.

Bibliography

Coedès, G. *Recueil des inscriptions du Siam. Première partie: Inscriptions de Sukhodaya*. Bangkok: Bangkok Times, 1924. 177 pp.

Cucherousset, Henri. *Quelques informations sur le Siam*. Hanoi: l'Éveil Économique, 1925. 124 pp.

de Schaeck, Ivan. *Promenade autour du monde avec S.A.I. le grand duc Boris de Russie*. Paris: Plon, 1910. 361 pp.

Gerini, Colonel G. E. *Siam and Its Productions, Arts, and Manufactures: A Descriptive Catalogue of the Siamese Section at the International Exhibition of Industry and Labour Held in Turin April 29–November 19, 1911*. London: Stephen Austin, 1912. 339 pp.

Graham, W. A. *Siam*. London: Moring, 1924. 2 vols.

Levenson, Joseph R. *Modern China and Its Confucian Past*. Garden City: Anchor Books, 1964. 246 pp.

Niramol Kangsadara. "The Buddhist Order under Prince Wachirayan (1898–1921)." Unpublished Master's thesis, University of Hawaii, 1972. 101 pp.

Norden, Hermann. *From Golden Gate to Golden Sun*. Boston: Small Maynard, 1923. 292 pp.

Oblas, Peter B. "'A Very Small Part of World Affairs': Siam's Policy on Treaty Revision and the Paris Peace Conference of 1919." *Journal of the Siam Society* 59, part 2 (July 1971): 51–74.

"The Pageant of Wild Tiger Traditions." *Wachirawutthanusǫn* (1953), pp. 1–49.

Powell, E. Alexander. *Where the Strange Trails Go Down*. New York: Scribner's, 1921. 279 pp.

Prachoom Chomchai. *Chulalongkorn the Great*. Tokyo: Centre for East Asian Cultural Studies, 1965. 167 pp.

Robinson, William Henry. *The Golden Legend, or Story of India's God-given Cynosure*. London: Luzac, 1911. 148 pp.

Sayre, Francis Bowes. *Glad Adventure*. New York: Macmillan, 1957. 356 pp.

———. *The Passing of Extraterritoriality in Siam*. New York: Institute of Pacific Relations, n.d. 60 pp. Reprinted from the *Atlantic Monthly*, November 1927, and the *American Journal of International Law*, January 1928.

Siamese Abuses in Patani. London: Wightman, 1923. 17 pp.

Skinner, G. W. "Change and Persistence in Chinese Culture Overseas: A Comparison of Thailand and Java." *Journal of the South Seas Society* 16, no. 1–2 (1960): 86–100.

———. *Chinese Society in Thailand: An Analytic History*. Ithaca: Cornell, 1957. 459 pp.

Smith, Malcolm. *A Physician at the Court of Siam*. London: Country Life, 1947. 164 pp.

Thornely, P. W. *The History of a Transition*. Bangkok: Siam Observer, 1923. 406 pp.

Vajiranana, Prince. *The Buddhist Attitude towards National Defence and Administration: A Special Allocution*. [Bangkok, 1916]. 26 pp.

Bibliography

———. *Right Is Right: A Special Allocution by His Holiness Prince Vajiranana, Supreme Patriarch of the Kingdom of Siam*. Bangkok, [1918]. 56 pp.

———. *The Triumph of Right: A Special Allocution*. Bangkok: Bangkok Daily Mail, [1919]. 39 pp.

Wales, H. G. Quaritch. *Siamese State Ceremonies: Their History and Function*. London: Bernard Quaritch, 1931. 326 pp.

Wenk, Klaus. *Die Ruderlieder—kap he ruo—in der Literatur Thailands*. Wiesbaden: Steiner, 1968. 177 pp.

William of Sweden, H.R.H. Prince. *In the Lands of the Sun: Notes and Memories of a Tour in the East*. London: Eveleigh Nash, 1915. 344 pp.

Wingfield-Stratford, Esmé. *The Victorian Cycle*. New York: Morrow, 1935. 3 vol. in 1.

Wyatt, David K. *The Politics of Reform in Thailand: Education in the Reign of King Chulalongkorn*. New Haven and London: Yale, 1969. 425 pp.

5. Newspapers and Journals

Ačhan. Monthly.
Bangkok Daily Mail. Daily.
Bangkok Times. Daily and weekly.
Čhotmaihet suapa. Monthly.
Dusit samit. Weekly.
Journal of the Siam Society. Monthly.
Khurusan. Monthly.
Nangsuphim thai. Daily.
Nawikkasat. Monthly.
New York Times. Daily.
Ratchakitčhanubeksa. Weekly.
Samutthasan. Monthly.
Sap thai. Monthly.
Sena suksa. Monthly.
Siam Observer. Daily.
Thawipanya. Monthly.
Times (London). Daily.
Triam udom suksa.
Wachirawutthanuson. Annual.
Warasan luksua. Monthly.
Witthayačhan. Monthly.

Index

Abdul Hamid, Sultan of Turkey, 68–69
Abhakara, Prince (Prince of Chumphon), 85, 120, 262, 265, 291 n.31
Advisers, foreign, 82–84, 86, 291 n.30, 312 n.112; Adviser in Foreign Affairs, 83, 84, 124, 182; General Adviser, 83, 84; legal adviser, 156
"Affairs of China, The," 247
Afghanistan, 88–89
Agriculture, Minister of, 168, 169, 285 n.15, 296 n.124
Alfonso XIII, 14
Amphawa Palace, 288 n.92
Amphon Palace, 19

Anantasamakhom Throne Hall, 18, 234, 277 n.18
Anirut, 235, 237
Anirut, Phraya, 264
Aphairacha, Chaophraya, 296 n.124
Archaeological Service, 205, 321 n.10
Army, 16, 21, 35, 45, 46, 47, 48–50, 56, 57, 58, 60, 85, 86–90, 95, 97, 112, 115, 127, 145, 147, 172, 186, 246, 248, 258, 259, 260–261, 262, 265, 267, 270. *See also* Aviation; World War I, Siamese Expeditionary Force
Army Chief of Staff. *See* Chakrabongs, Prince
Art, as an aspect of nationalism,

337

Index

178, 203, 230–235
Arthakar Prasiddhi, Phraya, 253
Arts and Crafts Fairs, 233, 246, 258, 259, 269, 317 n.116
As You Like It, 239
Asadang, Prince (Prince of Nakhǫn Ratchasima), 257, 258
"Asvabahu," 63, 99, 170, 192, 248, 252, 320 n.13
Auguries, 15–16, 229, 276 n.9
Australia, 86
Austro-Hungary, 2, 105, 111, 112, 185, 225
Aviation, 85–86, 114, 115, 119, 122, 127
Ayutthaya, 20, 119, 138, 146, 205, 206–207, 212, 244, 280 n.37

Baden-Powell, Sir Robert S., 29
Ban Pong, 41
Bang Pa-in Palace, 20, 138, 244, 263
Bangkok Daily Mail, 102, 254
Bangkok Times, 98, 102, 113, 129, 133, 141–142, 169, 184, 213, 246 251, 253, 255–256, 266–268
Beardsley, Aubrey, 9
Bejaratana, Princess, 158, 258
Belgium, 2, 102, 119, 251
Bhanurangsi, Prince, 291 n.32, 295 n.124
Bismarck, 94
Bǫdin, Čhaophraya, 296 n.124
Bǫribun Kosakǫn, Phraya, 254
Borneo Company, 172
"Bow and Arrows of Rama's Strength, The," 15, 16, 229
Boy Scouts (international), 29, 44
Boy Scouts (Thai), 42–44, 47, 49, 90, 127, 144, 151, 160, 163, 166, 167, 199, 232, 244, 246, 258, 259, 260, 261, 269, 270, 281 n.73, 281 n.80
Brahmanism, 3, 10, 14, 15, 16, 24, 67, 77, 114, 140–141, 181, 212–

213, 214, 220, 238
Buang man (Noose of Evil), 250
Buddhism, 3, 10, 15, 21, 24, 28, 36, 38, 77, 90, 92, 101, 104, 110, 111, 116, 118, 140, 143, 153, 156, 158, 161, 163, 177, 178, 195, 197, 203, 206, 214–228, 238, 246, 270, 314 n.31, 320 n.13
"Buddhist Attitude Towards National Defence and Administration, The," 225
Buri, Phraya, 104
Burma, 15, 30, 62, 65, 80, 103, 182, 204, 207, 208, 219, 222
Bushido, 89

Cambodia, 30, 62, 65, 81, 209, 210, 218–219, 222
Ceylon, 222
Chaiyo, ix, 100, 143–144, 211, 294 n.95, 302 n.63
Čhakkraphat, King, 206
Chakkri Day, 141, 142–143, 212
Chakkri dynasty, 65, 137, 141, 142, 204, 207, 208
Chakrabongs, Prince (Prince of Phitsanulok), 12, 16, 19, 20, 45, 47, 50, 53, 57, 58, 73, 84, 85, 86, 90, 106, 107, 109, 110, 114, 116, 140, 184, 185, 188, 192, 199–200, 234, 253, 257, 262, 263, 275 n.32, 278 n.40, 291 n.31, 295 n.121, 296 n.124, 297 n.155
Chalerm Vudhikosit, 256
Charoon, Prince, 46, 72, 80, 114, 117, 122, 123, 142, 143, 299 n.191
Čhatkan rap sadet (Preparing for a Royal Visit), 249
Chiangrai, 278 n.40
China, xiv, xvi, 30, 55, 56, 62, 64, 67–68, 70, 71, 74, 108, 128, 131, 153, 172, 182, 187, 188, 189, 194, 195, 200, 202–203, 218, 265, 285 n.6, 299 n.3, 310 n.68

Index

Chinese in Siam, xiv, xvi, 4, 6, 21, 44, 56, 67, 73, 78, 84, 99, 105, 131, 138, 149, 166, 171, 172, 173, 186–196, 197, 199, 208–209, 241, 256, 266, 270, 272, 285, n.6, 310 n.63, 310 n.65, 310 n.67, 310 n.68, 310 n.70, 310 n.78
Chino-Siam Daily News, 253–254
Chira, Prince (Prince of Nakhọn Chaisi), 20, 85, 285 n.7, 291 n.31, 291 n.32
Chitralada Palace, 161, 237
Čhotmaihet sửapa (Wild Tiger Documents), 34, 255
Christianity, compared with Buddhism, 214, 218, 219–220, 221
Christians in Siam, 228
Chronicle of the North, 209, 210
Chuai amnat! See Coup d'état!
Chudadhuj, Prince (Prince of Phetchabun), 257, 291 n.31
Chulalongkorn, King, xiv, 1, 2, 3, 4, 8, 10, 12, 13, 14, 17, 24, 25, 31, 34, 35, 54, 60, 63, 64, 73, 77, 82, 84–85, 141, 152, 153, 161, 164, 170–171, 187, 188, 191, 199, 205, 215, 224, 228, 230, 234, 235, 237, 239, 258, 262, 263, 264, 274 n.3, 274 n.7, 276 n.4, 276 n.9, 277 n.23, 284 n.3, 285 n.23, 289 n.107, 301 n.41, 306 n.174, 308 n.6, 312 n.4, 313 n.14, 317 n.118, 319 n.150, 320 n.6, 320 n.24
Chulalongkorn Day, 141–142
Chulalongkorn University, 164, 234, 269
Chumphọn, 246
"Clogs on Our Wheels," 247, 261
Coedès, G., 205, 206
Colombet, Father, 184
Communications, Department of, 102
Communications, Ministry of, 183, 232, 296 n.124
"Comparison of Surnames with Clan Names, A," 247
Conscription, 31, 85, 90
Constitutionalism, 55, 56, 58, 64–78, 256, 267, 289 n.99
Cooperative societies, 171
Council of Ministers, 3, 107–110, 140, 157, 253, 262–263
Coup d'état! (Chuai amnat!), 73–75, 249, 269
Coup party of 1912, 44–45, 47, 53–60, 73, 74, 265–266
"Court Circular," 251
"Cult of Imitation, The," 247

Daily Mail. See Bangkok Daily Mail
Damrong Rajanubhab, Prince, 15, 20, 37, 40, 41, 46, 136, 156, 164, 204, 205, 206, 207, 209, 233, 239, 263, 265, 300 n.7, 312 n.4, 313 n.14, 313 n.27
"Definition of Virtue, A." *See Sadaeng khunnanukhun*
Democracy. *See* Constitutionalism
Denmark, 82, 83
Dep Mori, Phra, 223–224
Devawongse, Prince, 20, 41, 73, 104–105, 106, 107, 139, 142, 156, 239, 257, 296 n.124, 300 n.7, 320 n.6
Dharma Jataka, 226–227
Doehring, Karl, 233–234, 317 n.123
Dọn Čhedi, 207
Don Muang, 85, 86
Durham Light Infantry Company, 103
Dusit Maha Prasat, 16, 17
Dusit Palace, 1, 2, 38
Dusit Park (Gardens), 19, 75, 288 n.92, 317 n.118
Dusit sakkhi, 255, 289 n.93
Dusit samai, 255, 289 n.93
Dusit samit, 65, 96, 162, 245, 256, 289 n.93
Dusit Thani, 75–76, 78, 255,

Index

288 n.92, 289 n.97, 289 n.99

Economic nationalism, 167–175, 244, 258–259, 268, 270, 307 n.200
Education, 7–8, 43, 73, 90, 145, 153, 154, 158–159, 160–167, 171, 192, 199, 209, 215, 268; Chinese schools, 187, 188, 189–190, 191, 192, 310 n.78; Primary Education Act, 159, 164, 165, 198–199, 244, 306 n.164; vocational education, 165–166, 171, 232–233. *See also* Chulalongkorn University; King Chulalongkorn's Civil Service College; King's College; Royal Naval College; Royal Pages College, Royal Pages College of Chiangmai; School of Arts and Crafts; Suan Kulap School; Vajiravudh College; War College
Education, Ministry of, 158, 159, 161, 164–165, 166, 167, 191, 296 n.124
"Education and Unrest in the East," 247
Edward VII, 14
Emden, 98
England, xiv, xvi, 2, 4, 7, 9–10, 12, 14, 19, 29, 30, 33, 38, 71, 72, 74–75, 80, 81, 82, 83, 84, 88–89, 94, 95, 98, 101, 102, 103, 105, 106, 107, 108, 109, 110, 112, 116, 119, 120, 123, 124, 137, 142, 144, 146, 147, 148, 150, 153, 156, 163, 171, 172, 182, 183, 184, 185, 186, 198, 214, 253, 258, 259, 264, 280 n.51, 291 n.30, 299 n.191, 310 n.60
Entertainments, Department of (Mahorasop), 235
Etymological Commission (Nirukkati Samakhom), 239

"Failure of the Young Turks, The," 247

Fenollosa, Ernest, 234
"Fiat Lux," 266
Fine Arts, Department of, 232
Football, 146–151, 154, 258
Foreign Affairs, Ministry of, 41, 84, 102, 104–105, 107, 139, 184, 296 n.124. *See also* Devawongse, Prince
France, 2, 12, 19, 29, 30, 52, 80, 81–82, 83, 84, 85, 94, 95, 102, 103, 106, 107, 108, 114, 117, 119, 120, 121, 122, 124, 184, 200–201, 290 n.27, 292 n.56, 297 n.159, 299 n.191
Franco-Prussian War, 94
Frankfurter, Dr. O., 206
"Freedom of the Seas," 247
French Indochina, 12, 30, 52, 80, 81, 84, 86, 102, 121, 124–125, 182, 200, 272
"Fruits of Turkish Constitutionalism, The," 247
Fund-raising campaigns, 117, 152, 244–246, 250; for army, 60; for aviation corps, 86, 244; for Red Cross, 244, 250; for Royal Navy League, 95–97, 98–101, 120, 121, 192, 193, 209, 212, 244, 246, 250, 260, 265, 294 n.83; for Siamese Expeditionary Force, 116, 192, 250, 261; for Wild Tigers, 50, 192, 244, 250

Gambling, 73, 144, 146, 151, 170
Ganesa, 10, 231, 239
George V, 19, 103, 186
Germany, 19, 29, 83, 84, 94, 95, 98, 101, 102, 103, 104, 105, 106, 107, 108, 109, 110, 111, 112, 113, 117, 122, 124, 172, 175, 183, 185, 218, 225, 245, 251, 253, 270, 296 n.132, 316 n.90
Grand Palace, 4, 19
Greece, 107
"Grinding Pepper Sauce in the

Index

River," 247

Hardie, Keir, 182
Hat Čhao Samran, 288 n.92
"Hermit," 256, 266, 267
Hinduism. *See* Brahmanism
Hiranhu (Hiranphanasun), 229–230
Historical Research Society (Borankhadi Samosǫn), 239
History, as an aspect of nationalism. *See* Vajiravudh, views on history
Ho hiw, 143
Hobbes, Thomas, 61, 131
Hua Hin, 41, 295 n.121
Huačhai nakrop (The Soul of a Warrior), 47, 92, 196, 239, 249, 251, 269
Huffman, P. A., 254

Inao, 235, 237
India, 30, 89, 103, 112, 128, 140, 149, 153, 185, 198, 222, 238, 320 n.13
Indians in Siam, 21, 103, 110, 191, 199
Indonesia, 203
Indra, 64, 139
Indrasakti Sachi, 158
"Instilling the Wild Tiger Spirit." *See* Plukčhai sửapa
Institute of Etymology and Orthography (Sapha Photčhanabanyat lae Akkharawithi), 239
Interior, Ministry of, 15, 38, 40, 76, 134, 146, 164, 188, 206, 233, 263, 296 n.124
International Exhibitions, 174, 233, 317 n.120. *See also* Leipzig Exhibition; San Francisco Exhibition; Turin Exhibition
Islam, 196–199, 218, 219
"Isn't a Four-Wheeled Vehicle More Stable Than a Two-Wheeled Vehicle?" 247
Italy, xv, 2, 174, 270

Japan, xiv, 2, 19, 30, 55, 63, 64, 70, 84, 89, 103, 109, 112, 124, 172, 185, 186, 188, 189, 191, 199, 234, 238, 253, 270, 291 n.30, 299 n.191
"Japan for Example," 247
Java, 30, 291 n.30
"Jews of the Orient, The," 193–194, 247
Joffre, Marshal, 122
Jones, Henry Arthur, 9
Judaism, 219, 220
"Junius," 255–256, 266, 267
Justice, Ministry of, 3, 54, 58, 60, 161, 254, 284 n.3, 296 n.124

Kaeo Samut, 172
Kamphaengphet, 204, 205
K'ang Yu-wei, 182
Kathin, 77, 191, 208–209, 214
Khanom som kap namya (The Right Amount of Noodles for the Sauce), 249
"Khǫ tham," 307 n.200
Khǫm damdin (The Cambodian Earth Diver), 250, 313 n.25
Khon, 4, 20, 235, 248
Khon Samak Len, 4
Khorat, 197, 212, 262
Khunying (Lady), 137
Khwamdi mi chai (The Triumph of Virtue), 249
King Chulalongkorn's Civil Service College, 164
"King, Nation, and Religion," xvi, 22, 33, 42, 52, 55, 60, 64, 91, 92, 98, 116, 120, 139, 140, 194, 216, 243, 249
King's College, 145, 161, 305 n.152
Kipling, Rudyard, 9, 116
Kittiyakara, Prince (Prince of Čhanthaburi), 296 n.124
Korea, 30
Krung Thep Daily Mail, 254
Kuomintang, 55, 188

Index

Lakhǫn. *See* Theater and plays
Lakshmi Lavan, Princess, 158
Lampang, 119
Lamphun, 227
Lao of Northeast Siam, 199–200
Laos, 81, 82, 200, 212
Law on Books, Documents, and Newspapers, 253
League of Nations, 141
Legislative Council (Ratthamontri Sapha), 73, 157
Leipzig Exhibition, 233, 317 n.120
"Lekhanukan," 292 n.53
Leng Sičhan, Dr. (Khun Thawaihanphithak), 57, 59
Lewin, P. A., 183–184
Lilit narai sip pang, 238
Lilit phayap, 238
Linguistic nationalism, 178, 239–242, 270, 319 n.150
Literary Society (Wannakhadi Samosǫn), 239
Literature, as an aspect of nationalism, 178, 203, 235–242
Lloyd George, David, 72
Local Government, Ministry of, 21, 41, 188, 189, 296 n.124
Lǫi krathong, 213
Looker-on, The, 274 n.11
Lopburi, 119, 205, 210
Lumphini Park, 174, 258, 271, 272
Lusitania, 104
Lyle, T. H., 184–185

Macaulay, Thomas, 88
Mahatama (The Mahatma), 100, 193, 196, 249, 250, 251
"Mahathiraratčhao," 323 n.25
Mahidol, Prince (Prince of Songkhla), 113, 291 n.31, 293 n.75
Malaya, 30, 80, 102, 146, 149, 153, 182, 291 n.30
Malaya-Borneo Exhibition, 174
Malays in Siam, 81, 156, 196–199

Marine, Ministry of, 40, 58, 85, 139, 172, 289 n.107, 296 n.124. *See also* Navy
Marriage law, 156–157
Marxism (Bolshevism), 67, 73, 74
Masao, T., 199, 312 n.112
Matthanapatha, 238, 239
Maxims of Phra Ruang, The, (*Suphasit phra ruang*), 212, 293 n.63
McLuhan, Marshall, 243
Médecin malgré lui, Le, 239
Merchant of Venice, 238, 239
"Might Is Right," 247
Mit mi chai (The Triumph of Friendship), 250
Mo, Khunying, 212
Molière, 239
Mon, 208, 219
Monarchy: Challenges to, 55–60, 267; defense of, 60–78, 178
Mongkut, King, xiv, 17, 24, 25, 84, 136, 137, 140, 141, 142, 155, 157, 161, 205, 214, 230, 242, 304 n.122, 312 n.4, 317 n.120
Mundie, W. H., 255
Muslims in Siam, 81, 156, 197–199, 228

Nai, 184–185
Nakhǫn Pathom, 6, 40, 41, 42, 43, 53, 119, 146, 185, 207, 280 n.37, 314 n.31
Nakhǫn Sawan, 99, 119
Nakhǫn Sithammarat, 146, 197, 249, 302 n.67
Nala and Damayanti. *See Phra non kham luang*
Nang (Mrs.), 137
Nangsao (Miss), 137
Nangsŭphim čhino, 254, 321 n.49
Nangsŭphim thai, 110, 251, 252, 254, 321 n.49
Naradhip, Prince, 154
Nares, Prince, 232, 296 n.124

Index

Naresuan, King, 111, 207–208, 211
Naris, Prince, 205, 234, 239, 313 n.25, 318 n.125
National Day. *See* Chakkri Day
National flag, 137–140, 244, 269, 301 n.52, 302 n.53
National holidays, 140–143
National Library, 3, 205, 206, 234, 237
National Savings Banks, 171
Navy, 17, 22, 57, 58, 85, 86, 90, 95–101, 112, 121, 127, 139, 145, 148, 150, 172, 223, 246, 258, 259, 260–261, 262, 265. *See also* Marine, Ministry of
Newspapers, 4, 6, 45, 73, 75, 102, 104, 117, 123, 129, 137, 144, 154, 169, 182, 187, 188, 189, 241, 242, 251–256, 266–268. *See also* Bangkok Daily Mail; Bangkok Times; Chino-Siam Daily News; Dusit sakkhi; Dusit samai; Krung Thep Daily Mail; Nangsuphim čhino; Nangsuphim thai; Sam samai; Siam Observer
"Nisit Ǫkfǫt" (Oxford alumnus), 302 n.67
Nǫi inthasen, 249
"Nǫila," 286 n.42
North Siam, 5, 160, 197, 199, 200, 204, 227,
Northeast Siam, 81–82, 197, 199–200

Ome Palangtirasin, 256
"On Becoming a Real Nation," 247
Othello, 239
Oxford, 2, 5, 302 n.67

Padoux, G., 156
Pageant of Wild Tiger Traditions, 39, 40, 47, 48, 265, 280 n.51
Pages. *See* Vajiravudh, relationship with courtiers
Palace, Ministry of, 36, 48, 78, 143

Pan-Thai idea, 200–201, 272
Paribatra, Prince (Prince of Nakhǫn Sawan), 20, 40, 46, 58, 73, 85, 139, 172, 253, 263, 265, 281 n.81, 289 n.107, 291 n.31, 291 n.32, 296 n.124, 301 n.52, 306 n.170
Parusakawan Palace, 54; model municipality in, 6, 288 n.92
Pattani, 80, 156, 199
Pawaret, Prince, 312 n.4
Persia, 30, 67, 70
"Perspectiva," 266–267, 267–268
"Phan Laem," 248
Phanthuprawat, Prince, 53
Phanung, 154, 160, 179
Phasin, 160
Phithakthepnakhǫn, Luang, 306 n.170
Phitsanulok, 146, 205
Phongphang (Fishtrap), 249, 269
Phra Chai Watthana, 215
"Phra Khanphet," 251
Phra non kham luang (The Story of King Nala in Classical Verse Forms), 235–237, 238, 239
Phra Pathom Čhedi, 229, 276 n.9
Phra Ruang, King, 95, 207, 209–212, 220, 314 n.31
Phra Ruang (naval vessel), 95–101, 120–121, 152, 192, 193, 209, 212, 245, 260, 265
Phra Ruang (play), 209–212, 238, 249, 251, 261, 269
Phǔan tai (Friends to the End), 249
Phuket, 48, 98, 99, 249
Phurai phlaeng (The Evil Doer), 249
Phya Thai Palace, 75, 229, 288 n.92
Pibulsonggram, Premier, 241, 269–272
Pinero, Sir Arthur Wing, 9
Plukčhai sǔapa (Instilling the Wild Tiger Spirit), 167, 247, 248
Portugal, 55, 67
Prajadhipok: Prince of Sukhothai, 158, 256, 257, 258, 259, 265,

Index

291 n.31; King, 52, 158, 168, 317 n.116, 322 n.61
Pramothai Theater, 235
Prasat Phra Thepbidǫn, 142
Prasit, Phraya. *See* Ramrakhop, Čhaophraya
"Principles of Government," 247
Privy purse, 50, 60, 95, 161, 171, 174, 267, 306 n.174
Priyadarshika, 238
Public Works, Ministry of, 232
Purachatra, Prince (Prince of Kamphaengphet), 85, 245, 291 n.31

Rabi, Prince (Prince of Ratburi), 54, 58, 157, 284 n.3, 285 n.15, 296 n.124
Railway Department, 81–82, 102, 103, 105, 111–112, 170, 183, 245
Rama, 16, 238, 248, 296 n.131; designation for Chakkri kings, 136–137, 141, 213; Order of Rama, 115, 120
Rama I, King, 66, 137, 142, 208, 276 n.4
Rama II, King, 137, 237, 258
Rama III, King, 137
Rama IV, King. *See* Mongkut, King
Rama V, King. *See* Chulalongkorn, King
Rama VI, King. *See* Vajiravudh
Rama VII, King. *See* Prajadhipok, King
"Ramachitti," 104, 110, 111, 124, 248, 296 n.131, 296 n.132
Ramathibǫdi, 137
Ramayana. See Rammakian
Ramkhamhaeng, King of Sukhothai, 205, 209, 212, 242, 277 n.16, 293 n.63
Rammakian, 235, 237, 238, 248, 249
Ramrakhop, Čhaophraya, 76, 147, 150, 151, 234, 264
Ramwong, 270

Ranǫng, 246
Red Cross, 103, 244, 250
Regency Council, 3
Religious Affairs and Education, Ministry of. *See* Education, Ministry of
"Right Is Right," 225–226
Romeo and Juliet, 239, 252
Royal Bangkok Sports Club, 120, 147, 148, 150
Royal Government Gazette, 48
Royal Naval College, 147, 150
Royal Navy League, 95–101, 103, 120, 121, 192, 193, 209, 212, 244, 246, 250, 255, 260, 265, 294 n.83
Royal Pages College, 62, 145, 150, 151, 161, 162, 163–164, 214–215, 216, 234, 246, 305 n.152
Royal Pages College of Chiangmai, 161, 305 n.152
Royal Pantheon (Prasat Phra Thepbidǫn), 142
Royal Plaza, 21, 111, 118, 120, 121
Royal Survey Department, 82
Russia, xiv, 9, 19, 29, 67, 73, 74, 80, 89, 94, 95, 103, 106, 107, 253, 290 n.27, 319 n.60
Russo-Japanese War, 89

Sadaeng khunnanukhun (A Definition of Virtue), 247, 248
Saiburi, 197
Sam samai, 253
Samakkhi sewok, 231–232
Samakkhichai House, 234
Samut Sakhǫn, 76
Samutthasan, 97, 103, 104, 255
San Francisco Exhibition, 174, 233
Sanam Čhan, 234
Sandhurst, 2
Samǫnratsirichet, Krommaluang, 257 n.17
Saowapha, Queen (Queen Mother), 1, 7, 8, 11, 20, 148, 152–153, 158, 199, 215, 234, 257, 258, 263,

Index

288 n.92, 306 n.174, 322 n.11
Sap thai, 255
Saranrom Palace, 1, 4–8, 12, 19, 27, 28, 34, 161, 235, 264, 275 n.24
Sathitya Semanil, 256
Satul, 156
Savitri, 238
Sawankhalok, 204, 205
Sayam manutsati, 269
"Sayamin," 301 n.41
Sayre, Francis Bowes, 124, 182
School for Scandal, 239
School of Arts and Crafts, 165–166, 232
Screech Owl, The, 274 n.11
Shakespeare, 238, 292 n.51
Shakuntala, 238
Shaw, George Bernard, 9, 182, 242
Sheridan, Richard Brinsley, 239
"Si Ayutthaya," 251
Si Intharathit, King, 209
Sia sala (Sacrifice), 249
Siam Cement Company, 171
Siam Commercial Bank, 83, 102
Siam Observer, 102, 251, 254, 321 n.50
Siamese Kingdom Exhibition, 174–175, 258–259
Siamese Steamship Company, 172, 244, 268
"Simplicitas," 266
Singapore, 184
Siva, 10
Siwichai, Phra, 227–228
Socialism, 181–182
Somawadi, Princess, 275 n.17
Sommot, Prince, 318 n.132, 318 n.139
Songkhla, 249
Songs, patriotic, 23, 34, 40, 42, 44, 88, 91–92, 118, 167, 228, 259, 260, 261, 262, 265, 269
Songtham, King, 206
Soul of a Warrior, The. See *Huačhai nakrop*

South Siam, 5, 48, 80–81, 106, 146–147, 156, 191, 196–199, 200, 246
Spain, 2, 14, 142
Sports, 7, 44, 50, 144–151, 154, 160, 164, 191, 244, 246, 258
Stevenson, Robert Louis, 255
Straits Settlements, 149
Suan Kulap School, 145, 233
Sucharit, Phraya, 264
Sucharit Suda, Phra, 158
Sukarno, 203
Sukhothai, 5, 204, 205, 206, 209, 210, 211, 212, 277 n.16, 293 n.63, 314 n.31
"Sukhrip," 248
Sumatra, 291 n.30
Sun Yat-sen, 67, 68, 182, 187, 310 n.68
Suphanburi, 207
Surasi, Čhaophraya, 296 n.124
Suriyothai, Queen, 212
Surnames, 128–136, 244, 260, 269, 300 n.7
Suvadana, Princess, 158
Svasti, Prince, 123, 156
Swinging Ceremony, 114–115
"Symbol of Civilization: The Status of Women, A," 247

Taksin, King, 66, 191, 207, 208–209, 211
Talaing, 208
Tang čhit khit khlang, 241
Temiya Jataka, 28
Tennyson, Alfred, 24
Thai (meaning free), 91, 98, 178, 212
"Thai Hua Het," 307 n.200
Thai nưa, 202
Thai tai, 200
Thaiyai, 199
Thamma, Čhaophraya, 296 n.124
Thammaracha, King, 206
Thammasakmontri, Čhaophraya, 164–165, 166, 281 n.81, 296 n.124
Thammathamma songkhram (The

345

Index

War between Good and Evil), 227, 250, 251
Thammathibet, Prince, 238
"Thanks to Our Chinese Friends," 192
Thao saen pom, 212, 238
Thawipanya, 5, 7, 255
Thawipanya Club (Thawipanya Samosǫn), 6–7, 27, 275 n.21, 275 n.22
Theater and plays, 2, 4, 7, 8, 9, 19, 20, 40, 47, 48, 50, 54, 73–75, 77, 78, 86, 88, 91, 92, 95, 100, 101, 103, 116, 120, 154, 191, 192, 193, 195–196, 209–211, 212, 216, 227, 235, 237, 238–239, 240, 241, 248–251, 261, 262, 275 n.24, 284 n.4. *See also* Khon
Theatre Royal, 19, 20
Thiao mùang phra ruang (A Visit to the Land of Phra Ruang), 209, 247
Tilleke, W. A. G., 321 n.31
Topta (Deception), 249
"Triumph of Right, The," 226–227
Turin Exhibition, 174, 233
Turkey, 67, 68–70, 71, 265. *See also* Young Turks

Umschau, 102
United States, 2, 19, 20, 29, 55, 68, 71, 74, 82, 86, 94, 103, 104, 105, 106, 110, 113, 122–123, 124, 174, 183, 299 n.191
"Uttarakuru," 181–182, 247
Utthaithani, 138

Vajira, 16
Vajira Hospital, 216
Vajiranana, Prince Patriarch, 28, 38, 215, 224–228, 239, 251, 257, 316 n.90, 316 n.95
Vajiravudh: as Crown Prince, 1–12, 54, 81, 91, 129, 144, 161, 204, 214, 229, 235, 238, 255, 264, 274 n.3, 274 n.7; tonsure of, 10, 11; as acting king, 3–4, 274 n.7; first coronation, 14, 121, 141, 142, 146, 163, 212, 213; second coronation, 14–26, 39, 77, 85, 141, 153, 191, 246, 276 n.4, 277 n.17; birthday celebrations, 39, 40, 141, 146, 212, 213, 225, 246, 258, 260; schooling, 2–3, 10, 146, 177, 214; reading habits, 5, 9; early interest in writing, 4–5, 274 n.11, 274 n.12; interest in theater, 2, 4, 7, 40, 54, 235, 248–251 (*see also* Theater and plays); poems of, 5, 64, 86, 88, 91–92, 95, 97–98, 116, 140, 159, 196, 209, 210, 211, 212, 216, 227, 231–232, 235–237, 238, 239, 240, 242, 248, 255; diary of, 5, 25, 51, 72, 85–86, 253, 274 n.12; pen names, 129 (*see also* "Asvabahu," "Lekhanukan," "Phan Laem," "Phra Khanphet," "Nisit Ǫkfǫt," "Nǫila," "Ramachitti," "Si Ayutthaya," "Sukhrip," "Thai Hua Het"); disinclination to marry, 8, 157–158; engagements and marriages of, 154, 155, 157–158; daughter of, 158, 258; relationship with courtiers, 5, 6–8, 27, 28, 35, 36, 37, 45, 47, 50, 51, 54, 75–76, 78, 150, 168, 264, 267; English influence on, 2, 7, 8–10, 12, 14, 23–25, 29, 33, 38, 110, 137, 144, 146, 163, 171, 176, 194, 214, 215, 280 n.51; general in British army, 103, 186; as a speaker, 246–247; fiscal policies, 25–26, 50–51, 54, 60, 168–170, 173, 174, 266–267, 306 n.174; views on history, 5, 16, 29–30, 40, 61, 64, 178, 202, 203–213, 270, 313 n.27
Vajiravudh College, *frontispiece*, 161, 269, 305 n.152. *See also* Royal Pages College

Index

Vajirunhis, Prince, 2, 12, 274 n.3, 275 n.17
Vallabha Devi, Princess, 154, 155, 157, 158, 160
Versailles, Siam at, 122–124
Victoria, Queen, 2, 9, 10, 23, 24, 142, 278 n.35
"Victory," 247
Vietnam, 30, 65, 117, 299 n.3
Vietnamese in Siam, 199
"Visit to the Land of Phra Ruang, A," 209, 247
Visvakarma, 231
Vudhijai, Prince, 291 n.31

Wachira, 16
Wachirayan, 237
"Wake Up, Siam," 172–173, 247
Walai, Princess (Princess of Phetburi), 22–23, 154, 159
War, Ministry of, 85, 86, 114, 183–184, 188, 254, 296 n.124
War College, 145
War games: of army, 48, 49, 58, 85, 95; at Saranrom Palace, 4, 5–6, 27, 28; of Wild Tigers, 38, 40–42, 43, 44, 47, 48, 49, 50, 52, 54, 95, 207
War of the Polish Succession, The, 274 n.11, 313 n.15
Wat Benčhamabǫphit, 317 n.118
Wat Phra Kaeo, 28, 111, 142
Wat Ratchaburana, 232
"We Don't Need Lizards," 124
Wembley Exhibition, 258, 259
Westernization, xiv–xvi, 15, 24–25, 29, 54, 55, 56, 64, 66, 70–72, 126–175, 176–177, 178–182, 203, 217, 230–231, 238, 240, 241, 270. See also Vajiravudh, English influence on; Constitutionalism
"What Is the Knowledge Attained by the Buddha on His Enlightenment," 247–248
White elephant, 15, 182
Wild Tiger Corps, 21, 27–52, 54, 56, 57, 60, 61, 62, 78, 79, 87, 88, 90, 93, 94, 95, 97, 127, 139, 143, 144, 145, 147, 152, 160, 163, 178, 179, 192, 199, 206, 207, 208, 216, 223, 224, 225, 226, 244, 246, 247, 248, 250, 255, 258, 259, 260, 261, 265, 267, 269, 278 n.5, 279 n.26, 280 n.51, 281 n.80, 282 n.84
Wilde, Oscar, 9
William, Prince, 20, 80
Wilson, Woodrow, 111, 122
Wisakhabucha, 163, 214–215, 216
Wiwaha phra samut (Neptune's Bride), 196, 249
Women, status of, 99, 151–160
Wongsa, Čhaophraya, 296 n.124
World War I, xiv, 29, 49, 51, 80, 86, 92–125, 140, 141, 168, 181, 206, 223, 225–226, 227, 244, 246, 250, 251, 296 n.132, 316 n.90; declaration of neutrality in, 93; declaration of war, 111–112; seizure of German ships, 111, 112, 172; Siamese Expeditionary Force, 113–117, 119–120, 227, 248, 262, 297 n.159; prisoners of war, 112, 185–186; treaty revision, 105, 106, 107, 108, 109, 113, 114, 122–124, 182; victory celebrations, 118–121

"Yellow peril," 187
Yi Ko-hong (Phra Anuwat Ratchaniyom), 192
Yiam Samut, 172, 307 n.192
Yommarat, Čhaophraya, 41, 46, 93–94, 188, 190, 253, 254, 261–262, 263, 296 n.124
Young Turks, 55, 68–70, 71
Yuan Shih-k'ai, 68, 187
Yugala, Prince (Prince of Lopburi), 20
Yuwachon, 270

Zimmerman Plot, 103

About the Author

WALTER F. VELLA, professor of history at the University of Hawaii, received his B.A., M.A., and Ph.D. degrees at the University of California at Berkeley. He was trained in the Thai language during his army service, and his first trip to Thailand was with the O.S.S. After acting as associate director of the Modern Thailand Project at Cornell and serving for five years as head of the John G. White Collection of Orientalia and Folklore in Cleveland, he came to Hawaii as the first permanent appointee in Southeast Asian history at the University of Hawaii. His research for *Chaiyo!* was conducted in Thailand with the aid of an A.C.L.S. grant. His wife, Dorothy Vella, a professional editor, assisted by researching all the English-language sources as well as by editing the book. Dr. Vella's other works about Thailand include *The Impact of the West on Government in Thailand* and *Siam under Rama III*. He has also edited G. Coedès' *The Indianized States of Southeast Asia* (An East-West Center Book, The University Press of Hawaii).